Lecture Notes in Computer Scie

Edited by G. Goos, J. Hartmanis and J. van

Springer
Berlin
Heidelberg
New York
Barcelona
Hong Kong
London
Milan
Paris
Singapore
Tokyo

Floor Koornneef   Meine van der Meulen   (Eds.)

Computer Safety, Reliability and Security

19th International Conference, SAFECOMP 2000
Rotterdam, The Netherlands, October 24-27, 2000
Proceedings

 Springer

Series Editors

Gerhard Goos, Karlsruhe University, Germany
Juris Hartmanis, Cornell University, NY, USA
Jan van Leeuwen, Utrecht University, The Netherlands

Volume Editors

Floor Koornneef
TU Delft, Safety Science Group
Jaffalaan 5, 2628 BX Delft, The Netherlands
E-mail: f.koornneef@tbm.tudelft.nl

Meine van der Meulen
SIMTECH
Max Euwelaan 60, 3062 MA Rotterdam, The Netherlands
E-mail: m.van.der.meulen@simtech.nl

Cataloging-in-Publication Data applied for

Die Deutsche Bibliothek - CIP-Einheitsaufnahme

Computer safety, reliability and security : 19th international
conference ; proceedings / SAFECOMP 2000, Rotterdam, The Netherlands,
October 24 - 27, 2000. Floor Koornneef ; Meine van der Meulen (ed.). -
Berlin ; Heidelberg ; New York ; Barcelona ; Hong Kong ; London ;
Milan ; Paris ; Singapore ; Tokyo : Springer, 2000
    (Lecture notes in computer science ; Vol. 1943)
    ISBN 3-540-41186-0

CR Subject Classification (1998): D.1-4, E.4, C.3, F.3, K.6.5

ISSN 0302-9743
ISBN 3-540-41186-0 Springer-Verlag Berlin Heidelberg New York

Springer-Verlag Berlin Heidelberg New York
a member of BertelsmannSpringer Science+Business Media GmbH
© Springer-Verlag Berlin Heidelberg 2000
Printed in Germany

Typesetting: Camera-ready by author, data conversion by DA-TeX Gerd Blumenstein
Printed on acid-free paper   SPIN: 10780880   06/3142   5 4 3 2 1 0

Preface

Welcome to Rotterdam and to the International Conference Safecomp 2000, on the reliability, safety and security of critical computer applications. This already marks the 19th year of the conference, showing the undiminished interest the topic elicits from both academia and industry. Safecomp has proven to be an excellent place to meet and have discussions, and we hope this trend continues this year.

People and organisations depend more and more on the functioning of computers. Whether in household equipment, telecommunication systems, office applications, banking, people movers, process control or medical systems, the often-embedded computer subsystems are meant to let the hosting system realise its intended functions. The assurance of proper functioning of computers in dependable applications is far from obvious. The millennium started with the bug and the full endorsement of the framework standard IEC 61508. The variety of dependable computer applications increases daily, and so does the variety of risks related to these applications. The assessment of these risks therefore needs reflection and possibly new approaches. This year's Safecomp provides a broad mix of papers on these issues, on progress made in different application domains and on emerging challenges.

One of the special topics this year is *transport and infrastructure*. One would be hard pressed to find a better place to discuss this than in Rotterdam. The reliability, safety and security of computers is of prominent importance to Rotterdam, as a few examples illustrate. Its harbour depends on the reliable functioning of container handling systems, on the safe functioning of its radar systems, and, as of recently, on the safe and reliable functioning of the enormous storm surge barrier at Hoek van Holland.

A new topic for Safecomp is *medical systems*. These progressively depend on – embedded – programmable electronic systems. Experience shows that the medical world lacks the methods for applying these systems safely and reliably. We welcome a group of people ready to discuss this topic, and hope, by doing so, to contribute to this field of applications of safe, reliable and secure systems.

Software process improvement also represents a special topic of Safecomp 2000. It proved to be the most fruitful of the three in terms of submitted papers. There were many contributions from a host of countries, which had to be spread amongst different session topics.

We wish to thank the International Program Committee's members, 41 in total, for their efforts in reviewing the papers and for their valuable advice in organising this conference. We are also grateful for their contribution to distributing calls for papers and announcements. Without their help the burden of organising this conference would have been much greater.

Finally, let us once again welcome you to Rotterdam, a truly international city and home to people of many nationalities. We hope you take the time not only to enjoy this conference, but also to find your way around the city, since it surely has much to offer.

Floor Koornneef
Meine van der Meulen

Table of Contents

Formal Methods

Invited Paper

Safety Guidelines, Standards and Certification

Hardware Aspects

Safety Assessment I

Design for Safety

Invited Paper

Transport & Infrastructure

Safety Assessment II

The Ten Most Powerful Principles for Quality in (Software and) Software Organizations for Dependable Systems

Tom Gilb

Result Planning Limited,
Iver Holtersvei 2, N-1410 Kolbotn, Norway
Phone: +(47) 66 80 46 88, Mobile: +(47) 926 67187
Gilb@acm.org
http://www.Result-Planning.com,

Abstract. Software knows it has a problem. Solutions abound, but which solutions work? What are the most fundamental underlying principles we can observe in successful projects? This paper presents 10 powerful principles that are not widely taught or appreciated. They are based on ideas of measurement, quantification and feedback. Our maturity level with respect to 'numbers' is known to be poor. Hopefully, as we move to higher maturity levels we will also begin to appreciate the power of measurement and numeric expression of idea. What can we do right now? I suggest the first step is to recognize that all your quality requirements can and should be specified numerically. I am not talking about 'counting bugs'. I am talking about quantifying qualities such as security, portability, adaptability, maintainability, robustness, usability, reliability and performance. Decide to make them numeric on your project. Draft some numeric requirements today, surprise your team tomorrow!

1   Introduction

All projects have some degree of failure, compared to initial plans and promises. Far too many software projects fail totally. In the mid 1990s, the US Department of Defense estimated that about half of their software projects were total failures! (Source: N Brown). The civil sector is no better [16]. So what can be done to improve project success? This paper outlines ten key principles of successful software development methods, which characterize best practice.

These 10 most powerful software quality principles are selected because there is practical experience showing that they really get us control over qualities, and over the costs of qualities. They have a real track record. This record often spans decades of practice in companies like IBM, HP and Raytheon. There is nothing 'new' about them. They are classic. But the majority of our community is young and experientially

F. Koornneef and M. van der Meulen (Eds.): SAFECOMP 2000, LNCS 1943, pp. 1-13, 2000.

new to the game, so my job is to remind us of the things that work well. Your job is to evaluate this information and start getting the improvements your management wants in terms of quality and the time and effort needed to get it.

"Those who do not learn from history, are doomed to repeat it" (Santayana, 1903, The Life of Reason).

Principle 1: Use Feedback

Experience of formal feedback methods is decades old, and many do appreciate their power. However, far too many software engineers and their managers are still practicing low-feedback methods, such as Waterfall project management (also known as Big Bang, Grand Design). Far too many also are checking the quality of their systems by relying on testing, 'late in the day', when they have finished producing their entire system. Even many textbooks and courses continue to present low-feedback methods. This is not from conscious rejection of high-feedback methods, but from ignorance of the many successful and well-documented projects, which have detailed the value of feedback.

Methods using feedback succeed; those without seem to fail. 'Feedback' is the single most powerful principle for software engineering. (Most of the other principles in this paper are really ideas, which support the use of feedback.) Feedback helps you get better control of your project by providing facts about how things are working in practice. Of course, the presumption is that the feedback is early enough to do some good. This is the crux: rapid feedback. We have to have the project time to make use of the feedback (for example, to radically change direction, if that is necessary). Some of the most notable rapid high-feedback methods include:

Defect Prevention Process (originated Mays and Jones, IBM 1983) The Defect Prevention Process (DPP) equates to Software Engineering Institute CMM Level 5 as practiced at IBM from 1983-1985 and on [14]. DPP is a successful way to remove the root causes of defects. In the short term (a year) about 50% defect reduction can be expected; within 2-3 years, 70% reduction (compared to original level) can be experienced and over a 5-8 year timeframe, 95% defect reduction is possible (Sources: IBM Experience, Raytheon Experience [5]).

The key feedback idea is to 'decentralize' the initial causal analysis activity investigating defects to the grass roots programmers and analysts. This gives you the true causes and acceptable, realistic change suggestions. Deeper 'cause analysis' and 'measured process-correction' work can then be undertaken outside of deadline-driven projects by the more specialized and centralized Process Improvement Teams.

The feedback mechanisms are many. For example, same-day feedback is obtained from the people working with the specification and, early numeric process change-result feedback is obtained from the Process Improvement Teams.

Inspection (originated Fagan, IBM 1975) The Inspection method originated in IBM in work carried out by M. Fagan, H. Mills ('Cleanroom') and R. Radice (CMM inventor). It was originally primarily focussed on bug removal in code and code design documents. Many continue to use it in this way today. However, Inspection has changed character in recent years. Today, it can be used more cost-effectively by focussing on measuring the Major defect level (software standards violations) in sample areas (rather than processing the entire document) of any software or upstream marketing specifications [9]. The defect level measurement should be used to decide whether the entire specification is fit for release (exit) downstream to be used, say for a 'go/no-go' decision-making review or for further refinement (test planning, design, coding).

The main Inspection feedback components are:

- feedback to author from colleagues regarding compliance with software standards.
- feedback to author about required levels of standards compliance in order to consider their work releasable.

Evolutionary Project Management (originated within 'Cleanroom' methods, Mills, IBM 1970) Evolutionary Project Management (Evo) has been successfully used on the most demanding space and military projects since 1970 [15], [13], [2], [8], [10]. The US Department of Defense changed their software engineering standard (2167a) to an Evo standard (MIL-STD-498, which derived succeeding public standards (for example, IEEE)). The reports (op. cit.) and my own experience, is that Evo results in a remarkable ability to delivery on time and to budget, or better, compared to conventional project management methods [16].

An Evo project is consciously divided up into small, early and frequently delivered, stakeholder result-focussed steps. Each step delivers benefit and build towards satisfaction of final requirements. Step size is typically weekly or 2% of total time or budget. This results in excellent regular and realistic feedback about the team's ability to deliver meaningful measurable results to selected stakeholders. The feedback includes information on design suitability, stakeholders' reaction, requirements' trade-offs, cost estimation, time estimation, people resource estimation, and development process aspects.

Statistical Process Control [originated Shewhart, Deming, Juran: from 1920's] Statistical Process Control (SPC) although widely used in manufacturing [4] is only to a limited degree actually used in software work. Some use is found in advanced Inspections [5],[18]. The Plan Do Study (or Check) Act cycle is widely appreciated as a fundamental feedback mechanism.

Principle 2: Identify Critical Measures

It is true of any system, that there are several factors, which can cause a system to die. It is true of your body, your organization, your project and your software or service product. Managers call them 'Critical Success Factors.' If you analyzed systems looking for all the critical factors, which caused shortfalls or failures, you would get a list of factors needing better control. They would include both stakeholder values (such as serviceability, reliability, adaptability, portability and usability) and the critical resources needed to deliver those values (such as people, time, money and data quality). You would find, for each of these critical factors, a series of faults, which would include:

- failure to systematically identify all critical stakeholders and their critical needs
- failure to define the factor measurably. Typically, only buzzwords are used and no indication is given of the survival failure) and target (success) measures
- failure to define a practical way to measure the factor
- failure to contract measurably for the critical factor
- failure to design towards reaching the factor's critical levels
- failure to make the entire project team aware of the numeric levels needed for the critical factors
- failure to maintain critical levels of performance during peak loads or on system growth.

Our entire culture and literature of 'software requirements' systematically fails to account for the majority of critical factors. Usually, only a handful, such as performance, financial budget and deadline dates are specified. Most quality factors are not defined quantitatively at all. In practice, all critical measures should always be defined with a useful scale of measure. However, people are not trained to do this and managers are no exception. The result is that our ability to define critical 'breakdown' levels of performance and to manage successful delivery is destroyed from the outset.

Principle 3: Control Multiple Objectives

You do not have the luxury of managing qualities and costs at whim. You cannot decide for a software project to manage just a few of the critical factors, and avoid dealing with the others. You have to deal with *all* the potential threats to your project, organization or system. You must simultaneously track and manage all the critical factors. If not, then the 'forgotten factors' will probably be the very reasons for project or system failure.

I have developed the Impact Estimation (IE) method to enable tracking of critical factors, but it does rely on critical objectives and quantitative goals having been identified and specified. Given that most software engineers have not yet learned to specify *all* their critical factors *quantitatively* (Principle 2), this *next* step, tracking progress against quantitative goals (this principle), is usually impossible.

IE is conceptually similar to Quality Function Deployment [1], but it is much more objective and numeric. It gives a picture of reality that can be monitored [8], [10]. See Table 1, an example of an IE table. It is beyond the scope of this paper to provide all the underlying detail for IE. To give a brief outline, the percentage (%) estimates (see Table 1) are based, as far as possible, on source-quoted, credibility evaluated, objective documented evidence. IE can be used to evaluate ideas *before* their application, and it can also be used (as in Table 1) to track progress towards multiple objectives *during* an Evolutionary project. In Table 1, the 'Actual' and 'Difference" and 'Total' numbers represent *feedback* in small steps for the chosen set of critical factors that management has decided to monitor. If the project is deviating from plans, this will be easily visible and can be corrected on the next step.

Principle 4: Evolve in Small Steps

Software engineering is by nature playing with the unknown. If we already had exactly what we needed, we would re-use it. When we choose to develop software, there are many types of risk, which threaten the result. One way to deal with this is to tackle development in small steps, one step at a time. If something goes wrong, we will immediately know it. We will also have the ability to retreat to the previous step, a level of satisfactory quality, until we understand how to progress again.

Table 1. An example of an IE table. This Impact table for project management gives the project manager constant realistic feedback based on actual measures of progress towards goals, alongside the cost information

	Step #1 A: {Design X, Function Y}	Actual	Difference - is bad + is good	Total	Step #2 B: {Design Z, Design F}	Actual	Difference	Total	Step #3 Next step plan
Reliability 99%-99.9%	50% ±50%	40%	-10%	40%	100% ±20%	80%	-20%	120%	0%
Performance 11sec.-1 sec.	80% ±40%	40%	-40%	40%	30% ±50%	30%	0%	70%	30%
Usability 30 min. - 30 sec.	10% ±20%	12%	+2%	12%	20% ±15%	5%	-15%	17%	83%
Capital Cost 1 mill.	20% ±1%	10%	+10%	10%	5% ±2%	10%	-5%	20%	5%
Engineering Hours 10,000	2% ±1%	4%	-2%	4%	10% ±2.5%	3%	+7%	7%	5%
Calendar Time	1 week	2 weeks	-1 week	2 weeks	1 week	0.5 weeks	+0.5 week	2.5 weeks	1 week

It is important to note that the small steps are not mere development increments. The point is that they are incremental satisfaction of identified stakeholder requirements. Early stakeholders might be salespeople needing a working system to demonstrate, system installers/help desk/service/testers who need to work with something, and finally, early trial users.

The duration of each small step is typically a week or so. The smallest widely reported steps are the daily builds used at Microsoft, which are useful-quality systems. They cumulate to 6-10 week 'shippable quality' milestones [3].

Principle 5: A Stitch in Time Saves Nine

Quality Control must be done as early as possible, from the earliest planning stages, to reduce the delays caused by finding defects later. There needs to be strong specification standards (such as 'all quality requirements must be quantified') and rigorous checking to measure that the rules are applied in practice. When the specifications are not of some minimum standard (like < 1 Major defect/page remaining) then they must be edited until they become acceptable.

- Use Inspection sampling to keep costs down, and to permit early, before specification completion, correction and learning.
- Use numeric Exit from development processes, such as "Maximum 0.2 Majors per page".

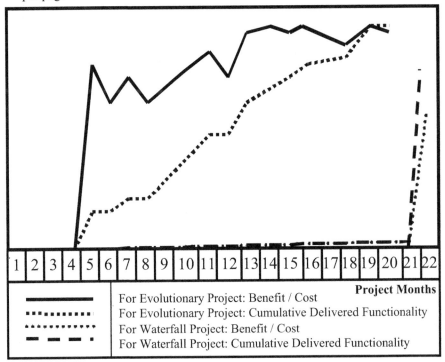

Fig. 1. From Woodward99: One advantage of Evo is that you can focus on delivering high value increments to critical stakeholders early. The upper line represents high value at early stages

It is important that quality control by Inspection be done very early for large specifications, for example within the first 10 pages of work. If the work is not up to standard then the process can be corrected before more effort is wasted. I have seen half a day of Inspection (based on a random sample of 3 pages) show that there were about 19 logic defects per page in 40,000 pages of air traffic control logic design (1986, Sweden). The same managers, who had originally 'approved' the logic design for coding carried out the Inspection with my help. Needless to say the project was seriously late.

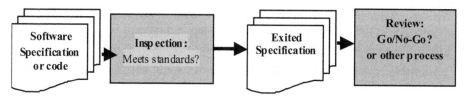

Fig. 2. Review comes after Inspection

In another case I facilitated (USA, 1999, Jet parts supplier) eight managers sampled two pages out of a 82 page requirements' document and measured that there were 150 'Major' defects per page. Unfortunately they had failed to do such sampling three years earlier when their project started, so they had already experienced one year of delay; and told me they expected another year delay while removing the injected defects from the project. This two-year delay was accurately predictable given the defect density they found, and the known average cost from Major defects. They were amazed at this insight, but agreed with the facts. In theory, they could have saved two project years by doing early quality control against simple standards: clarity, unambiguous and no design in requirements were the only rules we used.

These are not unusual cases. I find them consistently all over the world. Management frequently allows extremely weak specifications to go unchecked into costly project processes. They are obviously not managing properly.

Principle 6: Motivation Moves Mountains

Drive out Fear. W. Edwards Deming

Motivation is everything! When individuals and groups are not motivated positively. They will not move forward. When they are negatively motivated (fear, distrust, suspicious) they will resist change to new and better methods.

Motivation is itself a type of method. In fact there are a lot of large and small items contributing to your group's 'sum of motivation'. We can usefully divide the 'motivation problem' into four categories:

- the will to change
- the ability to change
- the knowledge of change direction
- the feedback about progress in the desired change direction.

Leaders (I did not say 'managers') create the will to change by giving people a positive, fun, challenge and, the freedom and resources to succeed.

John Young, CEO of Hewlett Packard during the 1980's, inspired his troops by saying that he thought they needed to aim to be measurably ten times better in service and product qualities ("10X") by the end of the decade (1980-1989). He did not demand it. He supported them in doing it. They failed. Slightly! They reported getting about 9.95 times better, on average, in the decade. The company was healthy and competitive during a terrible time for many others, such as IBM.

The knowledge of change direction is critical to motivation; people need to channel their energies in the right direction! In the software and systems world, this problem has three elements, two of which have been discussed in earlier principles:

- measurable, quantified clarity of the requirements and objectives of the various stakeholders (Principle 2)
- knowledge of all the multiple critical goals (Principle 3)
- formal awareness of constraints, such as resources and laws.

These elements are a constant communication problem, because:

- we do not systematically convert our 'change directions' into crystal clear measurable ideas; people are unclear about the goals and there is no ability to obtain numeric feedback about movement in the 'right' direction. We are likely to say we need a 'robust' or 'secure' system; and less likely to convert these rough ideals into concrete measurable defined, agreed requirements or objectives.
- we focus too often on a single measurable factor (such as '% built' or 'budget spent') when our reality demands that we simultaneously track multiple critical factors to avoid failure and to ensure success. We don't understand what we should be tracking and we don't get enough 'rich' feedback.

Principle 7: Competition Is Eternal

Our conventional project management ideas strongly suggest that projects have a clear beginning and a clear end. In our competitive world, this is not as wise a philosophy as the one Deming suggests. We can have an infinite set of 'milestones' or evolutionary steps of result delivery and use them as we need; the moment we abandon a project, we hand opportunity to our competitors. They can sail past our levels of performance and take our markets.

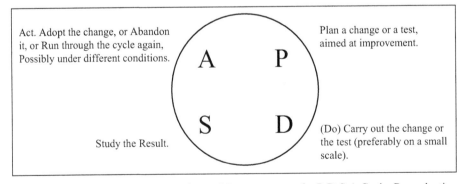

Fig. 3. The Shewhart Cycle for Learning and Improvement - the P D S A Cycle. Reproduction from a letter from W. Edwards Deming, 18 May, 1991 to the author

The practical consequence is that our entire mindset must always be on setting new ambitious numeric 'stakeholder value' targets both for our organizational capability and for our product and service capabilities.

Continuous improvement efforts in the software and services area at IBM, Raytheon and others [14], [5], [11] (Hewlett Packard, '10X', Young) show that we can improve critical cost and performance factors by 20 to 1, in five- to eight-year timeframes. Projects must become eternal campaigns to get ahead and stay ahead.

Principle 8: Things Take Time

> *"It takes 2-3 years to change a project, and a generation to change a culture."*
> W. Edwards Deming
> *"Things Take Time" (TTT). Piet Hein (Denmark)*

"Despite mistakes, disasters, failures, and disappointment, Leonardo never stopped learning, exploring, and experimenting. He demonstrated Herculean persistence in his quest for knowledge. Next to a drawing of a plow in his notebook Leonardo proclaimed, "I do not depart from my furrow." Elsewhere he noted, "Obstacles do not bend me" and "Every obstacle is destroyed through rigor."" [7].

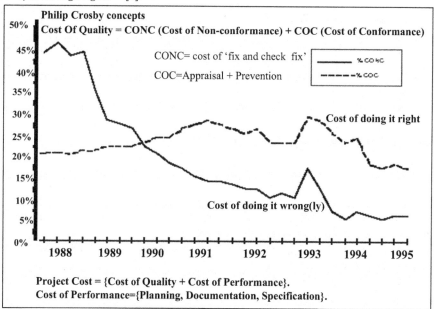

Fig. 4. Cost of Quality versus Time: Raytheon 95 - the 8-year evolution of rework reduction. In the case of Raytheon process improvements (Dion, 1995), many years of persistent process change for 1,000 programmers was necessary to drop rework costs from 43% of total software development costs, to below 5%

Technical management needs to have a long-term plan for improvement of the critical characteristics of their organization and their products. Such long-term plans need to be numerically trackable, and to be stated in multiple critical dimensions. At the same time visible short term progress towards those long-term goals should be planned, expected and tracked.

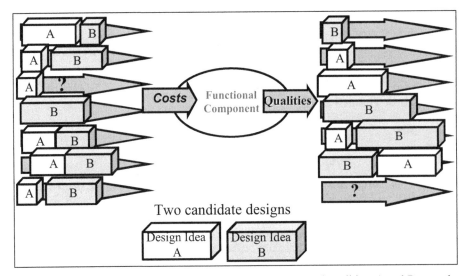

Fig. 5. The estimation of impact of the design ideas on costs and qualities: A and B are solutions / strategies / designs, the 'means' by which we intend to satisfy the 'quality' (stakeholder values) requirements. They each have an effect on many of the quality requirements, and on many of the cost budgets. The length of the bar indicates the degree of impact towards the goal or budget level (symbolized by the arrow point)

Principle 9: The Bad with the Good

In order to get a correct picture of how good any idea is, for meeting our purposes, we must :

- have a quantified multidimensional specification of our requirements; our quality objectives and our resources (people, time, money)
- have knowledge of the expected impact of each design idea on all these quality objectives and resources
- evaluate each design idea with respect to its total, expected or real, impact on our requirements; the unmet objectives and the unused cost budgets.

We need to estimate all impacts on our objectives. We need to reduce, avoid or accept negative impacts. We must avoid simplistic one-dimensional arguments. If we fail to use this systems engineering discipline, then we will be met with the unpleasant surprises of delays, and bad quality, which seem to be the norm in software engineering today. One practical way to model these impacts is using an IE table (as in Table 1).

Principle 10: Keep Your Eye on where You Are Going

"Perfection of means and confusion of ends seem to characterize our age" Albert Einstein

To discover the problem we have only to ask of a specification: "Why?" The answer will be a higher level of specification, nearer the real ends. There are too many designs in our requirements!

You might say, why bother? Isn't the whole point of software to get the code written? Who needs high level abstractions; cut the code! But somehow that code is late and of unsatisfactory quality. The reason is often lack of attention to the real needs of the stakeholders and the project. We need these high-level abstractions of what our stakeholders need so that we can focus on giving them what they are paying us for! Our task is to design and deliver the best technology to satisfy their needs at a competitive cost. One day, software engineers will realize that the primary task is to satisfy their stakeholders. They will learn to design towards stakeholder requirements (multiple concurrent requirements!). One day we will become real systems engineers and shall realize that there is far more to software engineering than writing code!

1. Rapid feedback allows rapid correction.
2. If you do not focus on the few measures critical to your system, it will fail.
3. If you cannot control multiple measures of quality and cost simultaneously, then your system will fail due to the ones you did not control.
4. You must evolve in small increments or 'steps' towards your goals; large step failure kills the entire effort. Early, frequent result delivery is politically and economically wise. 2% of total financial budget is a small step, one you can afford to fail on if things don't go according to plan.
5. Quality Control must be done as early as possible, from the earliest planning stages, to reduce the delays caused by finding defects later.
6. The 'best methods' work only when people are motivated.
7. Eternal Process improvement is necessary as long as you are in competition. (Paraphrasing Deming about PDSA cycle end).
8. Years of persistence are necessary to change a culture.
9. Any method (means, solution, design) you choose will have multiple quality and cost impacts, whether you like them or not!
10. You must keep your focus on the essential results, and never fall victim to the means.

Fig.6. The ten principles

2   Conclusion

Motivate people, towards real results, by giving them numeric feedback frequently and the freedom to use any solution, which gives those results. It is that simple to specify. It is that difficult to do.

3   References

1. Akao, Y. (Editor): Quality Function Deployment: Integrating Customer Requirements into Product Design. Productivity Press, Cambridge Mass. USA, (1990)

2. Cotton, T.: Evolutionary Fusion: A Customer-Oriented Incremental Life Cycle for Fusion. Hewlett-Packard Journal, August (1996) Vol. 47, No. 4, pages 25-38

3. Michael A. Cusumano and Richard W. Selby: Microsoft Secrets: How the World's Most Powerful Software Company Creates Technology, Shapes Markets, and Manages People. The Free Press (a division of Simon and Schuster), (1995) ISBN 0-028-74048-3, 512 pages

4. Deming, W.E.: Out of the Crisis. MIT CAES Center for Advanced Engineering Study. Cambridge MA USA-02139, (1986) ISBN 0-911-37901-0, 507 pages, hard cover

5. Dion, R.: The Raytheon Report.
    www.sei.cmu.edu/products/publications/95.reports/95.tr.017.html.

6. Fagan, M.E.: Design and code inspections. IBM Systems Journal, Vol. 15 (3), pages 182-211, 1976. Reprinted IBM Systems Journal, Vol. 38, Nos. 2&3, 1999, pages 259-287. www.almaden.ibm.com/journal

7. Gelb, M.J.: How to Think Like Leonardo da Vinci. Dell Publishing NY, (1998) ISBN 0-440-50827-4

8. Gilb, T.: Principles of Software Engineering Management.Addison-Wesley, UK/USA (1988) ISBN 0-201-19246-2

9. Gilb, T., Graham, D.: Software Inspection. Addison-Wesley, (1993) ISBN 0-201-63181-4. Japanese Translation, August (1999) ISBN 4-320-09727-0, C3041 (code next to ISBN)

10. Gilb, T. : Competitive Engineering, Addison-Wesley, UK (End 2000) There will always be a version of this book free at my website, http://www.result-planning.com

11. Kaplan C., Clark, R., Tang, V.: Secrets of Software Quality, 40 Innovations from IBM. McGraw Hill, ISBN 0-079-11975-3

12. Keeney, R.L.: Value-focused Thinking: A Path to Creative Decision-making. Harvard University Press, Cambridge Mass/London, (1992) ISBN 0-674-93197-1

13. May, E.L., Zimmer, B.A.: The Evolutionary Development Model for Software. Hewlett-Packard Journal, Vol. 47. (4) August (1996) 39-45

14. Mays, R.: Practical Aspects of the Defect Prevention Process. In: Gilb, T., Graham D.: Software Inspection, Chapter 17, (1993)

15. Mills, H.D.: IBM Systems Journal, (4) (1980) Also republished IBM Systems Journal, (2&3) (1999)

16. Morris, P.W.G.: The Management of Projects. Thomas Telford, London, (1994) ISBN 0-727-7169-3

17. Peters, T.: Reinventing Work, The Project 50. Alfred A. Knopf, New York, (2000) ISBN 0-375-40773-1

18. Florac, W.A., Park, R.E., Carleton, A.D.: Practical Software Measurement: Measuring for Process Management and Improvement. Guidebook from Software Engineering Institute, Reference: CMU/SEI-97-HB-003. Downloadable from SEI web site (Acrobat Reader): ftp://ftp.sei.cmu.edu/ for publications, and main site http://www.sei.cmu.edu. (1997)

19. Woodward, S.: Evolutionary Project Management. IEEE Computer, October (1999) 49-57

Empirical Assessment of Software On-Line Diagnostics Using Fault Injection

John Napier, John May, and Gordon Hughes

Safety Systems Research Centre (SSRC), Department of Computer Science,
University of Bristol, Merchant Venturers Building, Woodland Road,
Bristol BS8 1UB
J.Napier@bristol.ac.uk, J.May@bristol.ac.uk,
G.Hughes@bristol.ac.uk

Abstract. This paper is part of an on-going empirical research programme to develop an improved understanding of the implementation and evaluation of on-line diagnostics in software. In this study we have concentrated on the hypothesis that residual design errors exist because their coupling to the input space is very small, making them difficult to detect in normal testing. The objective of the reported experiment was basically to add a simple group of diagnostic checks to a reasonably complex program and use arbitrary fault injection to assess the error detection in relation to the coupling of the fault to the input space. The results were promising in that they demonstrated no significant deterioration in the effectiveness of the diagnostics as the fault coupling to the input space decreased. On this basis the use of diagnostics can be seen as supplementary to validation testing.

1 Introduction

Computer-based system failures are generated by either random hardware failures or by the systematic design errors incorporated into the hardware elements and architecture together with the embedded or application softwares. Random hardware failures are associated with time-dependent or 'wear-out' mechanisms which result in members of the same set of components (subjected to the same environment) failing randomly in-time. Fault tolerant design has its foundation in providing ways of detecting these random failures and ensuring continued system operation by the use of sub-system redundancy or recovery methods. However, the main problem for computer-based systems is providing fault tolerance for unknown (at the time of commencement of service) systematic design errors. Such residual systematic design errors only become apparent under specific conditions and, since they have not been detected by pre-operational testing, tend to have a long latency in normal operation. Indeed current design and assessment methods cannot ensure that software is error

F. Koornneef and M. van der Meulen (Eds.): SAFECOMP 2000, LNCS 1943, pp. 14-26, 2000.
© Springer-Verlag Berlin Heidelberg 2000

free and consequently fault tolerant techniques should play an important role in safety related systems to ensure safe software behaviour [1].

Fault detection in software can be obtained by the use of on-line diagnostics (e.g. executable assertions checking intermediate internal states) and fault tolerance achieved with appropriate exception handling [2] [3]. Utilising the fault coverage provided by on-line diagnostics at different operational states (external and internal) is a potential method of increasing software reliability. However, the flexibility and complexity of software means that there is extreme diversity in its modes of failure. In addition, there are generally an unlimited number and type of error checking functions that can be added in any complex application, and it is not clear which types of assertions are most effective. Whilst the benefits of executable assertions in software have been discussed in the literature over recent years [2], the empirical evidence to support the implementation and assessment of different on-line diagnostic solutions is lacking. Although on-line diagnostics seem to offer a distinct means of defence against general program failure, the current literature does not establish that a suitable defence against particular residual design errors is indeed achievable.

This paper is part of an on-going empirical research programme at the Safety Systems Research Centre (SSRC) which aims to develop an improved understanding of the implementation and evaluation of on-line diagnostics in software. The limited empirical evidence presented here is intended to provide a basis for further research which it is hoped will lead towards generalised guidelines for safety related software design and validation.

The focus of this paper is on one aspect of residual design errors, namely that some of them are only exposed by a small number of vectors in the input space over time and hence are difficult to detect during testing. It could be said that such a fault has a small *'footprint'*. Fault effects that are exposed to many points in the input space over time should be readily revealed under normal testing. The aim of the experiments described in this paper is to investigate the effectiveness of a simple diagnostic strategy when the degree of coupling between the fault initiator and the input space is relatively low. The basic hypothesis is that if the effectiveness of a diagnostic solution does not deteriorate as the coupling between fault and input space decreases, then the potential contribution of the approach as a defence against systematic error is much larger, since it can be assumed, by extrapolation, to target small faults that are hard to find by testing.

In one sense it is clear without experiment that a diagnostic is a special type of test with the power to reveal faults which are not related in an obvious way to the size of a fault's corresponding input domain (those inputs which expose the fault). Nevertheless, in common with tests, diagnostics are conceived based on a person's understanding of the software code, their conception of a fault model and their ability to improve ways of exposing/trapping the faults thus conceived. There are therefore many reasons to anticipate a degree of commonality in the fault -finding capabilities of the two approaches.

The experiments described here use fault injection techniques [4] to estimate the fault coverage of a diagnostic. A system is normally composed of a large number of low level software components and whilst it is possible to derive fault models for low level components it is very difficult to model fault propagation. Fault injection avoids this conceptual difficulty by simulating fault behaviour. The knowledge gained in this way may well be employed to improve diagnostics at a higher level in the code. Note that in general code execution is necessary and it is not feasible to take the knowledge of the simple component failure modes and directly conceive new high-level diagnostics. Also a quality of 'arbitrariness' in fault injection may prove to be an advantage. The idea is comparable to random testing of software, where tests are not conceived with any specific fault detection in mind, yet their fault detection ability remains powerful [5]. The preconceptions of testers lead them to miss classes of faults which random tests do not miss.

The following sections describe the design of an experiment to relate the effectiveness of diagnostics to fault size in the input space and provide a summary of the results.

2   Experimental Design

2.1   Objectives

Using a suitable software case study, the objectives of these experiments were: -

- to design a simple set of executable assertions to perform the on-line diagnosis and add these new functions to the original code.
- to develop a set of simulated faults for the software fault injection tests.
- to define an appropriate set of input test vectors. (A set of fault free results were used as a *gold* standard for comparison to identify system failure during fault injection.)
- to compare the proportion of faults detected with low input space coupling with the average success rate of the on-line diagnostics.

2.2   Case Study

The experiments were performed using a nuclear protection trip software from a previous project known as DARTS [15]. The aim of DARTS was to assess the contribution to reliability of diverse software versions in a multi-channel voting system. In the experiments discussed in this paper one channel is considered as an individual system. Each channel monitors various parameters from the nuclear plant environment and one of seven trips is output together with several data status signals under various circumstances. Once a trip is set it is latched until the software is reset. Two versions of the code - one in Ada and one in C - were available and in these experiments the C version was used. The choice was made on the basis that C presents less restrictions to the fault injection process than Ada. As discussed in [6], the freedom and arbitrariness of fault injection in Ada is restricted by the variable visibility of procedure parameters.

The code versions from the case study were developed specifically for experimentation, but this was done under commercial conditions to produce software representative of that used in practice. Various documentation was available from DARTS including the system requirements specification and the test specifications (accepted by the customer) for each software channel. The C version is reasonably complex consisting of approximately 2300 lines of code (LOC). To illustrate the design complexity a structure diagram of this software is shown in figure 1.

To simplify the focus of these experiments the use of recovery mechanisms was not included. If any assertions detected an internal error before system failure occurred then it was simply assumed that such information could be used to invoke a suitable form of recovery, such as switching to a stand-by system.

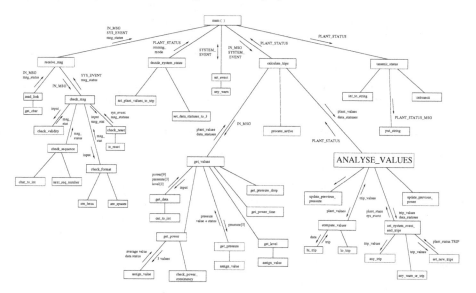

Fig. 1. Software Structure Diagram

2.3   Design of On-Line Diagnostics

Software fault diagnosis can be based on invariant assertions, which are derived from the specification. They can be diverse in nature, being used to verify intermediate results, final results and data flow. The data and control flow assertions are complementary; the data flow assertions check for errors within a given function while the control flow assertions check for valid execution sequences. The data flow assertions can be derived from formal definitions of the program behaviour (i.e. pre- and post-conditions). One useful categorisation of the different types of checks is provided in [7] and [8], and this was used as a starting point for the diagnostic design in this experiment. The classification is as follows.

1. *Replication* - involves replication of some parts of the code and comparison with approximate functions. Has a relatively high overhead in terms of extra code and so is generally limited to low level functions, which only replicate certain aspects of the system behaviour.

2. *Timing* - checks timing constraints where systems response is a requirement.
3. *Reversal* - where the input-output relationship of parts of the code is a one-to-one mapping, the module inputs can be re-computed from the output to check that they are the correct inputs for the given output. Unfortunately many modules/functions have a many-to-one mapping. Also problems can arise with floating point precision.
4. *Coding* - generally refers to data redundancy introduced purely for error checking of the non-redundant data parts, such as parity bits in binary codes.
5. *Reasonableness* - checks whether the states of various data objects are acceptable or reasonable. Examples include logical assertions that must be satisfied and simple out-of-range or correct data typing checks. Also includes checks of consistency between different objects possibly within the same data structure.
6. *Structural* - checks either the structural or semantic integrity of data structures.
7. *'Diagnostic'* - in the context of this categorisation this term specifically refers to checking the behaviour of individual components. Such checks exercise a component with a set of inputs, such as self tests in hardware. This term is slightly confusing - note that the terms *on-line diagnostics* and *diagnostics* are used interchangeably in this paper and refer to all 7 of these categories.

The other key factor to consider is the location of the diagnostics. Monitoring low level behaviour will not only increase the system complexity but may fail to detect errors caused by the interaction of components. Monitoring higher level behaviour provides diagnostic coverage over a wider range of components and their interactions and reduces the added complexity. However, this will allow the error to propagate further, possibly resulting in insufficient time for the system to recover and avoid system failure. The distribution of diagnostics throughout a system is the subject of on-going research [9].

Unfortunately there are generally an unlimited number and type of error checking functions that can be added in any complex application, and it is not clear which types of assertions are most effective. In these experiments the aim was to insert some relatively simple error checking functions, not to design an optimal diagnostic solution. The requirements specification and code design were studied in order to determine an appropriate set of assertions to reveal design and coding faults. Assertions related to the specification included out-of-range checks and consistency checks between data objects. Whereas assertions related to the code structure were largely based on reverse calculations, either where a one to one input-output mapping could be identified or where given the output of a function, input limits could be identified. No timing checks or coding checks were applicable to this case study. The checks were not intended to be exhaustive only exemplary and were limited to 18 for this simple diagnostic solution. The checks were all implemented at the same location in the code - as post-conditions to the *analyse_values* function (see figure 1). A considerable amount of data processing occurs within this function and in addition it makes use of the main data objects generated by previous functions. It was assumed that many fault effects would propagate to this point. Also assertions at this location would be able to trap the effects of faults prior to the system output being affected. The aim of further research at the SSRC is to compare the effectiveness of this initial solution with other diagnostic approaches using a range of techniques and a distribution of assertions throughout the code. The main restriction here being that low-level functions are not checked directly, assuming that any significant errors would propagate and be detectable at higher behavioural levels. In this experiment an average of 250 lines were added as diagnostic functions - approximately a 10% increase in the original code size. Minimising the increase in code size and complexity is an additional reason for using reasonable simple on-line diagnostics functions.

2.4   Approach to Software Fault Injection

Fault simulation in general is based on deliberately injecting faults (using a fault model) into a system, or a copy (such as a prototype or a simulation) to observe the effects of these faults on the system behaviour [4]. Whilst various software fault injection techniques have been used [4], [10] and [11] there are only two basic types. One is generally called mutation and there has been considerable research in this area over recent years [12]. In mutation the actual code is altered by replacing various statements or groups of statements with mutant code. Essentially the aim is determine if a set of tests can kill (expose as different) the mutant, providing evidence of the code coverage of those tests.

The second type of software fault injection aims to analyse the effects of injected faults on code behaviour and assess the fault tolerance of the software. It is primarily concerned with simulating the effects of systematic design errors, although it can also be used to simulate random hardware faults in the software's environment. This technique perturbs the information in a program's data state to model the effects of faults indirectly [4]. Possible perturbations of data states (and therefore data flow) include modifying an existing value (but not type definitions) or modifying branching conditions, which can be achieved by either modifying the value being tested or the condition itself. This paper focuses on this second type of software fault injection. In order to determine whether an error propagates to the system output a comparison against *fault free* results must be made.

One of the most difficult problems to overcome in any practical application is to determine how to simulate *realistic* faults. Unlike hardware fault injection where known and predictable random faults are the focus of most experiments [13], in software the focus is primarily on systematic faults: residual design errors, which by their very nature are unknown. In addition the number of possible ways and locations to perturb data or code in any complex system is unlimited. One possible approach is to speculate that all residual fault effects of any consequence - those leading to system failure - will manifest as internal errors in data as it is passed between the system modules [9]. Therefore simulated faults need only be located in data at the boundaries between system components and modules. However, there is still an unlimited number of ways to perturb the data at these boundary locations.

Rather than speculating about the nature of realistic fault sets, these experiments focused on a more pragmatic objective: utilising different types of hypothetical fault sets, randomly selecting sample faults from each and simply observing the experimental results from each set. If the results from each set agree then the confidence in the experiment as a whole is increased. In these experiments the following hypothetical fault types were used:-

1. Random data perturbations - data assignment locations in the code were selected at random and a data value within the assignment statement (or the result of the assignment) was perturbed at random.
2. Random code mutations - code statements which affected either data or control flow were selected at random and mutated such that the program still compiled and the system continued to produce some form of meaningful output.
3. Random module interface perturbations - based on the principle discussed above. Similar to the first fault set however data at the interfaces between modules were selected at random.

A total of 70 faults were introduced into the code separately and an executable version of the code produced for each. 10 locations from each set were selected and for fault sets 1 and 3, three perturbations for each fault were used. The coupling that resulted between simulated fault and input space was left to this process (i.e. not guided in any way) and it was hoped that the randomness in the process would lead to a range of coupling.

2.5   Design of Test Vectors

Within the context of this paper each test vector is considered to be one point in the input space (of test vectors), where each test vector is a temporal sequence of between 10 and 15 discrete environmental states, and each state is represented by a binary input code 80 bytes in length.

The ultimate goal of any fault injection experiment is to observe all the effects of the simulated faults. However, this can only be assured by testing the whole input space, which is an impractical task in most complex applications. So, in these experiments a practical test strategy was developed, with the aim of exposing a high proportion of the simulated fault effects. This strategy consisted of carefully chosen boundary value tests directed at critical areas of the code. Whilst exhaustive testing is not practical such tests are powerful - in the sense that fault footprints are assumed to be more concentrated in this test space than over the input space as a whole. In addition these tests vectors were based on the test strategies accepted by the customer during the DARTS project, which had been specifically designed to demonstrate compliance to the functional requirements specification.

For each infected version of code (and the fault free version) all 46 tests were performed resulting in a total of over 3000 tests. After each test the results were compared with the fault free test results to determine if a system failure had occurred and the numeric identifier of any assertion detecting the error was recorded. A summary of the results is provided below.

3   Summary of Results

3.1   Results

The results showed that 13 of the 70 faults produced no system failure for any of the input test vectors. Further examination of these faults revealed several reasons for this: the data perturbation was too small; the fault was in a code region not executed (either a conditional branch or in one case a function that is never called); or the fault was masked by re-assignment of the perturbed variable. Although these faults have a zero footprint in the space of test vectors, it is not correct to assume that they will have a zero footprint in the whole input space. They may well be revealed by different input vectors. As the effects of these faults were not observed during the experiment, it is not possible to know how effective the diagnostics may be in trapping them. The analysis that follows is only related to those fault effects that were observed during testing, and therefore these 13 faults are excluded.

Table 1. Results summary - success rates of error detection for a failed test vector

Fault Set	Coupling of fault to test space (46 different tests vectors in total)						All Faults
	High coupling			Low coupling			
	>41	>36	>31	<5	<10	<15	
Random	29%	36%	36%	23%	66%	59%	**40%**
Mutants	50%	50%	50%	0%	38%	29%	**45%**
Boundary	39%	39%	39%	55%	36%	27%	**39%**
All faults	**37%**	**39%**	**39%**	**35%**	**48%**	**38%**	**40%**

The results are summarised in table 1 and in figures 2 and 3. Table 1 summaries the diagnostic success rates for high and low coupled faults from each set and for all faults - the average success rate is 40%. The definitions of high and low couplings are taken over a range of arbitrary cut off points (i.e. the footprint size in the test space). There is some variation in the diagnostic success rates between fault sets particularly where the coupling is low – there is zero success detecting code mutants with a footprint of less than 5. However, the population of faults in this experiment set is quite small which may account for these variations (see section 3.3). Interestingly for the random and boundary data fault types some higher than average success rates are recorded. Expanding the analysis to cover all faults the variations are much less significant, which is encouraging.

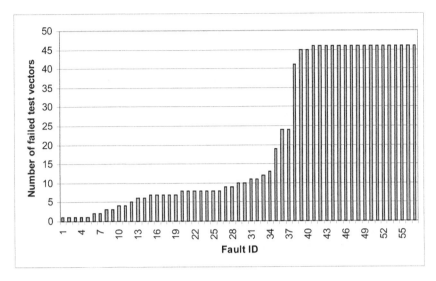

Fig. 2. The fault footprint in the test space

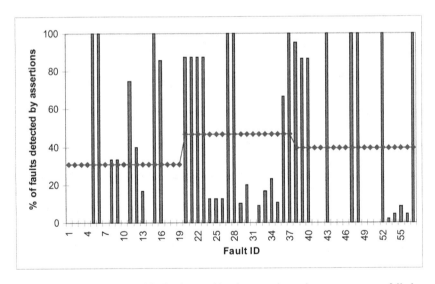

Fig. 3. The percentage of faults detected by the assertions given a test vector failed

In figure 2 the results from all 3 fault groups have been combined and ordered purely on the size of the footprint in the test space (zero footprint faults are excluded). A fault ID is assigned based on this ordering. The figure clearly shows the variation of fault footprint sizes in the test space. Figure 3 uses this same fault ID and shows the percentage of faults detected by the assertions given that a test vector has failed. This figure clearly shows that there is no discernible correlation between the footprint size and the diagnostic effectiveness. It is important that the effectiveness of a diagnostic solution does not deteriorate as the coupling between fault and input space decreases, as some residual design errors will have a very small footprint. In Figure 3 the faults are also coarsely grouped into low, middle and high footprint sizes and the average detection rate calculated over each group: low 31%, middle 46% and high 39%. There is some variation in these averages but again it is hoped that this would be reduced using a larger population of faults in further experiments.

These tests certainly do not provide conclusive proof that the diagnostics implemented would detect real residual design errors, but they do provide some evidence that even relatively simple diagnostic strategies can provide a defence against errors that are only revealed in rare operational circumstances. Although there is some variation between the results from each fault set the similarity of the results increases the confidence that these tests support this conjecture.

On average 60% of the errors were undetected. However the assertions were not designed as an optimal solution, only to be representative of possible solutions. It was observed that the fault effects trapped by out-of-range assertions generally had a large footprint in the test space. Whilst the reversal and consistency checks generally trapped subtler fault effects with smaller footprints. Beyond these basic observations no real attempt is made here to draw conclusions about the effectiveness of different types of error detection. It is difficult to generalise from experiments in one application as the types of checks employed in different applications will be largely influenced by the specific functions and code/data structures present. However, there may be some benefit in analysing the results from a number of different experiments.

3.2   Validity of Experiments

Experimental flaws could have resulted from the same programmer designing both the assertions and fault sets. The assertions were developed first to prevent biasing them towards particular fault types. Although every effort was made not to bias the faults towards or away from particular error checking functions, undoubtedly prior knowledge of the checking functions could have influenced these results. In addition the same knowledge of the underlying code/data structures was used to design both the diagnostics and the fault sets. It would be interesting to repeat the experiment using independent programmers for the design of the diagnostics and the simulated faults.

3.3   Discussion

The number of faults injected was governed by practical limitations of writing the code, storing the new executables and running the tests. However, to further increase the confidence in these results more faults should be injected utilising as many locations as possible. Although some simple automation routines were used here, further automation of the whole fault injection process is required. In [4] Voas describes the basic foundations for a software fault injection tool. The technique is slightly different to that used here: there is no need to store a new executable for each fault, and rather than compare tests results against a known standard, the criteria for system success must be specified in logical language with reference to the system input-output relationship. Whether a logical language could be used to sufficiently define the success criteria in this case study is an area for further research. Another study could explore more random variations of each fault perturbation, using a similar process to the homogeneity tests performed by Michael [14], in order to gain more information regarding the sensitivity of their detectability. The results showed that variations in the data perturbations certainly change the fault effect and footprint size.

Further analysis is now required to improve the effectiveness of the diagnostics in this application. Those tests where abnormal behaviour was not detected might provide useful insights. The improved fault coverage again would be measured using fault injection. A further study is needed to analyse the relationship between coupling and detection rates as coverage increased.

4   Conclusions

In this study we have concentrated on the hypothesis that residual design errors exist because their coupling to the input space is very small, making them difficult to detect in normal testing. The objective of the reported experiment was basically to add a simple group of diagnostic checks to a reasonably complex program and use arbitrary fault injection to assess the error detection in relation to the coupling of the fault to the input space. The results were promising in that they exhibited no discernible correlation between the effectiveness of the diagnostics and the fault coupling to the input space (test space). These tests certainly do not provide conclusive proof that the diagnostics implemented would detect real residual design errors, but they do provide some evidence that the fault tolerance achieved, by even relatively simple diagnostic strategies, can provide a degree of defence against errors which are only revealed in rare operational circumstances.

This paper is clearly based on limited experimental evidence and is intended to provide a basis for appropriate avenues of further research which could include:-

- More exhaustive testing using a larger number of input test vectors and environment simulation;
- Distributing diagnostics throughout the system, aiming to optimise the error checking whilst minimising the increased code complexity;
- Determining which types of assertions are most effective and which is the more appropriate recovery strategy - comparing results from several case studies, together with a relative comparison between several diagnostic solutions in each application;
- Examining the degree of independence between code programmer and diagnostic designer.

A wider aim of ongoing research must be to gain an improved understanding of the relationship between actual possible design errors and those simulated during software fault injection. This is important because quantification of the fault coverage provided is only relative to the set of faults simulated during assessment. Such experiments may lead to a practical taxonomy of faults.

Acknowledgements

The work presented comprises elements from the SSRC Generic Research Programme funded by British Energy, National Air Traffic Services, Lloyd's Register, Railtrack and the Health and Safety Executive. In addition elements of the Diverse Software Project (DISPO) are included, which is part of the UK Nuclear Safety Research programme, funded and controlled by the Industry Management Committee.

References

1.   **Michael, R. Lyu**, Editor, *Handbook of Software Reliability Engineering*, IEEE Computer Society Press (1996)
2.   **Rabajec, C**, On-line Error Detection by Executable Assertions, *Safecomp95*, Belgirate, Italy, (October 1995)
3.   **Leveson, N G,** *Safeware: System Safety and Computers*, Addison Wesley, (1995)
4.   **Voas, J M and McGraw, G**, Software Fault Injection: Inoculating Programs Against Errors, Wiley Computer Publishing, (1998)
5.   **Duran J.W. & Ntafos** S. *"An evaluation of random testing"* IEEE Transactions on Software Engineering, v10 n4 pp438-444, July 1984
6.   **Napier J, Chen L, May J, Hughes G**, *"Fault simulation to validate fault-tolerance in Ada"*, International Journal of Computer Systems: Science & Engineering, January 2000.
7.   **Anderson T and Lee PA**, *Fault Tolerance: Principles and Practice.* Englewood Cliffs, NJ: Prentice-Hall International, 1981
8.   **Leveson, N G, Cha, S S, Knight, J C, and Shimeall, T J,** The Use of Self Checks and Voting in Software Error Detection: An Empirical Study, *IEEE Trans. on Software Engineering*, **16**(4), (April 1990).
9.   **Napier J and Hughes G**, *Implementing Software On-Line Diagnostics in Safety Critical Systems*, Procs. of the 15th Annual UK Performance Engineering Workshop, Bristol, UK, July 1999.
10. **Clark, J A and Pradham, D K**, Fault Injection: A method for validating computer-system dependability, *IEEE Computer*, (June 1995) 47 - 56.
11. **Carpenter, G F**, Mechanism for evaluating the effectiveness of software fault-tolerant structures. *Microprocessors and Microsystems*, **14**(8), (Oct 1990) 505-510
12. **DeMillo RA, Lipton RJ and Sayward FG** *"Hints on test data selection: Help for the practising programmer."* IEEE Computer, 11(4) 34-41, April 1978.
13. **Lala PK**, "Fault Tolerant and Fault Testable Hardware Design", Prentice Hall Intl., 1985.
14. **Michael, C C,** On the uniformity of error propagation in software, *Procs. 12th Annual Conf. on Computer Assurance (COMPAS '97).* Gaithersburg, MD, (1997).

15. **Quirk, W.J. and Wall, D.N.,** *"Customer Functional Requirements for the Protection System to be used as the DARTS Example"*, DARTS consortium deliverable report DARTS-032-HAR-160190-G supplied under the HSE programme on Software Reliability, June 1991

Speeding-Up Fault Injection Campaigns in VHDL Models

B. Parrotta, M. Rebaudengo, M. Sonza Reorda, and M. Violante

Politecnico di Torino, Dip. di Automatica e Informatica,
C.so Duca degli Abruzzi 24, I-10129 Torino, Italy
{parrotta,reba,sonza,violante}@polito.it

Abstract. Simulation-based Fault Injection in VHDL descriptions is increasingly common due to the popularity of top-down design flows exploiting this language. This paper presents some techniques for reducing the time to perform the required simulation experiments. Static and dynamic methods are proposed to analyze the list of faults to be injected, removing faults as soon as their behavior is known. Common features available in most VHDL simulation environments are also exploited. Experimental results show that the proposed techniques are able to reduce the time required by a typical Fault Injection campaign by a factor ranging from 43.9% to 96.6%.

1 Introduction

In recent years, there has been a rapid increase in the use of computer-based systems in areas such as railway traffic control, aircraft flight, telecommunications, and others, where failures can cost lives and/or money. This trend has led to concerns regarding the validation of the fault tolerance properties of these systems and the evaluation of their reliability.

On the other side, the continuous increase in the integration level of electronic systems is making more difficult than ever to guarantee an acceptable degree of reliability, due to the occurrence of un-modeled faults and soft errors that can dramatically affect the behavior of the system. As an example, the decrease in the magnitude of the electric charges used to carry and store information is seriously raising the probability that alpha particles and neutrons hitting the circuit could introduce errors in its behavior (often modeled as Single Upset Errors) [1].

To face the above issues, mechanisms are required to increase the robustness of electronic devices and systems with respect to possible errors occurring during their normal function, and for these reasons on-line testing is now becoming a major area of research. No matter the level these mechanisms work at (hardware, system software, or application software), there is a need for techniques and methods to debug and verify their correct design and implementation.

F. Koornneef and M. van der Meulen (Eds.): SAFECOMP 2000, LNCS 1943, pp. 27-36, 2000.

Fault Injection [2] imposed itself as a viable solution to the above problems. Several Fault Injection techniques have been proposed and practically experimented; they can basically be grouped into *simulation-based* techniques (e.g., [3][4]), *software-implemented* techniques (e.g., [5][6][7][8]), and *hardware-based* techniques (e.g., [9][10]).

As pointed out in [2] physical fault injection (hardware- and software-implemented fault injection approaches) is more suited when a prototype of the system is already available, or when the system itself is too large to be modeled and simulated at an acceptable cost. Conversely, simulation-based fault injection is very effective in allowing early analysis of designed systems, since it can be exploited when a prototype is not yet available. The main disadvantage of simulation-based fault injection technique versus hardware- and software- ones is the high CPU time required to simulate the model of the system.

In the last years, VHDL has become a de-facto standard for describing systems in particular when automatic synthesis tools are exploited; therefore, several researchers have addressed the problem of how to perform fault injection campaigns on VHDL descriptions [3] [4]. These approaches are *simulator-independent*, i.e., injection is performed through the adoption of special data types or fragments of VHDL code that are dedicated to modify the system behavior. They do not rely on simulator features, nor require the modification of simulation tools, therefore can easily fit on any design flow.

The approaches proposed so far neglect the problem of reducing the time spent running fault injection campaigns. To deal with complex system new methods should be devised to *minimize the time* spent during simulations.

In this paper we address the problem of improving the efficiency of simulation-based fault injection and we show how simulation time can be dramatically shortened. The technique we developed analyzes the faults that will be injected in order to identify fault effects as early as possible and exploits the features provided by modern commercial VHDL simulators to speed-up injection operations. Our approach comprises three steps:

1. *golden run executions*: the system is simulated without injecting any faults and a trace file is produced, recording information on the system behavior. Moreover, the state of the simulator is sampled and stored allowing to resume the simulation at a given time instant;
2. *static fault analysis*: given an initial fault list, by exploiting the information gathered during golden run computation, we identify those faults which effects on the system are known a-priori, and remove them from the fault list. This step exploits a sub-set of already proposed fault collapsing rules [11];
3. *dynamic fault analysis*: during fault injection, the behavior of the system is periodically compared with the golden run. The simulation is stopped as early as the effect of the fault on the system becomes known, i.e., either the fault alters the system behavior or the fault does not produce any effect.

We exploit standard commands offered by commercial VHDL simulators for injecting faults and tracing system behavior. This technique minimizes the intrusiveness of our approach and, by exploiting standard commands that are usually provided by modern VHDL simulators, it is of general use.

To assess the effectiveness of our technique, we performed fault injection experiments on a benchmark target system composed by a single microcontroller. We analyzed the behavior of several programs, and we recorded a speed-up ranging from 43.9% up to 96.6%.

The remainder of this paper is organized as follows. Section 2 describes the system architecture where faults are injected. Section 3 describes the techniques we developed, while Section 4 reports some preliminary results assessing their effectiveness. Finally, Section 5 draws some conclusions.

2   The Target Architecture

The system we considered is composed of an Intel i8051 microcontroller equipped with an external RAM memory storing the code the i8051 executes. All the programs we have considered have a data segment that fits in the i8051 internal memory composed of 128 bytes of static RAM; therefore our target architecture does not exploit an external RAM for storing data. The whole system is described in VHDL at the Register Transfer (RT) level.

The fault model we are considering is the transient single bit flip. We injected faults in the following system components:

- i8051 control registers and internal SRAM
- external RAM storing the code.

This assumption allows us to evaluate the effects of single transient faults both in the data or in the code.

3   Proposed Approach

The purpose of our approach is to minimize the time required for performing fault injection campaigns. We addressed this problem by performing fault analysis (before starting and during the fault injection campaign) and resorting to simulator commands that can be used to quickly reach injection time. The proposed approach is based on the assumption that the simulation runs are deterministic, i.e. for a given set of inputs there is only one trace of the system golden execution.

To implement this approach the fault injection tool cooperates with a standard VHDL simulator, as Figure 1 shows. The fault injection manager issues commands (such as run commands or query commands) to the simulation back-end, which in turn sends responses to the Fault Injection manager.

In the following subsections we will detail how our technique can be implemented; in particular, subsection 3.1 describes the information we gather on the behavior of the system during golden run execution, then subsection 3.2 shortly recalls the fault-collapsing rules we exploited and subsection 3.3 details how dynamic fault analysis can be implemented. Finally, subsection 3.4 describes a technique which exploits simulator facilities and that allows to save the most of the time required to reach injection time.

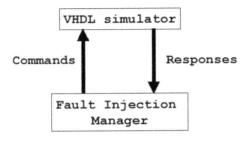

Fig. 1. Fault injection tool overview

3.1   Golden Run Execution

The purpose of this step is to gather information on the behavior of the system: given a set of input stimuli that will remain constant in the following fault injection campaigns, two sets of information are gathered, one for performing static fault analysis and one for performing dynamic fault analysis.

Static fault analysis requires:

- *data accesses*: whenever a data is accessed, the time, the type of access (read or write) and the address are stored;
- *register accesses*: whenever a register is accessed, the time, the register name and the type of access are stored;
- *code accesses*: at each instruction fetch, the address of the fetched instruction is stored in a trace file;

We collect the needed information resorting to ad-hoc modules written in VHDL, called *code/data watchers*, that we insert in the system model (Figure 2). This approach is not intrusive, since code/data watchers work in parallel with the system and do not affect its behavior.

Conversely, for performing *dynamic* fault analysis we sample the state of the system with a given sampling frequency. The state of the system reports the content of the processor registers and the content of the data memory. We gather this information by periodically stopping the simulation and observing the system state resorting to simulator commands. The values gathered during sampling are stored in main memory, where we record the time at which the sample is taken, the contents of processor control registers and the content of the processor memory.

This approach is very simple and effective because allows to capture snapshots of the system with zero intrusiveness. On the other hand, when addressing very large systems, it could require the availability of large amounts of both memory and disk space. As a consequence, the sampling frequency should be carefully selected.

3.2   Static Fault Analysis

Faults are removed from an initial fault list according to two sets of rules; one for faults intended to be injected in the data and one for faults in the code. The rules are applied by analyzing the information gathered during golden run execution.

We remove from the fault list a fault affecting data if it verifies at least one of the following conditions:

1. given a fault f to be injected at time T at address A, remove f from the fault list if A is no longer read after time T: this rule allows removing the faults that:
   - do not affect the system behavior, or
   - remain latent at the end of the simulation;
2. given a fault f to be injected at time T at address A, remove f from the fault list if the very first operation that involves A after time T is a write operation.

Conversely, we remove a fault in the code if it verifies the following condition: given a fault f to be injected at time T at address A, remove f from the fault list if the address A corresponds to an instruction that is no longer fetched after time T. This rule identifies faults that do not produce any effect and whose injection is therefore useless.

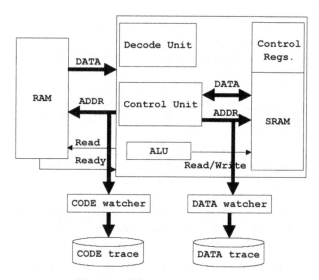

Fig. 2. Modified system architecture

3.3   Dynamic Fault Analysis

Dynamic fault analysis is based on the idea of identifying as early as possible the effect of the injected fault.

As soon as the effect of a fault become evident, we stop the simulation, potentially saving a significant amount of simulation time.

The fault injection routine we exploit is described in Figure 3.

```
result Inject( SAMPLE *L,  fault F)
{
  set_breakpoints();

  Simulate( F->time );
  FlipBit( F->location );
  P = get_first_sample( L, F->time );
  do {
    Simulate( P->time );
    res = Compare( P->regs, P->mem);
    if( res == MATCH ) return( NO_FAILURE );
    if( res == FAILURE ) return( FAILURE );
    /* res == LATENT */
    P = P->next;
  } while( P != end );
  return( LATENT );
}
```

Fig. 3. Fault injection routine

The fault injection routine starts by settings a set of breakpoints in the VHDL code of the system. Breakpoints are a feature of modern VHDL simulators that offers a simple mechanism to capture the following situations:

1. *program completion*: a breakpoint is set so that simulation is stopped after the execution of the last instruction of the program running on the system;
2. *interrupt*: in order to detect asynchronous events, a breakpoint is set to the VHDL statements implementing the interrupt mechanism activation;
3. *time out*: the simulation is started with a simulation time higher than the time required for program completion. A time out condition is detected if simulation ends and no breakpoint has been reached.

After all the required breakpoints have been properly set, we simulate the system up to the injection time, then we inject the fault. Injection is done by exploiting the VHDL simulator commands to modify signals/variables in the VHDL source. After injection we start a loop where the system is simulated up to a sample point and the state of the system is compared with the information gathered during golden run execution.

At each sample point, we check for the following situations:

1. *no failure*: the state of the system is equal to the state of the golden run at the same time, this implies that the fault effects disappeared from the system and that the fault has no effect on the system behavior; as a consequence, the simulation can be stopped;
2. the state of the system does not match the golden run; in this case two alternatives are available:
   - *failure*: the fault has affected system outputs, therefore its effect on the system is known, and simulation can be stopped;
   - *latent fault*: the fault is still present in the system but it has not affected system outputs, and therefore further simulation is still required.

3.4   Checkpoint-Based Optimizations

Modern VHDL simulators offer several features that can be exploited to effectively reduce simulation time of fault injection campaigns. In particular, we exploited the possibility of storing simulator state and then restoring it during simulations. The rationale behind this approach is shown in Figure 4.

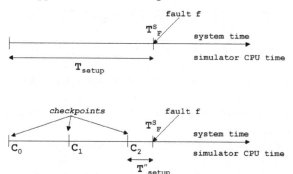

Fig. 4. Simulator-dependent optimization

Given a fault f to be injected at time T, a not-optimized fault injection tool will spend a time equal to T_{setup} to reach injection time. Conversely, during golden run execution, we sample the status of the simulator (and thus the status of the system under analysis) with a given frequency, and we store the information we obtain in a collection of *system status files*. Then, when fault f has to be injected, we resume the simulator from the first checkpoint before T (checkpoint 2 in the example of Figure 4 therefore, the time spent to reach injection time becomes T''_{setup}.

Two conditions must be satisfied for this approach to be effective:

1. let T_R be the time for restoring the status of the system at a given checkpoint, the following inequality must hold:

$$T''_{setup} + T_R < T_{setup} \tag{1}$$

2. the size of the checkpoints collection should be kept as small as possible.

As a consequence, the number of checkpoints should be carefully selected on the basis of both the time required for simulating the system and the size of the system.

4   Experimental Results

To evaluate the effectiveness of the proposed approach we wrote a prototypical implementation of the Fault Injection manager shown in Figure 1, which amounts to 790 lines of C code. During our experiments, we exploited Modeltech VSIM ver 5.1 to run VHDL simulations.

We wrote some simple benchmark programs and run them on the system architecture described in Figure 2 which amounts to 6,700 lines of VHDL code (380 lines are devoted to implement CODE and DATA watchers). The benchmarks characteristics are summarized in Table 1.

Table 1. Benchmarks description

Benchmark name	Description	Program Size [bytes]
MATRIX	3x3 matrix multiplication	409
BUBBLE	Bubble sort	327
TLC	Traffic light controller	533
ABFT	4x4 matrix multiplication with ABFT	1108

For each benchmark, we randomly selected 2,000 faults (1,000 in the data and 1,000 in the code) and we serially injected them in the system without resorting to any optimization. We then turned on dynamic fault analysis and checkpoint-based optimization and re-injected the selected faults. Finally, we collapsed the initial fault list resorting to static fault analysis and then injected the remaining faults. In the latter experiments dynamic fault analysis and checkpoint-based optimization are turned on. Results, gathered on a Sun SparcStation/5 running at 170 MHz and equipped with 128 Mbytes of RAM are reported in Table 2 and 3. Table 2 reports results gathered when injecting in the data, while Table 3 reports data gathered when injecting in the code. The columns have the following meaning:

1. *benchmark* reportsM• the name of the benchmark;
2. T_0 is the time required for injecting 1,000 faults (either in the data or in the code) when no optimizations are exploited;
3. T_1 is the time required by fault injection when dynamic fault analysis and simulator dependent optimization are exploited;
4. T_2 is the time required by fault injection when all the optimization previously described are exploited;
5. $1-T_1/T_0$ and $1-T_2/T_0$ are the speed-up we attain when the correspondent optimizations are turned on.

From the reported tables, we can observe that the complexity introduced in the Fault Injection manager to perform dynamic and static fault analysis and to exploit simulator facilities is worth paying, since it allows to speed-up simulated fault injection up to 96.6%. Moreover, static fault analysis plays a key role, since its adoptions always double the attained speed-up.

Our approach attains the best results when injecting faults in the data. This can be explained by considering that several faults exist that disappear from the system very soon after their injection (due to error detection and correction mechanisms or due to the system behavior) without affecting the system. Even if this faults cannot be eliminated by static analysis, the will be catch by dynamic analysis, thus saving a significant amount of CPU time.

Conversely, when faults in the code are concerned, if a fault is injected because it fails static analysis, it remains latent during all the program execution. Therefore, simulation can be stopped only when fault effects reach system outputs or when the program ends.

Table 2. Results on data

Benchmark	T_0 [sec]	T_1 [sec]	T_2 [sec]	$1-T_1/T_0$ [%]	$1-T_2/T_0$ [%]
MATRIX	27,019	13,393	2,088	50.4	92.3
BUBBLE	24,927	13,383	855	46.3	96.6
TLC	16,497	10,294	1,173	37.6	92.9
ABFT	25,545	10,777	6,505	57.8	74.5
Average				**48.0**	**89.1**

Table 3. Results on code

Benchmark	T_0 [sec]	T_1 [sec]	T_2 [sec]	$1-T_1/T_0$ [%]	$1-T_2/T_0$ [%]
MATRIX	24,315	16,390	8,754	32.6	63.9
BUBBLE	19,595	13,599	6,825	30.6	65.2
TLC	12,263	9,108	6,873	25.7	43.9
ABFT	24,441	15,732	6,245	35.6	74.4
Average				**31.1**	**61.9**

We evaluated the performance of our approach when varying the number of checkpoints. We considered the BUBBLE benchmark and we run four fault injection campaigns where 100 faults are injected and respectively 5, 25, 50 and 100 checkpoints are used. We recorded the time and the disk occupation each campaign required, and plotted them in Figure 5.

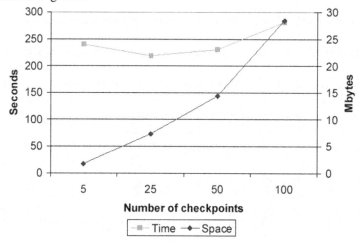

Fig. 5. Space occupation versus time

As this figure suggests, a trade-off exists between space required for storing checkpoints and the time for performing a fault injection campaign. For the benchmark we considered, 25 checkpoints offer the best trade-off since the experiment requires approximately 7 Mbytes of disk space and injects 100 faults in 219 seconds.

5   Conclusions

This paper presented some techniques for reducing the time required for performing simulation-based fault injection campaigns. Static and dynamic methods are proposed to analyze the list of faults to be injected, removing faults as soon as their behavior is known. Common features available in most VHDL simulation environments are also exploited. Experimental results show that the proposed techniques are able to reduce the time required by a typical fault injection campaign by a factor ranging from 43.9% to 96.6%.

References

1. M. Nikoladis, Time Redundancy Based Soft-Error Tolerance to Rescue Nanometer Technologies, IEEE 17th VLSI Test Symposium, April 1999, pp. 86-94
2. R. K. Iyer and D. Tang, *Experimental Analysis of Computer System Dependability*, Chapter 5 of Fault-Tolerant Computer System Design, D. K. Pradhan (ed.), Prentice Hall, 1996
3. E. Jenn, J. Arlat, M. Rimen, J. Ohlsson, J. Karlsson, *Fault injection into VHDL Models: the MEFISTO Tool*, Proc. FTCS-24, Austin (USA), 1994, pp. 66-75
4. T.A. Delong, B.W. Johnson, J.A. Profeta III, *A Fault Injection Technique for VHDL Behavioral-Level Models*, IEEE Design & Test of Computers, Winter 1996, pp. 24-33
5. G.A. Kanawati, N.A. Kanawati, J.A. Abraham, *FERRARI: A Flexible Software-Based Fault and Error Injection System*, IEEE Trans. on Computers, Vol 44, N. 2, February 1995, pp. 248-260
6. J. Carreira, H. Madeira, J. Silva, *Xception: Software Fault Injection and Monitoring in Processor Functional Units*, DCCA-5, Conference on Dependable Computing for Critical Applications, Urbana-Champaign, USA, September 1995, pp. 135-149
7. S. Han, K.G. Shin, H.A. Rosenberg, *Doctor: An Integrated Software Fault-Injection Environment for Distributed Real-Time Systems*, Proc. IEEE Int. Computer Performance and Dependability Symposium, 1995, pp. 204-213
8. A. Benso, P. Prinetto, M. Rebaudengo, M. Sonza Reorda, *EXFI: a low cost Fault Injection System for embedded Microprocessor-based Boards*, ACM Transactions on Design Automation of Electronic Systems, Vol. 3, Number 4, October 1998, pp. 626-634
9. J. Arlat, M. Aguera, L. Amat, Y. Crouzet, J.C. Fabre, J.-C. Laprie, E. Martins, D. Powell, *Fault Injection for Dependability Validation: A Methodology and some Applications*, IEEE Transactions on Software Engineering, Vol. 16, No. 2, February 1990
10. J. Karlsson, P. Liden, P. Dahlgren, R. Johansson, U. Gunneflo, *Using Heavy-Ion Radiation to Validate Fault-Handling Mechanisms*, IEEE Micro, Vol. 14, No. 1, pp. 8-32, 1994
11. A. Benso, M. Rebaudengo, L. Impagliazzo, P. Marmo, Fault-List Collapsing for Fault Injection Experiments, RAMS'98: Annual Reliability and Maintainability Symposium, January 1998, pp. 383-388

Specification and Verification of a Safety Shell with Statecharts and Extended Timed Graphs

Jan van Katwijk[1], Hans Toetenel[1], Abd-El-Kader Sahraoui[2]*,
Eric Anderson[3]**, and Janusz Zalewski[3]

[1] Delft University of Technology, 2600 AJ Delft, The Netherlands
{J.vanKatwijk,w.j.toetenel}@twi.tudelft.nl
[2] PATH/ITS, University of California, Berkeley, CA 94720, USA
kader@nt.path.berkeley.edu
[3] Dept. ECE, University of Central Florida, Orlando, FL 32816, USA
Eric.Anderson-1@kmail.ksc.nasa.gov jza@ece.engr.ucf.edu

Abstract. A new technique for applying safety principles, termed safety shell, eases the formal verification by segregation of the safety critical regions of the application into independent, well structured modules. This paper presents a practical use of formal methods for verification of the safety shell. A framework is proposed for the integration of semi-formal and formal notations, in order to produce a formal specification on which verification tools can be applied. The approach relies on the following steps. The first step consists in using adequately statecharts and support tools to guide the analyst's understanding of the system and produce a preliminary document. In the second step an XTG-based specification is generated from the preliminary document on the basis of predefined rules. The third step then is to verify the specification w.r.t. relevant specified properties. Tool support is being developed to assist in the second step, while tool support for verification is available through the TVS toolset.

1 Introduction

In modern designs of safety-related real-time computer systems, the control functions are separated from safety related functions, which are no longer built on the top of control functions. The obvious advantage of this approach to safety-critical software development is that safety functions can be activated independently, disregarding whether the control functions had been performed or not. This means that safety functions, when performed, may be applied to an environment that has changed already.

Recently, van Katwijk and Zalewski proposed a more cohesive approach by developing a safety architecture based on a concept of a "guard" [ ], which is a low-level construct that acts by detecting the danger and then forcing the system from a hazardous state into a safe state, if at all possible. The advantage

---

* Sahraoui is on leave from: LAAS-CNRS, 31077 Toulouse, France
** Anderson is also with NASA, Kennedy Space Center, FL 32899, USA

F. Koornneef and M. van der Meulen (Eds.): SAFECOMP 2000, LNCS 1943, pp. 37–52, 2000.
© Springer-Verlag Berlin Heidelberg 2000

of having a guard is that it receives all signals before the control system gets any related information. If there is no danger of reaching an unsafe state, all the guard does is just pass the signal values to the control system.

The concept of a guard is further developed by the technique called a safety shell, an alternative software architecture, which provides a hierarchical approach for the implementation of safety control in real time. The use of a safety shell can promote software safety in real-time systems without the cost of performing a full formal analysis of the entire system. This cost saving is particularly significant in systems with a high degree of maintenance. The authors previously showed the applicability of this technique for an example of a traffic light controller, whose behavior was verified with fault trees [ ].

One of the most challenging issues in system design today is the trade-off to be made between formal and rigorous approaches with respect to the "ease of use" – one may say semantics versus pragmatics. In this paper, we propose an approach combining the features of semi-formal methods (friendliness, communicativeness, etc.) and formal methods (rigor, precision, etc.). We use Statemate notations (especially statecharts and activity-charts) [ ] and an extension of timed automata [ ] (for which a toolset for model checking exists), as surrogates for the informal and formal specification languages, respectively. The proposed approach consists in giving structural guidance for the construction of a formal specification of the system which should then be used as a starting basis for the rest of the development process.

The paper is structured as follows. In Section 2 we overview the concept of a safety shell. In Section 3, we outline our approach based on integrating statecharts and the XTG notation. In Section 4, we briefly introduce the XTG notation, and in Section 5 we present an avionics case study, proposed by Aerospatiale Aircraft. We use it in Section 6 to illustrate our approach. Finally, in Section 7, we present conclusions and future work.

2   The Safety Shell Concept

Van Katwijk and Zalewski proposed a simplified architecture for maintaining safety in critical systems. In their "safety first" architecture, safety is primarily maintained by the use of a guard. The guard is a low-level construct which acts by detecting the danger and then forcing the system from a hazardous state into a safe state (Fig. 1). In many instances, this may be as simple as stopping the operation of the system, if necessary. The safety guard acts to encapsulate and protect the safety critical resources and detect violations of the safety rules.

From an architectural standpoint, the physical system being controlled is encapsulated by the guard and appears as a virtual system. The opposite is also true that from the system's point of view the controller appears as a virtual controller encapsulated by the guard. The guard must therefore control the controller-to-system communication in both directions. Thus the guard is able to react to erroneous commands sent from the controller and is able to react to erroneous physical responses input from the system.

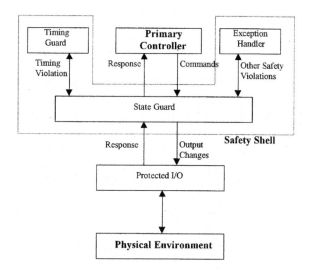

Fig. 1. Structure of the Safety Shell

The safety shell will encapsulate and constrain a mission critical application to enable the entire system to operate with safe limits. The safety shell operates as a stand-alone application, designed not through an analysis of system requirements as the application, but through a safety analysis of the system. Designed and operated independently from the controlling application, the safety shell allows efficient use of limited engineering resources for both the development and maintenance phases of the software's lifecycle [ ].

To accomplish the above, the safety shell must perform two functions: (1) detect conditions that, unchecked, will lead to a failure, and (2) respond to these conditions in a manner that the system will return to safe operation. Both of these functions may be implemented directly through the use of a fault tree of the system.

Detection of failures consists of three parts (Fig. 1). The shell must detect when a command issued by the controller will force the system into an unsafe state. The shell must check and 'approve' all commands issued by the controller before they reach the physical environment. Secondly, the shell must detect when the physical environment has independently entered a failure mode and must issue its own commands to restore the system to a safe state. Lastly, the shell must keep track of all timing constraints that may cause the system to enter failure modes and it must issue its own commands to prevent violation of these constraints. The shell must detect both system state and time variant failure modes.

3   Verification Approach

In a typical approach for verification of similar systems, such as the one proposed
by Zave [ ], all specification languages are assigned semantics in the same domain (first-order predicate logic). The semantics of the composition will be the
composition of the corresponding specificand sets. One of the main limitations
of this approach concerns the complexity of the translation of specification languages into first-order predicate logic. Other works were focused on combining
models as for the TCAS [ ], and Sacres [ ].

Our experience from the most recent work [, , ,] led us to the conclusion
that it is necessary to define another kind of strategy taking into account the
different aspects of a complex system and proposing a simple format for validation of the global specification. The best way to achieve this objective consists
in using a unified format for the integration of the partial specifications. The
global specification obtained should also take into account all different aspects
induced by the requirements (so the control aspects when relevant) [ ].

3.1   Selection of the Formalisms

The work described in this paper is based on these considerations. The approach
proposed here consists of combining two structured approaches:

- a top-down approach with statecharts [ ] which highlights the behavioral
  structure of the problem;
- a bottom-up approach, consisting in a systematic translation of the previous
  semi-formal specification into a formal specification notation using eXtended
  Timed Graphs (XTG) [ ].

Statecharts and activity-charts are both notations belonging to the Statemate approach [ ]. Statecharts are dedicated to modeling of reactive views and
activity-charts for the functional view. Activity-charts can be viewed as a multi-
level data-flow diagrams. They describe functions or activities, as well as data-
stores, all organized into hierarchy and connected via the information that flows
between them. The behavior of a non-basic activity is described by an associated
sub-activity, refered to as its *control-activity*. Each control-activity is described
by corresponding statecharts in the control view.

Statecharts represent an extensive generalization of state-transition diagrams.
They are based on multi-level states, decomposed in and/or fashion, and provide constructs for dealing with concurrency and encapsulation. Additional non-
graphical information related to the views and their flows of information is given
in a *Data Dictionary*.

The use of the formal notation is to a certain extent arbitrary, although
one would expect that the notation has semantics and a certain amount of tool
support for the use of the notation is available. At least simple support, such
as consistency checking of specification, should be available, although more advanced support, especially in verifying properties over specifications is desirable.
We use XTG as the common format because:

- it is state-based, essentially an extension of finite automata, so its semantic model fits well into Statemate based notations;
- it is supported by a toolset that allows verification through model checking of the properties of specifications.

3.2 Detailed Procedure

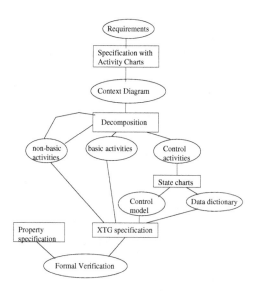

Fig. 2. The General Approach

The approach proposed in this paper starts with the preliminary specification of the system using Statemate, followed by the progressive translation of the obtained specification into XTG. The approach, illustrated in Fig. 2, consists of the following steps:

Specification with Activity-charts. Requirements analysis starts with the functional specification using activity-charts. The result consists mainly of the definition of a context diagram, composed by the top-level activity, the external processes and the information flows between the system and the environment.

Decomposition. The context diagram is then refined in a number of subactivities, data-stores and a control activity. This process is repeated for every subactivity until an acceptable level of detail is reached. In the end, we obtain a hierarchy of activities including a set of non-basic activities (activities which require further decompositions), a set of basic activities (activities which don't require other decompositions) and a set of control activities (activities describing the control behavior of their parent activities).

In our approach, the definitions of data and basic activities consist only of the graphical informations provided. It will not be necessary to give textual information through the Data Dictionary as it is normally the case with Statemate.

Specification with Statecharts. For each control-activity, we give a corresponding statecharts description. Textual information about these statecharts are also given in the Data Dictionary.

Translation into XTG. The Statemate specification obtained during the previous step is then translated into an XTG specification, one automaton for each process involved. At the end of this step, we have obtained a global formal specification which is used as the basis of the formal design.

4   XTG and Its Technology

In this section we summarize the XTG notation and briefly introduce the model checker PMC.

4.1   eXtended Timed Graphs

Timed automata [ ] are finite state machines augmented with clocks and data. Clocks are non-negative real-valued variables that uniformly increase. The increasing of clocks models the progress of time. Conditions on clocks and data can be used to constrain (by guards on edges) and enforce (by invariants on locations) the execution of transitions. Upon execution, a transition may update clocks and data.

XTG [ ] was developed at Delft University of Technology as the basis for a verification toolset. A key feature of XTG is that it provides a general form of urgency. Transitions can either be marked normal or urgent, indicating that they have to be executed immediately upon enabling, without letting time pass. This general form of urgency allows easy modeling of transitions that trigger on data and time conditions.

The communication model is based on the synchronous value passing model of CCS [ ]. In our version, a transition labeled with a synchronization $l!e$ must synchronize with a transition labeled with $l?v$, where l is a synchronization label (or channel name), e is value expression, and v is a variable. As a consequence the value of e is assigned to the variable v. Furthermore, processes can communicate through shared data. The first version of our notation is able to deal with systems that (besides clocks) have floats, integers, and enumerated variables.

The basic building blocks for XTG systems are *graphs*. An XTG specification is built from a composition of all graphs describing partial systems. The basic building blocks to compose graphs are locations and edges (Fig. 3). Each graph represents a single thread of control. Interprocess communication is modeled through synchronizing edges (Fig. 4). Synchronization is point-to-point, like in value passing CCS. Furthermore, edges can be guarded, as exemplified in Fig. 5. This figure shows an edge, indicating a transition that will be enabled when

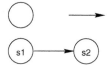

Fig. 3. XTG Basics: Locations and Edges

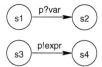

Fig. 4. XTG Synchronized Edges

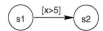

Fig. 5. XTG Guarded Edges

Fig. 6. XTG State Updates

$X > 5$. Predicates used in guards or invariants range over (global or local) state components. Currently the predicates are limited to simple linear forms. In Fig. 6, it is shown how edges may cause state updates The first graph depicts a state update of the clock variable c, the second one depicts a state update of the variable cnt. Edges can be marked *urgent* or *non-urgent*. Urgent edges (marked with a black blob at the starting point of the edge) should be taken immediately after enabling. Non-urgent edges may be taken at any time after being enabled (Fig. 7).

Locations can be guarded with a location invariant. The invariant forces control out of a location by taking an enabled edge as soon as the state of the system and the invariant are inconsistent. Combinations of location invariants and non-urgent edges form an elegant way of modeling time-interval semantics (Fig. 8). Edge attributes can be combined. The attributes consist of a predicate (default true), may hold up to one synchronization and a series of clock/state updates (Fig. 9). The automaton in Fig. 9 indicates that the location invariant of location $s1$ states that $c1 <= 20$, while the transition from $s1$ to $s2$ is enabled as soon as $c1 > 5$. Assuming that $c1$ is a clock, then it is specified here that the transition from $s1$ to $s2$ is taken at a moment when the clock value is $5 <= c1 <= 20$.

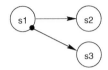

Fig. 7. XTG Edge Semantics

Fig. 8. XTG Guarded Locations

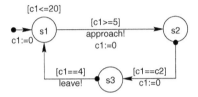

Fig. 9. XTG Combined Attributes

4.2 Specifying Properties

The purpose of having a specification is to be able to verify properties of the specification. XTG therefore supports a property specification language, a temporal logic based on CTL (Computation Tree Logic) [ ] and TCTL (Timed CTL) [ ]. The usage of these logics is strongly connected with the application of model checking verification.

The core syntax defines two temporal operators, AU and EU. The formula $(\phi_1 AU \phi_2)$ is satisfied in a state if for all computation paths starting from that state, there is a state along it which satisfies ϕ_2, and until that time ϕ_1 is satisfied. The formula $(\phi_1 EU \phi_2)$ is satisfied if there is at least one such computation path. Derived operators are: $EF\phi$ (there is path on which there is state satisfying ϕ), $EG\phi$ (there is a path of which every state satisfies ϕ), $AF\phi$ (on all paths there is some state satisfying ϕ), and $AG\phi$ (on all paths every state satisfies ϕ). There are two types of atomic properties in our CTL variant: boolean expressions over values of variables and clocks of both the system and the property, and location expressions. The latter are of the form $g@l$, and express the fact that the graph g of the system is currently at location l.

A property specification is defined by a tuple (C_p, V_p, ϕ), where C_p is a set of clocks, V_p is a set of variables, and ϕ is a CTL formula. Formulae are defined by the following syntax:

$$\phi ::= p \mid g@l \mid \neg\phi \mid \phi \vee \phi \mid \phi \wedge \phi \mid \phi\mathbf{AU}\phi \mid \phi\mathbf{EU}\phi \mid u.\phi$$

where p ranges over boolean expressions, u is a state manipulation assigning new values to variables from V_p or clocks from V_c, g denotes a graph identifier, l denotes a location identifier. Property specification variables and clocks in boolean value expressions p have to be bound by some earlier assignment operation.

XTG was not designed to be a user friendly language, therefore in addition to XTG, a notation was developed, with semantics very close to the XTG notation, but with more resemblance of a regular programming language [ ]. A discussion of this language (ACL) is outside the scope of this paper.

Given an ASCII description of an XTG specification with additionally the specification of CTL properties to be verified, the Prototype Model Checker (PMC) tool returns, if feasible within available resources, a positive or negative result for each property. The tool is furthermore able to generate traces that may clarify the verification result – for example a counterexample in case of a negative verification result for a safety property.

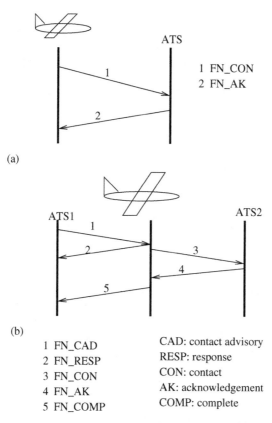

(a)

(b)

1 FN_CON
2 FN_AK

1 FN_CAD
2 FN_RESP
3 FN_CON
4 FN_AK
5 FN_COMP

CAD: contact advisory
RESP: response
CON: contact
AK: acknowledgement
COMP: complete

Fig. 10. AFN Messages

5   Case Study

In modern industries, especially those software-intensive, such as the aeronautical industry, the current trend is to develop systems that provide more functionality and higher performance. Consequently, the applications are more and more safety related. This is the case in avionics, where we initially tackled the problem of using a multi-formalisms approach for an onboard Airbus central maintenace and warning computer prototype [ ], [ ].

This case study involves the FANS (Future Air Navigation System), an avionics project of Aerospatiale Aircraft. The main purpose of the FANS is the improvement of the air traffic management. Among the main Data Link applications of the FANS, there are the CPDLC (Controller/Pilot Data Link Communication), the AFN (Air-traffic Facilities Notification) and the ADS (Automatic Dependant Surveillance). The CPDLC allows aircraft and ATC (Air Traffic Controller) center on the ground to communicate by data link (instead of vocally). Before the communication is iniated, connection should be established and maintained throughout the AFN. The fact that there is automatic communication between the ground and the pilot, causes that we can talk about a safety-related system.

In this case study, we are interested especially in the AFN. The AFN allows an ATC center, to obtain information about the data link capabilities of an aircraft and to exchange communication addresses. The AFN operates in two main phases:

The Log-On. This phase covers the connection between an aircraft and a ground ATC center (Fig. 10 (a)). It is initiated either on request of the pilot or automatically, by giving the address of the ATC center. A message FN_CON (contact) is then sent to the center, which should reply with another message labeled FN_ACK (acknowledgement).

Address Changing. When the aircraft reaches the border of the area covered by the current center, the latter sends to the pilot the message FN_CAD (contact advisory), in order to ask him to contact the next center (Fig. 10 (b)). At the receiving of this message, the aircraft should reply with a first message labeled FN_RESP (response) and, later, with a second message FN_COMP (complete) on completion of the contact with the next center.

6   Developing Specifications

The context diagram of the AFN system is presented in Fig. 11. The environment is composed of several external activities such as the onboard ATC control panel (for typing addresses), the aircraft database (references of onboard AFN applications, aircraft position, etc.), a ground ATC center and onboard indicators (presenting the success or failure of message exchange). We refine the top-level activity *AFN* during successive steps, so that an acceptable level of detail is reached. This will give rise to a hierarchy of activities composed of basic

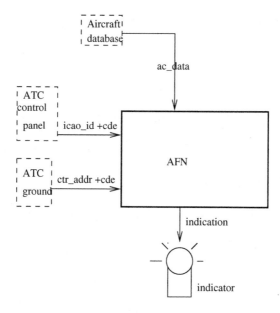

Fig. 11. The AFN Context Diagram

activities, non-basic activities and control activities. Basic activities and control activities are the most rudimentary and correspond to respective components (guards) of a safety shell. Fig. 12 gives an overview of this hierarchy.

The first level of refinement leads to two non-basic subactivities *BPROCESS* and *GPROCESS*, and a control activity *afn_sc*. *BPROCESS* describes the data transformations onboard, while *GPROCESS* corresponds to the ground transformations.

The activity *BPROCESS* is refined in two non-basic activities[1], *CONTACT* and *BCHECK*, a basic activity, *COMPLETE* and a control activity *bp_sc*, as follows:

- The purpose of *CONTACT* is to generate the message *FN_CON* on request of either the pilot or the ground ATC center; in the latter case, the message FN_RESP is also generated.
- The purpose of *BCHECK* is to check the validity of the message received onboard (i.e. FN_AK and FN_CAD) and to give to the pilot an indication concerning the success or failure of the process of message exchange.
- The purpose of *COMPLETE* is to generate the message *FN_COMP*.

The activity *CONTACT* is refined in four basic subactivities: *DSP* (transformation of the OACI code typed in by the pilot into a seven characters center

---

[1] It was brought to our attention during proofreading that the second level @BPROCESS block connects incorrectly to the top-level @GPROCESS, in Fig. 12. It should connect to @BPROCESS at the top level.

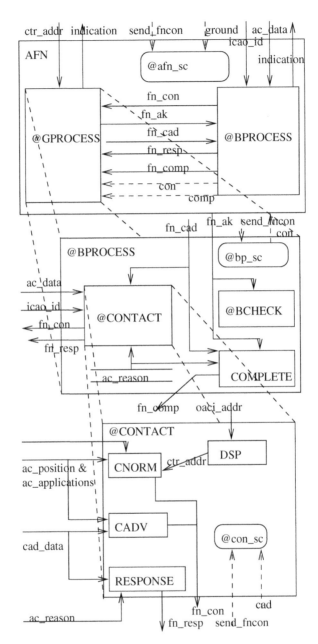

Fig. 12. The AFN Hierarchy

address), *CNORM* (generation of message FN_CON on pilot request or automatically), *CADV* (generation of message FN_CON on a ground ATC center request) and *RESPONSE* (generation of message FN_RESP).

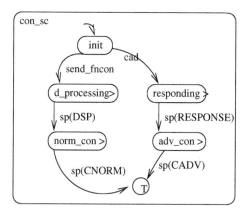

Fig. 13. Statechart for Control Activity con_sc

Control for all these models is described with statecharts. The statechart corresponding to *con_sc*, the control activity of *CONTACT* is represented in Fig. 13. The activity starts in state *init*; the generation of event *send_fncon* starts the execution of activity *DSP* in state *d_processing*, followed by the execution of activity *CNORM* in state *norm_con*, and then the deactivation in state *T*. The generation of event *cad* (contact advisory), when state *init* is active, leads to the execution of activity *RESPONSE* in state *responding*, followed by the execution of activity *CADV* in state *adv_con*.

Since the semantic base of both statecharts and XTG is finite state machines, translating statechart-based specifications into XTG is relatively straightforward. As an example, consider a fragment of the translation of the statechart presented in Fig. 13 into Fig. 14.

In this diagram, it becomes obvious that the combined triggering/action mechanism as used in the statechart formalism, can be replaced by the communication mechanism available in XTG. Each basic activity corresponds to an XTG graph that encodes the functionality of the activity, augmented with start and stop states that enable the activation of the activity. Space limits prevent giving a detailed description of the translation here, but the reader can find more information in [ ].

Typical properties that can be verified using our TCTL variant are safety and bounded liveness properties like deadlock problems and zeno-ness of the model. For example, the zeno-ness of the model is captured by the TCTL property $AG(z := 0.EF(z > 0))$, which expresses that in all possible futures it is always possible to have specification clock z incremented, i.e. time never stops. Timing of actions can be verified in a similar way. The TCTL property $AG\ CON\_SC@D\_P \implies (z := 0).AF(CON\_SC@NC \wedge z \leq t)$ expresses that the execution of action DSP in control activity CON_SC will be finalized within t time units.

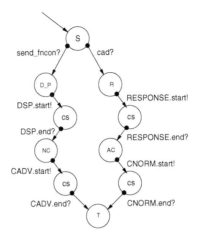

Fig. 14. Fragment of a Translation

It is not directly possible in (our) TCTL to address the occurrence of the actual synchronization events. High level properties that address the occurrence of events (messages) like FN_CON and FN_ACK in the statecharts should be transformed into low level properties over the XTG graphs. For example, the events can be modeled by actual messages sent over a virtual channel. Such a channel is subsequently modeled by a special XTG automaton that implements a test of the desired property. For instance, the property that a FN_CON event should always be followed by a FN_ACK event can be easily modeled this way. On a more abstract level, there are many different scenarios of the behavior of the AFN system in combination of incoming and outgoing planes related to critical safety.

7   Conclusion

Several case studies were successfully developed with the proposed approach, for example [ ]. In our view, the approach is practical for realistic systems development, although it needs some more work on describing the process in detail. We feel that the approach is capable of dealing with real-life applications in a convenient fashion.

Currently, we are developing fully automated support for the translation process. The tools are being interfaced with the Statemate environment of i-Logix [ ] and with the TVS toolset developed at Delft University of Technology. The translation carried out interactively will lead to a file containing the graph specification in XTG. The approach is being extended to safety dealing with issues in automated highways systems, based on work carried out in [ ].

References

1. Alur R., D. Dill. *The Theory of Timed Automata.* Theoretical Computer Science,Vol. 26, pp. 183–235, 1994. 42
2. Ammerlaan M., R. Lutje-Spelberg, W. J. Toetenel. *XTG – An Engineering Approach to Modelling and Analysis of Real-Time Systems.* Proc. 10th Euromicro Workshop on Real-Time Systems, pp. 88–97. IEEE Computer Society Press, 1998. 38, 40, 42
3. Anderson E., J. van Katwijk, J. Zalewski, *New Method of Improving Software Safety in Mission-Critical Real-Time Systems,* Proc. 17th Int'l System Safety Conf., System Safety Society, Unionville, VA, 1999, pp. 587-596 37, 38, 39
4. Beaufreton M., *SACRES: A Step Forward in the Development of Critical Avionics Systems,* Proc. HSCC'99, 2nd Int'l Workshop on Hybrid Systems Computation and Control. Springer-Verlag, Berlin, 1999. 40
5. Brink K., J. van Katwijk, H. Toetenel, J. Zalewski, *H-Astral and Its Use in the Development of Real-Time Control Systems,* Proc. 24th IFAC/IFIP Workshop on Real-Time Programming, pp. 123-128, Pergamon, Oxford, 1999 40
6. Clarke E. M., E. A. Emerson, A. P. Sistla. *Automatic Verification of Finite-State Concurrent Systems Using Temporal Logic Specifications.* ACM TOPLAS, Vol. 8, No. 2, pp. 244–263, 1986. 44
7. de Rooij R. C. M., J. van Katwijk *ACL Language Definition.* Technical Report, Faculty of Information Technology and Systems, Delft University of Technology (to appear). 45
8. Harel D., M. Politi, *Modeling Reactive Systems with Statecharts: The Statemate Approach,* John Wiley and Sons, New York, 1998. 38, 40
9. Henzinger T. A., X. Nicollin, J. Sifakis, S. Yovine. *Symbolic Model Checking for Real-Time Systems.* Information and Computation, Vol. 111, pp. 193–244, 1994. 44
10. van Katwijk J., J. Zalewski, *Merging Formal Specifications and Engineering Practice in Real-Time Systems Design,* Proc. 3rd Biennial World Conf on Integrated Design and Process Technology, Vol. 6, pp. 57-64, Society for Design and Process Science, Austin, Texas, 1998 40
11. Kornecki A., B. Nasah, J. Zalewski, *TCAS Safety Analysis Using Timed Environment-Relationship Petri Nets,* Proc. 9th Int'l Symposium on Software Reliability Engineering, Fast Abstracts and Industrial Processes, IEEE Computer Society, 1998, pp. 161-170 40
12. Lichtenecker R., K. Gotthardt, J. Zalewski, *Automated Verificataion of Communication Protocols Using CCS and BDDs,* pp. 1057-1066, Parallel and Distributed Processing, J. Rolim (Ed.), Springer-Verlag, Berlin, 1998 40
13. Lygeros J., D. N. Godbole, S. Sastry, *Verified Hybrid Controllers for Automated Vehicles,* IEEE Trans. Automatic Control, Vol. 43, No. 4, April 1998. 50
14. Lynch N., *High Level Modeling and Analysis of an Air Traffic Management System,* Proc. HSCC'99, 2nd Int'l Workshop on Hybrid Systems Computation and Control. Springer-Verlag, Berlin, 1999. 40
15. Milner R., *Communication and Concurrency.* Prentice Hall, Englewood Cliffs, NJ, 1989. 42
16. Sahraoui A. E. K., E. Anderson, J. van Katwijk, J. Zalewski, *Formal Specification of a Safety Shell in Real-Time Control Practice,* Proc. 25th IFAC/IFIP Workshop on Real-Time Programming, Mallorca, Spain, May 15-19, 2000 50

17. Sahraoui A. E. K., M. Romdhani, A. A. Jerraya, P. Chazelles *A Multiformalisms Approach for Specifying Avionics Systems*, First International Workshop on Hybrid Systems, Grenoble, 1996. 46
18. Sahraoui A. E. K., M. Romdhani, A. Jeoffroy, A. A. Jerraya, *Co-Specification for Co-Design in the Development of Avionics Systems*, Control Eng. Practice, Vol. 4, No. 6, pp. 871-876, 1996. 46
19. *The Languages of Statemate*, Technical Report, i-Logix, Inc., Burlington, Mass., 1987. 50
20. Toetenel W. J., J. van Katwijk, *Translation of Statecharts into XTG Graphs*, TVS Communications, Department of Information Technology and Systems, Delft University of Technology, 2000. 49
21. Zave P., M. Jackson, *Four Dark Corners of Requirements Engineering*, ACM Trans. on Soft. Eng. and Meth., Vol. 6, No. 1, January 1997. 40

Validation of Control System Specifications with Abstract Plant Models

Wenhui Zhang

Institute for Energy Technology
P.O.Box 173, N-1751 Halden, Norway
Wenhui.Zhang@hrp.no

Abstract. Automatic procedures and manual procedures play important roles in the control of power plants. Their correctness is of great importance to the safe operation of power plants. Testing of such procedures is difficult, especially because of the problem of errors in specifications. By verifying high level specifications of automatic procedures and formalised specifications of manual procedures against an abstract plant model and a set of correctness requirements, this problem can be overcome to some extent. This paper describes the basic idea of such verification. It suggests using the verification approach as a complementary aid to traditional verification and validation which may involve different aspects including human factors.

1 Introduction

Discrete event control is commonly used in implementing control tasks where many of the functional requirements can be specified by conditions telling what is acceptable and what unacceptable rather than as a criterion to be minimised. Designing discrete event control systems requires that many different situations be considered. There could be difficulties related to identifying different alternative behaviours of the plant, determining all the necessary preconditions of a successful control action and understanding all the possible consequences of a control action. Possible errors in the design are for instance incomplete exception handling and unforeseen side-effects.

Verification of control systems is difficult, especially because of the problem of errors in specifications. In [ ], Taylor suggested using plant models for logical validation of safety and control system specifications, in order to detect possible design and specification errors. Taylor argued that there were three reasons for using plant models instead of real plants for validation: the designer's mental model of the plant is a prime source of design information, and is available at an early stage in the design process; the model is available to mathematical analysis, whereas the real plant is not; and the plant model provides a way of validating safety before a control system is applied to a real plant.

In this paper, we further investigate the idea and suggest constructing abstract plant models for the validation of consistency between correctness requirements and specifications of control system units by using model checking

F. Koornneef and M. van der Meulen (Eds.): SAFECOMP 2000, LNCS 1943, pp. 53–63, 2000.
© Springer-Verlag Berlin Heidelberg 2000

techniques and tools [, ,]. The aforementioned reasons for using plant models instead of real plants for validation are also valid for the idea of using abstract plant models. The emphasis on abstractness is that we would like the models to be as simple as possible with respect to the need for the checking of consistency. This is due to the fact that model checking relies on building a finite model of a system and needs very much computation resource and hence there are limitations on the sizes of the problems and models that can be checked by model checking. The advantage of model checking is that it can utilise fully automated tools which require no intervention of the user and provide explicit information about what could be wrong when they fail to check a property. For the same reason, we explicitly state that our scope of the validation is specifications of control system units instead of specifications of complete control systems. For each such unit in consideration, we are only interested in the relevant part of the plant and the abstract plant model is restricted to this part of the plant, in order to limit the complexity of the models.

Discrete event control includes automatic control and manual control which are to be carried out by software programs and human operators. In this approach, we consider the technical part of the control system consisting of software programs and operating procedures (prescribing what an operator should do in various situations). A natural unit will be (possibly, a part of) a software program (which is referred to as an automatic procedure in the following) or (a part of) a manual procedure. The verification approach is equally applicable to both automatic procedures and manual procedures, since the verification approach concerns high level formal descriptions instead of low level executable instructions.

We try to describe the approach in generally understandable terms independent of specific verification tools. However for the formalisation of correctness requirements and verification of such, we follow the techniques and methods provided by the model checking tool Spin [ ]. Our view on how to model and what could be realistic complexity of models and abstraction level of models is affected by the available model checking techniques and tools. Further development in the field of model checking may lead to possibilities for automatically checking models with substantially higher complexity.

2   Correctness Requirements

In order to verify a specification of a control system unit, we need correctness requirements. The types of such requirements include the following [ ]:

- Functional specifications - descriptions of what a system should do.
- Safety specification - descriptions of what a system should not do.
- Performance specification - descriptions of how well a system should perform in terms of performance criterion.
- Reliability of risk specifications - statements of the maximum probability with which specified unwanted event may occur.

Functional and safety specifications are of particular interests for formal verification. According to [ ], such a specification can be expressed by statements such as:

- When A happens, X, Y, Z should happen.
- When A happens, if P is true, X, Y, Z should happen.
- When A happens, X then Y then Z should happen.
- A should never happen.
- A should never happen while P is true.
- P should always be true.
- Q should never be true.

where the terms "A, X, Y, Z happens" may be events or actions describing specific changes of states.

In addition to these finite state descriptions of events and conditions, there could be more flexible description forms such as continuous state and continuous time analytical descriptions. As we are considering using automated model checking tools which primarily rely on building finite state models, we only consider the finite state descriptions for verification.

3   Abstract Plant Models

As we are using automatic verification tools with limitation on the complexity of models, the number of involved processes should be kept as small as possible and the processes should be modelled as simple as possible. As a basic principle, we use discrete values instead of continuous values. For instance, if temperature varies from 0 to 100, we use a variable of type integer and not float-point to hold the value of the temperature. Second, we may use sets of values instead of single values whenever it is possible. For instance, if the only place involving the temperature is a test on whether "temperature ≥ 30", we may use two set-values Low and High to distinguish between values satisfying and not satisfying the condition.

There are different ways to model an object. One is using random simulation. For instance, whenever the value of the temperature is needed, we may randomly assign a value Low or High. This approach can be used if the system does not control the value of the temperature or the value of the temperature is difficult to model. If a property is checked to hold with this model (which is not very accurate) of the temperature, the property also holds with a more accurate model of the temperature. If we have information on how the state of an object changes, we may model the change of the state of the object by using a process. Assuming that there are three relevant set-values (Low, Medium, High) for the temperature and the temperature depends on the state of a heater. We may specify the change of the states of the temperature as follows:

Current State	State of Heater	New State
Low	On	Medium
Medium	On	High
High	On	High
Low	Off	Low
Medium	Off	Low
High	Off	Medium

For the specification of abstract plant processes, tables of this kind are very useful for many types of processes in our verification approach. Usually, one process controls the change of the states of one object and an abstract plant model consists of such processes that run in parallel.

4   Formalisation and Verification

In order to validate the consistency between correctness requirements and the specifications of a control system unit, we have to formalise the correctness requirements, the specifications of the control system unit, and the abstract plant model. The choice of languages for the formalisation depends on the tool to be used for the verification. The model checking tool we intended to used is Spin developed by the formal methods and verification group at Bell Laboratories We use propositional linear temporal logic formulas [ ] for formalisation of correctness requirements and use the language Promela (a process meta-language [ ]) for formalisation of abstract plant models and specifications of control system units. The propositional linear temporal logic formulas (translated into never-claims) and the descriptions in Promela can then be used as input to Spin for automated verification.

Correctness Requirements The finite state functional and safety specifications in section 2 can easily be specified by using temporal logical formulas. Since a logical expression has precise meaning, while meaning of a textual expression may be ambiguous, one has to be careful. For simplicity, we assume that "X then Y" implies "Y should happen at the same time as X happens or after X has happened" in the following translation of the textual finite state descriptions to logical expressions:

- When A happens, X, Y, Z should happen:
  $[](A \rightarrow (\Diamond X \wedge \Diamond Y \wedge \Diamond Z))$.
- When A happens, if P is true, X, Y, Z should happen:
  $[](A \rightarrow P \rightarrow (\Diamond X \wedge \Diamond Y \wedge \Diamond Z))$.
- When A happens, X then Y then Z should happen:
  $[](A \rightarrow (\Diamond(X \wedge \Diamond(Y \wedge \Diamond Z))))$.
- A should never happen: $[](\neg A)$.
- A should never happen while P is true: $[](P \rightarrow \neg A)$.
- P should always be true: $[](P)$.
- Q should never be true: $[](\neg Q)$.

where the symbol [] indicates that the statement following it should always be valid, the symbol ◇ indicates that the statement following it is valid at the current moment or will be valid at some time in the future, the symbols →, ∧ and ¬ are the usual symbols for implication, conjunction and negation, the symbols A, X, Y, Z in the formulas are propositions representing action events and the symbols P, Q are propositional formulas representing a condition or a system state. A natural way to associate a proposition to an action is to use an atomic sequence which includes the action and an assignment of the value *true* to the proposition and after the atomic sequence assign the value *false* to the proposition. In the specification of $[](A \rightarrow ◇X)$, this approach of associating a proposition to an action is sound if both actions are parts of the same process. However, additional mechanisms must be implemented, if the events are controlled by different processes (running in parallel with an interleaving semantics).

Formalisation of Procedures For automatic procedures, there already exist formal or semi-formal specifications. However they may not suit the purpose of verification. Abstraction or formalisation may be needed. For manual procedures, as many computerised operation manual systems have been developed [, ,] and manual procedures have been computerised in order to reduce operator stress and to enhance safety [,], the additional effort for formalisation and abstraction would be comparable to that of automatic procedures. However if the procedures are only informal text documents, this step may require significantly more effort. The result of the formalisation is processes representing the procedures (referred to as the procedure processes).

Abstract Plant Processes Specifications of abstract plant processes are translated into process descriptions in Promela, in order to be used as input to the model checking tool Spin. Given abstract plant processes in standard descriptions such as in special table formats, they can be translated to Promela processes automatically. However, correct translation of processes may not be sufficient. Sometimes, mechanisms for necessary synchronisation of execution of the processes are needed. This can be done by using communication channels or by using global variables and wait-statements. In addition to the processes representing how the state of objects changes, processes are needed for setting up initial states (or preparing states that satisfies the preconditions for starting the procedures) and for dealing with communication between the procedure processes and the rest of the system.

Verification There could be different verification sub-tasks and different strategies for verification. Normally, we run model checking for each correctness requirement together with the formalised procedure and the abstract plant model. In addition to the explicitly specified correctness requirements, we may also check standard correctness requirements such as whether there are instructions resulting in unintended infinite loops (that make it impossible to finish the procedure) or whether there are instructions resulting in situations that make the rest of the procedure not executable (both types of problems are referred to as execution errors in the following).

5   A Case Study

For the case study, we have chosen a not fully verified procedure (a temporary version not in use) that might have potential errors and applied the verification approach to this procedure, in order to show whether there are errors in the procedure and whether the verification approach is useful for detecting such errors.

The purpose of the procedure is to carry out a manual regeneration of cation resins. The size of the procedure is 7 pages and 421 lines. In addition, the procedure may initiate another procedure G-PIOI-4.3 which is information on safety precautions and handling of chemicals. The basic purpose of the procedure G-PIOI-4.3 is to guide the operator to read relevant information about different chemicals.

The Procedures For the main procedure, the main sequence of actions is as follows:

- Precheck
- Drain down the cation regeneration unit
- Terminate drain down and commence air rouse
- Terminate air rouse and commence backwash
- Terminate backwash and settle resins
- Prepare for injection of acid into the cation regeneration unit
- Commence acid injection into the cation regeneration unit
- Terminate acid injection and commence displacement rinse
- Terminate acid displacement rinse and begin acid rinse
- Terminate cation acid rinse

In addition, there are steps for taking corrective actions when problems occur in an execution of the main part of the procedure. For the procedure G-PIOI-4.3, there are steps for general information, for information on caustic soda, sulphuric acid, sodium hypochlorite, and salt and salt solutions.

Correctness Requirements The set of correctness requirements of the procedure includes:

1. If "the CRU (cation regeneration unit) valve 8/AA/19 is closed", then "the valve 7/8/AA/D21 is open".
2. The event "open CRU vent control valve 8/WC/V115" should never happen, while "the acid measure is not full".
3. The event "open CRU vent control valve 8/WC/V115" should never happen, if "the information on sulphuric acid has not been read".
4. The event "close valve 7/8A/ZA/45" should never happen while "the valve 7/8A/ZA/42 is open".

5. When the event "start the LP air blower" happens, the event "stop the LP air blower" should happen.
6. If "the CRU failed to drain", then "corrective actions" should be taken.
7. All executions of the procedure should terminate.

The first item is of the form $[]P$, the second, the third and the fourth are of the form $[](P \rightarrow \neg X)$, the fifth and the sixth are of the form $[](A \rightarrow \Diamond X)$, and the seventh item is the general requirement for checking whether the procedure is free of execution errors. We use the formula $\Diamond P$ to represent free of execution errors where P is a boolean to be assigned the value *true* at every possibly exit of the procedure. As explained earlier, we have to associate propositions to actions, in order to formulate items 2, 3, 4 and 5. For the formulation of the sixth item, an action (represented by a proposition) has to be associated to the statement which decides whether the draining process is successful (since "the cation regeneration unit failed to drain" is not a real action). The third item is the only correctness requirement that refers both to actions of the main procedure and to actions (or the results of these) of the procedure G-PIOI-4.3.

Formalisation of the Procedures Ideally, a procedure and the model of the procedure should have the same structure and there is exactly one statement in the model for each instruction of the procedure. However some extra features have to be added in the Promela model for the verification purpose. One of which is the indication of the end of a procedure execution for checking execution errors. Another is to add propositions and statements for associating the propositions to actions. Although this can be done systematically for all actions, propositions for actions are only added when they are necessary, due to the efficiency aspect of model checking. The two procedures are formalised as separated processes. Initiating the procedure G-PIOI-4.3 (by the main procedure) is modelled by starting the procedure process of the procedure G-PIOI-4.3 and waiting until it is completed. As an example, a part of the main procedure process specified in Promela is as follows (where $Value5uS$ is a value of conductivity, *check()*, *lt()*, *gt()* and *closeValve()* are macros for checking, comparing and changing the state of a given object):

```
STEP_10_INSTRUCTION_1: check(CationConduct);
   if
   :: lt(CationConduct,Value5uS); goto STEP_10_INSTRUCTION_2;
   :: gt(CationConduct,Value5uS); goto STEP_12_1_INSTRUCTION_1;
   fi;
STEP_10_INSTRUCTION_2: closeValve(Val7DED20);
```

Abstract Plant Processes In the case study, we have three simple processes for respectively modelling the relation between the development of the acid level and the state of a valve, modelling the relation between the development of the flow level and the state of a valve, and modelling opening and closing valves (which are modelled as a process that takes time to complete instead of instant actions). Random values are used for other objects whenever applicable (such as the reading of a cation conductivity meter). In addition, there are several processes for dealing with communication between the procedure processes and the rest of the system.

Problem Detection and Interpretation Following problems were detected by model checking:

1. A reference for the destination instruction of a conditional goto-instruction (i.e. an instruction of the form "IF condition THEN GOTO step A instruction B") is wrong.
2. An incomplete case analysis following a check of a system state.
3. Another problem related to the destination instruction of a goto-instruction.
4. Instructions in a sub-step are not reachable, as there are no references to the instructions.

The model checking times for detecting these problems are respectively 1, 2, 3 and 22407 seconds, when the procedure processes were checked against the requirement that the main procedure should be free of execution errors (i.e. requirement 7). The first and the third problems lead to loops, the second problem leads to an invalid stop. The last problem is not an error in the normal sense and the model checker had to search through the whole reachable state space. Some of these problems can be detected by checking other correctness requirements as well. For instance, the first problem which leads to a loop also leads to several unreachable statements. If we check requirement 1, we cannot find any error that violates that particular requirement. However at the end of the verification, the model checker Spin provides a report on unreachable statements and the problem can be detected by analysing these unreachable statements.

Formal verification provides reports of potential problems to a process expert. Whether the detected problems have to be considered as faults that must be corrected has to be interpreted by the process expert, since manual procedures do not have precise semantics and there may be different interpretations of the instructions. As the above problems are considered, the first and the third problems are typical problems when one copies a text from another part of the procedure and forgets to make all necessary changes. The second problem is that a trivial case is missing in a list of cases. An operator can usually figure out what to do if the case encounters, so this may or may not be considered as a real problem. Problems similar to the fourth problem may occur, if the procedure designer has first designed several methods (each resulting in an independent procedure step) to tackle a situation and later decided to use one method without removing the other methods.

Verification Times After the detected problems are corrected, we have to re-run model checking in order to verify that the procedure is correct with respect to the abstract models and the requirements. The following table shows the model checking times and memory usages for the seven correctness requirements:

Requirement No.	Time (in seconds)	Memory (in megabytes)
1	1033	57.3
2	1035	57.3
3	1023	57.3
4	1033	57.3
5	6841	98.3
6	2288	78.4
7	22460	76.4

The first four items are safety properties with the same complexity, hence the model checking times for these are expected to be the same. The last three are liveness properties, the model checking times vary very much depending on the complexity of the properties and the number of branches relevant to these properties.

6 Concluding Remarks

The important concepts of this paper include control systems, plant models, formal methods and model checking. Ideas of using plant models to the validation of control systems can be found in [ ], ideas of using theorem proving (with algebraic specification techniques) to the validation of discrete event control systems can be found in [ ] and ideas of using model checking to the validation of manual operating procedures can be found in [ ]. This paper combines these ideas and explains how to use model checking to the validation of discrete event control systems with abstract plant models. The described approach provides a way to validation of specifications of control system units against an abstract plant model and a set of correctness requirements.

It is worthwhile mentioning possible problems with this approach. One possibility is that the model may be wrong or conceived incorrectly (there is always a possibility that the designer misunderstands the way in which the plant works). Hence validation of the control system is not complete unless the plant model has also been validated. Another possibility is that the model may not be sufficiently detailed in all its aspects such that some parts of the correctness requirements cannot be checked. Both possibilities were discussed in [ ] and they are equally relevant with respect to our approach. In addition, since the approach aims at high level abstract specifications of control system units instead of the low level executable instructions, the verification does not guarantee the correctness of the actual implementation of the procedure (either by a software or by an operator).

¿From a practical point of view, the interest of verification is to find errors in the logic of specifications that could otherwise be hard to detect, and not necessary to prove the absolute correctness of control systems. Since a large portion of actual errors originates from specification errors, verification of high level specifications will help improve the total quality of the control systems and the verification approach may be used as a help to control system designers and procedure designers and as a complementary aid to traditional verification and validation which may involve different aspects including human factors [ ].

Acknowledgements

The research described in this paper was carried out at the OECD Halden Reactor Project at the Institute for Energy Technology, Norway. The author thanks G. Dahll, T. Sivertsen and other members of the project for their suggestions and comments. The author also thanks anonymous referees for their constructive criticisms that helped in improving this paper.

References

1. E. M. Clarke and E. A. Emerson and A. P. Sistla. Automatic Verification of Finite State Concurrent Systems Using Temporal Logic Specifications. Conference Record of the Tenth Annual ACM Symposium on Principles of Programming Languages: 117-126, January 1983. 54

2. S. Collier and M. Green. Verification and Validation of Human Factors Issues in Control Room Design and Upgrades. OECD Halden Reactor Project Report: HWR-598, Institute for Energy Technology, Norway. 1999. 61

3. E. A. Emerson. Temporal and Model Logic. Handbook of theoretical computer science, Volume B: Formal Models and Semantics (ed. Jan van Leeuwen). Elsevier. 1990. 56

4. P. Godefroid and G. J. Holzmann. On the Verification of Temporal Properties. Protocol Specification, Testing and Verification, XIII (C-16). A. Dantine, G. Leduc and P. Walper (Eds). 1993. 54

5. F. Handelsby, E. Ness and J. Teigen. OECD Halden Reactor Project: COPMA II On-Line Functional Specifications. OECD Halden Reactor Project Report: HWR-319, Institute for Energy Technology, Norway. 1992. 57

6. G. J. Holzmann. The Model Checker Spin. IEEE Transaction on Software Engineering 23(5): 279-295. 1997. 54, 56

7. M. H. Lipner and S. P. Kerch. Operational Benefits of an Advanced Computerised Procedure System. 1994 IEEE Conference Record: Nuclear Science Symposium and Medical Imaging Conference: 1068-1072. 1995. 57

8. L. Reynes and G. Beltranda. A Computerised Control Room to Improve Nuclear Power Plant Operation and Safety. Nuclear Safety 31(4):504-511. 1990. 57

9. H. Roth-Seefrid, J. Erdmann, L. Simon and M. Dull. SiROG: A Computer-based Manual for Situation Related Operator Guidance. Presentation at the Enlarged Halden Programme Group Meeting. Bolkesjø, Norway. October 1994. 57

10. T. Sivertsen and H. Valisuo. Algebraic Specification and Theorem Proving used in Formal Verification of Discrete Event Control Systems. OECD Halden Reactor Project Report: HWR-260, Institute for Energy Technology, Norway. 1989. 61

11. J. R. Taylor. Logical Validation of Safety and Control System Specifications Against Plant Models. Risø National Laboratory, Roskilde, Danmark. 1981. 53, 54, 55, 61

12. J. Teigen and J. E. Hulsund. COPMA-III - Software Design and Implementation Issues. OECD Halden Reactor Project Report: HWR-509, Institute for Energy Technology, Norway. 1998. 57

13. M. Y. Vardi and P. Wolper. An Automata-Theoretic Approach to Automatic Program Verification. IEEE Symposium on Logic in Computer Science 1: 322-331. 1986. 54

14. W. Zhang. Model Checking Operator Procedures. Proceedings of the 6th International SPIN Workshop on Practical Aspects of Model Checking (Lecture Notes in Computer Science 1680: 200-215). Toulouse, France. 1999. 61

A Constant Perturbation Method for Evaluation of Structural Diversity in Multiversion Software

Luping Chen, John May, and Gordon Hughes

Safety Systems Research Centre, Department of Computer Science,
University of Bristol, Bristol, BS8 1UB, UK
{Chen,jhrm,hughes}@cs.bris.ac.uk

Abstract. In this paper, fault simulation is discussed as a test method for diversity assessment of multiversion software and data flow perturbation is used as a main technique for implementation. More specifically, constant perturbation is introduced as a specific example of data-flow perturbation. Some quantitative metrics are proposed for the description of software diversity, and the parameters needed to calculate the metrics estimated by fault injection experiments. A case study is presented to illustrate that the diversity metrics are appropriate, and that constant perturbation is a practical fault injecting technique to estimate parameters necessary for assessing diversity.

1   Introduction

Software is a major source of systematic/design faults in safety-critical systems. A single version of software code, even of modest complexity, can never be considered to be fault-free, irrespective of the excellence of the design, verification and validation processes invoked. Therefore, the potential benefits of voted redundant systems incorporating diverse software versions have always been seen as a potential method to improve system reliability. The original approach to diverse design was to develop various versions of a program for a given task using separate teams with different experience/backgrounds, so that common design errors would be less likely and the resulting voted system more tolerant of any residual logical faults that can occur in software [1], [2]. This approach can be seen to follow the successful use of independence and redundancy in improving the fault tolerance of hardware.

The measurement and assessment of multiversion software is a longstanding topic of research [3]. However, to date no effective and realistic metric or model exists for describing software diversity. The independence assumption has been found inapplicable to model software diversity and the issue is the identified need to quantify "version correlation" [4], [5]. The correlation can be ascertained by revealing failure behaviours of each version in the system input space, but the traditional software testing methods and reliability models based on fault observation have been shown as not suitable for high reliability software. Normal software reliability models

F. Koornneef and M. van der Meulen (Eds.): SAFECOMP 2000, LNCS 1943, pp. 63-73, 2000.

are only useful for software with observed failure rates from 10^{-1} to 10^{-5} per hour. Safety critical software requires the failure rate to be below 10^{-7} to 10^{-9} per hour, and in general the reliability models can be considered inappropriate [6].

An alternative approach to the estimation of failure behaviour which has generated significant recent interest is the use of fault injection/error seeding methods [7], [8]. In software engineering, the fault simulation methods are mainly focused on assessment of single version software. Estimation of software diversity using fault injection is a potential but little explored approach. The fault-injection method has demonstrated its worth in the testing of some qualitative characteristics in single version software [9]. If a particular fault (represented by a data anomaly) seems unrealistic for the software in its natural environment then the benefit of injecting it may seem doubtful. However, it could still forewarn us of output anomalies resulting from "more realistic" data anomalies. Thus even "poor" choices of artificial data anomalies can potentially reveal undesirable output behaviours that were not known to be possible prior to fault injection being applied [10].

In this paper, a quantitative index is discussed for description of software diversity in section 2, based on the estimation of some parameters by fault injecting experiments. Constant perturbation is introduced as a type of fault injection method in section 3. In section 4, an experiment is set up to provide some confirmation that the constructed diversity index is reasonable, and that constant perturbation is a practical fault injection technique for estimating the parameters required to construct a diversity assessment.

2   Methods for Measurement of Software Diversity

Multiversions of software are likely to be similar because there are many common criteria used in their development, even by totally independent developers. Therefore independent failure behaviour cannot be easily assumed and to investigate this problem, Eckhardt and Lee firstly suggested a consideration of the failure probability of a randomly selected program on a random selected input (EL model) [4]. Littlewood and Miller developed the idea further for clarity and completeness (LM model) [5]. The issue is readily identified as "version correlation". If constructing two versions from two methods A and B was a process of randomly selecting two programs from the two respective populations, the LM model would describe the likely effectiveness of using multiversions i.e. the likely levels of diversity we could expect to achieve. However, this hypothetical model cannot be easily used for safety critical software as in a particular case the covariance depends on factors specific to the situation such as the developer's ability to avoid common faults and the tester's ability to reveal common faults which in turn depend on the actual S/W design chosen for the versions. Practical diversity assessment requires quantitative indexes to describe diversity as an inherent structural character of software as it presents in the particular case and not as an averaged population property. It can be seen from the theoretical model that, when the reliability of a multiversion software (with known version failure probabilities) is being evaluated, the overlapping of failure domains of the different versions is the crux of the problem. Overlapping can be analysed as a function of two more fundamental pieces of information. The first is the estimation of fault distribution patterns in software structures for different versions. For example, a simple assumption is that the faults are distributed proportionately according to Lines of Code(LOC), possibly factored with the difficulty of sub-tasks as in the EL model. The second is the connection of failure domains in the input space caused by the different faults in the different versions. The fault injection method as a "what if" technique which provides a convenient approach to discover the latter condition.

Similar to the definition of covariance, a relative quantitative index of software diversity can be introduced based on a comparison of the reliability of the combined software versions with that of each single version of the software. In order to describe the failure behaviour of the software versions based on fault injecting experiments, the new index is a calculation of the comparative common failure volume which can be measured by tracing the input failure points corresponding to faults [11]. The diversity of a pair of programme versions A and B is defined as:

$$Div(AB) = 1 - \frac{P(AB)}{Min\{P(A), P(B)\}} \tag{1}$$

where P(AB) is the coincident failure probability and P(A), P(B) are the respective failure probabilities of the single versions.

It is obvious that $0 \le Div \le 1$. Where 1 means the two versions have no coincidental failure, and 0 means there is no improvement over the single version. This basic concept can be extended for evaluation of the software diversity for a specific class of faults. If we assume a fault f_k is contained in version $*$, some tracing and space searching methods can be used to find the failure area and then find the corresponding failure probability $P(*|f_k)$ where:

$$P(*|f_k) = \sum_{\Omega_{*|f_k}} p(x) / \sum_{\Omega} p(x) = \sum_{\Omega_{*|f_k}} p(x) \tag{2}$$
$$= \sum_{\Omega} V_*(x) p(x) / \sum_{\Omega} p(x) = \sum_{\Omega} V_*(x) p(x)$$

where: $|f_k$ means the condition under which f_k occurred. Ω means the whole input space, $\Omega_{*|f_k}$ means the failure domain of the version $*$ when it contains fault f_k, $p(x)$ is the usage distribution over the inputs and its sum over Ω is 1, $V_*(x)$ is the score function of version $*$ which is defined normally: 1 when the version fails on x and 0 when it succeeds on x.

The following question suggests itself. If program A has the probability $\theta_A^{f_i}$ to contain the fault f_i and program B has the probability $\theta_B^{f_j}$ to contain the fault f_j, what is the diversity of the two versions assuming no other faults are possible? The following formula describes this quantity,

$$Div(AB|f_if_j) = 1 - P(AB|f_if_j)/Min\{P(A|f_i) \quad P(B|f_j)\} \tag{3}$$
$$= 1 - \theta_A^{f_i}\theta_B^{f_j} \sum_{\Omega_{A|f_i} \cap \Omega_{B|f_j}} p(x)/Min\{\theta_A^{f_i} \sum_{\Omega_{A|f_i}} p(x) \quad \theta_B^{f_j} \sum_{\Omega_{B|f_j}} p(x)\}$$

The above formula can be extended to estimate the combined software reliability if three elements are known, namely, reliability estimates for each single version, the possible fault distributions in each version, and Div for all inserted faults with full coverage of the software structure.

3   Fault Injection and Constants Perturbation

In common with other software testing methods, the application of fault simulation techniques to assess the software diversity must consider test adequacy criteria. It needs to consider fault selection analogously to test data generation, which may be manual, automated, or a combination of both, and requires stopping rules based on adequacy measures [12], [13]. Mutation testing and data flow testing are extensively regarded as effective for unit-level software testing, and mature enough to be used by industrial software developers [14]. Both techniques are thought of as white box methods providing a higher level of testing than older techniques such as statement and branch coverage. The theoretical analysis and experimental results show that both techniques have close coverage [15]. The approach suggested in this paper combines elements of these two techniques [16].

To obtain confidence in fault injection experiments the fundamental problem is finding adequate fault models. We need confidence that we have simulated an adequate range of abnormal events including specification errors, programmer faults, hardware and sensor failures and input/environmental anomalies, representative of real errors causing systematic failure.

A data definition of a variable is a code location where a value is placed in memory (assignment, input, etc.), and a data use is a location where the value of the variable is accessed. Uses are subdivided into two types: a computation use directly affects a computation or is an output, and a predicate use directly affects the flow of control. The former is considered to be on the nodes in the control flow graph and the latter is on the edges. The data values at these uses are decided by the code operations prior to the uses, the inputs and constants in the software, where "**constants**" refers to all parameters with predefined values in the program. In multiversion software, all versions typically contain the same constants deriving from the software requirements. There may be some other constants particular to individual versions used by developers to construct different software structures.

The data flow may be divided into two types. The first is from an input to an output combined with or controlled by some of the constants. Another is directly from an input to an output without any intervention from these constants. The second situation is very rare in practical software. The first situation is the main object for discussion in this paper. The effect of any software faults on software reliability can be seen as a disturbance of a data flow. A 'disturbance' might first manifest itself as an incorrect loading of state into memory within some control flow path, or as an incorrect redirection of control flow. The fundamental idea here is to use perturbation of constants as the fault injection method to simulate all data flow disturbances. The aim is to achieve high coverage; as good as data flow testing.

Constant perturbation is convenient when used on multiversion software. Each version contains largely the same constants. Therefore a single testing environment can be used to simulate the faults of both versions. Another benefit is that this kind of perturbation can be executed automatically.

4   Experimental Process and Results

4.1   The Background of the Software Version

The experiment was set up based on the DARTS project nuclear plant protection system software of UK HSE co-ordinated Nuclear Safety Research Programme. The software includes four channels programmed in different languages, all matching the same requirement specification. For clarity, **channel** is used here instead of 'version.' 'Versions' will refer to the different programs resulting from a channel as a result of different inserted faults. In all channels, there are a total of nine input signals to the software based on three important physical safety parameters from which seven trip formulae are to be calculated to produce the output. Each channel is required to complete the full cycle of data input (nine signals), trip calculations (seven trips) and outputs within 500 milliseconds. Therefore in the following, we will define an **"input"** as a data message representing the nine input signals and a **"output"** as a message comprising simple characters representing the seven trip results for each cycle. The **"input space"** is defined as the set of all possible inputs.

Two of the seven trips are based on the rate of change of certain signal values between two cycles. The C channel needs 3 and The Ada channel needs 4 cycles for initialisation after resetting and generally both channels need 2 to 4 cycles of output messages to respond correctly to an incident e.g. the maximum steam drum pressure or maximum pressure drop rate. Moreover, the channels respond to some incidents needs 5 to 8 cycles of outputs, e.g. on detection of a message format error the channel should indicate the appropriate signal status and thereafter the system should behave as if it has just been powered up. Therefore, **"a test"** in this experiment is defined as a sequence of inputs for either 10 or 15 cycles.

Two channels programmed in C and ADA were studied. In each case the final code resulting from the software development process was used as the **"golden version"**, and the "success" or "failure" behaviours of the versions derived by injecting faults into the golden versions were determined by comparing the outputs of these versions against their respective golden versions.

4.2   Fault Injection and Failure Detection

The test data sets for failure detection were generated from a combination of two approaches. The first was based on the test data provided by the acceptance testers, which was created for the verification of software functions according to the requirement specification. This element was assumed to provide test coverage of all requirement branches. The second was based on input-space searching, using the branch and bound method, to probe and establish the failure domains caused by an inserted fault into a version. The defined fault simulation made it possible to search the input space from some known failure point/s caused by the injected fault. The second approach is essential to estimate the diversity of channels because it allows the overlap of the failure domains of each version in the input space to be determined.

To simulate faults, 33 individual parameters labelled as case 1 to case 33 were selected for perturbation together with some special cases, like 34 which is combination of case 7 and 8. The parameters predefined as strings or characters in a program could be replaced with other possible ones, e.g. "safe" with "trip" or "warn". The enlargement or reduction of a parameter was called "Positive Perturbation (PP)" or "Negative Perturbation (NP)" respectively and could be performed within each parameter range limitation. The distributions of the insertion points for the ADA version can be see from Fig.1, which is based on the structural dependency graph of Ada modules provided by Darts Project. The numbers in the dashed frames represent the cases and the arrows indicate the objective module. Similarly, the distribution of inserted faults the C version modules can be seen in Fig. 2.

In order to reduce the complexity of the injection and detection processes, a basic assumption has been made:

Assumption For the same fault case, the failure domains caused by a large perturbation will contain those caused by a smaller one.

Where large bigger and smaller is a comparison of the absolute value used in NP or PP simulation, the meaning of "contain" implies the relation for both volume and position of the failure domains. This assumption was observed to be valid, without any exception for the following experimental cases.

Another empirical approach was also used to control the perturbation scale. The safety critical software has a high reliability, therefore the perturbations causing large failure domains can be ignored. So for each case, we needed to do 2-6 perturbation so that each version has 2-6 recompiled versions including an anomaly, and in total 93 anomalous versions were tested. Besides the 46 tests of the anomalous versions of each channel, 200-6111 tests were executed in a space searching experiment depending on the different size of the failure volume produced by the injected fault in each a case. The 6111 is maximum number of discrete points along the dimensional axis of a signal used as inputs to the channels. In some special cases like case 34, multi-dimensional searching is used to observe combined effects of coupled faults, which needed $O(10^6)$ tests.

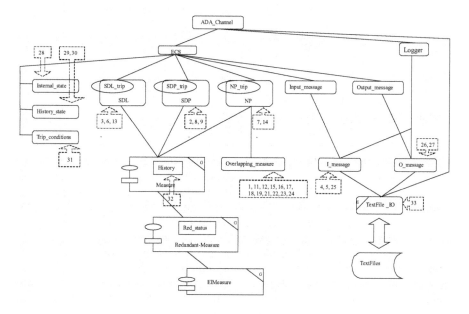

Fig. 1. The distribution of inserted fault cases for Ada channel

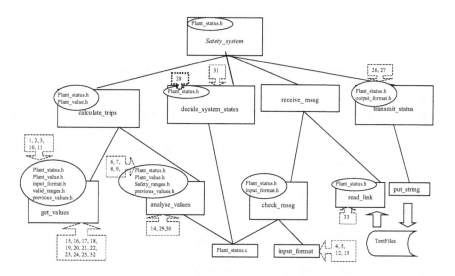

Fig. 2. The distribution of inserted fault cases for C channel

4.3   The Experimental Results

The parameter perturbation used can be regarded as inserting the same set of faults into different versions and the test results are summarised in table 1.

Table 1. The Connections of Failure Domains for Different Perturbation Case

	$C \supset ADA$	$C \subset ADA$	$C \equiv ADA$	$C \neq ADA$
46 tests	1, 10, 11, 23, 24, 25	12, 16, 21, 29, 30, 32	2. 3, 4, 5, 6, 7, 8, 9, 13, 14, 15, 17, 18, 20, 22, 26,27, 28, ,31,33,**34**	1*, 23*, 25*
Space searching	1*, 7, 10, 11, 23, 25	2*, 8*, 12, 16, 21, 22, 29, 30, 32	1, 2, 3, 4, 5, 6, 9, 13, 14, 15, 17, 18, 19, 20, 21, 24,26, 27, 28,31, 33	8, 25*, **34**

It is expected that the experiment can show the difference between the failure behaviours of two versions with the same inserted fault. This difference may reveal the internal structural characteristics of each software version, furthermore its quantitative description provides a basis to calculate the diversity index. The results are categorised in accordance with the relation of failure domains between two versions. If only from the point of view that both versions contain the same fault, the relations between two failure domains of Ada and C versions are of four types, as in set theory. Firstly, they have the same failure points as listed in column 3.i.e. their failure domains have the same volume and position in the input space. It is the worst situation to software diversity. Secondly, both of them separately have some particular failure points not belonging to each other as list in column 4. The more different points that exist between the two failure domains, the more diversity is achieved by the software channels for the specified fault. Thirdly and fourthly, one failure domain contains another one as in column 1 and 2. It is also an important to consider the diverse failure behaviours when the compound faults are considered like the following discussion for case 34.

In table 1, the recorded number for each case in fact represents several correspondent results of fault injection. The reason to record the case number but not each perturbation number is because the faults by different perturbation in respect to the same case usually causes the same relations between failure areas in input space. So the general case number demonstrates the most results of relative faults, and a few case numbers with a star representing the exceptional results of particular fault for this case. Generally, some phenomena and conclusions was observed and concluded as following:

- Comparing the first row and second row in the table, the results are some similar. But the normal acceptance tests are not enough to evaluate the software diversity. The input space searching is necessary in order to describe precisely the overlap of failure domains of different channels. So the following points will be discussed mainly based on the second row.
- It is quite difficult to achieve the explicit structural diversity. The majority of the cases produced same failure domains, and some formed containing relations between each other. Only a few cases presented the diverse failure behaviours. It supports the positive correlation explanations based on the hypothesis that the faults in two channels usually happened in the same data flow path for the same task because of the same difficult distribution [6], [7].
- The first and second situations are both the source of software diversity under same fault conditions. Normally the combination of cases in first column with the one in

second column can form a case belonging to column fourth. The case 34 is an example.

- For a same case, the rate of common failure points/points of smaller failure domain for two channels is usually going up with the growth of the perturbation margin. When comparing two channels respectively with the fault of different case, the varying trend of the rate kept the same although it might keep decreasing rather that increasing. This kind of results provide a convenience to estimate the upper bound of software diversity, e.g. for the situation with the same case, usually:

$$\max(O(Div(\text{case } i))) = O(Div(\text{case } i)|\text{observed minimum perturbation})$$

and the lower bound can be estimated by reason that of each single version failure probability is smaller than a specified value:

$$\min(O(Div(\text{case } i))) = O(Div(\text{case } i)|\text{maximum perturbation under control})$$

- In order to check the above conclusion 4, some random faults which may be represented by the case were inserted and the testing results showed that the diversity value was within the bounds.
- The fault injection by parameter perturbation can produce "satisfactory" coverage that may be illustrated by two aspects. The first is that every one of 46 tests can find a corresponding case. It means we can simulate a fault by constant perturbation, which was only checked out by the indicated one in the 46 tests. The second is that some inserted faults couldn't be found by the 46 tests, and were only detected by space searching.

5   Conclusions and Discussions

The task of estimating the reliability of mutiversion software is distinguished from single version in requiring knowledge of the coincidence of failure points between versions, the individual version failure probabilities provide insufficient information in themselves. The distribution of failure points is determined by the faults in the software and how the structure of the software maps an input to an output via these faults. The flexibility and complexity of software means that there is extreme diversity of possible faults in any non-trivial program.

In this paper, the constant perturbation method is proposed as a kind of fault injection technique to evaluate software diversity under specified fault conditions. By estimating fault patterns, the software diversity could be assessed but the problem is that no practical approach exists for the exact estimation of the fault distribution. The experimental results in this paper did not build the artificial fault distribution pattern and consequently was only able to discuss the quantitative metric in a qualitative manner, but there are already some suggested methods to estimate fault distribution. For instance, based on LOC or based on module complexity etc, which may be extended and developed further by incorporating extra information pertaining to developers' particular circumstance situations for each channel [17], [18]. Furthermore, white box statistical structural models, currently under development, may provide more useful information about the fault distribution based on the failure observation [19].

Further experimental results are now required from which to draw general conclusions about the effectiveness of fault injection to validate software diversity design. A wider aim of ongoing research must be to gain an improved understanding of the relationship between actual possible design errors and those simulated during software fault injection. This is important because quantification of the fault coverage and distribution provided is only relative to the set of faults simulated.

Acknowledgements

The work presented in this paper comprises aspects of a study (DISPO) performed as part of the UK Nuclear Safety Research programme, funded and controlled by the Industry Management Committee together with elements from the SSRC Generic Research Programme funded by British Energy, National Air Traffic Services, Lloyd's Register, Railtrack and the Health and Safety Executive.

References

1.   Avizienis, A.: The N-version approach to fault-tolerant software. IEEE Trans. Software Eng., Vol. SE-11(1985) 1491-1501
2.   Bishop, P. B., et al.: PODS-Aproject on diverse software. IEEE Trans. Software Eng., Vol. SE-12, No.9(1986) 929-940
3.   Knight, J., Leveson, N.: An experimental evaluation of the assumption of independence in multi-version programming. IEEE Trans. Software Eng., Vol. SE-12, no.1(1986) 96-109
4.   Eckhardt, D., Lee, L.: A theoretical basis for the analysis of multiversion software subject to coincident errors. IEEE Trans. Software Eng., Vol. SE-11, no.12(1985)1511-1517
5.   Littlewood, B., Miller, D.: Conceptual modeling of coincident failures in multiversion software. IEEE Trans. Software Eng., Vol. SE-15, no.12(1985)1596-1614
6.   Littlewood, B.: Predicting software reliability, Phil. Trans. Roy. Soc. London(1989) 95-117
7.   Voas, J. M., McGraw, G.: Software Fault Injection: Inoculating programs against errors. Wiley Computer Publishing", 1998
8.   Kawata, H., Yoshida, H., Nagai, M., Saijo, H.: Software testing. Journal of Information Processing, Vol.14, No.3(1991) 246- 253
9.   Laski, J., Szermer, W., Luczycki, P.: Error Masking in computer programs. Software testing. Verification, and Reliability, Vol.5(1995) 81-105
10.   Voas, J., et al.: `Crystal ball' for software liability. Computer, Vol.30, No.6 (1997)
11.   Napier, J., Chen, L., May, J., Hughes, G.: Fault simulation to validate fault-tolerance in Ada. Int. J Computer Sys. Sci. & Eng. 1(2000) 113-125

12. May, J., Hughes, G., Zhu, H.: Statistical Software Testing, and Test Adequacy. S. Gardiner, editor , Springer (1999): 155--170

13. Rapps, S., Weyuker, W. J.: Selecting software test data using data flow information. IEEE Transactions on Software Engineering, 11(4)(1985) 367-375

14. Frankl, P. G., Weyuker, E. J.: An applicable family of data flow testing criteria. IEEE Transactions on Software Engineering, 14(10)(1988) 1483-1498

15. Offutt, A. J., et al.: An experimental evaluation of data flow and mutation testing. SP&E 26(2)(1996) 165-176

16. Chen, L., Napier, J., May, J., Hughes, G.: Testing the diversity of multi version software using fault injection. Procs of Advances in Safety and Reliability, SARSS(1999) 13.1-13.10

17. Cottam, M., May J., et al.: Fault Analysis of the Software Generation Process - The FASGEP Project, Proceedings of the Safety and Reliability Society Symposium: Risk Management and Critical Protective Systems, Altrincham, UK October (1994)

18. May, J., et al.: Fault Prediction for Software Development Processes, Proceedings of Institute of Mathematics and its Applications Conference on the Mathematics of Dependable Systems, Royal Holloway,Univ. of London, Egham, Surrey 1-3 Sept.(1993)

19. Kuball, S., May, J., Hughes, G.: Structural Software Reliability Estimation. Lecture Notes in Computer Science, Computer Safety, Reliability and Security, 1698(1999) 336-349

Expert Error:
The Case of Trouble-Shooting in Electronics

Denis Besnard

Laboratoire de Psychologie Cognitive, Université de Provence
29, avenue Robert Schuman, 13621 Aix-en-Provence, France.
besnard@up.univ-mrs.fr

Abstract. An expert trouble-shooter is a subject who has a great deal of experience in his activity that allows him or her to be very efficient. However, the large amount of problems he or she has experienced tends to rigidify his or her strategies due to empirical learning and application of [symptom-fault] co-occurrence rules. We defend the hypothesis that experts' errors depend on the knowledge of these co-occurrences. Our experiment supported this point of view: expert trouble-shooters in electronics implement non-relevant actions in an atypical symptoms configuration.
From an operational point of view, human is an active component of systems and the final dependability partly relies on human reliability. More specifically, human operators are strongly involved in maintenance and trouble-shooting activities. One then has to know about the cognitive processes involved in expert error and integrate this knowledge in the design of systems.

1   Introduction

A lot of research has put in evidence the performance (rapidity of the actions) and the reliability (precision) of experienced operators in many domains of activity. The approach of this paper slightly deviates from this conception as it aims at exhibiting the limits of expertise in the core of its foundations. The experiment will show that an expert trouble-shooter in electronics may be sensitive to a bias. He may perform errors and activate non-relevant knowledge.

Research in problem-solving showed that experts are specialized in an automated processing mode. This preferred rule-based automatisation may imply that experts' errors mainly depend on this mode of reasoning. An atypical configuration of symptoms should then impair the reliability of expert trouble-shooters.

This article will mainly focus on expert trouble-shooters' activity in natural conditions of work in order to identify some psychological elements relevant to work situations. The paper begins by presenting some theoretical data about expertise in diagnosis. This will serve as a frame for the experiment. The discussion will then attempt to link the results with the existing theoretical data and to provide an operator-centered point of view about systems dependability.

F. Koornneef and M. van der Meulen (Eds.): SAFECOMP 2000, LNCS 1943, pp. 74-85, 2000.
© Springer-Verlag Berlin Heidelberg 2000

2   Expertise in Diagnosis

The theoretical position of this paper defends the idea that experienced operators (hereafter called experts) solve problems by extracting surface patterns of information from the environment in order to identify a possible solution [1]. The detection of such patterns permit the triggering of what Rasmussen [2] calls short-cuts, that is to say a matching process between a configuration of data and an action.

The need to make fast decisions favours diagnostic methods based on pattern recognition rather than on underlying processes [3]. Diagnosis operations of experts rely on probabilities [4, 5]. They activate tests of some elements of the system that, in the past, have most often explained the symptoms. These tests may be executed sequentially, from the most probable to the least probable [6].

Diagnosis can be considered as a form of reasoning whose goal is to identify causes of facts assessed as abnormal [7, 8]. Diagnosis is involved in a wide variety of situations where it regulates the activity. Such situations include among others the monitoring of a nuclear reactor [9], monitoring a furnace [10], piloting an aircraft [11], fire-fighting [12], decision making in an anti-aircraft defence system of a surface ship [13], decision making on an offshore platform [14]. Diagnosis is also present in static situations. This is the case of trouble-shooting. Studies that have dealt with natural trouble-shooting include an automobile ignition system [15], a running engine [16], an electronic circuit [17]. In these situations, fault-finding represents the main part of the activity and the diagnosis process mainly develops as a consequence of the operator's actions. In this research, diagnosis will be considered as a static trouble-shooting task.

Symptoms detection is a major phase in the trouble-shooting process. It is a selection of data. It is performed as a function of the weight that the operator assigns to the different available sources. This strategy relies on the knowledge of past occurrences of malfunctions and on their causes. It allows expert operators to implement a symptomatic trouble-shooting [7, 2, 4, 5]. This research strategy quickly reduces the number of components possibly at fault with very few tests. It is a pattern recognition process where symptoms are compared to possible causes in order to find a relation that will indicate a specific fault [8, 18]. The symptomatic strategy is generally opposed to the topographic strategy where fault-finding consists in searching for a fault by following a physical support such as a cable or a flux. It is processed at a knowledge-based level of control -typical of the novice operator- that implies heavy and numerous operations.

3   Theoretical Position

In the classical conception, expertise relies on a capacity to activate knowledge relevant to the task and to efficiently categorize problems [19]. This paper puts this conception of expert reasoning in question. The large amount of problems trouble-shooters meet through their experience tend to rigidify the strategies they implement. This is mainly due to empirical learning of [symptom-fault] co-occurrences. Expert trouble-shooters may then be sensitive to biases. They may produce errors and activate non-relevant knowledge, especially in an atypical configuration where the symptoms do not match the usual causes.

The experiment will attempt to show that experts' errors rely on a rule-based association that occurs when the situational data are not optimal for such an association. As novices' reasoning processes mainly rely on a knowledge-based level of control, they should not be sensitive to this bias. They are expected to show more efficient diagnostic reasoning processes in some phases of the trouble-shooting activity.

The general approach developed in this paper is a naturalistic one. It consists in studying a trouble-shooting task in the conditions of the real work. The psychological interest is to understand the mechanisms underlying expert error. This study also has an operational interest since an operator performing an error when trouble-shooting may impair the availability and the dependability of a system.

This research will study a trouble-shooting task on an electronic circuit where a fault was implemented. This fault exhibits frequent and well-known symptoms whereas the actual cause is rare. This discrepancy should be an interesting feature in order to study expert error in diagnosis.

4   Method

4.1   Subjects

All participants were male and volunteers. There were 10 expert and 9 novice electronics operators. Experts had between 8 and 40 years of experience (m=18,9; s=9,1). There were 8 military operators (Air Base 278 at Ambérieu and Naval Base at Toulon, France) and 2 civilians. All of them were professional operators. Novices were baccalaureat students in a technical school (Lycée Vauvenargues, Aix-en-Provence, France) who had been studying electronics for 2 years.

4.2   Materials

Diagnosis devices (multimeter, oscilloscope) and two technical diagrams (an implantation diagram and a theoretical diagram, in A4 format) were provided to the subjects. The implantation diagram (Fig. 1) is a representation of the topographic aspect of the circuit. The theoretical diagram (Fig. 2) represents the connections between the components.

4.3   Experimental Device

The device[1] subjects had to trouble-shoot was a simple low-frequency amplifier that comprised two amplification stages, each comprising an integrated circuit (IC). The

---

[1] The author wishes to thank Jean-Claude Gedin (LPC, University of Provence) for the design of the circuit.

first stage comprised the IC741 ; the second one comprised the IC386. The assembling of the circuit conformed to conventions. The board (24cm x 8cm) where the circuit was assembled allowed the subjects to visualize the tracks and the connections between the components. The inputs of the circuit were a FM radio signal plugged into the input jack (component J) and a DC 12V power supply. When the fault was located (see below) and the faulty component replaced, some FM music was broadcast through the loud speaker.

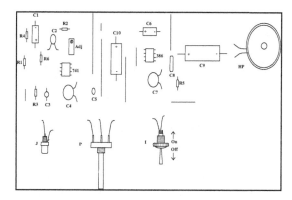

Fig. 1. Implantation diagram

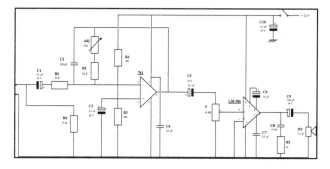

Fig. 2. Theoretical diagram

4.4   Description of the Fault

The fault was on the C7 condenser. Although this fault is very rare, it is similar to another fault -an integrated circuit (IC) failure- that can usually be diagnosed rapidly. C7 was short-circuited with a thin invisible weld wire. In this faulty condition, the condenser C7 switched the output signal of the IC386 to the mass track (Fig. 3). When subjects tested this IC, they tested the input, measured a signal, then tested the output and measured no signal. The symptoms led the subjects to suspect the connected IC386 as the cause of the fault.

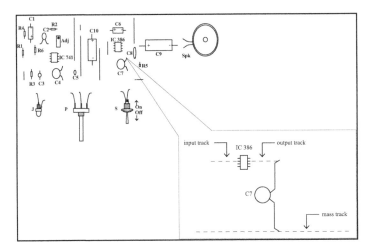

Fig. 3. Description of the fault

4.5   Procedure

The subjects worked in their usual workshop. After the instructions were read, the device was turned on (in configuration of fault) and the diagnosis began. The experimentation was videotaped in order to keep track of the operator's actions. The trouble-shooting process stopped when the subjects found the faulty component or when he gave up. No advice was given to the subject and there was no time limit. The experiment could stop with the cause of the fault not being discovered.

4.6   Variables

There is one between-subjects variable: expertise (expert *vs.* novice). Percentages in the total number of operations were computed for the variables 5 to 14. They allow the extraction and comparison of proportional data.

1 / *Fault located or not.*
2 / *Time.* This referred to the number of minutes that separate the beginning of the experiment to the localization of the fault or the moment when the subject gave up.
3 / *Total number of operations.* An operation is considered as a test (measure, disassembly, etc.) or the consultation of a source of information that is external to the circuit itself (e.g. diagrams).
4 / *Number of different elements covered by the operations.* This variable measures the diversity of elements tested by the subject.
5 / *Percentage of operations on the IC386.*
6 / *Percentage of operations on the IC741.*
7 / *Percentage of operations on the ICs (741 + 386).* ICs are active and fragile components. A high number of operations on these components highlights the implementation of a frequency heuristic.

8 / *Percentage of operations before the 1st operation on the IC386.*
9 / *Percentage of operations before the 1st operation on the IC741.*
10 / *Percentage of operations before the 1st operation on an IC.* This variable is an indication of the progression of the diagnosis before the 1st operation on an IC.
11 / *Percentage of operations on resistances and condensers.* Resistances and condensers are passive and reliable components. A high number of operations on these components indicates some remoteness from the frequency heuristic.
12 / *Percentage of operations on C7.* C7 is the component at fault. It is short-circuited but it is usually reliable. It is not a good candidate for the fault.
13 / *Percentage of operations before the 1st operation on C7.*
14 / *Percentage of operations after the 1st operation on C7.*

5   Predictions

Experts have the greatest amount of experience in this experiment (Variable 1). The total number of operations (V3) should be higher for experts than novices as the fault is an atypical one. However, this variable has to be considered in the context of the final result of the trouble-shooting process. On the other hand, the number of different elements covered should be lower for experts than novices since experts are expected to test a smaller diversity of components (V4).

The percentage of operations on the IC386, on the IC741 and on the ICs (V5, V6 & V7) should be higher for experts than for novices. In the same way, considering the expected saliency of the ICs, the percentage of operations before the 1st operation on the IC386, on the IC741 and on an IC (V8, V9 & V10) should be lower among experts. The hypothesized implementation of the frequency heuristic supports this set of predictions.

Through their extended practice, experts built an empirical knowledge about the relative reliability of the resistances and condensers. The percentage of operations on these components (V11) should be lower for these subjects.

Finally, as C7 is a very reliable component, the percentage of operations on C7 (V12) should be lower for experts than for novices. For the same reason, the percentage of operations before the 1st operation on C7 (V13) will be higher for experts.

The variables 2 (time) and 14 (% of operations after the 1st operation on C7), although not introducing any hypotheses, should provide some additional data.

6   Results

The data were analysed through an analysis of variance. Broadly speaking, results did not reject the hypotheses.

Experts located the fault more often than novices (5/10 experts versus 2/9 novices). Expertise, regarding the final state of diagnosis, remained a factor of competence. But some areas of the expert trouble-shooting process were sub-optimal.

The experiment stopped when the cause of the fault was located or when the subject gave up. Experts spent more time than novices before reaching this point (experts=47 min; novices=30,22 min) (F(1,17)=4,129; p=.058). Contrary to our prediction, experts and novices did not differ significantly on the total number of operations and on the elements covered by the operations.

As Fig. 4 shows, the percentage of operations on the IC386 is larger among experts (experts=25,9; novices=3,6) (F(1,17)=10,888; p=.004). These subjects also showed a larger percentage of operations on the IC741 (experts=13,2; novices=2,12) (F(1,17)=13,095; p=.002). On the whole, the percentage of operations on the ICs (741 + 386) was larger for experts than for novices (experts=39,2; novices=5,6) (F(1,17)=30,59; p=.0000). As predicted, expert operators over-valued the importance of ICs in the circuit.

Experts and novices differed significantly on the percentage of operations before the first operation on the IC386 (experts=4,66; novices=48,23) (F(1,15)=16,035; p=.001), on the percentage of operations before the first operation on the IC741 (experts=5,77; novices=26,39) (F(1,12)=6,414; p=.026) and on the percentage of operations before the first operation on ICs (experts=4,47; novices=43,7) (F(1,15)=11,881; p=.003). Generally speaking, experts performed fewer operations than novices before testing an IC. These findings were considered as evidence for the implementation of the frequency heuristic.

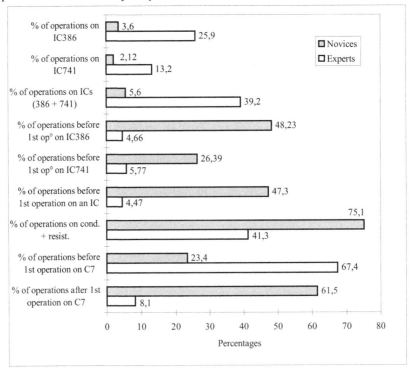

Fig. 4. Overview of significant results

The percentage of operations on resistances and condensers showed a significant difference (experts=41,3; novices=75,1) $(F(1,17)=11,34; p=.003)$. As predicted, the operations performed by experts on resistances and condensers represented, in comparison to novices, a small part of the activity.

The percentage of operations on C7 did not exhibit any difference between experts and novices but the percentage of operations before the first operation on C7 tended to be reliably different (experts=67,4; novices=23,4) $(F(1,10)=4,086; p=.07)$. Novices tested the faulty component sooner than experts. This result supported our hypothesis of a possible implementation of sub-optimal operations by experts. Nevertheless, the percentage of operations after the first operation on C7 showed that experts virtually finished trouble-shooting after having tested C7 for the first time (experts=8,15; novices=61,56) $(F(1, 11)=30,44; p=.0002)$.

7   Discussion

There were not any significant differences between the two groups of subjects on the number of operations and on the number of elements covered. On this latter point, one cannot conclude that the expert focused on a more narrow set of components than novices did. Subjects did not differentiate themselves on the percentage of operations on C7. Experts, when testing this component, noted that it was at fault. This measure marked the end of their trouble-shooting. On the other hand, novices hardly ever located the fault. As a consequence, they performed very few operations on C7. These two different behaviours explain the absence of any difference on this variable.

Among the experts who did not locate the fault (n=5), two performed operations on C7. How may an expert test C7 without locating the fault? One of these two subjects asserted, when measuring C7, that he had encountered "some difficulties in testing it". A possible explanation lies in the confidence of the operator in the measure. An alternative explanation refers to the consistency of a measure regarding the representation of the fault. If a component, even at fault, does not allow the operator to better understand the symptoms, then this component is not assessed as responsible for the symptoms.

Experts performed more operations on the IC386 and the IC741 than novices. They also tested ICs earlier and they perform less tests on resistances and condensers than novices. These data support the idea that experts use their knowledge of the relative reliabilities of components.

Novices tested the C7 component sooner than the experts although the latter virtually finished their diagnosis once C7 was tested. This result can be discussed in the light of the concept of cognitive economy. As resistances are reliable components, experts gave priority to ICs as candidates for the fault. Consequently, a small number of operations before the first test on this kind of component would be inconsistent with the principle of economy, even if it would lead the subject to locate the fault faster in our circuit.

The frequency heuristic associates symptoms to their causes depending on the past occurrences. It is a powerful tool in the case where symptoms reflect the structural state of the circuit. But this trouble-shooting method can generate errors when symptoms are not those usually associated to the fault. Then, the frequency of the past occurrences is no longer the best support of the diagnosis process as it causes experts to focus on non-relevant components.

7.1   Sub-optimality

Three points of sub-optimality were listed:

1. Experts performed more operations than novices before testing the faulty C7 for the first time.
2. Experts focused on ICs. Considering the current fault, this behaviour is sub-optimal since the ICs are not responsible for the fault. The concept of *frequency bias* may account for these two latter sub-optimal behaviours.
3. Experts spent more time than novices searching for the cause of the fault. Time is only a superficial indicator for cognitive activity since experts found the fault more often. However, one must keep in mind that speed is not an invariant among experts.

These points of sub-optimality support the idea a) that novices can exhibit more efficient behaviours that experts do and b) that expert errors mainly rely on a matching process used as a problem solving strategy. Expert operators tend to look for an optimal solution with a minimal cognitive expense even if there is not any guarantee about the results. This risk is constrained since, in most cases, the operator cannot reason in a systematic and exhaustive way on the whole data and hypotheses.

7.2   Limits of the Study

First, the conditions of the experiment are exceptional in comparison to the professional activity. Even if an error from an experienced operator is always possible whatever his field of activity, expertise is more a security factor than an error generator. Secondly, expertise, as in the present research, is often introduced as a binary concept. However, it is not a simple expert/novice distinction, even though such a dichotomy is experimentally useful. This conception does not fit the continuum of a life-scale process of knowledge acquisition.

7.3   What Link with Systems Dependability?

The interest in studying the dependability of systems goes far beyond the classical hazardous industrial processes (nuclear plants, transports, space, etc.). Nowadays, the existence and survival of some information systems totally relies on the availability of the components that underlie their security. In such systems (e.g. the stock exchange), when a physical problem occurs, the rapidity and precision of the intervention represent heavy operational stakes. For this reason, when a human operator attempts to recover the initial state of the system, he or she has to reach an optimal level of performance. If the intervention comprises sub-optimal phases (such as those reported in this paper), then some aspects of the dependability of the system may be impaired:

- the system may no longer be available to its users;
- continuity of the network in which the system may be inserted can be broken;
- confidentiality of the information in the system may be affected if a protection function is impaired.

The weight of humans' actions in information systems should cause the research in dependability to integrate a cognitive approach. Humans are parts of a system. This is a first reason why one should improve their level of performance, particularly if they are active components of dependability (e.g. maintenance operators). Moreover, cognitive ergonomics have qualitative and quantitative methods that can serve any domain of human activity. The dependability of computerized systems takes on some importance since:

- computers have an increasing role in all industrial and domestic tasks;
- human operators play a dynamic role in the interaction with machines.

There are at least two research orientations that may improve the reliability of human-machine interaction:

- keep on formalizing human activity in order to accurately identify the causes of (expert) operators' errors;
- integrating the possibility of human error occurrences in the system's architecture in order to implement tolerance margins.

8   Conclusion

This experiment was conducted in order to know on what expert error in trouble-shooting depends. From the experiment's results, it has been shown that expert operators in electronics trouble-shooting a circuit over-value the importance of the components that, most of the time, explain the symptoms. This behaviour, called *frequency bias,* explains why expert operators use intuitive statistical rules to implement actions. After previous similar results in electronics (Besnard & Bastien-Toniazzo, 1999) it seems that there is one more piece of evidence that experts use surface features when trouble-shooting. They tend to activate procedures from symptoms detection and this matching process forces them to accept a risk of error.

Accordingly, if one aims at building dependent systems where humans may have a role, then one has to take into account the cues and the cognitive processes upon which the expert error depends.

Acknowledgements

The author wishes to thank the DGA (French General Delegation for Armament) for financial support and Corinne Mazet (LAAS, Toulouse, France) for comments on previous versions of this paper.

References

1. Konradt, U. Strategies of failure diagnosis in computer-controlled manufacturing systems: empirical analysis and implications for the design of adaptive decision support systems. *International Journal of Human-Computer Studies*, 43, 503-521, 1995.
2. Rasmussen, J. Information processing and human-machine interaction. North Holland: Elsevier Science, 1986.
3. Simpson, S. A. & Gilhooly, K. J. Diagnostic thinking processes: evidence from a constructive interaction study of electrocardiogram interpretation. *Applied Cognitive Psychology* (11) 543-554, 1997.
4. Rasmussen, J. Technologie de l'information et analyse de l'activité cognitive. in R. Amalberti, M. De Montmollin & J. Theureau *Modèles en analyse du travail*. Liège: Mardaga, 49-73, 1991.
5. Patrick, J. Cognitive aspects of fault-finding training and transfer. *Le Travail Humain* (56) 187-209, 1993.
6. Bereiter, S. R. & Miller, S. M. A field-based study of troubleshooting in computer-controlled manufacturing system. *IEEE Transactions on Systems, Man and Cybernetics* (19) 205-219, 1989.
7. Rasmussen, J. & Jensen, A. Mental procedures in real life tasks. A case study in electronics trouble shooting. *Ergonomics* (17) 293-307, 1974.
8. Govindaraj, T. & Su, Y. D. A model of fault diagnosis performance of expert marine engineers. *International Journal of Man-Machine Studies* (29) 1-20, 1988.
9. Joblet, L. *Approches de conduite du nucléaire et répartition des tâches entre opérateurs*. Training course report. University of Provence, 1997.
10. Hoc, J-M. Effets de l'expertise des opérateurs et de la complexité de la situation dans la conduite d'un processus continu à long délai de réponse: le haut fourneau. *Le Travail Humain* (54) 225-249, 1991.
11. Amalberti, R. Safety and process control: An operator centered point of view. *Reliability Engineering and System Safety* (38) 99-108, 1992.
12. Brehmer, B. Dynamic decision making: human control of complex systems. *Acta Psychologica* (81) 211-241, 1992.
13. Kaempf, G. L., Klein, G., Thordsen, M. L. & Wolf, S. Decision making in complex naval command and control environments. *Human Factors* (38) 220-231, 1996.
14. Flin, R., Slaven, G. & Stewart, K. Emergency decision making in the offshore oil and gas industry. *Human Factors* (38) 262-277, 1996.
15. Weill-Fassina, A. & Filleur C. Représentation et fonctionnement cognitif dans une recherche de panne d'un système d'allumage en mécanique-auto. *European Journal of Psychology of Education* (4) 783-102, 1989.
16. Besnard, D. Erreur humaine en diagnostic. Doctoral dissertation, University of Provence, 1999
17. Besnard, D. & Bastien-Toniazzo, M. Expert error in trouble-shooting. An exploratory study in electronics. *International Journal of Human-Computer Studies* (50) 391-405, 1999.

18. Sanderson, P. M. Knowledge acquisition and fault diagnosis: experiments with PLAULT. *IEEE Transactions on Systems, Man and Cybernetics* (20) 255-242, 1990.
19. Sperandio, J.-C. Les aspects cognitifs du travail. in C. Levi-Leboyer & J.-C. Sperandio *Traité de psychologie du travail*. Paris: PUF, 646-658, 1987.

The Safety Management of Data-Driven Safety-Related Systems

A. G. Faulkner[1], P. A. Bennett[1], R. H. Pierce[1], I. H. A. Johnston[1], and N. Storey[2]

[1] CSE International Ltd
Glanford House, Bellwin Drive, Flixborough DN15 8SN, UK
Tel: +44 1724 862169
agf@cse-euro.com
[2] School of Engineering, University of Warwick,
Coventry. CV4 7AL UK

Abstract. Many safety-related systems are built from generic software which is customised to work in a particular situation by static configuration data. Examples of such systems are railway interlockings and air traffic control systems. While there is now considerable experience and guidance on how to develop safety-related software, and there are a number of standards in this area, the topic of safety-related configuration data is hardly mentioned in the literature. This paper discusses the desirable properties of safety-related data and sets out principles for the safety management of such data, including a data lifecycle which is analogous to a software development lifecycle. Validation and verification of the data, and the means used to achieve such validation and verification are given particular attention.

1   Introduction

Many Commercial Off The Shelf (COTS) computer systems are constructed from a generic software platform which implements the necessary algorithms for the particular class of application, and is customised for a specific application. Common sense and good practice often dictates the use of configuration data in one form or another, rather than changes to the software code itself.

Examples of such data-driven systems include:

1. Railway interlockings, where the signalling control tables for a particular track layout are represented in the form of data;
2. Railway signalling control systems where data is used to represent the track layout and the location of each signal, points and other trackside devices;
3. Air traffic control systems (such as radar displays and Flight Data Processing (FDP) functions) are also configured by extensive data (also known as adaptation data) which describe the layout of airways and control areas, the location of navigational aids and many other aspects of airspace design; and

F. Koornneef and M. van der Meulen (Eds.): SAFECOMP 2000, LNCS 1943, pp. 86-95, 2000.
© Springer-Verlag Berlin Heidelberg 2000

4. Telecommunication switches (exchanges) are also generic platforms that are customised to the needs of a particular network by data that provide the rules for call routing and associates telephone numbers with physical or logical circuits.

In these examples, the configuration data are often geographical in nature since the generic system needs to be adapted to the particular instances of a real physical environment.

The correct functioning of these data-driven systems is dependent on the correctness of the configuration data, just as it is dependent on the correctness of the software code. Errors in the configuration data can lead, in safety-related systems, to hazards and possibly to accidents.

Configuration data should be clearly distinguished from normal dynamic data maintained by the computer system. Configuration data represents the static model of the real world; dynamic data represents the current state of the model (as derived from sensors and human inputs). Configuration data input is part of the off-line system design and construction process, and should not be alterable in normal system operation. The safety management of configuration data is a topic that relates to both commercially available products (COTS) and specific applications developed in-house.

2   The Issues of Safety Management of Data

The desire amongst suppliers and operators to use COTS products [1] in safety-related systems for reasons of cost and timescale [2] raises a requirement for the safety management of data-driven safety-related systems.

McDermid [2] identifies that the construction cost of a system may be reduced by the purchase of COTS system. This COTS system will often consist of hardware and software elements, which will typically be tailored to the input domain by configuration data.

McDermid [2] further adds that the certification cost of this generic hardware and software may exceed the savings made by purchasing COTS products. This certification cost is incurred because the evidence required for approval of the COTS product may not be available to the buyer or may be inappropriate to the application domain.

The certification (or approval) cost of a data-driven system may be considered to be in two distinct parts:

1. That for the evidence for generic part of the safety-related system; and
2. That for the evidence for configuration data used to drive the safety-related system.

The generic part of a COTS solution (both the hardware and software) can be developed under existing standards such as IEC 61508 [3] using established tools and techniques as a means of achieving the necessary certification or approval. This is not to say that the achievement of such certification is necessarily straightforward particularly for a generic COTS solution. It is usually easier to achieve certification for a system developed for a particular application, which does not include the uncertainties associated with possible other uses.

Examples of high integrity COTS systems for specific applications are found in railway interlocking systems. Here generic hardware and software components have been developed to a high level of integrity and granted type certification by railway regulators. In such cases the problem of overall system validation is, in principle, reduced to that of ensuring the integrity of the configuration data.

The development of the hardware and software parts of a generic solution is extensively supported by safety-related literature in broadly the same way as the development of a custom solution for a particular application. There are established processes, and detailed guidance, for hardware and software that cover a wide range of equipment and systems. These range from application specific hardware based protection systems implemented with little of no software content, to complex monitoring and control software systems based upon standard computing hardware.

For the software element of such systems there are now development languages and translation tools specifically aimed at safety-related systems. The desirable characteristics of the software, such as code structure, are well understood, even if that understanding is sometimes patchily applied. The use of tools to measure the static and dynamic properties of the software is becoming common.

The configuration data that drives a COTS system in a particular instance is itself, in most cases, not COTS (although a counter-example is given later). This application specific part of a COTS solution is likely to be created by the system integrator, who in many cases will not be the COTS product supplier. It may be treated as a one-off application developed specifically for a particular instance of the system.

The issues raised by the use of configuration data in data-driven safety-related systems are not directly addressed in the safety community literature. The need for data integrity commensurate with the SIL of the software is recognised in some standards such as IEC 61508 [3], Def Stan 00-55 [4], and CENELEC prEN 50128 [5]. However, these standards provide very little guidance on how data integrity is to be achieved, although prEN 50128 [5] is the most useful in this respect and at least recognises the need for a defined data lifecycle. As a result there is no established guidance on the process for generating such data, or on methods of achieving certification for it.

The problems of configuration data are most acutely seen where there are large volumes of real-world configuration data to be captured. Many systems need some form of configuration data, but if this is confined to a few scalar parameter values then the effort in validating these values will be small and the risk associated with this data correspondingly small. The real concern arises where large volumes of data are required.

The remainder of this paper sets out to identify the important issues and to indicate how these issues might be addressed either by using existing techniques or by developing new ones. The central issues are those of validation and verification, process evidence, data structure, tools and techniques. There is also a need for an agreed set of requirements for configuration data for a range of integrity levels, for example SIL1 to SIL4 in IEC 61508 [3].

3   Hazard Analysis for Configuration Data

The safety requirements of any system are identified through a process of hazard and risk analysis. Hazard analysis should consider the problems produced by incorrect data alongside problems associated with faults within hardware and software. In this way an integrity requirement should be assigned to the configuration data of a system, as for other system components. Standards such as IEC 61508 [3] give guidance on techniques to investigate hazards associated with hardware and software, but say little about the data within systems.

Hazard analysis involves the investigation of the functionality provided by the system and the consequences of the failure and failure modes of the identified functionality.

A variant of the Failure Modes and Effects Analysis (FMEA) method would be a possible basis for such an analysis. In the case of data the FMEA should consider both errors in data types and where necessary in individual data entities or values.

As an example, consider a flight data processing (FDP) system. The purpose of such systems is to distribute data on the proposed flight plans of aircraft to allow the air traffic controller to be aware of the presence and intentions of aircraft in his or her sector of airspace or shortly to enter it. Such information aids the controller in maintaining the mental "picture" of the air traffic and how to control it, and also acts an important reversionary measure in case of loss of radar surveillance data. Flight data is presented in the form of flight (progress) strips, either printed or on electronic displays. Typically an FDP system will generate a flight strip for a given sector some time in advance of the time a flight is expected to enter the sector. Since airspace design changes from time to time, it is usual to store sector boundaries as configuration data. The data failure mode "sector boundary in wrong position" may cause the system to fail to produce a flight strip for a given flight, or direct it to the wrong sector, which would lead in turn to a hazardous system failure mode "flight strip not produced when required". This kind of error would become more critical if the "free flight" concept becomes widely used (airliners being given direct routing from point to point rather than following linear airways) in which case flights could enter sectors at many different places.

The above example shows an FMEA analysis of a data *type*, since there are many sector boundaries in a typical FDP system.

An FMEA analysis applied to individual data *elements* might consider the trip threshold values entered for individual sensors in reactor or plant protection systems. A wrong data value might delay a trip until a hazardous plant state had been reached. Each element value would have to be considered individually since some may be more critical than others.

Systems such as railway interlockings and telecommunications systems make extensive use of configuration data. Railway interlockings are a specific example of a safety-critical system that clearly illustrates the use of configuration data.

In the example of the railway interlocking the generic part of the system is customised to the application instance by configuration data. A hazard analysis of the railway interlocking should identify not only the consequence of failure of the generic hardware or software, but also the consequences of inaccurate, erroneous or corrupted configuration data.

Configuration data failures may range from gross errors due to random failures in hardware, to systematic errors in the data preparation. Systematic errors in data preparation are due to failures of the data generation (collection) and management, or as a consequence of changes to the real world which that data represents. Changes to the real world may be as a consequence of a maintainer exchanging equipments for different makes, models or issues of the existing equipment.

4   Validation and Verification

Validation and verification of configuration data is central to the safe operation of any data-driven safety-related system. The definition of the configuration data and the closeness of its representation to the real world, which it aspires to describe, will be key factors in maintenance of the configuration data once the safety-related system enters service.

A system that uses terrain data to guide an aircraft between two points, or in a ground proximity-warning device, may be taken as an example.

What risk would be posed by terrain data which contained errors? In the case of a guidance system for low flying, it could lead to 'negative ground clearance' and the loss of the aircraft. In this case, the severity of the hazard is high and the integrity of the data must be correspondingly high to achieve a tolerable accident rate. If the terrain data is being used in a ground proximity warning system (GPWS), there has to be an error on the part of the pilot before the GPWS is needed, and although the severity of the resulting accident is the same, the likelihood of it is reduced and a lower integrity can be tolerated for the data.

The degree of rigour used in validation of configuration data should therefore be commensurate with the risk (hazard severity and likelihood) posed by errors in the configuration data and the degree to which the safety-related system could tolerate errors in the data.

What measures, tools and techniques could be used to reduce errors in the terrain data to an acceptable level? One possibility is to consider how the data is represented within the computer.

In the above example, the terrain data could be represented as a collection of heights above sea level on a grid representing the surface of the Earth. Such an array of values contains no inherent structure with which to perform on-line or off-line validation. Rules could be devised to identify the maximum height of a mountain, and the lowest part of a valley, within particular geographical areas. These minimum and maximum values could then provide range checking to detect gross errors. However, plausible error values could exist between the identified minimum and maximum values. Wire frame computer models, which consist of many triangles to describe the surface of the terrain, offer the opportunity to introduce further diversity and self-checking capability into the representation of the terrain. Any single point within the terrain would be represented as the corner of a number of triangles. The relationship between each of the constituent triangles and the point which makes up a corner of these constituent triangles provide an inherent structure which can assist in the validation the terrain. For example, missing triangles (apparent "holes" in the terrain surface) or non-contiguous areas may be detected, indicating some corruption in the data.

The representation of terrain as a wire frame model will require more computing power than a simple grid model, so there may be a trade off between speed of computation and the ability of the data to reveal errors.

Another problem with geographical data, which is common to all representations, is that changes in the real terrain, such as the erection of a radio mast, must be reflected in the data. This is a particularly difficult problem in cases where real world changes are not within the control of the data user or originator. Geographical data is an example of data which may itself be COTS in that it is typically produced by a mapping agency rather than by the user of the application system.

5   Process Evidence

Configuration data for safety-related systems should be created and managed under some systematic set of processes. The definition and design of the data structures, and of tools to manipulate and maintain the data content, should be derived in some systematic manner. This set of systematic processes may be collectively termed a data lifecycle. A lifecycle does not include evidence, but may include provision for generating process-based evidence.

Errors in configuration data used for data-driven safety-related systems will, as noted above, lead to risk. Established safety management tools and techniques should be used to analyse the risk presented by errors in configuration data.

Process evidence from the construction lifecycle for the generic part of the system will be derived from the hardware and software components of the system. The construction lifecycle should also include design evidence for the configuration data.

The population of the configuration data for a specific application instance of the data-driven safety-related system should also provide evidence for assurance purposes. The maintenance and management of the configuration data must continue over the life of the system.

The means of data preparation should be such as to minimise the likelihood of errors being introduced and maximise the likelihood of errors being detected. Data entry methods and formats should be as close to the real world representation as possible. For example, when entering data from a map, it is preferable to use a digitiser than to read off the coordinates of points of interest by eye and enter them by keyboard. This is an obvious example, but the principle is one which should be applied more generally.

The configuration data lifecycle should include:

1. The definition of the internal structure of the data, and its external representation;
2. The data validation techniques to be used;
3. A suite of test datasets;
4. Software tools to manage the configuration data (including translation between internal and external data representation); and
5. The definition of processes and procedures to manage the configuration data and the process evidence required for assurance purposes.

When testing the safety-related system, consideration should be given to coverage measurements of the data. In other words, it should be known what proportion of the data elements have been accessed by the software. Ideally 100% of the data elements should be accessed during system test, but whether this is possible, practicable or even sensible depends on the nature of the data and the application.

Software development should generate a number of test harnesses by which functional groupings of code may be exercised under the controlled conditions of a test specification. A corresponding structure for testing configuration data would be a test data set.

A suite of test data sets should be used to exercise the data-driven system under predetermined test conditions, these test conditions being described by each data set. Each data set should represent operation in either a normal or degraded mode with specified input conditions such as alarms and a description of the expected response from the safety-related system. The data-driven safety-related system should provide an opportunity to periodically test the system either for assurance of the systems continued safe operation or for fault determination. The data-driven system offers an opportunity to validate the system in the operational domain. The test data sets should be suitably separated from the operational domain so as not to become confused with the normal operation of the system.

Configuration data will probably require a set of software tools to manage and manipulate both the configuration data and the test data sets. These software tools should facilitate the offline validation of the configuration data.

The definition of processes and procedures for the configuration data recognises that people will be involved in the installation or operation of the safety-related system, or both. These processes are intended to provide a systematic framework, to be refined through experience and use, to reduce systematic errors in the configuration data.

6   Configuration Data Structure

Design features of the configuration data should be selected which reduce the likelihood that hazardous errors will remain in the data when the system goes into service and ease the task of data validation.

The data structure of the configuration data should be such as to enable demonstration that there is sufficient modularity to reduce side effects when the configuration data is maintained or extended. The configuration data should be complete, and it should not contain elements or structures which are not required. Where the configuration data has other features or structures then evidence should be provided that these features or structures are independent of the requirements of the application instance. Data elements (data content), which are not required for the application instance, should be removed from the configuration data, unless it is not reasonably practicable to do this.

Validation and verification should be a prime design consideration for configuration data. Design options which ease, or make feasible, online or offline validation of configuration data should be chosen in preference to those design decisions which simply ease the design of other elements of the system such as software, hardware or fit with a current data set. Where possible the design option for the data structure of the configuration data should be requirement driven, and solution independent. The current data set may not lend itself to the validation requirements and hence be unsuitable for use in the safety-related data-driven system.

7   Tools and Techniques

What tools and techniques are appropriate to configuration data used for safety-related systems? The tools and techniques used for data preparation and data maintenance should be appropriate to the risks posed by the use of configuration data in a data-driven safety-related system.

Current standards such as IEC 61508 [3] identify development, verification and validation and techniques for software, which are recommended, based upon the required safety integrity level (SIL1, SIL2, SIL3 and SIL4), with more rigorous techniques being used for higher integrity levels.

The definition of what tools and techniques are necessary for configuration data for a particular safety integrity level requires further debate amongst the safety community as a whole.

Examples required could include the following:

1. Techniques for data validation and verification could include inspection of the data by individuals independent of those who originally collected and entered the data;
2. Where the data is translated from an external human readable representation to an internal representation (which is normal), measures should be devised to check that the translation process does not corrupt the data, for example by reverse translation and checking against the original data;
3. The data entry format should be such as to minimise the chances of error. For example, where map data is to be entered, it would make sense to use a drawing tool rather than lists of co-ordinates of lines and points in numeric form (there is at least one FDP system which requires the latter, and despite internal validation checks in the data translator the system in question has failed in operation due to errors in the data); and
4. System testing will clearly be an important means of validating the data together with the software design and implementation. However, tests should be designed specifically to check that the software has accessed each data item. In the example of the FDP system given above, simulation data could be used to ensure that a flight strip is produced at the correct time when a flight crosses every sector boundary in the airspace.

8   Requirements for Configuration Data Used for Safety-Related Systems

The design of the configuration data should facilitate the validation of the data content and structure as appropriate to the risk presented by errors in the data set. If safety analysis exposes a high risk based upon failure of the configuration data content or structure, then the system requirements should include online validation (dynamic checking of the data).

The representation and means used for configuration data preparation should be as intuitive, convenient, and close to conventional real-world representations as possible, to minimise the likelihood of the data preparation process introducing errors.

Care must be taken in collecting the source information from which the configuration data will be created, to ensure that it is an adequately correct representation of "ground truth" (the source information may include geographical map data, engineering drawings, photographs, plant specifications and even human memories). This can be a particularly time consuming exercise if the source information is known to be out of date or unreliable, or there are doubts about its accuracy. New geographical or engineering surveys may be required.

A configuration data definition should support the concept of modularity, where this is logically feasible. A module of data should be self-consistent, complete, and contain no unresolved internal references, to facilitate automated rule-based validation.

Where references to other data items and data structures are made within a configuration data module these references should be made in such a way as to facilitate their validation. Data references (keys) should be based upon compound data structures. These compound data keys contain sufficient information to identify the referenced item without any addition external data. These compound keys would be in contrast to integer based keys, which would only allow range-based validation checks.

9   Conclusion

It has been argued above that there is a need for the safety management of configuration data, and a number of principles have been outlined. These principles are in addition to the requirements or guidance found in a number of standards, which is in most cases very weak.

More work is required in the area of data driven safety related system to establish clear guidance as to the design and management of data driven systems. The assurance of the configuration data should be supported by process evidence from an identifiable lifecycle for the system as a whole that should include the configuration data.

The population of the configuration data should be supported by process and procedures to reduce systematic error. These processes and procedures should not only be capable of the reduction of systematic error in the creation of configuration data, but also be used for the management of the configuration data through the system life. These processes and procedures should not only be concerned with control of the introduction of errors but also the detection of errors.

The design of the configuration data should aide and facilitate the validation and verification of the data through data structures that lend themselves to rule based automation. The configuration data should support the use of 'data sets' that may be used to calibrate, test, and exercise the entire system. These data sets are created as separate modules to fully exercise the system in all functional conditions allowing demonstration of normal and degraded modes. These data sets would allow the system administrator to either detect faults in the system operation or to gain confidence in the continued correct operation of the system.

References

1. R. H. Pierce, S. P. Wilson, J. A. McDermid, L. Beus-Dukic and A. Eaton, "Requirements for the use of COTS operating systems in safety-related air traffic services", Proceedings of Data Systems in Aerospace, Lisbon, Portugal, 17 May 1999
2. J. A. McDermid "The cost of COTS", IEE Colloquium - COTS and Safety critical systems. January 1998
3. International Electrotechnical Commission, Functional Safety: Safety-related Systems, International Standard IEC 61508, January 2000.
4. UK Ministry of Defence (MoD) Def Stan 00-55: Requirements for Safety Related Software in Defence Equipment Issue 2 – Dated 1st August 1997
5. European Committee for Electrotechnical Standardisation CENELEC   prEV 50128: Railway Applications: Software for Railway Control and Protection Systems Final DRAFT June 1997.

Software Support for Incident Reporting Systems in Safety-Critical Applications

Chris Johnson

Department of Computing Science, University of Glasgow
Glasgow, G12 8QQ, UK.
Tel: +44 (0141) 330 6053 Fax: +44 (0141) 330 4913
johnson@dcs.glasgow.ac.uk
http://www.dcs.gla.ac.uk/~johnson

Abstract. Incident reporting systems are playing an increasingly important role in the development and maintenance of safety-critical applications. The perceived success of the FAA's Aviation Safety Reporting System (ASRS) and the FDA's MedWatch has led to the establishment of similar national and international schemes. These enable individuals and groups to report their safety concerns in a confidential or anonymous manner. Unfortunately, many of these systems are becoming victims of their own success. The ASRS and MedWatch have both now received over 500,000 submissions. In the past, these systems have relied upon conventional database technology to support the indexing and retrieval of individual reports. However, there are several reasons why this technology is inadequate for many large-scale reporting schemes. In particular, the problems of query formation often result in poor precision and recall. This, in turn, has profound implications for safety-critical applications. Users may fail to identify similar incidents within national or international collections. This paper, therefore, shows how several alternative software architectures support incident report systems in safety-critical applications.

1 Introduction

Incident reporting schemes are increasingly being seen as a means of detecting and responding to failures before they develop into major accidents. For instance, part of the UK government's response to the Ladbroke Grove crash has been to establish a national incident-reporting scheme for the UK railways. At a European level, organizations such as EUROCONTROL have been given the responsibility of establishing international standards for the reporting schemes that are operated by member states. In the United States, the Senate recently set up the Chemical Safety and Hazard Investigation Board to coordinate incident reporting throughout the

F. Koornneef and M. van der Meulen (Eds.): SAFECOMP 2000, LNCS 1943, pp. 96-106, 2000.
© Springer-Verlag Berlin Heidelberg 2000

chemical industries. The popularity of these schemes depends upon their ability to elicit reports from operators. This, in turn, depends upon individuals receiving the feedback that is necessary to demonstrate that their participation is both valued and worthwhile. People will only submit if they believe that their contributions will be acted on. In part this depends upon the confidentiality of the system. Individuals must not fear retribution providing that they are not reporting criminal activity. However, an effective response and individual participation also rely upon our ability to analyze and interpret the submissions that are made to incident reporting schemes.

In the past, most incident reporting schemes in safety-critical industries have operated at a local level. For instance, chemical and steel companies have developed proprietary systems that operate within their plants [1]. In the UK health service this has led to a situation where there are many different local schemes with no effective means of sharing data between hospitals. This situation is not as pathological as it might appear. Local schemes have the benefit that individual contributors can directly monitor the impact of their contributions on their working environment. The people maintaining these systems can also inspect the systems and environments in which incidents occur [2]. However, the disadvantages are equally apparent. There is a danger that the lessons learnt in one institution will not be transferred to other organizations. There is also a danger that individual incidents may appear as isolated instances of failure unless there is confirmatory evidence of similar incidents occurring on a national and international scale [3]. For all of these reasons there is now an increasing move towards national and international systems. Later sections will describe how this is introducing new problems of scale that can only be solved with software support.

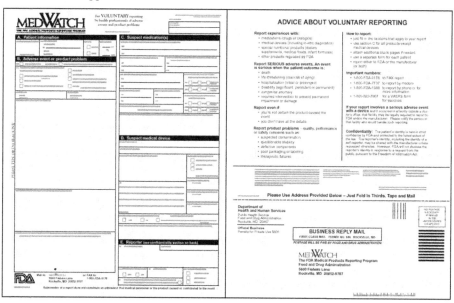

Figure 1: FDA Incident Reporting Form for Medical Devices

Figure 1 provides an example of the forms that are used to elicit information about incidents, including software failures, in safety-critical industries. It illustrates the format that is used by the US Food and Drug's Administrations MedWatch program. This particular form is intended for healthcare professionals to report incidents involving medical devices. As can be seen, this form only asks for rudimentary details about particular incidents. This is justified because the system is confidential and not anonymous. The operators of the MedWatch programme can, therefore, contact the respondents to elicit further information. Figure 2 presents two MedWatch reports that deal specifically with software "failures" in medical devices.

Access Number: M484728   Date Received: 12/13/93
Product Description:
BOEHRINGER MANNHEIM-HITACHI CLINICAL CHEMISTRY ANA
Manufacturer Code: BOEHMANN
Manufacturer Name:
BOEHRINGER MANNHEIM CORP., 9115 HAGUE ROAD, INDIANAPOLIS,
Report Type: MALFUNCTION   Model Number: 911
Catalog Number: NI   Product Code: JJC
Panel Code: CLINICAL CHEMISTRY   Event Type: FINAL
Event Description: clinical chemistry analyzer erroneously printed out a value of >5 as the result of a lipase control, but transmitted the correct value of 39 to the laboratory's host computer. The software for the analyzer was evaluated by its mfr and was found to contain a software bug which caused the inappropriate printing of a qualitative parameter when the laboratory host computer and data printing accessed the qualitative data processing program at the same time. Software mfr has modified the software, and an evaluation of the revised software is in progress at this co. (*)

Access Number: M830568   Date Received: 09/25/95
Product Description: PRX SOFTWARE DISK   Manufacturer Code: CARDPACE
Manufacturer Name:
CARDIAC PACEMAKERS, INC., 4100 HAMLINE AVE N, ST. PAUL, MN 55112
Report Type: MALFUNCTION   Model Number: 2860
Catalog Number: NA   Product Code: LWS
Panel Code: CARDIOVASCULAR   Event Type: FINAL
Event Description: co received info from a field clinical engineer that while using software module during a demonstration with a non functional implantable cardioverter defibrillator, noted that two of the keys were mapped incorrectly. The field clinical engineer then changed to another software module, same model, serial number 006000. And experienced the same results. Corrective action: co has recalled and requested the return of affected revision 11.2 software modules and replaced them with the appropriate version. (*)

Figure 2: Examples of Software Failure from the FDA's MedWatch Programme

The records shown in Figure 2 are typical of the information that is lodged with incident reporting schemes. A number of categories are used to help index the data and to support subsequent statistical analysis. In the case of the MedWatch programme, this includes information about the particular types of devices that were involved, the Product Code. The classification information also includes the clinical area that the device was being used in, the Panel Code. Free text is also used to provide details about how the incident was detected and was resolved, the Event Description.

2   The Problems

Incident reporting systems have become victims of their own success. The FAA has maintained a consistently high participation rate in the ASRS since it was established in 1976. It now receives an average of more than 2,600 reports per month. The cumulative total is now approaching half a million reports. Medwatch, illustrated by Figures 1 and 2, was set up by the FDA as part of the Medical Devices Reporting Program in 1984. It now contains over 700,000 reports. These figures are relatively small when compared to the size of other data sets that are routinely maintained in many different industries. However, the safety-critical nature of these reports creates a number of unique problems that frustrate the development of appropriate software support.

2.1   Precision and Recall

Precision and recall are concepts that are used to assess the performance of all information retrieval systems. In broad terms, the precision of a query is measured by the proportion of all documents that were returned which the user considered to be relevant to their request to the total number of documents that were returned. In contrast, the recall of a query is given by the proportion of all relevant documents that were returned to the total number of relevant documents in the collection [3]. It, therefore, follows that some systems can obtain high recall values but relatively low precision. In this scenario, large numbers of relevant documents will be retrieved together with large numbers of irrelevant documents. This creates problems because the user must then filter these irrelevant hits from the documents that were returned by their initial request. Conversely, other systems provide high precision but poor recall. In this situation, only relevant documents will be returned but many other potential targets will not be retrieved for the user.

In most other areas of software engineering, the trade-off between precision and recall can be characterized as either performance or usability issues. In incident reporting schemes, these characteristics have considerable safety implications. For instance, low-recall systems result in analysts failing to identify potentially similar incidents. This entirely defeats the purpose of compiling national and international collections. More worryingly in a commercial setting it leaves companies open to litigation in the aftermath of an accident. Failure to detect trend information in previous incident reports can be interpreted as negligence. Conversely, low-precision approaches leave the analyst with an increasing manual burden as they are forced to continually navigate "another 10 hits" to slowly identify relevant reports from those that have no relation to their information needs. Again this can result in users failing to accurately identify previous records of similar incidents.

2.2   Data Abstractions and Dynamic Classifications

A number of further problems complicate the software engineering of tool support for incident reporting systems. In particular, incidents will change over time. The introduction of new technology and working practices creates the potential for different forms of hardware and software failure as well as different opportunities for operator "error". Any data abstractions that are used to represent attributes of incident reports must also be flexible enough to reflect these changes in incident classification schemes. This problem arises because the incident classification schemes that regulators use to monitor the distribution of events between particular causal categories are, typically, also embodied in the data abstractions of any underlying tool support.

There are two general approaches to the problems of developing appropriate data models for incident reports. The first relies upon the use of generic categories. These include "software failure" rather than "floating point exception" or "human error" rather than "poor situation awareness". These high-level distinctions are unlikely to be extended and refined over time. However, they also result in systems that yield very low precision. A query about "floating point exceptions" will fail if all relevant reports are classified as "software failures". Further problems arise if inheritance mechanisms are used to refine these high level distinctions. The addition of new sub-types, for instance by deriving "floating-point exceptions" from "software failures", forces the reclassification of thousands of existing reports.

The second approach that addresses the changing nature of many incidents is to develop a classification scheme that is so detailed, it should cover every possible adverse event that might be reported. To provide an illustration of the scale of this task, the US National Co-ordinating Council for Medication Error Reporting and Prevention produces a Taxonomy of Medication Errors. This contains approximately 400 different terms that record various aspects of adverse incidents. EUROCONTROL have developed a similar taxonomy for the classification of human "error" in incident reports. There is no such taxonomy for software related failures. This is a significant issue because retrieval systems must recognise similar classes of failures in spite of the different synonyms, euphemisms and colloquialisms that are provided in initial reports of "bugs", "crashes", "exceptions" and "run-time failures". There are further more general problems. In particular, if safety-critical industries accept detailed taxonomies then software tools may exhibit relatively poor recall in response to individual requests. The reason for this is that many existing classification systems are exclusive. As can be seen from Figure 2, incidents tend to be classified by single descriptors rather than combinations of terms. As a result, many incidents that stem from multiple systemic failures cannot easily be identified. There is also the related problem that national and international systems must rely on teams of people to perform the analysis and classification. This introduces problems of inter-classifier reliability. Systems that are based on a detailed taxonomy increase the potential for confusion and ultimately low recall because different classifiers may exhibit subtle differences in the ways in which they distinguish between the terms in the taxonomy.

3   Solutions: Relational Data Bases

There are two central tasks that users wish to perform with large-scale incident reporting systems. These two tasks are almost contradictory in terms of the software requirements that they impose. On the one hand, there is a managerial and regulatory need to produce statistics that provide an overview of how certain types of failures are reduced in response to their actions. On the other hand, there is a more general requirement to identify trends that should be addressed by those actions in the first place. The extraction of statistical information typically relies upon highly-typed data so that each incident can be classified as unambiguously belonging to particular categories, such as those described in the previous section. In contrast, the more analytical uses of incident reporting systems involve people being able to explore alternative hypotheses about the underlying causes of many failures. This, in turn, depends upon less directed forms of search. Unfortunately, most incident reporting systems seem to be focussed on the former approach. Relatively, few support these more open analytical activities.

Many incident reporting systems exploit relational database techniques. They store each incident as a record. Incident identifiers, such as the classified fields before the free text descriptions in figure 2, are used to link, or join, similar records in response to users' queries. It is important to emphasize that many existing applications of this relational technology have significant limitations. They are, typically, built in an ad hoc manner using mass-market database management systems. The results are often very depressing. For example, Boeing currently receives data about maintenance incidents from many customer organizations. Each of these organizations exploits a different model for the records in their relational systems. As a result, the aircraft manufacturer must attempt to unify these ad hoc models into a coherent database. At present, it can be difficult or impossible for them to distinguish whether a bolt has failed through a design fault or through over torquing by maintenance engineers. Sam Lainoff recently summarized the problems of populating their relational database in the following way:

> "There is no uniform reporting language amongst the airlines, so it's not unusual to find ten different ways of referring to the same thing. This often makes the searching and sorting task a difficult proposition... The data we have won't usually permit us to create more refinement in our error typing. But at times it will give us enough clues to separate quality problems, and real human error from pure hardware faults." [4].

This quotation illustrates a couple of points. Firstly, it identified the commercial importance of these problems within safety-critical industries. Secondly, it is indicative of the problems that people face when attempting to correctly assign values to the fields that are defined in relational databases. This problem stems from the diverse and changing nature of incident reports that was described earlier. However, this quotation does not reveal all of the problems that are created by relational approaches. In particular, it can be extremely difficult for people who were not involved in the coding and classification process to develop appropriate queries. One example query in a relational incident reporting system within the steel industry was expressed as follows:

$ SEL 1; USE EMP; INDEX SEV TO T1; SEL 2; USE DEPT;
INDEX SEV TO T2; SET REL EMP SEV; DISP NAME SEV ID DATE

Even professional software engineers fail to retrieve correctly indexed records using relational query languages such as SQL [5]. These findings are not significantly effected even when graphical and menu-driven alternatives are provided.

4   Solutions: Free-Text Retrieval and Probabilistic Inference

Information retrieval tools provide powerful mechanisms for indexing and searching large collections of unstructured data. They have supported numerous applications and are ubiquitous on the World Wide Web. It is, therefore, surprising that they have not been more widely adopted to support incident reporting systems. One explanation for this is that they cannot, in their pure form, be used to collate the statistics that are more easily extracted using relational systems. However, they avoid many of the problems associated with database query languages. In particular, they offer a range of techniques for exploiting semantic information about the relationships between the terms/phrases that appear in a document and the terms/phrases that appear in the users' query. These techniques enable analysts to ensure that queries that include concepts such as "software failure" will also be associated with terms such as "Floating point exception" or "Null pointer error".

Information retrieval systems, typically, perform several indexing processes on a data set before it can be searched [6]. For instance, variations on Porter's stemming algorithm can be used to unify terms such as "failure", "failing" and "failed". This preliminary analysis also includes the compilation of dictionaries that support query expansion. For example, "Numeric Error Exception" and "Floating Point Exception" occur in similar contexts but are not synonyms. As a result, they may not be grouped within standard thesauri. Programmers and analysts can, however, provide this semantic information so that a retrieval engine will locate both forms of incident in response to a user's query about numeric software failures. These rather simplistic techniques are supported by more complex concept recognition. Information retrieval tools can exploit probabilistic information based on the relative frequencies of key terms [6]. The system can rank documents according to whether or not it believes that documents are relevant to a query. If a term such as "floating point exception" occurs in a query but is only used infrequently in the collection then those documents that do contain the term are assigned a relatively high probability of matching the query. This process of assigning probabilities can be taken one stage further by supporting relevance feedback. In this process, the user is asked to indicate which of the documents that the system proposed were actually relevant to their query. The probabilities associated with terms that occur amongst several of the documents that are selected can then be increased.

Figure 3: Integrating Information Retrieval and Relational Techniques
(http://www.accessdata.fda.gov/scripts/cdrh/cfdocs/cfMAUDE/Search.cfm)

Figure 3 illustrates how the FDA have recently exploited some of the techniques mentioned above in their medical devices reporting system. As can be seen, this system also retains the ability to exploit the fields that were encoded in earlier relational approaches mentioned in the previous section. Unfortunately, these approaches still have a number of disadvantages when providing software support for incident reporting schemes. In particular, it is still difficult to tune queries in retrieval engines and in relational databases to improve both the precision and recall of particular searches. As a result, it is entirely possible for users to issue queries that fail to find similar incidents or which return almost every report in a collection of well over half a million incidents. We have recently conducted a number of tests to support this argument. We began by manually tagging any incident reports that dealt with a loss of separation in the last 100 ASRS Air Traffic Control submissions. These nine tagged reports provided a base case that enables us to judge whether the retrieval engine performed as well as manual retrieval. We then indexed the same set of reports using the Inquery [6] search engine and issued a query using the phrase "Aircraft loss of separation". As mentioned, rrecall is defined to be the number of relevant items retrieved divided by the number of relevant items in the database. In the first of our tests, all nine relevant reports were retrieved giving a maximum recall value of 1. However, precision is defined to be the number of relevant items retrieved divided by the total number of items retrieved. Our query yielded 46 possible hits giving a precision of 0.19. In practical terms this meant that any investigator would manually have to search through the 46 potential hits to identify the 9 relevant reports. This relatively poor precision can be improved by refining the query or by improving the internal weightings that Inquery uses for key terms, such as Aircraft, that may have biased the results of our query [6, 7]. There are, however, alternative means of providing software support for incident reporting systems.

5   Solutions: Conversational Search and CBR

Case Based Reasoning (CBR) offers a further alternative to information retrieval techniques and relational databases. In particular, conversational case based reasoning offers considerable support for the retrieval of incident reports within safety-critical industries. For instance, the US Naval Research Laboratory's Conversational Decision Aids Environment (NaCoDAE) presents its users with a number of questions that must be answered in order to obtain information about previous hardware failures [8]. For instance, if a user inputs the fact that they are facing a power failure then this will direct the system to assign greater relevance to those situations in which power was also unavailable. As a result, the system tailors the questions that are presented to the user to reflect those that can most effectively be used to discriminate between situations in which the power has failed. NaCoDAE was initially developed to support fault-finding tasks in non-safety critical equipment such as printers. We have recently extended the application of this tool to help analysts perform information retrieval tasks in large-scale incident reporting systems, including the FAA's ASRS. Figure 4 illustrates this application of the NaCoDAE tool. After loading the relevant case library, the user types in a free-text query into the "Description" field. This is then matched against the cases in the library. Each case is composed of a problem description; some associated questions and if appropriate a description of remedial actions. The system then provides the user with two lists. The first provides "Ranked Questions" that the system believes are related to the user's original question. This helps to reduce the query formation problems that have been noted for other systems. The second "Ranked cases" list provides information about those cases that the system currently believes to match the situation that the user is confronted with. A particular benefit of this approach is that Stratified Case Based Reasoning algorithms can be used to ensure that questions are posed in a certain order. They can help to ensure that users move from general questions that partition the case base at a gross level to increasingly precise questions that may only yield specific cases in response to their interactive search [8].

The previous paragraph indicates the critical nature of the questions that are encoded within the NaCoDAE system. Our study began by deriving these questions directly from the fields that are encoded in the MedWatch and ASRS systems. Users navigate the case base by answering questions about how the incident was resolved, what the consequences of the anomaly were, who identified the anomaly etc. If the user selected Cockpit/FLC as an answer to the question "Who detected the incident?" then all cases in which the flight crew did not detect the incident would be automatically moved down the list of potential matches. Each incident report only contains answers to some of these questions. For instance, the person submitting the form may not know how it was resolved. Once a set of similar cases has been identified, it can look for questions that can discriminate between those cases. For example, if some highly ranked cases were resolved by the Aircrew and others were resolved by Air Traffic Controllers then the system will automatically prompt the user to specify which of these groups they are interested in. This iterative selection of cases and prompting for answers from the user avoids the undirected and often fruitless query formation that is a common feature of other approaches [8].

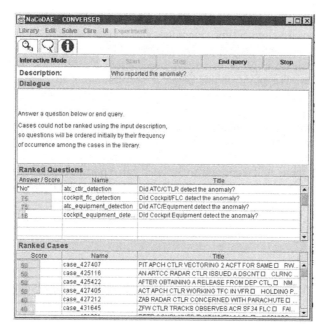

Figure 4: Using Conversational CBR to Support Incident Reporting

6   Conclusion and Further Work

This paper stresses the growing importance that incident reporting systems have in many safety-critical industries. Unfortunately, many of these schemes currently rely on ad hoc implementations running on relational databases [4]. These systems suffer from a number of problems. Poor precision and low recall may be dismissed as usability issues in other contexts. For safety-critical applications they may prevent analysts from identifying common causes both to software related incidents and other forms of failure. These problems are compounded by the difficulty of query formation in relational systems and by the problems of developing appropriate data models that reflect the ways in which incident reports will change over time. In contrast, information retrieval tools relax many of the problems that frustrate query formation in relational databases but they also make it difficult for users to assess the effectiveness of "naïve" queries. By "naïve" we mean that users may have no understanding of the probabilistic algorithms that determine the precision and recall of their query. Finally, we have proposed conversational case-based reasoning as a means of avoiding these limitations. This approach uses a combination of free-text retrieval techniques together with pre-coded questions to guide a user's search through increasingly large sets of incident reports. The application of tools, such as the US Navy's Conversational Decision Aids Environment, can be extended from fault finding tasks to support the retrieval of more general accounts of systems failure, human 'error' and managerial 'weakness'.

It is important to emphasize that more work remains to be done. There are many alternative software-engineering techniques that can be applied to support national and international incident reporting systems. For example, our experience of information retrieval engines is largely based around extensions to Bruce Croft's Inquery tool [6]. The point of this paper is not, therefore, to advocate the specific algorithms that we have implemented or the systems that we have applied. It is, in contrast, to encourage a greater participation amongst software engineers in the design and maintenance of incident reporting software. If this is not achieved then the world's leading aircraft manufacturers will continue to have considerable difficulty in searching the incident data that is provided by their customers [4]. If this is not achieved then there will continue to be medical reporting tools that fail to return information about incidents that users know have already been entered into the system [9].

References

[1]   W. van Vuuren, Organizational Failure: An Exploratory Study in the Steel Industry and the Medical Domain, PhD thesis, Technical University of Eindhoven, Netherlands, 1998.

[2]   D. Busse and C.W. Johnson, *Human Error in an Intensive Care Unit: A Cognitive Analysis of Critical Incidents*. In J. Dixon (editor) 17th International Systems Safety Conference, Systems Safety Society, Unionville, Virginia, USA, 138-147, 1999.

[3]   M.D. Dunlop, C.W. Johnson and J. Reid, Exposing the Layers of Information Retrieval Evaluation, Interacting with Computers, (10)3:225-237, 1998.

[4]   S. Lainoff, *Finding Human Error Evidence in Ordinary Airline Event Data*. In M. Koch and J. Dixon (eds.) 17th International Systems Safety Conference, International Systems Safety Society, Orlando, Florida, 1999.

[5]   P. E. Reimers and S. M. Chung, Intelligent User Interface for Very Large Relational Databases. Proc. of the Fifth International Conference on Human-Computer Interaction 1993 v.2 p.134-139

[6]   H.R. Turtle and W.B. Croft, Evaluation of an inference network-based retrieval model. ACM Transactions on Information Systems, 9(3):187-222, 1991.

[7]   P. McElroy, Information Retrieval/Case-Based Reasoning for Critical Incident and Accident Data. Project Dissertation. Department of Computing Science, University of Glasgow, Scotland. May 2000.

[8]   D. Aha, L.A. Breslow and H. Munoz-Avila, Conversational Case-Based Reasoning. Journal of Artificial Intelligence (2000, to appear).

[9]   C.W. Johnson, Using Case-Based Reasoning to Support the Indexing and Retrieval of Incident Reports. Accepted and to appear in the Proceedings of European Safety and Reliability Conference (ESREL 2000): Foresight and Precaution, 2000.

A Dependability-Explicit Model
for the Development of Computing Systems

Mohamed Kaâniche[1], Jean-Claude Laprie[1], and Jean-Paul Blanquart[2]

[1] LAAS-CNRS / LIS
7 av. du Colonel Roche, 31077 Toulouse Cedex 4, France
{kaaniche,laprie}@laas.fr
[2] ASTRIUM / LIS
31 rue des Cosmonautes, 31402 Toulouse Cedex 4, France
jean-paul.blanquart@astrium-space.com

Abstract. This paper presents a development model focused on the production of dependable systems. Three classes of processes are distinguished: 1) the system creation process which builds on the classical development steps (requirements, design, realization, integration); 2) dependability processes (i.e., fault prevention, fault tolerance, fault removal and fault forecasting); and 3) other supporting processes such as quality assurance and certification. The proposed approach relies on the identification of basic activities for the system creation process and for the dependability processes, and then on the analysis of the interactions among the activities of each process and with the other processes. Finally, to support the development of dependable systems, we define for each system creation activity, a checklist that specifies the key issues related to fault prevention, fault tolerance, fault removal, and fault forecasting, that need to be addressed.

1 Introduction

Design faults are generally recognized as being the current bottleneck for dependability in critical applications. As design faults have their origin in the development process, this leads naturally to pay attention to development models. Conventional development models, either for hardware or for software, do not explicitly incorporate all the activities needed for the production of dependable systems. Indeed, hardware development models traditionally incorporate reliability evaluation (see e.g., [3]), but pay less attention to verification and fault tolerance. On the other hand, traditional software development models (waterfall [9], spiral [2], etc.) incorporate verification and validation activities but do not mention reliability evaluation or fault tolerance.

F. Koornneef and M. van der Meulen (Eds.): SAFECOMP 2000, LNCS 1943, pp. 107-116, 2000.

Designing a dependable system that is able to deliver critical services with a high level of confidence is not an easy task. On the one hand, one has to face the increasing trend in the complexity of computer based critical applications that is related to the evolution towards large scale and distributed architectures. On the other hand, the diversity of the classes of faults at the origin of system failures (be they accidental or intentionally malicious) and of their consequences and severity, requires the implementation and integration of multiple overlapping and complex fault tolerance mechanisms. Therefore, as stressed in our previous papers [5, 6] as well as by other authors, e.g. [1], there is a need for a systematic and structured design framework that integrates dependability concerns at the very early stages of the development process. This is especially important for systems that have to satisfy several, and sometimes conflicting, dependability objectives. Such a framework can hardly be found in the many standardization efforts: as a consequence of their specialization (telecommunications, avionics, rail transportation, nuclear plant control, etc.), they usually do not consider all possible sources of failures which can affect computing systems, nor do they consider all attributes of dependability.

It is our opinion that the means for dependability (i.e., fault prevention, fault tolerance, fault forecasting and fault removal) should be explicitly incorporated in a development model focused at the production of dependable systems. In this paper, we present such a model, which can be termed as *dependability-explicit development model*. It identifies three classes of basic processes: 1) the system creation process which builds on the classical development steps, (i.e., requirements, design, realization, integration); 2) dependability processes (i.e., fault prevention, fault tolerance, fault removal and fault forecasting); and 3) other processes such as quality assurance and certification. Basic activities are defined for each dependability process and the interactions between these processes and the system creation process are analyzed. Finally, these activities are detailed and a list of guidelines addressing the critical points to be covered during the main stages of the development process are outlined.

This paper elaborates on our previous work reported in [7]. It is important to point out that the main objective of the paper is not to give a tutorial on the techniques to be used to build dependable systems, but rather to define a generic framework allowing dependability-related activities to be structured and incorporated into each stage of the system creation process. As a matter of fact, all the techniques and methods proposed in the literature to achieve fault tolerance, fault forecasting, fault removal and fault prevention (see e.g., [4] for a recent summary of the state of the art) can be naturally integrated into our model.

The paper is structured into four sections. Section 2 presents the basic model proposed. Section 3 gives a list of guidelines focusing on dependability related key issues to be addressed during the requirements and the design development stages. Finally, Section 4 draws up the main conclusions of the paper.

2   Basic Model

The production of dependable systems such that a justified confidence can be placed on the services delivered to the users requires the application of complementary activities aimed at fault prevention, fault tolerance, fault removal and fault forecasting. These activities can be carried out iteratively, in a sequence or in parallel, according to the lifecycle model chosen. The dependability related activities can be grouped into separate processes interacting with the system creation process and with other supporting processes. Such dependability focussed process-oriented development approach, that generalizes for instance the model proposed in the DO178B standard [10], provides a structured framework that is well suited to explicitly identify the dependability-related key issues that are needed during the development and to ensure that these issues are correctly implemented.

Following this concept, our basic model (Fig.1) identifies three classes of processes:

- the system creation process, which builds on the classical development steps, i.e., requirements, design, realization, integration;
- the dependability processes: fault prevention, fault tolerance, fault removal and fault forecasting;
- other processes such as quality assurance and certification.

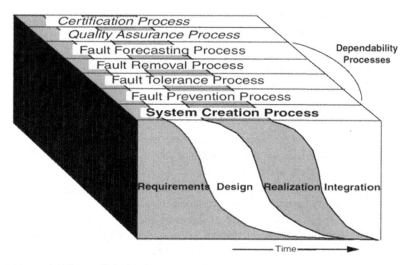

Fig. 1. Dependability-explicit development model

2.1   System Creation and Dependability Processes Basic Activities

The *system creation process* orchestrates the activities performed within the other processes.

The requirements activities of the system creation process encompasses the activities leading to the statement of users needs, and the description of these needs in the form of a specification (formal or informal). These two types of activities are differentiated, sometimes, by defining two distinct life cycle phases. Usually, this is supported by differences, on the one hand, in the levels of details and formalism and, on the other hand, in terms of responsibilities. Nevertheless, both activities are of the same nature and share a single objective, that of defining the needs and services that the system has to fulfil. Therefore, we decided not to make a distinction between them. The design and realization activities correspond to the usual development steps leading respectively to the definition of the system architecture and the implementation of each component according to its specification. As regards integration, it includes usual integration activities (i.e., assembling system components according to the architecture defined during the design stage and implemented during the realization stage) as well as the final system integration into its operational environment before delivery.

As regards the dependability processes, we have identified the key activities that best characterize each process, and we have searched for the minimum number of classes needed to group these activities according to their nature and objectives. This analysis led us to define three main classes of activities for each dependability process. Such classification is aimed at facilitating, on the one hand, the identification of the key issues to be considered with respect to fault prevention, fault tolerance, fault removal and fault forecasting and on the other hand, the analysis of the interactions that exist among the different processes. Each dependability process and the corresponding classes of activities are briefly presented in the following.

The *fault prevention process* is structured into three major classes of activities:

- choice of *formalisms and languages* for the different activities to be performed during the development process,
- *organization* of the project, including its breakdown into tasks and the allocation of the necessary resources to each tasks,
- project *planning* and *evaluation of risks* incurred from the system development.

The *fault tolerance process* is composed of three main activities:

- the study of the *behavior in the presence of faults*, aimed at eliciting the faults against which the system will be protected,
- the *system partitioning*, aimed at structuring the system into error confinement areas, and at identifying the fault independence areas,
- the *fault and error handling*, aimed at selecting the fault tolerance strategies, at determining the appropriate mechanisms, without forgetting the protection of those mechanisms against the faults which are likely to affect them.

The fault assumptions produced by the study of the behavior in the presence of faults constitute a basis for system partitioning, and inputs for the fault and error handling.

The *fault removal process* is composed of three main classes of activities:

- *verification,* that consists in checking whether the system adheres to properties termed the verification conditions, using techniques such as reviews, inspections, modeling and behavior analyses, testing, etc.

- *diagnosis*, that consists in searching for the faults preventing the verification conditions from being met,
- system *modification* to perform the necessary corrections.

The *fault forecasting process* is composed of three classes of activities:
- statement of dependability *objectives*,
- *allocation* of objectives among system components,
- *evaluation* of measures to assess whether the system satisfies the objectives or not.

The definition of the dependability requirements and the fault tolerance mechanisms to be implemented in the system should result from a global analysis and iterative refinements that take into account all the dependability processes as well as the system creation process. This leads to several interactions between these processes and among the dependability processes themselves. This can be illustrated for instance by the need, on the one hand, to verify evaluation results and on the other hand to evaluate the progress of verification activities (through the evaluation of test stopping criteria, test coverage, etc.). Another example concerns the interactions between the fault tolerance and the fault forecasting processes. In particular, the dependability properties to be taken into account for fault forecasting should be defined precisely and related to the dependability requirements derived from the analysis of the system behavior in the presence of faults performed within the fault tolerance process. This includes the definition of the acceptable degraded operation modes as well as of the constraints imposed on each mode, i.e., the maximal tolerable service interruption duration and the number of consecutive and simultaneous failures to be tolerated, before moving to the next degraded operation mode. This analysis should be done iteratively at each system decomposition step to define the criticality levels of system functions and components and the minimum level of fault tolerance to be implemented in the system. This also leads to the need to evaluate the system's capability to tolerate faults by assessing the fault tolerance coverage with respect to the fault assumptions as well as the validity of these assumptions (see §2.2).

The model proposed is in fact a meta-model. It is not a classical life-cycle model as it defines for each process the logical links between the activities to be conducted irrespective of their temporal sequencing. The system components can be developed according to various strategies as illustrated in the example given in Fig. 2. Indeed, similarly to the model of DO-178B, groups of activities can be instantiated several times in order to accommodate several approaches in the development of a given system. In the example presented in Fig. 2, the system consists of four subsystems. The first one is developed in accordance with the waterfall model. The second one is reused but a number of customizations are introduced to meet the requirements. The third one is reused without modification. The last one is developed following a prototyping approach. Finally, the integration of the system is performed progressively, first within the different subsystems and then, between the subsystems, to arrive at the final product.

2.2   Fault Assumptions

Fault assumptions constitute a key point in the development of dependable systems. At each system description abstraction level, associated fault assumptions should be defined taking into account the fault assumptions established at the higher levels [11]. This leads to a hierarchy of fault models. Ensuring the consistency of these fault models is a difficult task that requires a thorough examination and in-depth analysis. In particular, it is essential to study how the faults that occur at a given manifest and propagate to the higher and lower levels. Error propagation analysis is important for the specification and the design of error containment barriers. It is also important for the optimization of fault tolerance verification experiments based on fault injection [12].

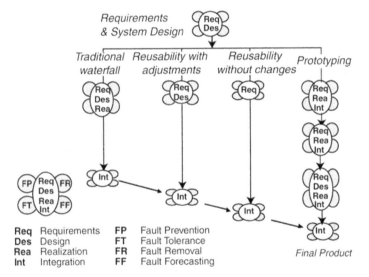

Fig. 2. Example of application of the dependability-explicit model

It is worth noting that fault assumptions related to the fault prevention, fault tolerance, fault removal and fault forecasting processes are generally not identical. Faults to be prevented are not the same as those to be tolerated or as those to be removed. For example, some verification techniques are only suitable to reveal the presence of some specific faults, depending on the location of the faults and on observability and controllability constraints. On the other hand, the fault assumptions examined during fault forecasting activities should be, generally, weaker than those considered by the other processes because of the need to validate the system under pessimistic conditions that are as close as possible to the actual operation environment. Therefore, each dependability process activity should have clearly stated and justified associated fault assumptions. The assessment of the activity outputs is to be performed in accordance with the corresponding assumptions and to be accompanied by an evaluation of the validity of these assumptions [8].

3   Checklists and Guidelines for the Development

To support the development of dependable systems, we define for each system creation activity, an annotated checklist and guidelines that specify the key issues related to fault prevention, fault tolerance, fault removal, and fault forecasting, that need to be addressed. Only key aspects to be stressed during the development of a dependable system are detailed. The main objective is to ensure that these issues are not overlooked. For the sake of illustration, the checklists corresponding to the Requirement and Design system creation activities are given in Fig. 3 and Fig.4, respectively.

System Creation Process
- Functional specifications
   - Definition of system functions (expected values and timing behavior)
   - Description of mission phases and their sequencing (phased systems)
   - Preliminary task distribution between the operators and the computing system
- Definition of the operational environment
   - System boundaries, utilization environment and user profiles
   - Operation and maintenance modes
- Development, validation and operating constraints
   - Physical constraints (weight, technology, etc.), Maintenance and operation constraints
   - Foreseeable evolutions, Reusability, Portability, Interoperability, Testability

Fault Prevention Process
- Formalisms and languages
   - Standards, rules and certification requirements, development environment, formalisms and tools
- Project organization
   - Definition of life-cycle models, Assignment of tasks to project teams, Resource management
- Project planning and project risk assessment
   - Identification of risks and means for risk reduction
   - Selection of development strategies and technologies
   - Planning of development stages and definition of transition criteria between stages
   - Project reviews planning, Configuration management planning

Fault Tolerance Process
- Description of system behavior in presence of failures
   - Identification of relevant dependability attributes and necessary tradeoffs
   - Failure modes and acceptable degraded operation modes
   - Maximum tolerable duration of service interruption for each degraded operation mode
   - Number of consecutive and simultaneous failures to be tolerated for each degraded operation mode

Fault Removal Process
- Verification Planning
   - Static verification techniques, Testing strategies (testing criteria, test generation techniques)
   - Specification of test-beds and environment simulators
- Verification assumptions
   - Classes of functions, behavior and expected faults to be analyzed by each verification technique
   - Predicates to be verified
- Verification of the requirements
   - Functional and behavioral analyses , Reviews and inspections of the specification
   - Prototyping, User-based validation, Expert reviews

Fault Forecasting Process
- Expression of dependability objectives
   - Definition of quantification measures and assignment of quantified targets
- Analysis of failure modes and their consequences on delivered service
   - Identification of failure modes
   - Classification of failures by severity
   - Specification of the classes of faults and failures to be addressed
- Fault forecasting assumptions
   - Modeling assumptions and parameters
- Function-by-function dependability allocation
   - Classification of system functions by criticality levels
- Fault forecasting planning
   - Selection of appropriate methods and tools for qualitative analysis and quantitative evaluation
   - Definition of a data collection environment
- Data collection and analysis
   - Feed-back from existing products , Follow-up of the product under development

Fig. 3. Checklist and guidelines corresponding to the Requirements phase

System Creation Process
- Architecture definition
  - Structure: Decomposition into layers and/or components (human operators, hardware, software)
  - Behavior: System states and events for each layer and interaction between layers
  - Data types, data flow and interfaces between components
- Selection of development technologies
  - Identification of hardware and software components
- Identification of reusable components
  - Definition of necessary adjustments
- Operation and maintenance procedures preparation
- Integration plan preparation
  - Architecture integration strategy
  - Planning of system integration in its operational environment

Fault Prevention Process
- Formalisms and languages
- Project management
- Project planning and project risk assessment

Fault Tolerance Process
- Description of system behavior in presence of faults
  - Fault assumptions (faults considered, faults discarded)
- System partitioning
  - Fault tolerance structuring: (Fault containment regions, Error confinement regions)
  - Fault tolerance application layers
- Fault tolerance strategies
  - Redundancy, Functional diversity, Defensive programming, Protection techniques, etc.
- Error handling mechanisms
  - Error detection, Error diagnosis, Error recovery
- Fault handling mechanisms
  - Fault diagnosis, Fault passivation, Reconfiguration
- Identification of single points of failure

Fault Removal Process
- Verification assumptions
  - Classes of expected faults to be analyzed, Predicates that should hold
- Verification of the design
  - Behavioral analyses
  - Reviews and inspections of the design
  - Prototyping and simulation for human-machine interfaces verification
  - Design verification against the requirements
- Verification of fault tolerance mechanisms
  - Error and fault handling algorithms (formal) verification
  - Simulation-based fault injection (fault models)
- Unit and integration testing planning
  - Testing strategies (testing criteria, test case generation methods)
  - Fault injection strategies
- Definition of functional and structural verification scenarios
- Verification of evaluation results

Fault Forecasting Process
- Fault forecasting assumptions
- Analysis of failure modes and their consequences on the service to be delivered
- Component-by-component dependability allocation
- Preliminary assessment of the system dependability
  - Analytical models, Simulation
  - System scaling: Redundancies (human operators and computing system), Coverage
- Data collection and analysis

Fig. 4. Checklist and guidelines corresponding to the Design phase

4   Conclusion

The dependability-explicit development model presented in this paper provides a general framework allowing the different activities performed during the development of dependable systems to be structured and organized. Grouping fault prevention, fault tolerance, fault removal and fault forecasting activities into supporting processes that interact with the system creation process and with each other, aims to ensure that dependability related issues are not overlooked, but rather considered at each stage of the development process. The dependability-explicit development model is generic and can be applied to a wide range of systems and application domains. For a given system, a number of customizations might be needed. Some activities could be discarded if, for example, some system components are reused or if the dependability objectives to be satisfied do not require the implementation of these activities. The checklists proposed to support the development of dependable systems can be applied, irrespective of the development methods used (conventional functional approach, object-oriented, etc.). These guidelines focus on the nature of activities to be performed and the objectives to be met, rather than on the methods to be used to reach these objectives. Indeed several complementary techniques and practices could be used to reach the same objectives. The selection of optimal solutions depends on the complexity of the system, the dependability attributes to be satisfied, the confidence level to be achieved, and the constraints related to cost limitation or imposed by the certification standards. Especially, the model proposed can be used as a reference to support the ongoing standardization efforts towards the definition of application sector specific standards focused on the development and certification of dependability related issues. Indeed, the proposed framework can be used as a baseline to define and to structure the objectives and the requirements related to dependability to be satisfied by the product to be assessed. Also, it can be used to define the evidence to be provided to show that the product to be delivered to the users satisfies the dependability requirements assigned to it. These requirements are to be defined taking into account the specific constraints and needs of each application sector.

References

1. Avizienis, A. *Building Dependable Systems: How to Keep Up with Complexity.* in *25th International Symposium on Fault-Tolerant Computing (FTCS-25)-Special Issue.* Pasadena, CA, USA, IEEE Computer Society Press (1995), 4-14.
2. Boehm, B.W., *A Spiral Model of Software Development and Enhancement.* IEEE Computer, **21**(5) (1988), 61-72.
3. BSI, *Reliability of Constructed or Manufactured Products, Systems, Equipment and Components, Part 1. Guide to Reliability and Maintainability Programme Management*, 1985, British Standard Institution.
4. FTCS-25, *Proc. 25th Int. Symp. on Fault-Tolerant Computing (FTCS-25). Special Issue.* 1995. Pasadena, CA, USA: IEEE Computer Society Press.
5. Laprie, J.-C. *Software-based Critical Systems.* in *15th Int. Conf. on Computer Safety, Reliability and Security (SAFECOMP'96).* Vienna, Austria: Springer. (1996), 157-170
6. Laprie, J.-C. *Dependability of Computer Systems: from Concepts to Limits.* in *1998 IFIP Int. Workshop on Dependable Computing and Its Applications (DCIA98).* 1998. Johannesburg, South Africa (1998), 108-126.
7. Laprie, J.-C., *et al.*, *Dependability Handbook.* 1995-96, Toulouse, France: Cépaduès. *(in French)*

8.   Powell, D. *Failure Mode Assumptions and Assumption Coverage*. in *22nd IEEE Int. Symp. on Fault-Tolerant Computing (FTCS-22)*. Boston, MA, USA: IEEE Computer Society Press (1992).

9.   Royce, W.W. *Managing the Development of Large Software Systems: Concepts and Techniques*. in *WESCON* (1970).

10.   RTCA/EUROCAE, *Software Considerations in Airborne Systems and Equipment Certification*, Report n°. 591-91/SC167-164, DO 178B.5, 1991, RTCA/EUROCAE.

11.   Siewiorek, D.P. and R.S. Swarz, *Reliable Computer Systems - Design and Evaluation*. Bedford, MA, USA: Digital Press (1992).

12.   Yount, C.R. and D.P. Siewiorek, *A Methodology for the Rapid Injection of Transient Hardware Errors*. IEEE Transactions on Computers, **45**(8) (1996), 881-891.

Deriving Quantified Safety Requirements in Complex Systems

Peter A. Lindsay[1], John A. McDermid[2], and David J. Tombs[1]

[1] Software Verification Research Centre
University of Queensland, Australia
{pal,tombs}@svrc.uq.edu.au
[2] High Integrity Systems Engineering Group
Dept of Computer Science, University of York, United Kingdom
jam@cs.york.ac.uk

Abstract. A variety of hazard analysis techniques have been proposed for software-based systems but individually the techniques are limited in their ability to cope with system complexity, or to derive and prioritise component safety requirements. There is also confusion in practice about whether the techniques are being used to assess risk or to assign targets. This paper proposes a way of integrating hazard analysis techniques to solve these problems. The resulting process enables functional safety requirements to be derived for logically complex components such as software, together with target (maximum acceptable) failure rates.

1 Introduction

The complexity of modern computer-based systems challenges existing notions and methods for demonstration of safety. A typical system has multiple failure modes. Individual components have their own characteristic fault behaviour, and lead to system failure in unexpected ways. In particular, design error dominates over physical failure for software and other logically complex elements. It is difficult to derive satisfactory and realistic safety targets for software.

The objective of this paper is to develop a process to derive safety requirements for all system components, including software. Broadly, component safety integrity has two aspects:

- a *functional* aspect, relating to what the component is supposed to do or not do;
- a *quantitative* aspect, relating to the degree to which the system can tolerate failure of the function and yet operate with acceptable risk.

To address both aspects, we set up a framework to classify potential accidents and system hazards, to show how functional failures of the system lead to hazards, to analyse system failures, and to identify combinations of component faults that may cause them. Using a quantified risk model based on the tolerable occurrence rate of different classes of accident, and exploiting known component

F. Koornneef and M. van der Meulen (Eds.): SAFECOMP 2000, LNCS 1943, pp. 117–130, 2000.

failure rates where possible, we derive quantified integrity requirements on remaining components, including software.

IEC 61508 [ ] and other international and sector-specific safety standards [, ,] reflect practical experience rather than academic theory. The total safety of the system is viewed as a function of the reliability of its components, but little guidance is given on how to derive safety targets for components whose failure rates are not known. In particular, it is difficult to derive satisfactory and realistic safety targets for complex elements such as software. The process described in this paper differs from that of IEC 61508 in a number of subtle but significant ways. First, a clear distinction is made between the concepts of 'failure', 'hazard' and 'accident', and our process relates them through quantifiable, structured methods. Second, known and target failure rates are distinguished: if the failure rate of a component cannot be estimated, our method derives a quantified target *safety integrity requirement* which it must satisfy during development. The safety integrity requirement will decide which development, verification and validation methods to use on the project; choice of method is beyond the scope of this paper. In contrast, the notion behind the Safety Integrity Level, or SIL, defined in IEC 61508 and other standards, is to assure a system by assessing the SILs achieved by its components. There is no universally applicable process for setting SILs in advance. Overall, it might be said that our process is *prospective*, and IEC 61508 is *retrospective*.

We expect our approach to make the assurance effort in system and software development more efficient. Our process integrates existing analysis techniques into a complete, quantitative system risk assessment, assesses the robustness of the system to component failure, and derives meaningful integrity requirements on software and other components. It also provides a means for comparing different designs and bringing out safety considerations early in the design process. This paper demonstrates the objectives of each phase of the process and draws conclusions. An SVRC technical report [ ] contains a more complete application.

2   Process Outline

We model the target system as a collection of components whose functions combine to achieve system functions. The term component is used here in its broadest sense, and covers anything from major subsystems to individual software modules or even human operating procedures. Independence of component failures decides the appropriate level of granularity. With the system model as a foundation, a risk analysis process classifies software functional requirements and failure modes according to their criticality in the target system, and provides traceability of safety features and risk reduction mechanisms.

The process combines into a single framework aspects of a number of established techniques, including Fault Tree Analysis [ ], Functional Failure Analysis [ ] and Event Tree Analysis [ ]. The modelling framework is sufficiently rich to capture safety issues for a wide variety of systems and component types. It addresses failures in hardware, software, and human factors like operator or procedural fault. It covers hazard initiators and co-effectors from within the system and from the external environment, and considers the effect of fault propagation, detection and protection mechanisms. Finally it addresses common mode failure, which is a serious concern with the application of many safety standards. In outline, the steps of the process described in this paper are:

1. Construction of a System Conceptual Design model which defines the scope of the system and the functions of its components (Section 3).
2. Identification and classification of system hazards (Section 4). Functional Failure Analysis is the suggested tool for this step.
3. Identification of system safety functions and protective measures through consideration of accident sequences (Section 5). Event Tree Analysis is the suggested tool for this step.
4. Construction of a detailed cause and effect model, to record how faults propagate through the system from component level to system level, and to identify possible common causes (Section 6). Fault Tree Analysis is the suggested tool for this step.
5. Allocation of a budget of safety integrity requirements, using the models from previous steps to justify quantitative targets (Section 7).

In simple terms, the steps address respectively: how does the system work; what can go wrong; how might it go wrong; why might it go wrong; how likely it is to go wrong. No assumptions are made about when in the system development life-cycle this process would be applied.

We have previously suggested that Cause Consequence Analysis (CCA) [ ] should be used to analyse complex systems and to set safety targets [ ]. CCA is a combination of FTA and ETA that enables both the causes and consequences of hazards to be investigated within a single framework. In this paper we define more precisely the process to derive safety requirements and targets for use in CCA.

The body of the paper is written in the form of a "top-down" iterative process for allocating and refining safety integrity requirements from system level down to component level. The terminology of IEC 61508 is used where possible.

A simple running example is used to illustrate the concepts, terminology and main features of the process. However, because of space limitations, the example is very simple, and to avoid any possible confusion it is important to be clear about the exact purpose of the example. It is not intended to be representative of the complexity of the systems we are targeting: in fact, the process will seem like overkill for the example. Nor do we claim that it is a safe design. Similarly, it does not illustrate the process in full: for example, completeness of coverage is an important goal of the process that cannot be demonstrated here, even on this simple example. However, the example includes sufficient features to illustrate many of the subtleties of analysis.

The (hypothetical) example concerns a large industrial press such as might be used to mould body parts for motor vehicles. An SVRC report [ ] contains a description of the machinery. The press consists of a heavy (50 tonne)

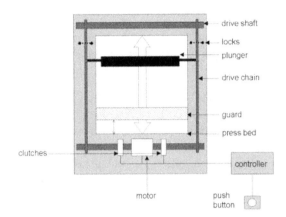

Fig. 1. Hydro-mechanical structure of the Press

"plunger" which is raised seven metres above the "press bed" by means of a hydro-mechanical plunger-drive mechanism (see Figure 1). An operator loads sheet metal (an "unformed work-piece") onto the press bed, and then moves away to the press-control panel and pushes a button which causes the press to close: the plunger is released and falls to the bottom under gravity, thereby pressing the work-piece into shape. The press then reopens, by means of the plunger drive. As safety features, there are locks to hold the plunger at the top, and a physical guard blocks operator access to the press bed while the plunger is falling. Finally, at times the operator may decide to abort operation prematurely in order to adjust the work-piece: the plunger drive activates to slow and reverse the plunger's fall and return it to the top.

3   System Conceptual Design

The first step in our safety process is to develop a suitable model of *System Conceptual Design* (SCD) as a basis for integrity allocation. The model should clearly define system scope and operational concept, and describe system functionality at a suitable level of abstraction. It should identify the main system components and their functions, and explain how system functions are allocated to components (sometimes known as the system conceptual architecture).

For the purposes of the safety process, the SCD model should meet the following criteria:

1. The relationship between the system and the environment is defined sufficiently clearly that it is possible to identify how system failures may cause harm (i.e., the system boundary is delineated).
2. The operation of the system is defined sufficiently clearly to indicate how normal or abnormal operation might cause system failure, and how the consequences of system failure depend upon the operational state or mode.

3. The system's design is modelled sufficiently accurately to identify the major components that may fail, and how their failure can affect the rest of the design. The model is sufficient to identify chains of cause and effect that represent the failure behaviour of the system.
4. The model is sufficient to identify mitigation functions that may be triggered by a failure and chains of cause and effect that describe the system's failure and recovery behaviour.

The model should not be too detailed, for manageability and breadth of coverage. Functions chosen must not be too deep. The inclusion of human operators is an issue of judgement.

Ideally the model should be produced by the designers; however our experience is that it may be necessary to refine existing design models to enable effective hazard and safety analysis. If this is done, the model should be referred back to the designers and ideally adopted by them; at minimum it should be reviewed and accepted by them. A diagram that indicates clearly the system boundary, its major components and their interconnections helps.

For the press example, the operational cycle provides a suitable SCD model. There are four main phases:

- Open: the press is held fully open while the operator loads and unloads work-pieces.
- Closing: initiated by the operator, the guard closes and the plunger is released and allowed to fall under gravity.
- Opening: when the plunger is at the bottom, the guard opens and force is applied to drive the plunger back to the top.
- Abort: initiated by the operator, force is applied to the falling plunger to slow and reverse its descent, and the guard opens.

A full safety analysis would also consider phases for start-up, emergency shutdown, maintenance, etc. In a full analysis, human-factors issues would also have to be considered in detail.

4   Hazard Identification and Analysis

Identification and classification of system hazards is central to the process. We define a *system hazard* to be a system condition or state that can cause an accident. Roughly, a hazard defines a failure mode or state of the system, where the chain of cause and effect crosses the system boundary. A system hazard is thus 'larger' than a component failure but 'smaller' than an accident. For our running example, "operator's hand crushed in press" would be termed an accident, whereas "press closes unexpectedly" is an example of a system hazard. This concept of hazard is consistent with the majority of standards but they sometimes use different terminology. For example, IEC 61508 defines a hazard as a "potential source of harm" where harm is physical injury, and Def Stan

00-56 [   ] defines it as "a physical situation, often following from some initiating event, that can lead to an accident".

Because they lie on the system boundary, system hazards represent the limit of what can be controlled and are thus the natural place to set and agree tolerable-risk targets. The process described in this paper takes a complete and concise set of system hazards as its origin.

In a full safety process, the system hazard list would form the basis of the hazard log through which subsequent analysis and resolution of hazards would be tracked. The system hazard list should therefore be as complete as possible and should cover all circumstances that can reasonably foreseen. Methods for identifying potential hazards and accidents are commonplace (see e.g. IEC 61508 and Def Stan 00-56). Typically they involve group-based exploratory analysis and use checklists and historical data, such as knowledge of incidents that have arisen previously. Sources of hazard might include energetic materials (explosives and fuels); corrosive materials; electromagnetic radiation; chemicals and biochemicals; electrical power; heavy machinery; and simple things such as obstacles in the working environment.

Following on from hazard identification, the system should be analysed at the functional level. There are two reasons to do this: to reveal the system-wide effect of functional failures; and to confirm and refine the lists of hazards. This step corresponds to the task of 'Preliminary Hazard Analysis' in many standards [,]. In ARP 4761 [ ] there is a comprehensive worked example of an equivalent task, which is discussed by Dawkins et al [ ]. There are various techniques that could be used, including HAZOP or a high-level fault-tree analysis [ ]. From experience, we propose *Functional Failure Analysis* (FFA) [,]. FFA is essentially a form of Failure Modes and Effects Analysis carried out on system functions rather than components - an SVRC report [ ] describes it in more detail. FFA requires a well-defined set of system functions, and forces the analyst to consider how each function can fail.

Table 1 contains part of the FFA for the press, for the function "apply upward force to plunger". The drive mechanism and the locks perform this function together, but we do not distinguish them in the functional model. Guidewords are taken from a common set of definitions, and the 'phase' column refers to phases of the SCD model. The right hand column identifies the associated hazard, if any. In particular, the first two entries confirm the hazard "press closes unexpectedly" mentioned previously and reveal two separate cases for analysis.

5   System Safety Functions

In the next step of the process, we undertake a more methodical, structured analysis of system hazards. The purpose is to analyse how functional failures contribute to accidents and to identify protective measures in the design. The suggested tool for this step is *Event Tree Analysis* (ETA). Other forms of consequence analysis could be substituted (e.g. risk graphs) but ETA has the advantage of being more structured and amenable to quantitative analysis. The Fault

Table 1. FFA for "apply upward force to plunger"

Guideword	Phase	Local Effect	Coeffectors	System Effect
Function not provided	Open	Plunger falls unexpectedly	Guard open	Press closes unexpectedly, while guard open
	Open	Ditto	Guard closes & traps operator's hand	Press closes unexpectedly, with operator's hand trapped
	Closing	N/a		N/a
	Opening	Plunger falls unexpectedly	Guard open	Plunger released before reaching top
	Abort	Plunger falls to bottom	Guard opens	Press closes (& guard opens) despite abort
Function provided when not intended	Closing	Plunger descent slowed but not stopped	Plunger beyond PONR (see explanation)	Plunger drive activated while plunger falling beyond PONR
	Others	N/a		N/a
Function provided incorrectly	All	Plunger drive applied unevenly		Plunger falls asymmetrically

Tree Handbook [ ] presents a full discussion of ETA and the SVRC report [ ] describes how to construct them as part of our process.

ETA is a graphical technique for analysing and recording accident sequences - sequences of events from some initiating event through to particular outcomes. Initiating events can be human actions, external failures (e.g. of the power supply), or technical failures of the system. Branch points in event trees correspond to coeffectors or interventions to control and mitigate the consequences of the initiating event. Other possibilities include failure of internal or external protective measures, abnormal actions or actions with a restricted exposure time. Qualitative analysis of event trees derives minimal cutsets of events needed to cause each accident, while quantitative analysis calculates the likelihood of each accident cutset given its initiating event (see Section 7).

Figure 2 presents an event tree corresponding to part of the FFA presented in Section 4, for the hazard "press closes unexpectedly". The tree refines the hazard into two events:

a. upwards force on plunger released;
b. support mechanism fails to hold plunger.

Once the hazard has arisen, two operator actions are needed for an accident to occur:

c. operator's arms inside press;
d. operator does not notice falling plunger, or cannot take avoiding action.

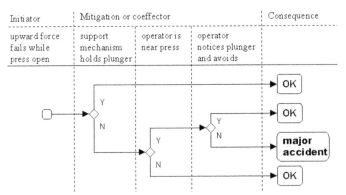

Fig. 2. ETA for hazard "press closes unexpectedly"

Together, the four events form the cutset for the accident. Note that this description is purely functional and does not attempt to identify component failures inside the system.

6   Fault Propagation and Dependent Failures

The next step in the process is to refine the SCD model to component level and to trace the cause of system functional failures down to the level of independent component failures. The analysis follows on from ETA and accident cutset determination, and determines how failures in individual components contribute to the accident sequences previously identified.

Functional failures, such as those identified during FFA and ETA, often have complex causes. While many system functions appear to be primarily assignable to specific components, closer inspection usually reveals a subtler situation. For example, the "apply upwards force to plunger" function is primarily the responsibility of the plunger-drive mechanism, but the locks also play a role when the plunger is at the top. The controller plays a role in activating the plunger drive, and possibly also in opening the locks, and it in turn relies on inputs from sensors and commands from the operator via the control panel. A failure of the "apply upwards force" function could be due to a fault in any of these components, or some combination of failures.

Some form of *causal analysis* needs to be undertaken to identify and record the logic of fault propagation, and to break high-level functional failure into "basic events" (component failures and coeffectors). A number of different causal analysis techniques could be applied at this step. We have chosen to illustrate the step using *Fault Tree Analysis* (FTA) [ ] since it is widely known and used and can be applied quantitatively, but other techniques could be substituted (e.g. Markov Analysis). An earlier paper [ ] describes the way our process uses FTA. Important aspects are clear descriptions of top, intermediate and base events, emphasis on causal chains of failure, and identification of common events.

Figure 3 shows partial fault trees for the two functional failures that contribute to the hazard "press closes unexpectedly" in Figure 2. The terminology in the fault trees reflects the switch in perspective from functional failures to component failures and intermediate faults. Component failures due to physical causes have been taken into account, such as breakage of the plunger drive mechanism and locks. The trees have been developed as far as a common node, where the controller commands the locks to open and the plunger to be released. This failure might itself be elaborated as a fault-tree to separate errors in software, hardware and input data.

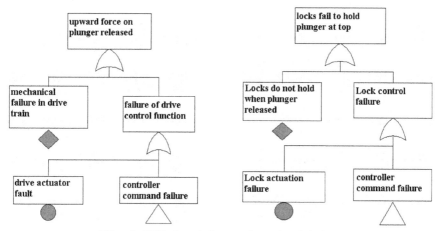

Fig. 3. FTA breakdown of top-level failures

As a first qualitative analysis on the fault-tree, we extract component cutsets. These are distinct from the accident cutsets in Section 5. Cutset extraction is a precursor to quantitative analysis (Section 7) and identifies minimal sets of base events that together cause a hazard and features like common mode faults. In the current design, the controller is a possible single point of failure: a software error might lead to the plunger drive being deactivated and the locks being opened without a command from the operator. This is unlikely to meet the integrity requirements of modern safety standards and the press may require redesign. One option is to construct an interlock so that the controller cannot autonomously release the locks.

Leaf events in a complete tree designate component faults or necessary, and perhaps unavoidable, coeffectors Safety requirements are derived by expressing that these faults shall not occur. There are two different kinds of component safety requirement. Both may be assigned a quantitative likelihood (see Section 7).

- *Non-initiation requirements* to avoid component failures that have hazardous outcomes (e.g. "drive actuator shall not fail").

– *Mitigation requirements* to provide protective measures, to control or mitigate the effects of events with hazardous outcomes (e.g. "locks shall hold
  falling plunger").

The combination of the system design models, event trees and fault trees
together build up a detailed cause-and-effect description of the whole system.
In this way it serves a similar purpose to a Cause Consequence Analysis (CCA)
model, but also provides a systematic development method. The models and
fault trees should be validated (e.g. by independent review) and any assumptions
noted and discharged during installation, operation, training and maintenance.

7   Allocation of Quantitative Targets

For complex systems, it is generally impossible to guarantee that a given requirement will be satisfied 100% of the time. System design and engineering involves
trade-offs between cost and reliability: a given requirement can generally be implemented in many different ways, some safer and more reliable than others.
Risk assessment is the process of judging the safety risk of different designs and
deciding between them. It should be quantified as far as possible, and should
address the risk of failure of both physical components, where there is a chance
of random failure, and of logical components, where there is a chance of design
failure.

This section outlines how the SCD model and safety integrity requirements
developed in the preceding sections facilitate a rigorous quantitative risk assessment. Our theory uses the metaphor of a *safety integrity budget*, since the
problems are akin to balancing a budget. We describe the theory and indicate
some of the practical difficulties in applying it. At the end of the section we and
apply it to part of the running example.

7.1   The Process

Quantification of risk starts by determining tolerable accident rates. This typically involves defining a number of accident severity classes and a policy regarding the acceptable maximum occurrence rate for accidents in each class.
Accident severity is usually expressed in terms of human harm but may also include environmental or equipment damage. The safety authority for the system
will normally decide tolerable accident rates, based on domain-specific standards;
the issue is outside the scope of this paper. We assume we have a requirement
for each class of accident, from which we which we must derive target failure
rates for system components.

In principle it is simple enough to do this. The accident requirement is first
divided between the different accident cutsets (Section 5). For each cutset, events
whose occurrence rate can reasonably be predicted are factored out, leaving a
residue failure rate "budget" to allocate amongst the remaining events. Each such
top-level event has a causal decomposition (Section 6), and failure rates may be

assigned to primitive events out of the top-level budget. Some component failure rates are known or can be reasonably predicted. However, there are other events, notably concerning software, for which no meaningful failure rate can be claimed. The budget is allocated among these events, thus quantifying the safety integrity requirements derived in Section 6. The process is far more difficult than this description might suggest, however, due to the complexity of cause and effect. Allocations frequently require readjustment along the way, when feasibility of meeting lower-level targets becomes questionable.

Likelihood should be quantified in appropriate units. Factors to take into account in choosing units include the type of safety requirement, the analysis tools and types of models used, and the system itself. Thus one might use "probability of failure" for an on-demand function, "mean time to failure" (MTTF) for a physical component, "failure rate" for a human action or a continuously applied function, and so on. Failure rates might be specified per year, per hour or per second, or perhaps using a time unit directly relevant to the system, such as per operational cycle or per processor cycle. The same issue drives choice of analysis method: fault trees work best with probabilities; Markov Analysis is better for MTTF calculations. We do not prescribe particular units in what follows, but simply note that they should be used consistently and that a clear justification should be given when converting from one unit to another.

Failure rates are known or calculable for many different kinds of component. Manufacturers supply reliability data for physical hardware devices, such as switches. Tables exist that predict the human performance of different tasks. Historic reliability data for similar systems, which indicates the relative significance of different classes of component, is helpful when allocating budgets. Potentially, reliability documentation exists for some off-the shelf software (COTS). When relying on historic data, care should always be taken that it was gathered in a comparable context.

The arithmetic to combine failure rates is well understood (e.g. AND and OR gates for FTA). Again, however, one should take care to use the right units. When an event or failure depends on an earlier event, one must determine the conditional probability of the second event occurring, not its overall failure rate. The same event may have different conditional probabilities if it arises in different accident sequences, because its precursors are different.

The principal difficulty with quantification is that budget allocation must take into account the potential for common-mode failure. If a component failure can cause multiple failures in the same event cutset, then the budget for that cutset cannot be allocated in a simple manner. Common-mode failure occurs in subtle and unexpected places and consequently the event cutset budget may be unsatisfiable. Instead, it should be used to guide assignment of component failure rates. Failure rates should be calculated globally, not just for a single event in a fault tree.

For these reasons, balancing a budget is an iterative process that often entails a period of trial-and-error. In our process, the qualitative safety analysis becomes more progressively more refined. As this happens, the budget must be rebalanced. Tool support to automate calculations is a necessity.

7.2   Running Example

Consider the "operator's hand crushed in press" accident in accident in our running example. Let us suppose this is classed as a major accident, and that the tolerability target for such an accident is a rate of occurrence not more than 10^{-2} per year. Since the system hazards are described in terms of press operational phases, we shall use "probability per operational cycle" as the common unit for quantifying likelihood. Let us assume a normal operational cycle takes about a minute and that there would normally be about 10^5 operations of the press per year. Thus accidents should have a probability of less than 10^{-7} per operation.

The next step in the allocation process is to apportion the budget between accident cutsets. For the sake of illustration, let's suppose there are 10 accident cutsets and we decide to apportion the budget evenly between them, so that each accident cutset has a target probability of 10^{-8} per operational cycle.

Now consider the system hazard "press closes unexpectedly". Suppose that this hazard occurs in exactly one of the accident cutsets, with the following coeffectors, taken from the event tree in Section 5: operator has hands in press and fails to avoid the falling plunger. Suppose it is estimated that the operator's hands are in the press for approximately one tenth of the time that the press is open, but that the environment is so noisy that the operator might not hear the plunger falling. This means we can assign a probability of 10^{-1} to the coeffector, leaving a budget of 10^{-7} per operation for occurrence of hazard. Note that if the hazard appeared in more than one cutset, its budget would need to be reduced proportionally.

This hazard budget is then apportioned between the corresponding component-level cutsets derived from the fault trees (Section 6). Suppose a budget of $2 * 10^{-8}$ is allocated to the controller command fault. Recall that this is a single point of failure in the original design. If the design is left unchanged, this implies a software integrity target stricter than $2 * 10^{-8}$ per operation, which is simply not credible [ ]. This confirms the qualitative analysis of Section 6, and the design must be amended.

Assume now that an interlock is placed between the controller and the locks. The cutset containing the controller error now has two faults: software commands press to close without receiving a valid input signal; and the interlock fails. Suppose an integrity target of 10^{-4} per hour has been set for the failure rate of the interlock. Assuming there are about 50 operations per hour, the probability of interlock failure can be taken as $2 * 10^{-6}$ per operation. Hence we set an integrity target of 10^{-2} per operation for the software. That is, the degree to which the system is relying on the software to not command the press to close before receiving a valid button signal is 10^{-2} per operation.

The outputs of this step are integrity targets for each of the functional safety requirements identified in the previous step, together with documented assumptions about likelihood of external coeffectors. The integrity targets should be consistent with the cause-and-effect models generated in previous steps, and should meet the tolerable accident rates assigned.

8   Conclusion

We have developed a process to carry out a hazard and risk assessment for complex, safety-related systems. The process provides a theoretical underpinning for system standards such as IEC 61508, which require that components and software meet specific system safety targets, but give only general guidance on the derivation of component safety requirements. The novelty of the work lies in the way well-known analysis techniques are integrated into a single process to derive well-defined, quantifiable safety integrity requirements on components, both hardware and software.

The process may be used to provide an early indication of system risk and the relative safety and reliability of competing designs. Iteration as the design evolves produces more refined analyses and more accurate integrity budgets. The process does address how to predict hardware component failure rates, nor how to achieve a safety integrity target for a software component. However, the assembled evidence forms a basis for a safety case for the completed system.

Acknowledgements

The authors gratefully acknowledge Brenton Atchison, Tim Kelly and Neil Robinson for their feedback about the ideas in this paper, and David Leadbetter for his assistance with typesetting.

References

1. B. Atchison, P. A. Lindsay, and D. J. Tombs. A case study in software safety assurance using formal methods. Technical Report 99–31, Software Verification Research Centre, University of Queensland, Australia, November 1999. 119
2. R. W. Butler and G. B. Finelli. The infeasibility of experimental quantification of life-critical software reliability. *ACM SigSoft*, 16(5), 1991. 128
3. S. K. Dawkins, T. P. Kelly, J. A. McDermid, J. Murdoch, and D. J. Pumfrey. Issues in the conduct of the PSSA. In *Proceedings of the 17th International System Safety Conference*, 1999. 122
4. E. J. Henley and H. Kumamoto. *Probabilistic Risk Assessment*. IEEE Press, New York, 1981 & 1992. 119, 122
5. International Electrotechnical Commission. *IEC 61508, Functional Safety of Electrical / Electronic / Programmable Electronic Safety Related Systems, Parts 1-7*, 1999. 118
6. N. G. Leveson. *Safeware: System Safety and Computers*. Addison-Wesley, 1995. 118, 122
7. P. A. Lindsay and J. A. McDermid. A systematic approach to software safety integrity levels. In P. Daniel, editor, *Proceedings of 16th International Conference on Computer Safety, Reliability and Security (SAFECOMP'97)*, pages 70–82, Berlin, September 1997. Springer. 119

8. P. A. Lindsay, J. A. McDermid, and D. J. Tombs. A Process for Derivation and Quantification of Safety Requirements for Components of Complex Systems. Technical Report 99-46, Software Verification Research Centre, University of Queensland, Australia, December 1999. 118, 122, 123, 124

9. N. H. Roberts, W. E. Vesely, D. F. Haasl, and F. F. Goldberg. *Fault Tree Handbook*. Systems and Reliability Research Office of U. S. Nuclear Regulatory Commission, 1981. 118, 122, 123, 124

10. Society of Automotive Engineers, Warrendale PA. *SAE ARP 4754, Certification considerations for highly-integrated or complex aircraft systems.* 118, 122

11. U. K. Ministry of Defence Directorate of Standardisation, Glasgow. *Def Stan 00-56, Safety management requirements for defence systems*, December 1996. 118, 122

12. U. S. Department of Defense. *MIL-STD-882C, System safety program requirements*, September 1996. 118, 122

Improving Software Development by Using Safe Object Oriented Development : OTCD

Xavier Méhaut and Pierre Morère

Ada & Safety Skill Center, AONIX
66-68 avenue Pierre Brossolette, F-92247 Malakoff, France
{xavier.mehaut,pierre.morere}@aonix.fr

Abstract. Starting in early 90's with the first COTS certifiable executive (C-SMART), and continuing through the end of the decade with the first certifiable implementation of the Ravenscar profile (ObjectAda Raven™), Aonix has had a long history of experience in Ada language based Safety Critical applications, especially in transportation (avionics or rail). Aonix has developed a solution which takes advantage of a fully object oriented approach related to three major emerging trends in this domain: the use of Object Oriented methodology (in analysis, design and coding) in the real-time embedded market, the birth of new areas for certification such as the space industry (for both ground-based and on-board missions) and the increasing complexity of the applications which need to be certified. The main point of this process is called OTCD- Optimized Technique for Certification of Dispatching. This paper explains the main phases of the process and the potential cost reduction benefits.

1   Introduction

The use of an Object Oriented approach is not new in embedded mission critical applications. Some companies in the military aircraft, space, and ground transportation industries have used and continue to use an OMT or HOOD design approach[8], although the use of Ada83 features during implementation may not allow those companies to translate their designs in straightforward and natural ways. With Ada95, there exists greater traceability between the design and the implementation (eg. benefiting from the use of data extension features). Aonix has been involved in several certification projects and in particular in the SAE (Safe Ada Executive) project which is currently in use on the ATV (Automatic Transport Vehicle) under the name T-SMART [1]. Aonix is now working on a definition of a UML subset and an extension to the Ada95 subset known as the Ravenscar's Profile [2]. In this paper we will first describe the state of art regarding the use of object oriented in Safety Critical system. In a second step we will present a simple system used for the purpose of illustration. We will describe the current way to implement this kind of system using Ada83 approach. We will propose an implementation using

F. Koornneef and M. van der Meulen (Eds.): SAFECOMP 2000, LNCS 1943, pp. 131-140, 2000.

new Ada95 features. We will compare the two kinds of implementation. Finally, we will describe the OTCD approach; an approach primarily designed for applications needing to be certified at the highest levels (Level A and B of DO-78B [3], or SIL 4 and SIL 3 of EN-50128 [4]).

2   Use of Object Oriented Programming in Safety Critical System

1994 [4] points out that with regard to safety aspects, it is not clear whether object-oriented languages should be preferred to conventional ones. It is amazing to note that 6 years later this is still not clear. On the one hand, the use of abstraction and encapsulation is fully accepted and even highly recommended in several standards or norms. On the other hand, the use of any non-deterministic and dynamic feature linked to object-oriented programming is forbidden. Therefore, constructors/destructors as well as dynamic object creation are not allowed. Moreover the use of access types is restricted to static structures only.

Today the Ada community agrees on the fact that the dynamic features of Ada95 should be excluded for use in High Integrity Applications [9]. Nevertheless a large number of applications which use these kinds of features have been certified. This is due to the fact that some of these feature are safe as a result of special implemention characteristics. In general, high level restrictions (based on language semantics) may be eased due to implementation details. In this paper we will see how an a-priori forbidden feature (dynamic dispatching) might be used because the characteristics of its implementation.

3   Object Oriented System Description

The implementation of a protocol has been chosen in order to illustrate the advantages of using Object Oriented programming for improving the software development process. Two distant systems communicate through a message passing mechanism. The messages may be of various lengths, containing different kinds of frames (see Fig 1.).

4   Development without Dispatching

There are several features in Ada83 which support Object Oriented Design such as, encapsulation and abstraction (private and limited types), polymorphism (overloading of subprograms) and inheritance without data extension (derived types). In order to ensure upward compatibility these features have been kept in Ada95. The use of unconstraint records with discriminants with default values can be used to implement type hierarchies. The use of such a feature requires a specific approach with respect to certification. This is mainly due to compiler behavior. For instance, during the life of the application, it is possible for objects declared with discriminants with default values to undergo structural changes as a result of complete assignments. Given the fact that the size of such objects can change, a compiler might choose to create these objects :

1. in the heap : If the size changes, the compiler allocates a new structure and frees the old one. Of course such a solution is forbidden for use in safety applications. For this reason, this kind of type is not permitted to be used in high integrity software.
2. on the stack : The maximum size is allocated on the stack, and all the structural changes of the object are done in this area. Of course this solution is memory consuming, but with such an approach, the use of these kinds of types is allowed by the certification authority.

In the solution explained hereafter, we assume that the second solution[1] is supported by the compiler, and is acceptable to the certification authority.

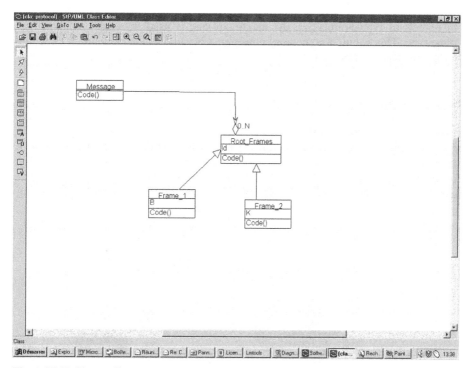

Fig. 1. UML Classes diagram

---

[1] A compiler could use these two approaches, for example in AdaWorld cross 68k (Aonix compilers), transient records with a maximum size less than 8 kilo-bytes are allocated on the stack whereas objects with a maximum size greater than 8 kilo-bytes are allocated in the heap. A technical note on this subject is available upon demand.

4.1   First Version

The code of the high level package which describes the frame type is the following.

```
package All_Frames is
    type Frame_Kind is (Frame_1, Frame_2);
    type Frame (Kind : Frame_Kind := Frame_1) is record
        Id : Integer;
        case Kind is
            when Frame_1 => B : Boolean;
            when Frame_2 => K : Integer;
        end case;
    end record;
    type Index is range 1 .. 2;
    type Frames_Set is array (Index) of Frame;
    procedure Code (F : in Frame);
end All_Frames;
```

For objects of type Frame_Set, the maximum size is used for each component of Frame type. This solution is memory consuming but allows the declaration of arrays with component of variable size.

4.2   Evolution

In order to accommodate the introduction of a new kind of frame, the enumerated type used for the definition of the record needs to change. This implies a recompilation of the entire system, and all the code needs to be re-tested. One consequence of such an approach is that those objects which require no functional changes are also impacted by this change. This impact is shown in the following figure.

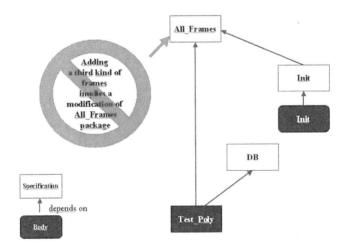

Fig. 2. Dependence graph for Ada83 implementation of the protocol sample

5   Using New Ada95 Features

Ada95 provides new functionality such as tagged type (equivalent to the class notion in C++), inheritance, polymorphism and dispatching. The polymorphism is the fact that the same operation may behave different on different object classes. In conjunction with polymorphism the notion of dispatching is supported by Ada95. The dispatching is the capability to call the correct depending on the actual type of an object addressed through an access. The dispatching could be static (the actual type of the object is known at compile time) or dynamic (the actual type of the object is known at execution time). In the following implementation we will use all these new features.

5.1   First Version

The design implementation is conceived in such a way as to minimize the dependence between Ada units (see Fig 3). This is achieved for example, by introducing an abstract type which encompasses all the attributes and methods common to all frames and the methods that will be used to encode and decode messages.

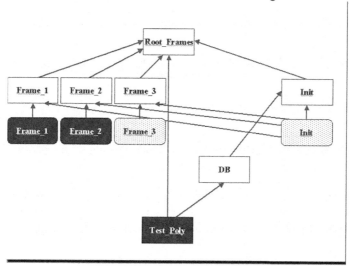

Fig. 3. Dependence graph for Ada95 implementation of the protocol sample

Only the code for the units directly involved in the main subprogram : Root_Frames, DB (for DataBase) and Test_Poly is given

Root_Frames specification package :

```
package Root_Frames is
    type Frame is abstract tagged record
        Id : Integer;
    end record;
```

```
        -- use for the dispatching
        type A_Frame is access all Frame'Class;
        type Index is range 1 .. 2;
        type Frames_Set is array (Index) of A_Frame;
        procedure Code (M : in Frame);
    end Root_Frames;
```

DB specification package

```
with Root_Frames;use Root_Frames;
with Init; use Init;
package DB is
    Table : constant Frames_Set :=Init_Message_Array;
end DB;
```

Test_Poly subprogram body :

```
with DB; use DB;
with Root_Frames;use Root_Frames;
procedure TestPoly is
    PA : A_Frame;
begin
    for I in Table'Range loop
        PA := Table (I);
        Code (PA.all);
    end loop;
end;
```

In the Test_Poly main program, the correct Code subprogram is chosen at runtime using the tag of the object which is managed by the compiler.

5.2   Evolution

Adding a new kind of frame implies only a modification of the package body Init. The units which have not been modified do not need to be re-tested (unitary, functional, coverage tests). - with the exception of Test_Poly. For this unit, we need only to test that the new kind of frame is properly handled. In this simple sample, only one unit out of nine need be revalidated. The same evolution using the Ada83 solution implies a new complete validation of the application.

6   Comparison between the Two Implementations

Although the first implementation is still used in Ada95, we will call it the Ada83 solution. We have chosen several criteria covering the entire life cycle.

Traceability: both solutions provides good traceability between the design and the code. Nevertheless the Ada95 solution allows a better mapping between a UML class and an Ada class which is defined in only one package.

Modularity: in the Ada83 solution a message needs to have access to the definition of the frame. In general this implies the creation of a large package containing all the type definitions needed for the declarations of the Message type.

Performance: the dispatching code of Ada98 is faster than the code used in the Ada83 implementation.

Control flow determinism: the Ada83 implementation is fully deterministic. The Ada95 implementation requires the use of procedure addresses.

Execution determinism: with the Ada95 solution the time needed to execute the call to the correct operation (depending on the actual type of the object) is constant. This is not the case with the Ada83 solution where the execution time for the selection of the correct operation depends on the evaluation order within the case statement.

Maintainability: the Ada95 solution provides better maintainability as a result of the loose coupling modules.

Certification: the main advantage of the Ada83 solution is that several applications using this approach have been previously certified.

Miscellaneous: Another advantage of the Ada95 solution is its look &feel is familiar to developers who are used to using other Object-Oriented Programming languages such as C++.

As this short non-exhaustive list shows, the main inconvenience of an Ada95 implementation is that it is a new approach whose dynamic aspects are not sufficiently field tested to give confidence to certification authorities. OTCD is a technique which solves this issue by reducing the dynamic aspects of the approach.

7   OTCD Optimized Technique for Certification of Dispatching

OTCD is based on a knowledge of ObjectAda code generation. The use of this technique has an impact on both the design of the system as well as on the coding phase of development. The main steps are explained hereafter, the whole approach is available upon demand.

7.1   Design and Coding

There are two main aspects which need to be taken into account during the design phase. The first one is limiting the dependence between data structures and various units. The second one is the handling of static data. The OTCD approach implies that each object subject to dispatching is accessed through reference rather than directly. The link between the message and the frame is created during the elaboration phase of execution, this is done in order to reduce dependencies between units and to avoid unnecessary recompilation. With such an approach, the implementation of a Message object is functionally equivalent to a large static structure (contiguous representation) which declares all the potential frames within. This kind of representation is not compatible with the dispatching capability of Ada95.

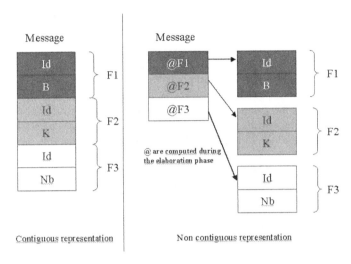

Fig. 4. Comparison between two ways to implement composition

7.2   Static Verification

Static verification of the program, requires generating the assembly file corresponding to the Ada units. For example, the following code, using ObjectAda Raven for PowerPC, is generated for the Root_Frames.Frames_1 specification package.

```
# ************* Constant segment :
|               .align 8
|               .global root_frames__frames_1__frame_1___dispatch_table
| 000000        root_frames__frames_1__frame_1___dispatch_table:
|               .word   root_frames__frames_1__frame_1___expanded_name
|               .word   root_frames__frames_1__frame_1___external_tag
|               .word   root_frames__frames_1__frame_1___ancestor_table
|               .word   root_frames__frames_1__frame_1___su_size
|               .word   0x00000000
|               .word   0x00000000
|               .word   root_frames__frames_1__frame_1___equal
|               .word   root_frames__frames_1__frame_1___assign
|               .word   0x00000000
|               .word   0x00000000
|               .word   0x00000000
|               .word   0x00000000
|               .word   root_frames__frames_1__code__2
```

Fig. 5. Constant section used for the support of dispatching operations

This table needs to linked to the code generated for the dispatching operation done in the test_poly subprogram. The *root_frames__frames_1__code_2* is located at the offset 48 of the constant section known under the generic name of "dispatch table".

```
# Source Line # 8        Code (PA.all);
   8| 00003C 80610008      lwz    r3,8(sp)       # STATIC_FRAME_SEG PA
   8| 000040 90610010      stw    r3,16(sp)      # STATIC_FRAME_SEG
   8| 000044 81810010      lwz    r12,16(sp)     # STATIC_FRAME_SEG
   8| 000048 81610010      lwz    r11,16(sp)     # STATIC_FRAME_SEG
   8| 00004C 814B0000      lwz    r10,0(r11)
   8| 000050 812A0030      lwz    r9,48(r10)
   8| 000054 386C0000      addi   r3,r12,0
   8| 000058 7D2903A6      mtspr  ctr,r9
   8| 00005C 4E800421      bctrl
```

Fig. 6. Code generated for the dispatching operation

In the above code the offset used in order to call the correct subprogram is not computed but is hardcoded. This is due to the technology of the ObjectAda compiler (and is platform-independant). It is easy to verify, in a static way, that all the offsets correspond to the correct offset in the constant table. This is very important because one of the issues when using class type programming and dispatching in high integrity software, as pointed out in [6], is that no static analysis can be in such a case. Using OTCD, the data structures are static, the dispatching tables are static and the offsets are known at compile time.

7.3   Test

Of course code coverage should be performed in conjunction with static verification,. This code coverage needs to be performed at the assembly level as mandated in chapter 6.2.4 of [3] in order to be compliant with the level A of criticality. This can be achieved by using a qualified tool such as AdaCover[2] which is fully integrated with ObjectAda Raven technology. One should note that that the generated low level code is sequential, greatly simplifying the coverage test design. The complexity of testing (and of verification) can be compared to the complexity involved in an Ada83 like approach. In the integration phase, the tests need to verify that correct coverage is achieved regarding the actual contents of a message. In case of modification only the new class need be tested.

8   Conclusion

OTCD allows for an incremental approach for developing safety related software while streamlining cumbersome testing phases at each development iteration. This

---

[2] AdaCover is a coverage tool qualified against the DO-178B to the CC2 level.

approach is mainly suitable for applications which are data oriented (protocol, data base) and which have a degree of predictability in their future modifications. Using dispatching (as described by OTCD) enables direct traceability between design (eg using UML) and implementation. OTCD also exists for less critical systems whose rules are relaxed in regards to low level coverage and data organization.

It is important to note that the generation of static offsets guaranteed by the ObjectAda technology is linked to the fact that Ada95 does not explicitly support multiple inheritance (see [7]). For other object oriented languages which support multiple inheritance, the offset can not be known at compile time and so no static analysis may be performed.

Related work is currently underway by Aonix in order to describe OTCD as a certifiable design pattern and to associate this approach with a specific test design pattern.

References

1. Morère, P.: Certifiable Multitasking Kernel: from T-SMART to Raven, DASIA'99, Lisboa 99
2. Dobbing, B.: Real-Time and High Integrity Features of Ada95 using Ravenscar Profile, Ada-Belgium'98, Decmber 1998
3. DO-178B/ED-12B, « *Software considerations in airborne systems and equipment certifications* », RTCA/EUROCAE, December 1992.
4. EN 50128, "Software for railway control & protection systems (CENELEC)."
5. « *Ada 95 Reference Manual* », International Standard ANSI/ISO/IEC-8652:1995, January 1995.
6. "Ada 95 Quality and Style: Guidelines for Professional Programmers"SPC-94093-CMC Version 01.00.10 October 1995 AJPO.
7. "Ada 95 Rationale", January 1995, Intermetrics. Inc
8. Méhaut, X. and Richard-Foy, M.: Enhancing critical software Development using HOORA/HOOD and UML/ROOM, DASIA'99, Lisboa 99
9. HRG Working Group: [GUIDANCE] "*Guidance for the use of the Ada Programming Language in High Integrity Systems*" September 1997

A Safety Licensable PES for SIL 4 Applications

Wolfgang A. Halang[1], Peter Vogrin[1], and Matjaž Colnarič[2]

[1] Faculty of Electrical Engineering, FernUniversität
58084 Hagen, Germany
Fax: +49-2331-987-375
Wolfgang.Halang@FernUni-Hagen.de
[2] Technical Faculty, University of Maribor
2000 Maribor, Slovenia
Colnaric@Uni-Mb.si

Abstract. The architecture of a programmable controller especially suited for automation applications of highest safety criticality, i.e., on Safety Integrity Level 4, is presented. Its main characteristics are input conditioning by low resolution analogue-to-digital converters and inference by look-up in cause/effect tables or rule set tables. This programmable electronic system consists of a few elements, only. Thus, it is reliable, safe, verifiable, cheap and small. Owing to the simplicity of both its hardware and software, safety licensing of the controller is facilitated. With regard to software, this can easily be carried out by inspection of the table content. The controller is very fast, with its speed mainly determined by the table access time, and works almost jitter free. Operating in a strictly cyclic fashion, the controller exhibits fully predictable real time behaviour. Its hardware operation is supervised by a fail safe logic immediately initiating an emergency shut-down in case of a malfunction.

Keywords: Safety critical industrial automation, Safety Integrity Level 4, safety licensing, programmable electronic system, predictable real time behaviour, fail safe behaviour.

1 Introduction

Safety critical devices and control systems are employed in many application areas of vital importance. In the past, safety proofs were often carried through by considering the reaction of certain devices in case of failures. In general, safety licensing is still an unsolved problem due to the complexity of hardware and software. Hitherto, it was impossible to establish that safety critical systems consisting of hardware and, particularly, software were error free. Therefore, in designing such control systems the approach of diversification is usually taken.

In this paper, a novel programmable electronic system is described, which addresses safety issues not by diversity but by perfection. It is not suitable for arbitrary computing or industrial automation tasks, but for a large class of control tasks as typically found in applications having to meet the requirements of Safety Integrity Level 4 as defined in IEC 61508 [ ]. The presented design

F. Koornneef and M. van der Meulen (Eds.): SAFECOMP 2000, LNCS 1943, pp. 141–150, 2000.

fascinates by its simplicity as, in contrast to conventional controllers, it avoids any kind of sequential programs and arithmetic calculations. Nevertheless, the controller's behaviour is easily programmable by just inserting other memory modules containing different tables. Thus, the controller can be adapted to the requirements of any technical process.

The programmable controller conditions its input domains by relatively coarse rastering carried out in hardware, viz., by linear or non-linear low resolution analogue-to-digital converters. This leads to an inference scheme which does not require any numerical or Boolean computations, but just look-ups in tables containing rule sets. Thus, the controller neither needs a general purpose processor nor software in form of sequential computer programs, both of which would make the controller's safety licensing practically impossible considering the present state-of-the-art. Instead, software only takes the form of rules in tables or of cause/effect tables, lending itself to rigorous verification by inspection [ ]. By design, the controller consists of a rather limited number of relatively simple and long established hardware modules whose correct operation is permanently supervised by an inherently fail safe circuitry. Upon any irregularity, this supervisor immediately causes an emergency shut-down of the controller and the technical process. Thus, safety licensing of the hardware can follow well understood and already proven procedures.

2   An Electronic System Programmed by Rule Sets

As shown in Figure 1, a programmable controller is designed with a condition interface producing rastered values of several input variables. These are then subjected to an inference engine co-operating with a rule base. The outputs from the inference engine are directly provided to an action interface, which finally performs process actuation.

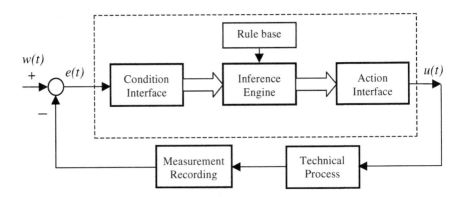

Fig. 1. Block diagram of a programmable controller

As inputs several analogue signals, such as speed and angle of rotation, are provided to the controller in form of control errors, i.e., differences between actual measured values and desired values. For reasons of algorithmic simplification in the controller, and to use proven hardware as widely as possible, these differences are determined in analogue form with operational amplifiers.

The transfer behaviour of the programmable controller can be described by the static relations between its input and output values. Thus, if the raster intervals of the inputs are small enough, it is possible to approximate any static control algorithm with this type of controller. Moreover, dynamic controllers can be composed by adding integrators and differentiators.

The main component of the controller is the inference engine. It operates under a strictly cyclic regime, such as industrial programmable logic controllers. In contrast to the latter, however, each loop execution takes exactly the same amount of time, because the same operations are carried out in every iteration. Thus, the controller's real time behaviour is fully deterministic and easily predictable.

Every loop execution comprises three steps:

1. input data generation by analogue-to-digital conversion in the condition interface,
2. inference by determining appropriate control rules, and
3. control actuation via digital-to-analogue converters in the action interface.

These steps as well as the overall operation cycle are strictly synchronised with a system clock.

2.1 Condition Interface

The control errors are fed into the condition interface. The domains of the input variables are subdivided into intervals and, thus, a (coarse) discretisation of the input data is obtained. As the input values are given in analogue form, the most simple and straightforward way to directly obtain the corresponding digital coding is to employ analogue-to-digital converters. Thus, if the intervals are equally long, the condition interface reduces to a set of standard A/D converters, whose number equals the number of input variables.

By discrete implementation of the A/D converters (or by non-linear pre-amplification in the input stage), non-equidistant domain partitions can be realised, thus providing different precision in different ranges. Typically, higher precision is selected around reference points.

2.2 Inference Engine

The inference engine's rule base consists of one table for each output variable to be determined. Logically, these tables have the form as shown in Table 1: A value of an output variable is assigned to any conjunctive combination of the values corresponding input variables can assume. Such tables are most easily implemented as random access memories which, for safety reasons, should be readable only, i.e., as ROMs, PROMs, or EPROMs. Actually, Boolean conjunction of input variables is not performed. Instead, the binary codes of the input values are concatenated [ ] to form addresses of table entries, i.e., memory locations, containing digital equivalents of the desired actuations.

Figure 2 shows the principle of the controller. An input latch is needed to prevent jitter on address lines. The state of inputs is sampled and latched to provide the address bits of an EPROM. The thus read out data represent the output value associated with the given inputs. Latches hold the output values until new ones are provided. A sequencer, implemented with a PAL and consisting of a clock generator and dividers (counters), controls the latching of inputs, the generation of outputs, and their latching in a sequential way.

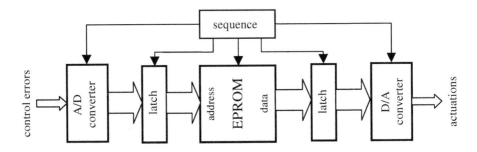

Fig. 2. Basic principle of the programmable controller

2.3   Action Interface

The EPROM read-outs are finally provided to the action interface. In the design presented here any further transformations are avoided by directly storing in the rule base tables (EPROM) the digital equivalents of the desired actuations. Hence, the action interface reduces to a standard digital-to-analogue converter for each output signal to be generated by the controller. It operates cyclically, starting conversion every fourth controller cycle.

2.4   Fail Safe Supervision

In order to make the controller apt for utilisation in safety critical or vital environments, it is endowed by a device supervising correct operation. In case of a malfunction this supervisor generates a signal which can be used to initiate an emergency shut-down of both the controller and the technical process. Owing to these requirements, the supervisor must be implemented in a fail safe logic. To this end, a dynamisation principle is applied. As shown in Figure 3, a detailed functional diagram of the controller, each functional unit provides a ready signal indicating successful operation. These signals are logically conjugated, by fail safe And gates, with the clock signals initiating the particular operations to form enable signals provided to the subsequent operation each. The last digital-to-analogue conversion performed in the action interface enables the first analogue-to-digital conversion in the condition interface to realise cyclic control operation. All enable signals are also input to a fail safe Or gate whose output drives an RC element. The temporal behaviour of the voltage at the capacitor C is depicted in Figure 4. Only when the enable signals continue to permanently re-load the capacitor via the Or gate and the resistor R, the voltage at C remains higher than a certain threshold. If the signals cease for any reason whatsoever, the capacitor discharges causing a relay to switch to emergency-off.

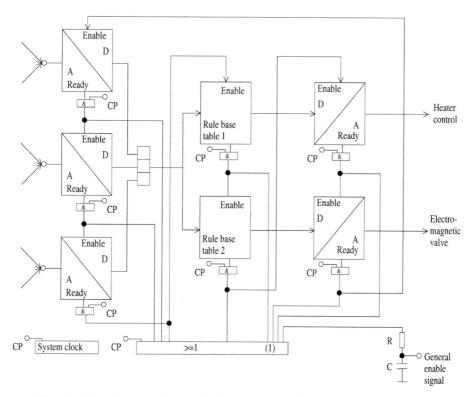

Fig. 3. Fail safe supervision of the programmable controller's operation

3   Software Safety Licensing

The contents of the rule base tables is the only "software" contained in the controller. All other functions are implemented in hardware. Here software does

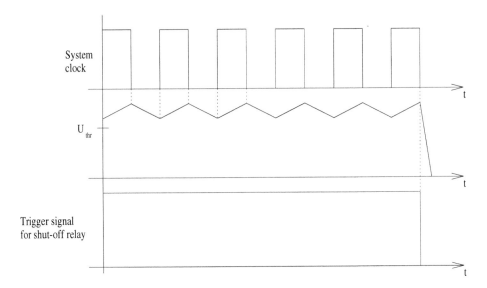

Fig. 4. Dynamisation principle for fail safe supervision

not mean executable sequential programs fetched from writable memory as in the classical von Neumann computer architecture. Instead, it is better described as a parametrisation with which a general purpose controller is configured to perform a specific function. Since coded rule bases should always reside in some kind of read-only memories, the software takes on the form of firmware.

Rigorous software verification is, in general, still an unsolved problem due to the complexity of software. Moreover, for purposes of safety licensing object code, i.e., the only version of a program actually visible to and executed by a machine, must be considered, because the transformation of a program's representation from source to object code by a compiler or assembler may introduce errors into the object code. The architecture of the controller presented here greatly facilitates the rigorous verification of the software contained under the constraint that object code needs to be examined. Owing to the software's very limited complexity, it is feasible to employ the safety licensing method of inspection. This method was developed by a licensing authority, viz., TÜV Rheinland, and consists of reading loaded object code out of a machine and having it analysed and checked by human licensors [ ]. If they work without mutual interaction, the process fulfills the requirements of diversity. Inspection is essentially informal, easily understandable, and immediately applicable without training. Its ease of understanding and use inherently fosters error free application of the method.

Since rule base tables are machine executable on one hand, but also consti-tute formal problem specifications on the other, there is, *by design*, no semantic gap, except coding, in the controller's architecture between the levels relating to humans and to the machine. Inspecting object code thus means to verify an implementation and to validate a problem specification at the same time. The effort involved to verify rule base tables and their correct implementation is by orders of magnitude less than for licensing sequential software and is, therefore, also economically feasible.

4   Case Study: Rotation Control of a Pointer

The following simple example shows, in principle, the way to construct a rule based controller. Angle of rotation control of a pointer without friction or any other damping is considered, to provide for the most difficult case to control. As the pointer moves on a vertical plane, the gravity needs to be considered, and usually a torque is needed to hold the pointer at the desired angle. Let the pointer's mass be 1 kg and its length 1 m. Therefore, the rotation of the pointer is mathematically described by the following differential equation for the angle ϕ as a function of time:

$$\frac{d^2\phi}{dt^2} = 3 \cdot (M_C + M_D + 4.9 \cdot \sin \phi) \qquad \text{and} \qquad M_C = 5 \cdot I$$

with M_C being the torque controlling the pointer, M_D the torque disturbing it, and I the current leading to the torque M_C.

If the control deviation is larger than 2 rad and M_D is not too big, the pointer moves to the desired rotation angle with an angular velocity between 10 and 15 rad/s, and the controller works as speed controller. After the acceleration period the pointer moves to the desired angle nearly without actuations. Therefore, if the control error is 2 rad, the angular velocity is between 10 and 15 rad/s. It is easy to construct and to improve a rule based controller for this narrow speed range. If the control deviation is smaller than 2 rad, the controller works as angle of rotation controller. It is also possible to control the speed of the pointer dependent on the control deviation. This approach could reduce the regulating time. Higher speed, however, certainly leads to higher mechanical forces. These considerations lead to the structure of a rule based controller as shown in Figure 5.

For the domains of the input variables non-equidistant partitionings with higher precision around zero as shown in Figures 6 and 7 are selected, which can be implemented using corresponding analogue-to-digital converters or non-linear input pre-amplification.

The number of words required in the EPROM corresponds to the product of the numbers of input intervals. In this example 63 words are needed. Table 1 shows a part of the rule base table, in which I_D is the digital equivalent of the current leading to the torque M_C. These values are stored in the EPROM.

Experiments and measurements were carried out [ ] to compare the performance of a rule based controller as described above and of the best possible classical PID controller. They revealed that, in addition to the ones already mentioned, the rule based controller has many advantages as compared to controllers with conventional structures such as PID:

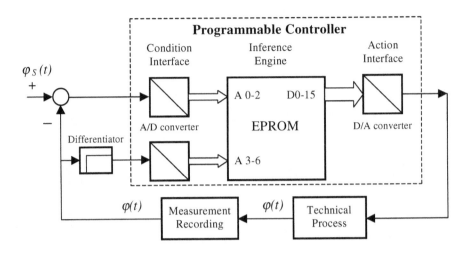

Fig. 5. Structure of a rule based rotation controller of a pointer

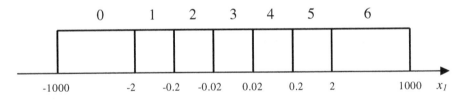

Fig. 6. Input intervals of the control deviation of the rotation angle (A0–2)

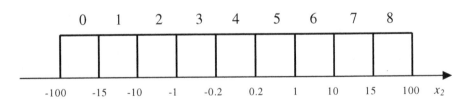

Fig. 7. Input intervals of the angular velocity (A3–6)

Table 1. Section of a rule base table for one output variable

Interval of input x_1	Interval of input x_2	Actuation I_D
2	6	1.3
2	7	3
2	8	5
3	0	-5
3	1	-4
3	2	-1.8
3	3	-0.3
3	4	0

- The overshoot after a set-point jump is much smaller (less than 0.1 rad) independent of the set-point.
- The output error is smaller than 0.1 rad in a much shorter time.
- If the disturbing torque M_D is not too large, it is possible to freely determine the maximum speed of the pointer.

This case study also shows that it is possible to build a rule based controller with an EPROM of a very small capacity, only. Nevertheless, its performance turns out to be much better than the performance of a conventional approach. Moreover, it is easily feasible to improve the performance of the rule based controller. The range of permanent control errors can, for instance, be reduced by

- providing more input intervals, especially for the control deviation x_1, close to zero, or by
- providing an additional controller input for the integral of the rotation angle's control deviation.

5   Conclusion

The major advantages of the programmable controller described in this paper are its inherent safety and speed. Its main characteristics are input conditioning by analogue-to-digital converters and inference by look-up in rule tables. The controller consists of a few relatively simple, industry standard hardware modules. Hence, safety licensing of the hardware can follow well understood and long established procedures. The main task of a safety proof is to verify an implemented rule set's correctness by inspection. This method leads back in one easy step from machine code to problem specifications. For the architecture presented, the effort required to utilise inspection to safety license control software is by several orders of magnitude smaller than to verify sequential programs running on von Neumann computers. Owing to its simple construction and its software form's utmost simplicity, the controller can be licensed for applications with the highest safety requirements, i.e., those of Safety Integrity Level 4. Working in a strictly periodic fashion with (almost) no jitter, the controller's real time behaviour can be predicted in full. Its hardware operation is supervised by a fail safe logic immediately initiating an emergency shut-down in case of a malfunction.

Basically, it is possible to approximate any control algorithm by this type of rule based controller. In general, the better the approximation and the larger the number of inputs the higher is the EPROM capacity needed, which may be very large. Fortunately, there exist possibilities to reduce these capacity requirements. In practice, it turns out that this space is often very small. The controller presented here is, therefore, able to solve difficult control tasks very easily and transparently. It can be adapted to the requirements of any technical process.

We have built a prototype of the controller with a 64 Kword EPROM. It is cheap and small, and runs very fast with a loop execution time of 800 ns. Controllers often need to provide certain functions such as timers, counters, or internal storage. Also, digital and analogue inputs and outputs must be dealt with. A range of such modules was implemented which can be plugged into the prototype.

References

1. M. E. Fagan: Design and Code Inspection to Reduce Errors in Program Development. *IBM Systems Journal* 15, 3, 182 – 211, 1976 142
2. R. Hampel, H. Stegemann, F. Worlitz and N. Chaker: Verfahren zur Regelung zeitkritischer Prozesse durch einen High Speed Matrix Controller. (German) Patent-Offenlegungsschrift DE 197 56 507 A 1, July 1999 144
3. Draft International Standard IEC 61508-1: *Functional Safety of Electrical/Electronic/Programmable Electronic Systems: Generic Aspects — Part 1: General Requirements.* Geneva: International Electrotechnical Commission 1998. 141
4. H. Krebs and U. Haspel: Ein Verfahren zur Software-Verifikation. *Regelungstechnische Praxis rtp,* 26, 73 – 78, 1984 146
5. P. Vogrin: *Safety Licensable and High Speed Programmable Digital Controllers Providing Any Required Control Behaviour.* Fortschr.-Ber. VDI Reihe 8 Nr. 814. Düsseldorf: VDI Verlag 2000, ISBN 3-18-381408-0, ISSN 0178-9546 147

Safety and Security Issues in Electric Power Industry

Zdzisław Żurakowski

Institute of Power Systems Automation
ul. Wystawowa 1, 51-618 Wroclaw, Poland
zurako@isat.iase.wroc.pl

Abstract. The paper presents, the main types of hazards for personnel, equipment and electric power systems which should be taken into consideration in the design of computer-based systems applied in electric power industry, as well as threats to the systems from security point of view. Additionally, examples of problems are described which appeared in carrying out, for the first time in Polish electric power sector, the safety analysis of a extra-high voltage substation software interlockings. The problems were mainly connected with the lack of standards or guidelines on the design of computer-based systems applied in power substations and the lack of exact data on failures of substation components, breakdowns and accidents at substations and large failures of the national electric power system. The data which are used for the traditional relay-based control systems design are insufficient. In conclusion some suggestions are given to improve the situation.

1   Introduction

Safety as a crucial issue of computer applications in such fields as nuclear power stations, space industry, aircraft industry, process industry, or railways is well recognized by a wide spectrum of experts of these fields as well as by software experts.

Safety issues associated with computer system applications in electric power industry are touched upon very rarely during conferences organised by electric power engineers and hardly ever during conferences organised by software experts. The same refers to professional journals, books and any other publications concerning this problem [1]. One can get a wrong impression that safety of computer systems in this field is not important and that there is no demand for R&D on this issue.

In fact, applications of computer-based systems in the conventional electric power sector (excluding nuclear power plants), are not regarded by a wide group of IT experts which are not involved with electric power sector by profession, as related to safety applications. The only opinions which can be met are that these applications are related to reliability. But even when considering the reliability requirements, the applications of computers are not considered to be critical from a reliability point of view because in case of failure, as it is claimed, it is easy to provide additional, reserve power supplies due to a quite high degree of redundancy existing in power grids. The reality however is much more complex than this feeling at first sight might suggest.

F. Koornneef and M. van der Meulen (Eds.): SAFECOMP 2000, LNCS 1943, pp. 151-164, 2000.
© Springer-Verlag Berlin Heidelberg 2000

Also, security of computer-based systems in the electric power industry becomes more and more important. Until now computer security in electric power sectors was derived mainly from traditional physical, administrative, communications, and personnel security techniques. The move from the architecture of "islands of computing" to a networked architecture, provide significant operational benefits for electricity companies, however it also increases the exposure to modification and loss of data.

The aim of this paper is to present to the dependable computing community the industry sector which towards the end of this century emerged as the most critical sector, in the sense explained below, for the national security, economic prosperity and social well-being. At the same time the sector offers the community a wide range of issues which are both basic for the future of the sector and interesting and challenging for the community. Due to space limitation in the paper only basic concepts and pieces of information are given. The paper consist of four parts. First, the structure of the electric power industry is briefly presented. Then examples of   hazards for people and equipments in power stations and substations are given and the safety concept with reference to an electric power system is presented together with some current trends aiming at power systems safety enhancement. Afterwards some remarks are given on security issues. Then examples of problems are presented which appeared during specification of requirements for software inter-lockings case study and further plans. In conclusion final remarks are given.

2   Structure of the Electric Power Industry

The electric power industry in each country consists of many different companies involved in generating of electric power, bulk transmission of energy from power stations to loading centres and its distribution to customers. In order to perform their functions and to attain suitable effectiveness, all power stations, substations, power lines forming power grids, the related control centres and other components are interconnected, although they belong to various companies, forming an electric power system (EPS). Usually this interconnection is now the strongest at the national level, forming a national power system. However an increasing tendency can be observed, for example in Europe, aiming to build up more and more stronger connections between the separate EPS-s existing in the individual countries. Energy related policy of the European Union aims at building Trans-European networks in order to provide a sound basis for free and competitive electricity market in Europe and strengthening security of energy supply.

The physical network of generation, transmission and distribution subsystems forming an EPS is coupled with the EPS telecommunication network that is used for communication and transmission of data between power generating stations, substations and control centres for remote signalling, metering, control and fault protection. In the last decade due to the process of computerisation of the EPS-s the data network is used on increasingly larger scale for transmitting the data that are critical to safe and reliable operation of an EPS and for the power grid - related financial transactions.

To illustrate the degree of complexity imposed on a data network in EPS by the physical and organisational structure one can state that in the Polish EPS, being a middle – sized system, the national transmission network is operated by one company, the Polish Power Grid Company. The regional distribution networks are operated by 33 public utility companies. The transmission network includes 106 extra-high voltage substations (220 kV and above). 1264 substations 110 kV and thousands substations of lower voltages are situated within the distribution networks. There are six control centres to operate the electric power system in the transmission network and dozens local control centres within the distribution networks. Power stations which are connected to national transmission system are operated by 17 power generating companies. At present in Poland there are no unmanned substations. However in West – Europe most of the substations are already unmanned and fully remotely controlled from control centres through the data network. The control centres also adjust the output power of the power stations connected to the transmission network.

3   Safety Issues

Current applications of safety-related computer systems in electric power industry concern mainly some applications in power stations, substations and control centres.

Most hazards which appear in power stations and substations are hazardous for people and equipment and are connected with the technological process of energy production or switching operations performed at substations. Those kind of hazards are approximate to the kind of hazards appearing in other sectors of industry. Their nature is rather obvious and in this paper they will not be analysed in detail. Examples of these hazards are given below in Section 3.1.

However in the electric power industry there are also hazards whose nature is fundamentally different from the nature of those occuring in other sectors. These hazards are connected with concept safety of electric power system, which is presented in Section 3.2.

3.1   Hazards for People and Equipment

An example of safety-related function in steam power stations can be starting the oil burners upon disappearance of flame in the boiler combustion chamber in order to prevent the damping of flame because a very dangerous explosion could take place through a repeated ignition of coal dust burned under the boiler producing vapour.

Substations form vital nodes in power networks because, among others, they enable modifications in the configuration of networks during the operation of the EPS using switching devices that can be controlled by computer-based control systems applied in the substations. Initiation of the control procedure may be performed locally by substation operators or remotely from the EPS control centres. They contain mainly switching devices and busbars to which lines and transformers are connected, as well as control and protection devices.

Main hazard for substation staff and equipment is connected with the fact, that for design reasons, the disconnectors are not able to switch on or off the current (e.g. to switch on or off the loaded line) and are used only to ensure the required isolation clearance between disconnected elements which due to design restrictions cannot be achieved by a circuit breaker. In order to take these limitations into consideration switching off a line for example must be performed according to the following sequence (compare Figure 1):

- breaking of the current using a circuit-breaker (Q19);
- opening of the line disconnector (Q39) in order to achieve isolation clearance between the disconnected line and the circuit-breaker;
- opening of the busbar disconnector (Q31 or Q32, depending on which busbars, 1A or 2, the line is conncted to) in order to achieve the isolation clearance between the circuit-breaker and busbars.

If this sequence is carried out in an incorrect way, the signal for opening would be sent at first to the disconnector (e.g. busbar disconnector), an electric arc will arise between the contacts of the disconnector accompanied by high rate optic and acoustic phenomena, spraying melted metal etc. The arc would travel to neighbou-ring phases, resulting in an inter-phase short circuit. It would look like an explosion. The faulty line and the busbars which the line was connected to, would be switched off by short-circuit protection. This failure would cause considerable material losses because of complete destruction of the disconnector and possibly also other components in the substation, disturbance in substation operation and interruption of ener-gy supply to consumers. Sprayed melted metal could seriously injure personnel if accidentally someone of the personnel is near an exploding disconnector. To avoid such cases software interlockings in substation control systems are applied, which block the opening or closing of a disconnector when circuit breaker interlocked with the disconnector is closed.

Depending on the situation in a given EPS, the incorrect sequence of switching operation could also cause even large power system failure and collapse a part of the EPS, i.e. it could creates hazard for safety of the EPS. More detail it is presented in Section 3.2 and 5.

3.2   Safety Concept with Reference to an Electric Power System

In electric power systems engineering safety of an EPS is described by means of the word "security", although in less formal descriptions the word "safety" is also used. Because further on security aspects are presented for computer systems application in EPS, to avoid misunderstanding, later the paper refers to the safety of EPS by means of the word "safety" in the sense defined below.

In the history of the electric utility industry, safety as it is understood today is a relatively recent concept, which emerged after the famous 1965 blackout that left almost 30 mln people of northeastern United States and Ontario, Canada, without electricity.

Through the first two-thirds of this century, the term "safety" was not used and the safety of an EPS was subsumed with its reliability and implemented into the system in the system planning process by providing a robust system that could withstand any "credible" sudden disturbances without a serious disruption. The condition of reliable work and operators' main concerns were to make sure that sufficient so-called spining reserve was on line to cover unforecasted load increases or loss a generator, and to check the consequences of possible removing a line or other EPS component for maintenance. As it is given in very well written the tutorial paper [2], perhaps the epitome of this approach was midcentury American Electric Power system, which in 1974 withstood five simultaneous major tornadoes, losing eleven 345 kV lines, one 500 kV line, two 765 kV lines, and three major switching substations, without interraption of service to customers.

Such practices even if technically feasible are no longer considered economically or environmentally feasible. Following the 1965 blackout the concept of "safety" was introduced. Possibly the first mention in publications of "safety" in its present sense was in the *Proceedings of The Second Power Systems Computation Conference* in 1966 [2].

The focus in the safety concept was shifted from system robustness, which was designed into the system at the planning stage, onto risk aversion, which is based on automatic protection and control devices and still to a considerably high degree on intervention of a system operator in real time in an emergency state.

In this approach safety of an EPS is a property that has to be considered at the electric power system level and according to widely accepted definition given by the North American Electric Reliability Council (NERC) it is *the ability of the bulk power electric system to withstand sudden disturbances such as electric short circuits or unanticipated loss of system components.*

Generally speaking, if all generators connected to an EPS work synchronously and the voltage and the frequency in the EPS is within the required limits, then this is a normal, stable state of an EPS. In case of sudden disturbances, e.g. sudden increase of the load, or disconnecting of an important transmission line due to a fai-lure in a substation computer control or protection system, the stable state of operation is disturbed. Each EPS is designed with a certain stability margin. When the disturbance is greater than the stability margin it results in loss of stability and collapse of the EPS, which may be total, and this is called a black-out, or partial. The loss of stability is understood in the sense applied in dynamical systems, it means generators fall - out of synchronism and then generators emergency shut-down by automatic protection devices in order to protect them against destruction and emergency stop of power stations. Economic and social results of the loss of stability by a EPS are always very serious. This is the reason why maintaining stability of an EPS is the main requirement for the EPS planning, operation and control. Hazard for stability is equivalent to hazard for safety of an EPS. Major blackouts are rare events, but as it has been stated in one publication, their impact can be catastrophic. In fact as it follows from the examples below the events are not so rare.

According to one of CIGRE (Conference Internationale des Grands de Reseaux Electriques a Haute Tension) publications, within the period of 1978-1985 there were 24 system failures outside the United States. The following are two examples of the large system failures called major disturbances in electric power engineering:

- 1978 France - the whole electric power system practically collapsed and about 90% of consumers were devoid of power supply, economic loss 150 millions USD;
- 1983 Sweden - consumers were devoid of power supply of 11,400MW, 67% of load, interruption time: about 9 hours.

A large system failure which happened in 1977 in New York blacked out the city, that is caused that the city was without an electricity supply. Losses were estimated at 310 millions USD.

During the recent 15 years (1984-1998) American electric power companies informed the Department of Energy about 434 cases of system disturbances in the United States. Eighteen cases included large system disturbances which resulted in the loss of a supply for at least 1.5 milion customers or 3000 MW load. One of the failures, which took place on 10 August 1996, left 7 500 000 customers without electricity and resulted in the loss of 30 525 MW of firm system loads. It has been estimated that the finansial losses suffered by California industry - due to lost production, spoilage, etc. - was in the range of 1-3 bilion USD [3].

The last large system disturbance in Poland occurred in January 1987, in effect the northeastern Poland was without electricity.

NERC defines *reliability* of an EPS as comprising of two components: *safety* (defined the above) and *adequacy*. According to the NERC definition, adequacy exist if there are sufficient generation and transmission resources installed and available to meet projected needs plus reserves for contigencies. If in the concept of EPS reliability, adequacy can be to some extent considered as negotiable (guaranteed through contracts with customers) then safety is non-negotiable characteristic. Large disturbances in EPSs spread almost instantaneously according to the laws of physics and are not affected by any negotiations.

In the latest published reports [3], [4], [5], [6] and in all other publications on this issue, safe operation of power systems is considered so important as it never was in the past, and is getting more and more important. Residential, commercial and industrial electricity users increasingly rely on uninterrupted electricity. Households rely on high-quality power for home computing, telecomputing and, increasingly, networking. Commercial and industrial customers depend on uninterrupted power for sensitive information systems and manufacturing processes. In addition, at the end of the century an electric power system has emerged as one of the most critical or even the most critical infrastructure, because all other infrastructures including transport, telecommunication, oil, gas and financial systems depend on electric power infrastructure to energise and control their operations. This dependence means that failure of the EPS can easily propagate multiplying damages associated with EPS failures to other infrastructures. The current costs of power quality disruptions for the USA, are estimated for dozens billion of USD annually (more than 30 billion USD according to [4]).

The understanding of the term "safety" is conditioned by culture and in the traditional approach a computer system is considered as safety-related if a failure of the system leads to the identified hazard understood as physical situation with a potential for human death or injury. Significant part of computer systems already play important role in a EPS where failure of one of these systems can endanger the safety of the EPS according to the NERC definition. Large material losses and chaos in social life caused by large EPS failures give grounds for including the systems into socially critial systems and aiming at ensuring high level safety of the systems. However, it is worth to note that there is rather no doubt that large material losses and social chaos endanger human life and health too although in general not so directly - though directly can also happen - as hazards created by failure of safety-related systems used for example in railways, process industry or medical applications.

3.3   Some Current Trends Aiming at EPS Safety Enhancement

Safety nets. Because safety tools today are to computationally intensive to allow real-time safety monitoring of the EPS, using off-line methods it is possible to determine the location of break-points which would allow effective islanding once disturbances occur. The idea is to contain a disturbance as it occurs and limit the cascading effect to a small area. This "safety net" approach is being examined in the Western Interconnection (WSCC) of the North American electric power system [5].

On-line analysis and control. The first Wide-Area Management System (WAMS) based on satelite communications is currently being installed in the western U.S. power grid. According to the reports [4], [5] the WAMS network, comprised of sophisticated digital monitoring equipment, interactive control data network tools, and high-power electronic controllers, when fully deployed, will enable precise real-time monitoring and control of the grid.

Self-healing infrastructures. Large-scale networks, like electric power grids, are characterized by many points of interaction among variety of participants-owners, operators, sellers, buyers. These complex interactive networks are too complex for a single entity to evaluate, monitor and manage in real time. These networks also are vulnerable to attacks and local disturbances which can lead to wide spread failure almost instantaneously and are too complex for convential mathematical methodologies. In the United States a Government Industry Collaborative University Research (GICUR) programme has been funded. The aim of this initiative is to develop among other things [4], [5], [7]:

– Methodologies for robust distributed control of heterogeneous, widely dispersed, yet interconnected systems.
– Tools to prevent/ameliorate cascading effects through and between networks.
– Tools/techniques which enable large-scale and interconnected infrastructures to: self-stabilize, self-optimize, and self-heal.

4   Security Issues

Almost all available publications on security issues in electric power industry have been published in the US and concern US electric power industry. Some of the publications are also available on www pages of such institutions as Critical Infrastructure Assurance Office and the North American Electric Reliability Council.

In 1997 an extensive report was published by the President's Commission on Critical Infrastructures Protection [6]. The report defines *critical infrastructures* as *"infrastructures which are so vital that their incapacitation or destruction would have a debilitating impact on defence or economic security"*. Eight infrastructures were mentioned as critical in the given sense i.e.: telecommunications; electrical power; gas and oil storage and transportation; banking and finance; transportation; water supply;

emergency services (including emergency medical services, police, fire and rescue); and government services. Some findings of the report:

- More than a thousand reported incidents directed against the US energy system (including electric power, oil, and natural gas) have been documented by the Department of Energy over the last 15 years. Some of the incidents involved outages and significant damage. In recent years, cyber incidents, including deliberate as well as accidental malfunctions, have begun to appear.
- Applied in electric power Supervisory Control and Data Acquisition (SCADA) systems are vulnerable because of use of commercial off-the-shelf (COTS) hardware and software, connections to other company networks, and the reliance on dial-back modems that can be bypassed. Also, the conclusions on electric power vulnerabilities state that from the cyber perspective, SCADA systems offer some of the most attractive targets to disgruntled insiders and saboteurs intent on triggering a catastrophic event.
- More training and awareness in infrastructure assurance is needed, focusing on risk management, vulnerabilities, performance testing, and cyber security.
- Adopting uniform physical and cyber security guidelines, standards or best practices would enhance protection.

The report [5] notice that electricity is also the only commodity whose price varies dramatically from hour to hour and from one location to another. As a result, an enormous financial incentive exist to deliberately disrupt power markets.

5   The Software Interlocking Case Study

As shown in Section 3.1 to ensure the safety of switching operations the order of switching sequences must be strictly preserved. In order to meet the condition mutual interlockings between disconnectors, circuit breakers and earthing switches are applied.

Conventional interlockings, in a substation with relay-based control system, use only a small amount of information available at the substation, which are in fact limited to a condition of auxiliary contacts of high voltage switches participating in a given switching operation. The use of computer systems made it possible to design software interlocking which provides access to all information available at a given substation and thus minimises a number of switching operations performed without any interlocking. It also makes it possible to construct more advanced interlocking, for example by extension of their range to neighbouring substations and larger parts of network. The above facts, together with the growth in the computer-based automation of substations and EPSs, the large scale introduction of remote controlled unmanned substations etc., increases the importance of interlockings. This leads to the growth in the importance of problems associated with ensuring their appropriate safety level.

The software interlocking case study has been carried out for the Mosciska 400 kV substation. It is a recently built substation situated at Warsaw constituting an important node of the grid supplying energy to the capital city. The substation consist of two busbar systems and eight bays. The case study was focused on the bay number 1, to which the line to Milosna substation is connected. Schematic diagram of the bay is shown in Figure 1. All the substation bays are identical and to some extent typical for all extra-high voltage substations.

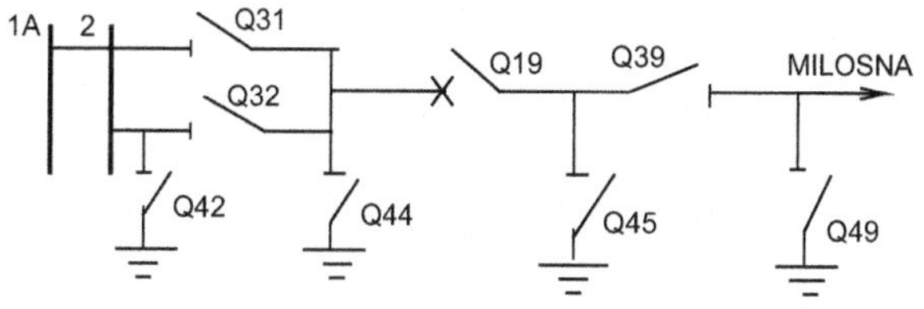

Fig. 1. Simplified schematic diagram of the bay number 1 in Mosciska 400 kV substation

The aim of the case study was to prepare the specification of requirements for software interlockings for substation computer control system which control switching operations and to make safety analysis of the interlockings. Due to the space limitations this paper does not include full description of the specification of requirements and the case study results. Below only examples of problems are presented which appeared during the hazard and risk analysis phase in specification of requirements for substation computer-based control system. The problems to some extent are typical for all on-line systems applied in a EPS. Full description of the case study is presented in [8], [9]. Object oriented models of the bay and results of safety analysis regarding the methods applied during safety analysis are presented in [10].

The case study was considered as a pilot case study and was carried out in Polish electric power sector for the first time.

5.1   Examples of Problems which Appeared in Hazard and Risk Analysis Phase

In this section event sequences are presented for one of the initiating events considered in the case study which lead to hazardous events. The *initiating event* is: switching off the line by the disconnector Q31, Q32 or Q39. This event create hazards for:

(a) bay (substation) equipment,
(b) EPS,
(c) substation staff.

Case (a). Hazards for bay (substation) equipment.
Main hazard is for the disconnector and other equipment in its close vicinity.
Accident. Arising electric arc between contacts of the disconnector, accompanied by high rate optic and acoustic phenomena, spraying melted metal, etc., and short-circuit.
Consequences. The minimal consequence is the complete destruction of the disconnector only, and damage in this case includes:

- cost of new disconnector: ca 21,000 USD (in Poland);
- cost of disconnector replacement (replacement time ca. 2 days);
- removing the line in the bay number 1 within the replacement time of disconnector in case of the failure of the disconnector Q39 (in case of the failure of the disconnector Q31, the line could be supplied from the busbar 2 through the disconnector Q32, whereas in case of the of the disconnector Q32 - from the busbar system 1A through the disconnector Q31).

Risk. Actually for the Polish EPS the risk has not been identified. In every case, when the loaded line is switching off by the disconnector, the accident occurs. According to existing experience frequency of accidents could be classified as occasional (see the following Discussion).

Case (b). Hazard for EPS.
Hazards depend upon the state of the EPS while initiating event is occurring. Generally there are possible hazards for:

- regional EPS,
- national EPS.

Accidents. Accidents depend very much on the state of EPS and on such factors as:
- season of the year,
- weather conditions,
- level of industrialisation of the community,
- preparation level of the power sector and the community to the big EPS failures, etc.

Exemplary accidents are as follows:

- cascading outages resulting in a collapse of a part of regional EPS and considerable outages;
- large EPS failure, which causes sectioning of the national EPS and collapse of one or more system parts (islands) which was formed as a result of sectioning of the EPS;
- collapse of the national EPS (blackout).

Consequences. Consequences depend on many factors, including the above-mentioned in *Accidents.* The accidents are mentioned according to the consequences they can cause, but generally in any case damage is considerable and can be disastrous. The smallest damage takes place generally in the first one of the above-mentioned accidents. The costs, updated to July 1987, of one kW interrupted and one kWh not delivered to industrial plants and commercial buildings in the United States and Canada are as follows [11]:

- all plants .... 4.69 USD/kW + 6.65 USD/kWh.
- all commercial buildings..................14.65 USD/kWh not delivered

Assuming rather little outages, e.g. 1000 MW, costs of interruption only, and costs for "all plants", the damage in this case, caused only by the interruption costs, can amount to approximately: 4.69 millions USD.

Risks. Risk strongly depend on the situation at the moment of initiating event occurring, and actually for the Polish EPS has not been identified. On the grounds of existing experience, without going too much into detail, it is possible to state, that the probability of a big system failure in Poland is about one failure for several up to a dozen or so years. Damages in case of a failure:

- Material: medium high (several to a dozen or so million US dollars) or high (more than that).
- Social: probably has never been assessed by anyone; they depend on the level of industrialisation (management standard, applied technologies, etc.) and social development (utilisation of electric appliances, level of organisation of social life, value of individual and common time of society members etc.).

Case (c). Hazards for the substation staff, concern the maintenance and repair staff which was working in the direct vicinity of the disconnector subject to failure (not only dispatching staff).

Accident. Injury by liquid metal spread at the time of a disconnector failure, which appears to be like an explosion.

Consequences. Personal injury, sometimes even very serious (e.g. eyes).

Risk. No appropriate information was found in publications, very short time of the project did not allow to gather information about any accidents of this type in the past. However, due to strict regulations concerning people entering the area of a substation, it seems that the probability of such an accident is small.

Discussion. Strict specification of hazards for a given EHV substation would require full analysis of hazards and risks for the whole EPS in a given country and the monitoring of possible influence of interconnected EPS's of other countries on a given EPS. Such an analysis has never been carried out in Poland, because in fact such a need rather did not exist up to the present. In Poland, the national electric power system has only existed since the beginning of the 1960s (in leading countries the origins of first electric power systems came into being as early as in the 1930s). At the start of development of the electric power industry, there were separated power stations and local systems. Since the 1960s, the EPS in Poland and coupled with it data transmisson network have become more and more complex.

Even if the hazard analysis for EPS would have been done, hazards and risks for a given substation would depend on the current situation in the EPS. For example in the normal state of the EPS, switching off a line by a disconnector may create only hazard described in case (a), that is the occurrence of the accident would result in the destruction of the disconnector and short circuit which would be turned off by the substation protection system.

In the case of for example a shut-down of a number of power stations (e.g. severe winter, coal shortage) the same activity may also cause serious hazards (e.g. for the local EPS), described in cases (a) and (b). One of the reasons for the above-mentioned situation is that in spite of the fact that location of the substation in question has not changed, the grid to which the substation is connected has changed.

Also even if hazards, consequences of accidents and frequency of accidents would be defined it has not been come up against guidelines concerning risks classification for EPS. If for example one would like to define the risk classes for e-xamples presented in this section according to the IEC 61508 draft standard, only intuitive and very tentative classification is possible, because at present there is not a frame of reference for "consequence" (negligible, marginal, critical, catastrophic), and "frequency" (incredible, improbable, remote, occasional, probable, frequent), used in the standard for the risk classification. Similarly, there is not a frame of reference for factors influencing the frequency of hazardous event like the "possibility of avoiding the hazardous event" or the "probability of the unwanted occurence".

6   Final Remarks

1. The shift of the idea how to provide an EPS safety and reliability from robustness of the EPS into control of the EPS during an emergency state will increasingly challenge the state of the art in EPS monitoring, communications, and control which must be based on high dependable computer systems. The challenge will also be strongly influenced by the emerging free market of electric power. On the other hand, in the field of distributed generation technologies revolutionary developments are expected in the next ten years and beyond [4], and the further increase in requirements for very high level of power quality. If there is no success in fulfilling these requirements through the development in EPS control, more and more of customers with critical power quality needs will find it necessary to self-generate if they cannot get the quality they need from the grid. Therefore, one can reasonably fear that it might result in the decrease of interest in EPSs development, and consequently in degradation of the distribution systems and even the whole EPSs. Hence, there has been emerging a concept of *distributed utility* based on mixture of distri-buted and central generation, which is supplied to the given distribution system by the transmission system. However the distributed resources must be dispatchable. This will require adding a variety of remote monitoring, communications, and control functions to the system as a whole [4]. Hence, in the concept of distributed utili-ty ensuring reliability of energy supply will also require high dependable computer systems.

2. A report [5] states that a recent presidential panel concluded that the electric power grid and telecommunications infrastructure are the most vulnerable to sabotage and cyber-attack in the United States. It should be taken into account that, due to the energy which exists in the electric power grids, the modification of programes which control switching operations could not only disrupt operation of a substation or cause outages of energy supply to customers, but also the physical destruction of substation components (e.g. by switching of a line by disconnector, see Section 3.1 and 5).

3. During the case study, it has turned out that the existing data on failures of substation components, breakdowns and accidents at substations, and large failures of the national EPS, are insufficient for assurance in an efficient way in the design stage high quality of computer systems applied in the EPS with regard to safety and security requirements as well as all other required quality attributes. The similar remark refers to the lack of analysis of hazards of the whole national EPS. The exis-ting current EPSs have been evolving for many years basing on another concept of its reliability assurance. Also they have never been designed for the free market of electric-

ity. Hence, in present completely different conditions and with another concept of reliability assurance, their behaviour is to some extent unknown. It has been confirmed to some extent by a study of significant disturbances made in the USA. From the study it follows that relays of EPS protection systems were in one way or another involved in 75% of major disturbances which took place in the USA between 1984-1988. A common scenario of these disturbances was that a relay (or a protection system) had an "hidden defect" not detected during a normal operation, calibration or maintenance that was exposed due to conditions created by other disturbances (e.g. nearby faults, overloads, or reverse power flows) [12].

4. The case study has confirmed what has already been written in publications, that there is the need to prepare an electric power sector standard or guidelines on design of safety-related computer systems applied in this sector. Probably the sector standard could be based on the international standard IEC 61508. Preparation of the standard or guidelines would require collection of data on failures and accidents in electric power sector in an appropriate and systematic way (preferably according to an international standard or guidelines on the data collection), and co-operation on international level.

5. The increasing organisational complexity of the sector, connected with the development of the free market of electric power, privatisation and division of the national power system into many independent companies, strongly heightens the necessity for legal regulations concerning computer systems design, commissioning and maintenance.

6. The automation of a power station, a power substation or a control centre, similarly like automation of other objects, is more and more based not only on hardware but also on software solutions. This fact should be taken into account by Univer-sities. The experience gained during the case study shows that programmes of electrical engineering faculties should at least include *Requirements Engineering* (lectures, classes and laboratory) to the extent which enables graduates specification of requirements on their own, and co-operate with software engineers during validation of models used in the safety analysis, carrying out the safety analysis, evaluation of results etc. With reference to students of software engineering at computer science departments it is worth considering if it would be useful they learn the basis of engineering (electrical diagrams, mechanical diagrams, etc.) in order to co-operate better with engineers from different sectors of industry which apply computer systems.

Acknowledgements

The case study presented in Section 5 has been carried out within EU Joint Research Project "Copernicus" CP'94 1594 *Integration of Safety Analysis Techniques for Process Control Systems (ISAT)*.

References

1. Żurakowski Z.: Review of Standards and Current Practices: Review of Dependability in EHV Substations. TR ISAT 97/20, Institute of Power Systems Automation, Poland (1997)
2. Balu, N., Bertram, T., et al.: On-Line Power System Security Analysis. Proceedings of the IEEE, Vol. 80, No. 2 (1992) 262-280
3. Department of Energy: Maintaining Reliability in a Competitive U. S. Electricity Industry. Final Report of the Task Force on Electric System Reliability (1998)
4. Electric Power Research Institute (EPRI): Electricity Technology Roadmap: Powering Progress - 1999 Summary and Synthesis. EPRI, Palo Alto (1999)
5. Electric Power Research Institute (EPRI): Issues and Solutions: North American Grid Operations (2000-2005). EPRI (1999)
6. Critical Foundations, Protecting America's Infrastructures. The Report of the President's Commission on Critical Infrastructure Protection, available at http://www.ciao.ncr.gov/default.html (1997)
7. Executive Summary: EPRI/DOD Initiative On Complex Interactive Networks/Systems. www.epri.com (1999)
8. Babczyński T., M. Borgosz-Koczwara M., Żurakowski Z.: Specification of Requirements for Extra-High Voltage Substation Software Interlocking Case Study Using i-Logix STATEMATE. TR ISAT 97/12, Institute of Power Systems Automation, Poland (1997)
9. Żurakowski Z.: Identification and Preparation of Case Studies - Extra-High Voltage Substation Software Interlocking Case Study. TR ISAT 97/8 (updated February and April 1997), Institute of Power Systems Automation, Poland (1997)
10. Nowicki, B., Górski, J.: Object Oriented Safety Analysis of an Extra High Voltage Substation Bay. In Proceedings of the 17th International Conference SAFECOMP'98. Lecture Notes in Computer Science, Vol. 1516. Springr-Verlag, Berlin Heidelberg (1998) 306-315
11. ANSI/IEEE Std 493-1990: IEEE Recommended Practice for the Design of Reliable Industrial and Commercial Power Systems. Second Printing (1995)
12. Phadke, A.G., Thorp, J.S.: Expose Hidden Failures to Prevent Cascading Outages. IEEE Computer Applications in Power, July (1996) 20-23

Dependability of Computer Control Systems in Power Plants

Analytical and Experimental Evaluation

Cláudia Almeida, Alberto Arazo, Yves Crouzet, and Karama Kanoun

LIS/LAAS-CNRS
7, Avenue du Colonel Roche, 31077 Toulouse Cedex 4 - France
{almeida,arazo,crouzet,kanoun}@laas.fr

Abstract. The work presented in this paper is devoted to the evaluation of the dependability of computer control systems in power plants. Two complementary approaches are used to analyze and evaluate the dependability of such systems, based respectively on analytical modeling and experimental validation. Both approaches as well as examples of their mutual interactions are briefly illustrated on a subsystem of a specific computer control system. The analytical approach allows evaluation of dependability measures such as availability and identifies the most influential dependability parameters. Fault injection provides the numerical values of the above mentioned parameters and allows identification of specific behaviors that may not have been considered by the analytical model.

1 Introduction

The work presented in this paper is devoted to the evaluation of the dependability of *Computer Control Systems* (CCSs) in power plants. Our study focuses on a subset of a CCS that provides the necessary means for the operators to control the power production.

The considered system is partially composed of *Commercial-Off-the-Shelf* (COTS) hardware and software components. Hence, only partial information is available for system validation, and we cannot rely only on this information to characterize the system and to acquire enough confidence for its use in critical applications. More generally, the use of COTS components in such systems raises the question of their acceptance by the proper authorities.

Our study emphasizes the combined use of two approaches to analyze and evaluate the dependability of the CCS, based on analytical and experimental evaluation.

The purpose of the analytical approach is to provide stochastic models that will be used to evaluate the dependability of the CCS. Modeling is done by means of *Generalized Stochastic Petri Nets* (GSPNs). One of the major problems in stochastic modeling is to have the most realistic values for the parameters. If for rates like failure or repair, we can rely on statistical data obtained by feedback

F. Koornneef and M. van der Meulen (Eds.): SAFECOMP 2000, LNCS 1943, pp. 165–175, 2000.

on similar components or systems, when it comes to the parameters directly related to the fault tolerance mechanisms (*e.g.*, coverage), a specific analysis has to be done in order to measure them. However, all such parameters may not have significant impact on system dependability. A sensitivity study enables the identification of the most influential one. Analytical evaluation helps to focus the experimental evaluation on the parameters with strong impact, thus reducing the number of experiments.

By forcing the system to react to undesirable inputs (the faults), fault injection aims at evaluating the efficiency of the fault tolerance algorithms and mechanisms, through measurement of some dependability parameters such as coverage factor, fault dormancy, error latency, etc [ ]. On the other hand, fault injection may identify specific failure modes of the system that have not been taken into account by the modeling approach. This may lead to introduce some modifications on the analytical model improving its representativity.

The above approaches are complementary and their combined use provides accurate dependability measures [ ].

The remainder of the paper is organized as follows. Section 2 briefly presents the CCS. Section 3 is devoted to analytical modeling where examples of models are presented to illustrate the needs for experimentation. Section 4, addressing the experimental approach, discusses the way fault injection will be performed according to the features of the CCS. Finally, Section 5 concludes the paper.

2   CCS Presentation

For the sake of simplicity, in what follows, the subset of the CCS considered in our work will be referred to simply as the CCS. The CCS is a distributed system with five nodes connected by a *Local Area Network* (LAN). It performs five main functions: *Processing* (PR), *archiving* (AR), *management of configuration data* (MD), *human-machine interface* (HMI) and *interface with other parts of the CCS* (IP). The functions are not totally independent and they exchange information through the LAN. The mapping between the various nodes and the functions is given in figure 1. Note that while HMI is executed on four nodes, node 5 runs three functions.

Nodes 1 to 4 are composed of one computer each. Node 5 is fault-tolerant: It is composed of two redundant computers, one of them acting as a primary (its outputs are the only considered) and the other as a backup (called secondary). The primary computer executes three primary software replicas (corresponding to AR, PR, and IP), while the secondary computer executes a subset of these functions. All nodes have several *Fault-Tolerance Mechanisms* (FTMs).

The computers are commercial workstations running COTS operating systems and protocols. Indeed, the whole CCS is itself a COTS system constituted by COTS software and hardware components to which specific proprietary software has been added by the CCS provider. Roughly speaking, we can consider that each node has three layers. The lowest layer corresponds to the COTS hardware and software components. On top of it runs the second layer constituted

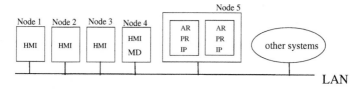

Fig. 1. CCS architecture

by the distributed middleware (for system configuration, system fault-tolerance, real-time services, etc.), on top of which run the main functions sketched above.

From a dependability point of view, very little knowledge about the CCS development and integration is available. As a consequence, its use in critical applications may be questionable. However, we will see later that this lack of knowledge may be compensated by information resulting from their widespread use in other systems. Nevertheless, such systems require a lot of validation before being accepted in critical application systems, hence the need for a complete validation approach.

3   Analytical Approach

The purpose of the analytical approach is to provide stochastic models to evaluate measures of dependability such as availability, reliability and safety. The evaluation is based on Markov chain models.

The modeling approach is modular, taking benefit from the systems' modularity. It is an incremental approach, similar to the one described in [ ]. Model construction is based on GSPNs (see *e.g.*, [ ]): The Markov chain is derived from the processing of the GSPN. In a first step, we build the GSPNs of all nodes and of the LAN independently. The system's GSPN is obtained by composition of the above GSPNs, taking into account the dependencies between the nodes and between the nodes and the LAN. Indeed, two sources of dependencies are to be considered:

- functional dependencies due to the communication between system functions, and
- dependencies due to maintenance (when several nodes are in failure, repair may be performed in successive steps if not enough repairmen are available).

Due to all these dependencies, the resulting global model is very complex. This complexity is increased by the fact that, within each node, several dependencies resulting from the interactions between the hardware and software components have also to be considered. Examples of dependencies internal to each node are: Software stop following hardware failure, error propagation from hardware to software or from software to software, switching from the primary computer on to the secondary computer. Because of this complexity, it is not possible to present in this paper the complete model of the whole CCS. We will thus consider one node, Node 5. In addition, as our purpose in this paper is to emphasize the combined use of the analytical and experimental approaches for system validation (more specifically for dependability evaluation), we have selected a small part of Node 5 to illustrate this objective.

In the rest of the section, we will first present the GSPNs of the two software replicas of function DP running on Node 5, then the GSPN of the switch from the primary computer on to the secondary computer. These examples have been chosen so as to introduce some significant parameters that can be evaluated by fault injection. An example of results is then commented before discussing how fault injection can help.

3.1   Examples of GSPN Models

Figure 3.1 gives the GSPNs of two software redundant replicas: The primary and secondary replicas running respectively on the two redundant computers. To model these replicas, the following assumptions and notations are used: .

- the activation rate of a software fault is λ_p (Tr$_1$) in the primary and λ_s (Tr$_4$) in the secondary;
- a software fault is detected by the FTMs with probability d (tr$_2$ and tr$_4$). The detection rate is δ (Tr$_2$ and Tr$_5$);
- the effects of a non detected error are perceived with rate π (Tr$_3$ and Tr$_6$);
- errors detected on the secondary are of two categories: Those requiring to stop the primary (tr$_5$), and those necessitating only a secondary reset (tr$_6$);
- the reset rate is ρ (Tr$_7$) and the probability that an error induced by the activation of a permanent software fault disappearing with a reset is r (tr$_7$);
- if the error does not disappear with the software reset, a re-installation of the software is done. The software re-installation rate is σ (Tr$_8$).

A detected or perceived (tr$_2$ and Tr$_3$) software error in the primary induces a *switch* (P$_{sw}$) from the primary computer to the secondary. And, as mentioned above, certain detected errors in the secondary software (tr$_5$) component may also induce a switch between computers.

Note that an error in the primary software may propagate to the secondary (tr$_{11}$). Indeed tr$_{11}$ models the common modes failures (probability p) of the primary and secondary (λ_p = common mode failure rate).

The second example of GSPN concerns the switch between the two redundant computers (figure 2(b)). As seen in figure 3.1, a switch between the two software replicas may occur when either an error is detected or perceived in the primary or detected in the secondary software components. Indeed, switching of replicas involves switching the computers on which the replicas are running. In addition, an error detected or perceived in the primary hardware induces a switch.

The switch mechanisms in figure 2(b), are characterized by two parameters: The *switch rate* (β) and the *switch coverage factor* (c). c is the probability that the service is re-established when a fault affects a given component in an operational context.

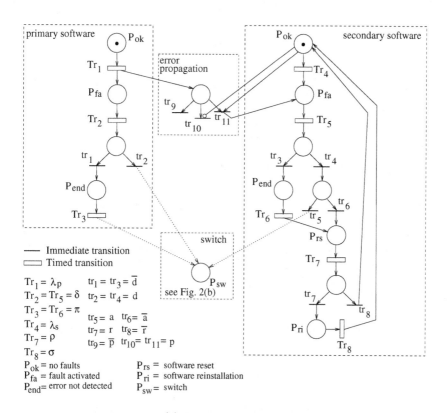

(a) Software of Node 5

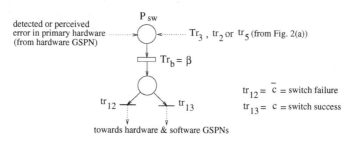

(b) Computer switch

Fig. 2. Examples of GSPNs

3.2   Model Parameters

In order to process the model to obtain the desired measures of dependability, numerical values should be given to the various model parameters (*i.e.*, event rates and probabilities). One of the major problems is to have the most realistic values for these parameters.

As mentioned earlier, the system is composed of COTS. In spite of all the drawbacks the use of COTS in critical systems may have, there are some advantages. Among them, there is one in particular that directly affects the analytical approach: *Feedback information*. Feedback information can help the analytical approach insofar as to give realistic values to some of the models' parameters.

If for rates like failure or repair, we can rely on statistical data obtained from feedback, when it comes to the parameters directly related to the fault tolerance mechanisms, a specific analysis has to be done in order to measure them. The experimental approach through fault injection is perfectly suitable to help the analytical method in this point.

Usually, we perform sensitivity analysis to point out the parameters that affect significantly the dependability measures evaluated. This means that the model is processed with different values of the parameters to check how strongly they affect these measures. Only the parameters with strong impact will be evaluated experimentally, to reduce the number of experiments.

For the CCS, we have considered nominal values for the failure and repair rates obtained by analogy with other systems and we made sensitivity analysis for the other parameters. The objectives were twofold: Identify the most significant ones to measure them experimentally and, for those that cannot be measured experimentally, make sensitivity analysis to evaluate a range for the dependability measures. The model has been processed using the SURF-2 tool [ ]. The unavailability, evaluated in hours per year (with a repair time of 10 hours) according to c and β is given in table 1.

It can be seen that both parameters have significant impact. It is obvious that the smallest unavailability is obtained for the shortest switch time and the best coverage factor. This table shows that an annual unavailability of approximately 2h may be obtained for (0.99; 5min) and (0.98; 1min or 30s). Since β an c are not known at this stage, we cannot make any conclusions. Fault injection will help us to identify the accurate result.

Table 1. Node 5 annual unavailability

$c\backslash 1/\beta$	30s	1min	5min	10min
0.99	**1h34min**	**1h38min**	**2h06min**	2h45min
0.98	**2h00min**	**2h04min**	2h33min	3h11min
0.95	3h20min	3h23min	3h52min	4h31min

4   Experimental Approach

We have developed an efficient fault injection strategy taking advantage of the main basic characteristics of the CCS, which are: i) the modular and multilayer design and implementation paradigms, and ii) the use, at the lowest layer of the system's architecture, of standard COTS components.

In the rest of the section, we explain the features of our fault injection strategy resulting from the early integration of the above characteristics. After that, we show how a prototype tool, supporting our strategy, can be used to obtain the set of expected measures.

4.1   A Modular and Multilevel Approach

To take into account the multilayer and modular design of the system, our fault injection strategy is *multilevel*. Also, the notion of *fault region* around both hardware and software components plays an important role. The integration of these two concepts enables us to a) design fault models emulating with a high accuracy the real faults affecting the CCS at any architectural layer, and b) refine progressively fault injection campaigns. Refinement is not only needed to improve analytical analysis results, but also to obtain other diagnostic information, increasing our knowledge about the CCS behavior in the presence of faults. The two following paragraphs explain these concepts and their relation with the CCS characteristics.

In a modular, distributed and multilevel computation approach, one can consider that each component is associated to a fault region. For example, a node can be considered as a fault region at a high level of abstraction. At a lower level of abstraction, a computer or a software replica can also be considered as a fault region. Each failure mode of each component is seen by the other interacting components, as being a fault model.

Our fault injection approach is intended to be used at any level of abstraction. This enables us to refine the outcomes of fault injection campaigns. The same fault injection protocol is used for emulating both high-level faults affecting link communication between software replicas, and low-level real hardware faults affecting the memory or internal processor units. The templates emulating a real fault and the means to inject and to observe their consequences, are instantiated in a strong relationship with the granularity of the target injection and monitoring levels. For example, at the low system layer, a well-known bit-flip model is considered as a good representation of the consequences of real electromagnetic perturbations (hardware faults). By an error propagation analysis, this multilevel approach would give us the means to observe, at a higher system layer, the consequences of the same low-level fault. Such analysis is necessary for emulating, with a coarse, yet satisfactory, high-level software fault models, low-level real faults. The corollary of this schema is a good coverage of the real fault types considered by the analytical approach. Both the injection and the observation activities are carried out by means of agents placed in different places of the system.

4.2   Exploiting Standard COTS Component Features

As stated earlier, the CCS is composed of proprietary software running on top of the distributed middleware that is running on top of standard software and hardware COTS. The middleware provides, among other services, fault-tolerance mechanisms to protect the services required by the upper functions from errors propagated from the lowest layer. Because very little information of CCS's structure, specification, development and integration is available, sometimes we will be constrained to place our fault injector Agents out of the proprietary CCS software. Ideally, they will be placed between the low layer (constituted by COTS components) and the CCS middleware services. Thus, the implementation of CCS on top of COTS components is an interesting benefit for the fault injection point of view. Because services, features and structures of standard COTS are well documented, we can easily interface the target node and use them to generate "COTS-level" faults, emulating real hardware and software faults.

4.3   Implementation of the Fault Injection Strategy

Fault injection campaigns give us an estimation of the parameters identified by the analytical approach, by means of readouts (R) obtained during the CCS operational activity (A), in presence of well selected sets of faults (F). Moreover, further unknown CCS operational behaviors under faulty conditions may be detected by a set of readouts correctly placed in the nodes. The desired measures (M) are obtained by processing the readouts.

Our fault injection strategy is built around a *Software Implemented Fault Injection* (SWIFI) approach. As recent works (see *e.g.*, [,]) have shown, SWIFI approaches take full advantage of features provided by standard hardware and software COTS. Their main advantages are their ability for: i) emulating a wide variety of fault models (F), ii) programming, in time and space, the point of impact of the injections, iii) placing, almost wherever we want, the readouts (R) to observe the consequences of emulated faults, and iv) automating the experimental campaign by script file orders addressed to injector Agents.

Our tool platform is based on the SPARC^{TM} hardware architecture, running Solaris 2.5.1 Operating System^{TM}. It is depicted in figure 3 where the target node is assumed to be Node 5. Because a large degree of portability is necessary for covering the evaluation of a wide variety of CCSs, we have separated the tool into a portable high-level software, and a small system-dependent part (which depends on the target platform). For this purpose we have adopted a *"Host-Target"* paradigm, separating the *campaign computation tasks* (design, experiment control and measures) running on the host, from *fault injection and monitoring tasks* achieved by *Agents* running on the target node (more precisely on the two workstations of the node, WS1 and WS2). The Agents have three main roles:

- program when and where the fault is to be injected according to the scripts received;
- perform the fault injection;
- record and send the results (through the readouts).

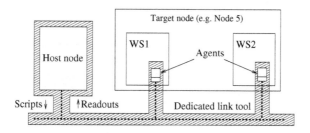

Fig. 3. Fault injection platform

4.4 Contributions of Fault Injection to the Analytical Approach

In the model described in figure 2(b), $1/\beta$ corresponds to the switch duration following any failure origin (detected or perceived failure in the primary hardware, failure of the primary software or a subset of errors in the secondary software). Even though the three origins have been distinguished, it is assumed that the switch rate and the coverage factor are independent from the origin. Fault injection may be performed separately, keeping record of the failure origin. If the results show significantly different switching times or coverage factors, this means that the analytical model should be modified to distinguish the three cases. Otherwise, if the switch duration and coverage factor are independent from the switch origin, there is no need to modify the model. This shows an example of how fault injection results can lead to modify the model or to strengthen our confidence on the assumptions supporting it. In the following, we comment the campaign aiming at evaluating $1/\beta$.

The first step is to select a satisfactory abstraction level for the experiments. This selection is done according to both our knowledge about the CCS components, and the degree of details required by the GSPN model. For the purpose of our example, the *middleware* layer is a satisfactory target level. This choice results from the fact a large part of the CCS activities (A) are instantiated on top of this layer, and also the hardware error detection and fault tolerance mechanisms (provoking the switch) are in this layer. The second step concerns the description of the aims of the experimental campaign. For this purpose, we rely on the approach described in [ ] that proposes two domains for fault injection characterization: The *output domain* (measures, M and readouts, R) describing the objectives of the campaign (here the measure of $1/\beta$), and the *input domain* (faults, F and activities, A) describing the means employed to reach these objectives.

The campaign for measuring the switch time $1/\beta$ implies the definition of a set of commands to be sent to the injector and monitoring Agents. Here, three campaigns (taking into account different Fault sets (F)) must be programmed, since system switch may result from three cases as recalled above. However, the goal being the same, a subset of common class of readouts (R) can be defined for the three campaigns. Here, the first part of R is defined as a set of reads of the internal clock to compute the time spent between error detection and service restart. This time is computed and recorded by the Agents[1]. For this clock service we rely on the hardware and operating systems COTS features. The second part of R concerns the observation of the consequences of F (the switch) and, in this case, the objective is the evaluation of the coverage factor with respect to the sets F. This subset of R is closely related to the definition of F for each campaign.

In order to emulate the three sets F, we rely on some structural aspects according to the level of abstraction chosen and the R set. First of all, we identify the set of computational objects (a subset of the activities (A)) concerned by the experiments. Here, these computational objects are the set of tasks provoking the start of the switch mechanisms. In order to program a fault emulation, we define a series of actions using the resources provided by the COTS components: Breakpoint registers, clock ticks register, task control blocks, etc. Indeed, the first step of the fault injection experiment is to stop, for a very short of time, the nominal behavior of the WS at the application layer, by modifying the nominal behavior of the underlying layer (here the middleware layer). After this, we emulate the fault. After resuming the CCS activity, the Agents analyze the behavior of the computation objects under faulty assumptions and record, for a pre-defined period of time, the results of the fault-tolerance mechanisms and the time of switch in readouts. At the end of the three campaigns, the readouts recorded are used by the host node to calculate the three values of $1/\beta$ and c.

5   Conclusions

In this paper an evaluation of the dependability of computer control systems (using standard COTS components) in power plants has been presented. More precisely, a strategy combining the use of two complementary approaches based respectively on analytical and experimental evaluation has been discussed.

It is shown how an optimization of the fault injection campaign is obtained by making sensitivity analysis on the analytical models. Thus, only the parameters that affect the most the system's unavailability and for which no feedback information has been given, will be evaluated by fault injection campaigns. Also, we have discussed the way results of the experimental evaluation may influence the analytical models and how fault injection takes advantage of the use of standard COTS components in the sytem.

The work is still under progress. Particulary the fault injection is under implementation. Even though the paper was devoted to a specific CCS architecture, our work is intended to be more general. Its aim is to support the industrial company for which this work is performed, in several ways:

- select, based on dependability analysis and evaluation, among other things the most suitable system among those proposed by systems' integrators;
- characterize more precisely the selected system.

---

[1] We assume that nodes' clocks of the CCS architecture are synchronized by an external mechanism

The modeling and the fault injection approaches can thus be applied with progressive knowledge of the system: For system selection, high level approaches are sufficient, whereas for accurate system characterisation, more precise, low level approaches are needed.

References

1. Arlat, J., Crouzet, Y., Laprie, J.-C. "Fault Injection for Dependability Validation of Fault-Tolerant Computing Systems", in *Int. Symp. on Fault-Tolerant Computing (FTCS-19)*, Chicago, IL (USA) (1989) 348–355. 173

2. Arlat, J. "Informatique Sûre de Fonctionnement: défis et solutions", in *Journal Européen des Systèmes Automatisés*, vol. 30, n. 10 (1996) 1433-1465, (in french). 166

3. Béounes, C., et *al.* "SURF-2: A Program for Dependability Evaluation of Complex Hardware and Software Systems", in *Proc. 23rd. Int. Symp. on Fault-Tolerant Computing (FTCS-23)*, Toulouse, France (1993) 668–673. 170

4. Carreira, J., Madeira, H., Silva, J. G. "Xception : A Technique for the Experimental Evaluation of Dependability in Modern Computers", in *IEEE Trans. on Software Engineering*, vol. 24, no. 2 (1998) 125–135. 172

5. Clark, J. A., Pradham, D. K. "Fault Injection : A Method for Validating Computer-System Dependability", in *IEEE Computer*, vol. 28 (1995) 47–56. 166

6. Kanoun, K., Borrel, M., Morteveille, T., Peytavin, A. "Availability of CAUTRA, a Subset of the French Air Traffic Control System", in *IEEE Trans. on Computers*, vol. 48, n. 5 (1999) 528–535. 167

7. M. Ajmone Marsan, G. Balbo, G. Conte, S. Donatelli and G. Franchescinis, *Modelling with Generalized Stochastic Petri Nets*, Series in Parallel Computing, Wiley (1995). 167

8. M. Rodríguez, F. Salles, J. Arlat and J.-C. Fabre, "MAFALDA: Microkernel Assessment by Fault Injection and Design Aid", in *3rd European Dependable Computing Conference (EDDC-3)*, Prague, Tcheck Republic (1999) 143–160. 172

A Method of Analysis of Fault Trees
with Time Dependencies

Jan Magott and Paweł Skrobanek

Institute of Engineering Cybernetics, Technical University of Wrocław
Wybrzeże Wyspiańskiego 27, 50-370 Wrocław, Poland

Abstract. Safety is one of the biggest concerns in the design of computer–aided control systems. In order to make the system as safe as possible a number of analysis techniques has been developed. One of them is Fault Tree Analysis. Fault tree (FT) represents causal and generalization relations between events (e.g. between hazard and its causes). However, original FT cannot express either time relations between events or times of: detection of a danger situation and protection. A new method based on systems of inequalities and equalities for analysis of FTs with time dependencies is proposed in the paper. The method can be used for analysis of protections too. FT analysis and modelling of protection using systems of inequalities and equalities will be illustrated by an example.
Formal models of FT gates used in the paper have the same expressive power as Timed Petri Net (TPN) models of FT gates from the paper [5]. However, present analysis method has greater decision power than classic TPN analysis method because the present method can be applied for much greater FTs. Additionally, the present approach results in more clear final conclusions.

Keywords: Safety–Critical System, Fault Tree, Time Dependency, Time Petri Net, Protection

1 Introduction

In order to make the system as safe as possible a number of analysis techniques has been developed: Failure Mode and Effect Analysis [1], Event Tree Analysis, Fault Tree Analysis [9]. Fault trees are studied in the paper. Fault tree (FT) represents causal and generalization relations between events (e.g. between hazard and its causes). Original Fault Tree cannot express either time dependencies between the hazard and its causes or times of: detection of a danger situation and protection. But it is the knowledge of that relationship which is useful in constructing protections.

In the paper, an analysis method for FTs with time dependencies is proposed. This method can be used to introduce protection against a hazard. Having system description, a FT with time dependencies for selected hazard event is constructed.

F. Koornneef and M. van der Meulen (Eds.): SAFECOMP 2000, LNCS 1943, pp. 176-186, 2000.
© Springer-Verlag Berlin Heidelberg 2000

Then, a system of inequalities and equalities (IES) for the FT is built. The IES is analyzed to determine whether the hazard event can occur. The IES represents so called static and dynamic conditions for the hazard to occur. Then a minimal set A of events that can cause the hazard is chosen. Next the system is extended by facilities to detect the set A and by a protection to avoid the hazard. Time characteristics of the detection and the protection have to be modelled. Then the extended system is verified to determine whether the detection and protection subsystem is quickly enough to avoid the hazard. The similar analysis can be preformed for the other minimal sets of events that can cause the hazard.

The paper is organized as follows.

In Section 2, the example of fault tree for a gas burner and formalization of the tree according to the papers [4], [5], [6] is given. In Section 3, for the definitions of FT gates from the paper [5], the static and dynamic conditions (IES) for the gates are presented. Case studies are included in Section 4. Comparison of computation times for IES method and classic TPN analysis method is given in Section 5. Section 6 contains conclusions.

2 Fault Trees

Fault tree technique is a top-down approach. It is started from identifying hazards, i.e., dangerous situations. Subsequently, for each hazard, a set of events that can cause the hazard is generated. A gas burner system and its model [5] will be used as an example. The system and its informal FT are presented at Fig.1. h (hazard), x, y, t, u, v, w are events while G1, G2, G3 are gates.

The hazard happens only when both x and y occur together for an adequately long period of time. The description of the gates from Fig.1 is as follows:

G1 –causal AND

$occur(h) \Rightarrow occur(x) \wedge occur(y) \wedge duration(x \wedge y) \geq t_{dmin} \wedge$
$$max(\tau(xs),\tau(ys)) + t_{dmin} \leq \tau(h) \leq max(\tau(xs),\tau(ys)) + t_{dmax}$$
where:

$occur(h)$ - predicate: the hazard h has occurred,

$occur(x)$ - predicate: the event x had occurred,

t_{dmin} - length of time interval when both events: x and y had occurred,

$\tau(xs)$ - time instance when the event x started,

t_{dmin}, t_{dmax} – respectively: the earliest and the latest time after which the gas concentration reaches an unsafe level.

G2 –causal OR

$occur(x) \Rightarrow (\exists x \bullet (duration(t) > t_{d1min} \wedge \tau(ts) + t_{d1min} \leq \tau(xs) \leq \tau(ts) + t_{d1max}))$
$\vee (\exists u \bullet (duration(u) > t_{d2min} \wedge \tau(us) + t_{d2min} \leq \tau(xs) \leq \tau(us) + t_{d2max}))$
where:

$\bullet$ - satisfying,

t_{d1min}, t_{d1max} – respectively, minimal and maximal times of opening of the gas valve,

t_{d2min}, t_{d2max} – respectively, minimal and maximal delays between event u and event x

G3 –generalization OR

$occur(y) \Rightarrow (occur(v) \wedge y = v) \vee (occur(w) \wedge y = w)$

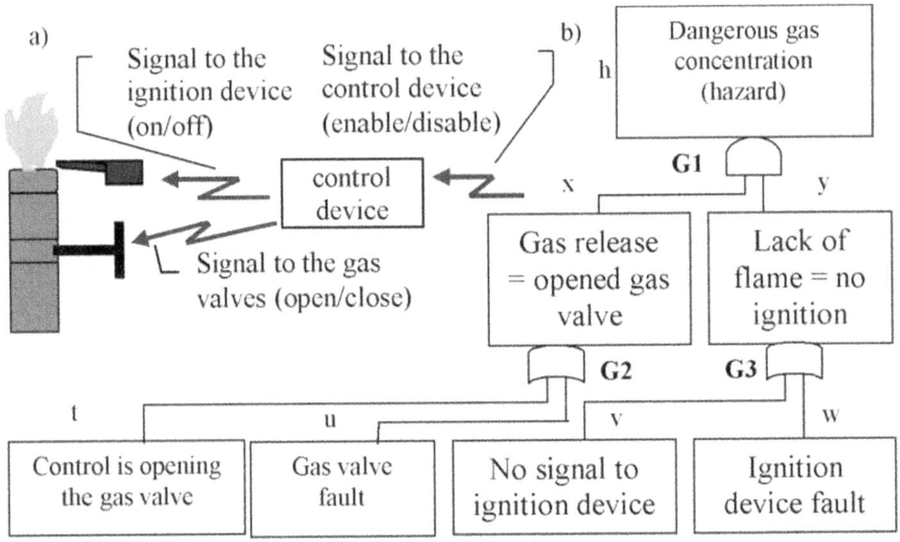

Fig. 1. a) A gas burner system, b) A fault tree of the gas burner

3   Method of Analysis of Fault Trees

In order to analyze fault trees with time dependencies, two kinds of conditions will be examined.

A hazard can occur if both kinds of conditions are satisfied:

1. **Static conditions** (SC) are such conditions that if they are not satisfied then no sequence of events will end in a hazard.
2. **Dynamic conditions** (DC) consist of some additional relations concerning starting and final moments of events in event sequences.

Static and dynamic conditions will be expressed by systems of inequalities and equalities.

The advantages of the static conditions are:

- they are relatively simple when compared to dynamic conditions,
- there exists very effective algorithm to verify static conditions.

If static conditions are not satisfied then there is no need to examine dynamic conditions.

3.1   Inequalities for Fault Tree Gates

In the papers [4], [5], [6], there are definitions of fault tree gates with time dependencies. In our paper, the definitions of FT gates from the paper [5] will be used. Our method is based on the presentation of the particular gates using adequate IES.

CAUSAL AND:

$$\text{occur}(z) \Rightarrow \text{occur}(x) \wedge \text{occur}(y) \wedge \text{duration}(x \wedge y) \geq t_{dmin} \wedge$$
$$\max(\tau(xs), \tau(ys)) + t_{dmin} \leq \tau(zs) \leq \max(\tau(xs), \tau(ys)) + t_{dmax}$$

The sequence above should be read as follows: if z has occurred then x and y have occurred as well, and they have lasted together at least t_{dmin}; moreover, z started in the time interval ###t_{dmin}, t_{dmax}### with regard to latest start of an event from the x, y pair of events. A time belonging to the above interval expresses time delay between causes: x, y and effect z.

In further presentation, the following notations will be used:

xs, xe , respectively, represents: start transition, end transition, respectively, of the event x,

$\tau(xs), \tau(xe)$, respectively, are time instances when the event x started, ended , respectively,

$\alpha^S_{xe}, \beta^S_{xe}$, respectively, are: minimal, maximal, respectively, duration times of the event x,

α^S_d, β^S_d , respectively, are: minimal, maximal, respectively, time delays between causes: x, y and effect z, i.e., $\alpha^S_d = t_{dmin}, \beta^S_d = t_{dmax}$.

Now let us consider the static (SC) and dynamic conditions (DC):

$$\text{SC:} \quad \alpha^S_d \leq \beta^S_{xe} \text{ and } \alpha^S_d \leq \beta^S_{ye} \qquad (1)$$

If $\alpha^S_d > \beta^S_{xe}$ or $\alpha^S_d > \beta^S_{ye}$ then requirement: duration$(x \wedge y) \geq t_{dmin}$ would not be satisfied.

DC: Let us suppose that the event zs started at time instance $\tau(zs)$. Dynamic conditions consist of such additional relations concerning starting and final moments of the events: x and y that have to be fulfilled if the event zs started at time instance $\tau(zs)$. Two cases: $\tau(ys) \leq \tau(xs)$ and $\tau(xs) \leq \tau(ys)$ have to be considered.

1. $\tau(ys) \leq \tau(xs)$ and $\tau(zs) - \beta^S_d \leq \tau(xs) \leq \tau(zs) - \alpha^S_d$ and $\tau(xe) \geq \tau(zs)$ and $\tau(ye) \geq \tau(zs)$
or 2. $\tau(xs) \leq \tau(ys)$ and $\tau(zs) - \beta^S_d \leq \tau(ys) \leq \tau(zs) - \alpha^S_d$ and $\tau(xe) \geq \tau(zs)$ and $\tau(ye) \geq \tau(zs)$

The relations: $\tau(zs) - \beta^S_d \leq \tau(xs) \leq \tau(zs) - \alpha^S_d$ are a consequence of relations: $\max(\tau(xs), \tau(ys)) = \tau(xs)$ and $\tau(xs) + \alpha^S_d \leq \tau(zs) \leq \tau(xs) + \beta^S_d$. The cases as presented above have to be supplemented with missing formulae describing a given moment of time, when the transitions ys and xs can occur at the earliest. Knowing that $\tau(xe) \geq \tau(zs)$ and $\tau(ye) \geq \tau(zs)$ – because events x and y can only end after the occurrence of event z, and $\tau(xs) \geq \tau(xe) - \beta^S_{xe}$, $\tau(ys) \geq \tau(ye) - \beta^S_{ye}$ -finally we can express these formulae as follows:

1. $\tau(ys) \leq \tau(xs) \leq \tau(zs) - \alpha^S_d$ and $\tau(zs) - \min\{\beta^S_d, \beta^S_{xe}\} \leq \tau(xs)$ and $\tau(ys) \geq \tau(zs) - \beta^S_{ye}$ $\qquad (2)$
and $\tau(xe) \geq \tau(xs)$ and $\tau(ye) \geq \tau(zs)$

The formula $\tau(zs) - \min\{\beta^S_d, \beta^S_{xe}\} \leq \tau(xs)$ is obtained from the formulas:

$$\tau(zs)-\beta^S_d \leq \tau(xs) \text{ and } \tau(xe)-\beta^S_{xe} \leq \tau(xs), \ \tau(zs) \leq \tau(xe)$$

2. $\tau(xs) \leq \tau(ys) \leq \tau(zs)-\alpha^S_d$ and $\tau(zs)-\min\{\beta^S_d,\beta^S_{ye}\} \leq \tau(ys)$ and $\tau(xs) \geq \tau(zs)-\beta^S_{xe}$ **(3)**

$$\text{and } \tau(xe) \geq \tau(zs) \text{ and } \tau(ye) \geq \tau(zs)$$

CAUSAL OR:

occur(z) $\Rightarrow$ ($\exists x \bullet$(duration(x) > t_{d1min} $\wedge$ $\tau(xs)$ +$t_{d1min} \leq \tau(zs) \leq \tau(xs)$ +t_{d1max})) $\vee$

        ($\exists y \bullet$(duration(y) > t_{d2min} $\wedge$ $\tau(ys)$ + $t_{d2min} \leq \tau(zs) \leq \tau(ys)$ +t_{d2max}))

where:

t_{d1min}, t_{d1max}, (t_{d2min}, t_{d2max}), respectively, represent: minimal, maximal, respectively, time delays between the occurrence of the cause x (y) and the effect z. The following symbols will be used:

$\alpha^S_{di} = t_{dimin}$, $\beta^S_{di} = t_{dimax}$, $i \in \{1,2\}$.

SC and DC: one of the following expressions is satisfied:

1. $\alpha^S_{d1} \leq \beta^S_{xe}$ and $\tau(zs)-\min\{\beta^S_{d1},\beta^S_{xe}\} \leq \tau(xs) \leq \tau(zs)-\alpha^S_{d1}$ and $\tau(xe) \geq \tau(zs)$ **(4)**

2. $\alpha^S_{d2} \leq \beta^S_{ye}$ and $\tau(zs)-\min\{\beta^S_{d2},\beta^S_{ye}\} \leq \tau \ (ys) \leq \tau \ (zs)-\alpha^S_{d2}$ and $\tau(ye) \geq \tau(zs)$ **(5)**

GENERALIZATION OR:

occur(z) $\Rightarrow$ (occur(x) $\wedge$ x = z) $\vee$ (occur(y) $\wedge$ y = z)

SC and DC: because this is the *generalization or* type gate, the event z is identical to one of the causes. Two cases ought to be considered:

1. $\tau(xs)=\tau(zs)$ and $\tau(xe)=\tau(ze)$ **(6)**

2. $\tau(ys)=\tau(zs)$ and $\tau(ye)=\tau(ze)$ **(7)**

GENERALIZATION AND:

occur(z) $\Rightarrow$ occur(x) $\wedge$ occur(y) $\wedge$ overlap(x, y) $\wedge$

        max($\tau(xs)$, $\tau(ys)$) =$\tau(zs)$ $\wedge$ min($\tau(xe)$, $\tau(ye)$) = $\tau(ze)$

where:

overlap(x,y) – predicate: the events x and y overlap in time.

SC and DC: because this is *generalization and* type gate, the event z occurs only if both causes occur simultaneously.

Four cases ought to be considered:

($\tau(ys) \leq \tau(xs) \leq \tau(ye)$ and $\tau(ye) \leq \tau(xe)$ and $\tau(xs)=\tau(zs)$ and $\tau(ye)=\tau(ze)$)   **(8)**

or ($\tau(xs) \leq \tau(ys)$ and $\tau(ye) \leq \tau(xe)$ and $\tau(ys)=\tau(zs)$ and $\tau(ye)=\tau(ze)$)

or ($\tau(ys) \leq \tau(xs)$ and $\tau(xe) \leq \tau(ye)$ and $\tau(xs)=\tau(zs)$ and $\tau(xe)=\tau(ze)$)

or ($\tau(xs) \leq \tau(ys) \leq \tau(xe)$ and $\tau(xe) \leq \tau(ye)$ and $\tau(ys)=\tau(zs)$ and $\tau(xe)=\tau(ze)$)

The restrictions: $\tau(xs) \leq \tau(ye)$ in the first case and $\tau(ys) \leq \tau(xe)$ in the fourth case are required in order to overlap the events x and y.

3.2   Equalities for Fault Tree Gates

We begin by identifying the time interval, when hazard can occur. Then, we consider the causes that can lead to hazard and time relations for causes and hazard occurrences.

Let us denote: $<\alpha_t,\beta_t>$ - time interval, when the transition t (t is start or end of an event) can lead to the occurrence of hazard. α_t (β_t) is the earliest (latest) time instance.

In order to carry over an analysis, one need to choose a time instant as zero time. It is supposed that the hazard h is started in the time interval

$$<\alpha_{hs},\beta_{hs}>=<0,0> \tag{9}$$

Next we specify the time intervals for the particular events of the FT or conclude that such an interval does not exist for a given event. For each gate using expressions (1-8), we have:

CAUSAL OR

Let us consider the IES given by the expression (4):

$\alpha^S_{d1}\leq\beta^S_{xe}$ and $\tau(zs)-min\{\beta^S_{d1},\beta^S_{xe}\}\leq\tau(xs)\leq\tau(zs)-\alpha^S_{d1}$ and $\tau(xe)\geq\tau(zs)$

We know that $\alpha_{zs}\leq\tau(zs)\leq\beta_{zs}$ so:

$\alpha_{zs}-min\{\beta^S_{d1},\beta^S_{xe}\}\leq\tau(zs)-min\{\beta^S_{d1},\beta^S_{xe}\}\leq\tau(xs)\leq\tau(zs)-\alpha^S_{d1}\leq\beta_{zs}-\alpha^S_{d1}$

$=> \alpha_{zs}-min\{\beta^S_{d1},\beta^S_{xe}\}\leq\tau(xs)\leq\beta_{zs}-\alpha^S_{d1}$

Because $\alpha_{xs}\leq\tau(xs)\leq\beta_{xs}$ therefore:

$\alpha_{xs}=\alpha_{zs}-min\{\beta^S_{d1},\beta^S_{xe}\}$ and $\beta_{xs}=\beta_{zs}-\alpha^S_{d1}$

Finally, for event zs to occur the following conditions must be satisfied:

$$\alpha^S_{d1}\leq\beta^S_{xe} \text{ and } \alpha_{xs}=\alpha_{zs}-min\{\beta^S_{d1},\beta^S_{xe}\} \text{ and } \beta_{xs}=\beta_{zs}-\alpha^S_{d1}$$
$$\text{and } \alpha_{xe}=\alpha_{zs} \text{ and } \beta_{xe}=\beta_{xs}+\beta^S_{xe} \tag{10}$$

where $\alpha_{xe}=\alpha_{zs}$ comes out from: $\tau(xe)\geq\tau(zs)$.

Values: α_{xs} and β_{xs} define the time interval, when occurring of the transition xs can lead to occurring of the transition zs. $\#\#\#_{xs}$ and $\#\#\#_{xs}$ are related to a given moment of time chosen as "0". Similarly, from expression (5) one obtains:

$$\alpha^S_{d2}\leq\beta^S_{ye} \text{ and } \alpha_{ys}=\alpha_{zs}-min\{\beta^S_{d2},\beta^S_{ye}\} \text{ and } \beta_{ys}=\beta_{zs}-\alpha^S_{d2}$$
$$\text{and } \alpha_{ye}=\alpha_{zs} \text{ and } \beta_{ye}=\beta_{ys}+\beta^S_{ye} \tag{11}$$

As the result of a similar analysis performed for the successive gates, we have:

CAUSAL AND

$$\alpha^S_d\leq\beta^S_{xe} \text{ and } \alpha^S_d\leq\beta^S_{ye} \tag{12}$$

and

$$(\alpha_{xs}=\alpha_{zs}-min\{\beta^S_d, \beta^S_{xe},\beta^S_{ye}\} \text{ and } \beta_{xs}=\beta_{zs}-\alpha^S_d \text{ and } \alpha_{ys}=\alpha_{zs}-\beta^S_{ye} \text{ and } \beta_{ys}=\beta_{xs}$$
$$\text{and } \alpha_{xe}=\alpha_{zs} \text{ and } \beta_{xe}=\beta_{xs}+\beta^S_{xe} \text{ and } \alpha_{ye}=\alpha_{zs} \text{ and } \beta_{ye}=\beta_{ys}+\beta^S_{ye} \tag{13a}$$

or

$$\alpha_{ys}=\alpha_{zs}-min\{\beta^S_d, \beta^S_{xe},\beta^S_{ye}\} \text{ and } \beta_{ys}=\beta_{zs}-\alpha^S_d \text{ and } \alpha_{xs}=\alpha_{zs}-\beta^S_{xe} \text{ and } \beta_{xs}=\beta_{ys}$$
$$\text{and } \alpha_{xe}=\alpha_{zs}, \beta_{xe}=\beta_{xs}+\beta^S_{xe} \text{ and } \alpha_{ye}=\alpha_{zs} \text{ and } \beta_{ye}=\beta_{ys}+\beta^S_{ye}) \tag{13b}$$

GENERALIZATION OR

$$\alpha_{xs}=\alpha_{zs} \text{ and } \beta_{xs}=\beta_{zs} \text{ and } \alpha_{xe}=\alpha_{ze} \text{ and } \beta_{xe}=\beta_{ze} \tag{14}$$

or

$$\alpha_{ys}=\alpha_{zs} \text{ and } \beta_{ys}=\beta_{zs} \text{ and } \alpha_{ye}=\alpha_{ze} \text{ and } \beta_{ye}=\beta_{ze} \tag{15}$$

GENERALIZATION AND

$$(\; \alpha_{xs}=\alpha_{zs} \text{ and } \beta_{xs}=\beta_{zs} \text{ and } \alpha_{xe}=\alpha_{ye} \text{ and } \beta_{xe}=\beta_{xs}+\beta^S_{xe} \tag{16}$$
$$\text{and } \alpha_{ys}=\alpha_{xs}-\beta^S_{ye} \text{ and } \beta_{ys}=\beta_{xs} \text{ and } \alpha_{ye}=\alpha_{ze} \text{ and } \beta_{ye}=\beta_{ze} \;)$$

or

$$(\; \alpha_{ys}=\alpha_{zs} \text{ and } \beta_{ys}=\beta_{zs} \text{ and } \alpha_{ye}=\alpha_{ze} \text{ and } \beta_{ye}=\beta_{ze}$$
$$\text{and } \alpha_{xs}=\alpha_{ye}-\beta^S_{xe} \text{ and } \beta_{xs}=\beta_{ys} \text{ and } \alpha_{xe}=\alpha_{ye} \text{ and } \beta_{xe}=\beta_{xs}-\beta^S_{xe} \;)$$

or

$$(\; \alpha_{ys}=\alpha_{zs} \text{ and } \beta_{ys}=\beta_{zs} \text{ and } \alpha_{ye}=\alpha_{xe} \text{ and } \beta_{ye}=\beta_{ys}+\beta^S_{ye}$$
$$\text{and } \alpha_{xs}=\alpha_{ys}-\beta^S_{xe} \text{ and } \beta_{xs}=\beta_{ys} \text{ and } \alpha_{xe}=\alpha_{ze} \text{ and } \beta_{xe}=\beta_{ze} \;)$$

or

$$(\; \alpha_{xs}=\alpha_{zs} \text{ and } \beta_{xs}=\beta_{zs} \text{ and } \alpha_{xe}=\alpha_{ze} \text{ and } \beta_{xe}=\beta_{ze}$$
$$\text{and } \alpha_{ys}=\alpha_{xe}-\beta^S_{ye} \text{ and } \beta_{ys}=\beta_{xs} \text{ and } \alpha_{ye}=\alpha_{xe} \text{ and } \beta_{ye}=\beta_{ys}-\beta^S_{ye} \;)$$

4   Case Study

4.1   Static and Dynamic Conditions for Fault Tree of the Gas Burner

We assume the following values of relevant quantities for the gas burner system (see Section 2.):

G1: $\alpha^S_{hs} = 0$ $\beta^S_{hs} = 0$ $\alpha^S_d = 10$ $\beta^S_d = 20$ $\beta^S_{xe}=\infty$ $\beta^S_{ye}=\infty$
G2: $\alpha^S_{d1}=60$ $\beta^S_{d1}=90$ $\alpha^S_{d2}=0$ $\beta^S_{d2}=0$ $\beta^S_{te}=\infty$ $\beta^S_{ue}=\infty$
G3: $\beta^S_{ve}=\infty$ $\beta^S_{we}=\infty$

E.g. $\beta^S_{xe}=\infty$ means that time when "gas is released" is unbounded.

For the above values, we have the following time intervals $<\alpha_t,\beta_t>$, see Fig. 2.

Now, we can look at the temporal relations between the occurrence of particular events for the hazard to happen. First, we analyze the relations for expression (13a). The diagram below illustrates those temporal relations:

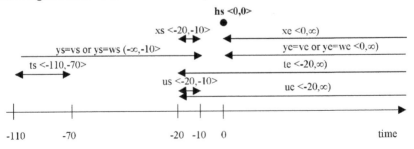

In order to avoid the hazard, one can require that the gas cannot be released at zero time. Therefore, the system ought to be modified or equipped with an adequate protection.

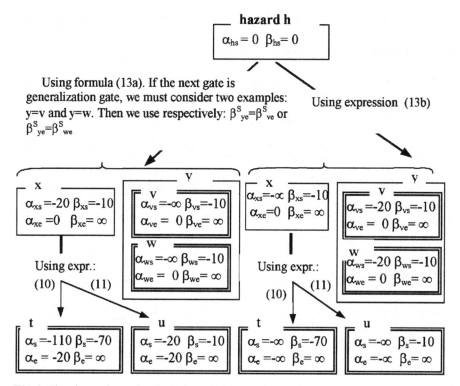

Fig. 2. Time intervals $\langle \alpha_t, \beta_t \rangle$ for fault tree of the gas burner from Fig. 1

4.2   Gas Burner with Protection

Now, the above gas burner system with a protection will be studied. Let the protection be combined from a safety valve and synchronization of the gas valve opening with ignition signal sending.

If the system works correctly, then first, the control starts the opening of the gas valve and second, sends immediately a signal to ignition device. Let control fault means: "No signal to ignition device" (see Fig.1) in spite of sending the signal to open the gas valve. Therefore, the control fault can occur only after start of the event "control is opening the gas valve". It is not possible to represent such a case in original FT.

The protection works as follows. Immediately after start of the event "control is opening the gas valve", the detection of control fault is activated. After recognizing of the control fault, immediately the closing of the safety valve is started.

The following delays characterize the protection:

d3 –time of recognizing of the control fault, d4 –time of closing of the safety valve.

Let $\alpha^S_{d3}=20$ and $\beta^S_{d3}=40$, respectively, be minimal and maximal times of recognizing of the control fault, respectively.

We have to define such minimal α^S_{d4} and maximal β^S_{d4} times of closing the safety valve that the gas cannot be released at zero time (see diagram of temporal relations). The above purpose will be achieved if: $\beta^S_{d3} + \beta^S_{d4} < -\beta_{ts}$.

In the above relation there is the symbol $-\beta_{ts}$ because recognizing of the ignition fault can be started after the event ts. Because $\beta^S_{d3}=40$ and $\beta_{ts}= -70$, so the maximal time of closing the safety valve should be less than 30 time units.

For the formula (13b), $\beta_{ts}= -70$ too. Therefore, the solution presented above is quickly enough.

Now, let us consider the event u: "Gas valve fault". Because $\beta_{us}= -10$, so the protection as the above is not sufficient. In this case, let d5 be the time of recognizing of the coincidence of events: u and y: "Lack of flame". Hence, the relation $\beta^S_{d5} + \beta^S_{d4} < -\beta_{us} =10$ have to be satisfied. Let us suppose that a protection which satisfies this relation has been constructed. Therefore, previous protection which contains the synchronization of the gas valve opening with ignition signal sending is not required.

5   Computation Results

Subtrees of the FT from Fig. 1 with 1, 2, and 3 gates have been investigated. Computation times for the IES based method and the classic TPN analysis one are given in the Table 1. For the IES method, the computation time is a time required to generate all combinations of values α_{xs}, β_{xs}, α_{xe}, β_{xe} for all events x from the FT according to the expressions from (10), (11), (12), (13), (14), (15). For the classic TPN method [8], the computation time is a time required to generate state class reachability tree [2], [3] until reaching a class with a token in the place that represents a hazard event. For the IES method and the classic TPN one, respectively, average computation time for each FT has been obtained as arithmetic mean from 100 and 10 computations, respectively. The computations have been performed on the personal computer AMD K5, 100 MHz, 48 MB RAM.

Table 1.

Gates	Average computation time [s]	
	IES method	Classic TPN method
G1	$33,23 \bullet 10^{-6}$	0,057
G1 and G2	$66,63 \bullet 10^{-6}$	0,329
G1, G2 and G3	$81,01 \bullet 10^{-6}$	2,760

It is clear that the IES method is much more effective than the classic TPN method.

6   Conclusions

New method for analysis of FTs with time dependencies has been proposed in the paper. The method can be used for analysis of protections too.

Two kinds of conditions: static and dynamic ones have been defined. If these conditions are not satisfied then hazard cannot occur (provided that a FT represents all causes of a hazard). Static conditions are such conditions that if they are not satisfied then no sequence of events will end in a hazard. Dynamic conditions consist of some additional relations concerning start and end time instances of each event in event sequences. Static conditions are relatively simple when compared to dynamic ones. There exists very effective algorithm to verify static conditions. If static conditions are not satisfied then there is no need to examine dynamic conditions.

Our method has the following limitations. We have limited ourselves to single-cause effects for Causal OR gate, i.e., only such events are considered for with two input events only.

Formal models of FT gates used in this paper have the same expressive power as Timed Petri Net (TPN) models of FT gates from he paper [5]. The IES method is much more effective than the traditional technique of analyzing of time dependencies in TPN models of FTs. Therefore, the IES method has greater decision power than classic TPN analysis method. Additionally, the present approach results in more clear final conclusions.

References

[1]   *Analysis techniques for system reliability –Procedure for Failure Mode and Effect Analysis*, International Electrotechnical Commission, IEC Standard, Publication 812, 1990

[2]   B. BERTHOMIEU, M. DIAZ, *Modelling and Verification of Time Dependent Systems Using Time Petri Nets*, IEEE Transaction of Software Engineering, vol. 17, no. 3, March 1991

[3]   B. BERTHOMIEU, M. MENASCHE, *A State Enumeration Approach for Analyzing Time Petri Nets*, 3. European Workshop on Applications and Theory of Petri Nets, Varenna (Italy), September 1982

[4]   J. GÓRSKI, *Extending Safety Analysis Techniques With Formal Semantics,* In Technology and Assessment of Safety Critical Systems, (F.J. Redmill, Ed.), Springer-Verlag, 1994

[5]   J. GÓRSKI, J. MAGOTT, A. WARDZIŃSKI, *Modelling Fault Trees Using Petri Nets*, SAFE COMP'95, Belgirate (Italy), 1995

[6]   J.GÓRSKI, A. WARDZIŃSKI, *Formalising Fault Trees*, Safety Critical Symposium, Brighton (UK), February 1995

[7]   N. LEVESON, J. STOLZY, *Safety Analysis Using Petri Nets*, IEEE Transaction of Software Engineering, vol. SE-13, no. 3, March 1987

[8]   P. SKROBANEK, *Fault trees with time relations applied for introduction of protections into the systems* (In Polish), Real -Time Systems'97, Szklarska Poręba, Poland, 1997

[9]   W. E. Vesely et el., *Fault Tree Handbook,* NUREG 0492, US Nucleary Regulatory Commission, 1981

A Formal Methods Case Study: Using Light-Weight VDM for the Development of a Security System Module

Georg Droschl[1], Walter Kuhn[2], Gerald Sonneck[2], and Michael Thuswald[2]

[1] Technical University of Graz
Institute for Software Technology
droschl@ist.tu-graz.ac.at
[2] Austrian Research Centers
Department of Information Technology and Telematics
{kuhn,sonneck,thuswald}@arcs.ac.at

Abstract. This paper describes a formal methods case study in which one module of an existing security system was re-developed using the light-weight Vienna Development Method, supported by the IFAD Toolbox. With respect to the original version, formal methods – even in its light-weight form – has increased software quality while the development efforts were comparable. The team that has used conventional methods for the development of the original version discusses the relevance of the findings.

1 Introduction

Formal software development methods are methods that exploit the power of discrete mathematics – set theory and predicate calculus. As [   ] point out, *"formal methods are one of a number of techniques that when applied correctly have been demonstrated to result in systems of the highest integrity"*.

One of the best known formal methods is the Vienna Development Method (VDM) [   ]. VDM is a development method in the sense that rules are given to verify steps of development. Today the discussion is confined to its specification language VDM-SL. This is because only recently, engineers have started using VDM-SL in a more light-weight manner than it was originally intended within the original framework of VDM. Rather than making use of formal proof, validation and verification are approached by applying test cases to the specification [   ].

In a case study, the Subsystem Driver 0E (SSD-0E) of the Compilable Security System [   ] was re-developed using light-weight VDM given the original requirements (cf. Fig. 1). The new version of SSD-0E was compared with the original one in terms of development effort and the degree of conformance with the requirements. For this purpose, test cases were deduced from the requirements.

F. Koornneef and M. van der Meulen (Eds.): SAFECOMP 2000, LNCS 1943, pp. 187–197, 2000.
© Springer-Verlag Berlin Heidelberg 2000

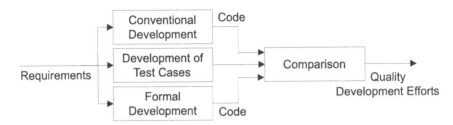

Fig. 1. Project Overview: Parallel Development and Comparison

Related Work. There are numerous reports from various domains on the practical application of formal methods. However, the number of projects where code was developed is considerably smaller. [   ] describe the formalization of parts of IBM's Customer Information Control System. The application of the formal method Z [   ] has lead to an overall improvement of software quality and to an earlier detection of errors found in the process. [   ] report on the development of a metro signaling system that was designed at reducing the separation times between trains. The system developed using the B method [   ] met its requirements: increased throughput and certification. [   ] discuss the development of a distributed system which is capable of tracking rail traffic across Europe. An object-oriented version of VDM – VDM++ – was used for modeling. The main benefit was in the capacity to provide early feedback due to the formal model. [   ] studied the parallel development of a secure message handling system. The development efforts were comparable. The VDM version has revealed a special condition that was left undiscovered in the conventional version. [   ] used a combination of VDM and B for the development of a middle-ware software which allows applications to communicate via a simple application programming interface. The main conclusion is that using formal methods, faults may be found early. [   ] report on a process improvement experiment of a code generator. Most surprisingly, the C++ code created by the IFAD Toolbox out of the VDM specification was twice as fast as the handwritten code. This is attributed to a better design in the formal path. [   ] applied the B method for the development of metro vehicle control system. The project stayed within budget and schedule and lead to good software quality. [   ] describe the development of the control software for a storm surge barrier using Z. Modules that were specified formally turned out to require little maintenance and rework.

The most closely related work is reported in [   ] and [.   ]. [   ] discusses prototype development using formal methods. In his "system study" – which is very thoroughly written – an access control system serves as an example. In a sequence of refinement steps, the B method is used to develop a concrete model of an access control system. [   ] has applied verification based on linear programming on a similar type of system as Abrial. It has been modeled as a set of communicating automata.

However, the concept of guardrounds has not been studied using formal methods before. The functionality of the systems described by [,   ] is restricted to granting employees access to buildings. Second, in contrast to the present work, [,   ] defined their own (very clear) requirements. The authors of SSD-0E's requirements wrote down much of their domain knowledge. This lead to a high level of detail in the description, and made the development quite challenging. In particular, it has been shown that parts of the requirements are contradictory and incomplete [   ].

2   A Security System Module

The Compilable Security System (CSS) was developed using conventional development methods [   ] by the Austrian Research Centers (ARCS) on behalf of Philips. CSS has been successfully installed at various sites from different domains including banking, insurance, industry, military, and research. CSS has a wide range of features including digital video recording, automatic door control, intrusion detection, night-guard supervision, etc.

The SSD-0E module supports night guards on duty. It interfaces with the (human) operator of CSS, a number of night guards, and the rest of the system.

The task of a *guard* is to monitor a pre-defined area which is defined in terms of a one-way path called a *round*. It contains a list of *stations* which shall be visited one after another. Examples of such stations are card-readers, terminals, and simple buttons. The act of visiting a station is referred to as a "hit".

There are doors and intrusion circuits restricting where the guard may go. These are called *obstacles* and can be in one of two states: unblocked, and blocked. For the guard there is no easy way of toggling these devices. Instead, SSD-0E must perform state changes automatically.

The task of the *operator* is to assign guards to rounds, to supervise the guards on duty, and to interfere at exceptional conditions: for example, a guard may signal a "silent alarm" to the operator once he or she feels threatened by an intruder.

Informal Requirements. The desired functionality of SSD-0E is defined in terms of 58 informal requirements [   ]. The following are requirements (in *italics*) plus some annotations: *every round contains at least one station. For each station, several switches can be defined.* Given a station, a switch is a logical link to an obstacle to be unblocked after the guard has hit the station and to be blocked again after the guard has hit the following station.

The first station of a round must be codable. When the guard hits a station, the system may determine the identity of the guard if and only if the station is codable. An example for a non-codable station is a simple button.

There are three round selection modes: (1) selected for recording, (2) selected for executing by one guard, (3) selected for executing by two guards, (4) deselected. The selection mode should be chosen by the operator when selecting a round. At any time, a round can only be selected once. A guard round can only be selected for executing if it has been programmed and recorded. If a round has been programmed, then it has a list of stations assigned to it. If a round has been recorded, then the system is aware of the time it may take the guard from each station to the next one.

Formal Specification of SSD-0E. [   ] contains the entire formal VDM-SL specification. In this paper, we will show 8 out of 200 declarations. Fig. 2 contains a few simple data type declarations, function- and operation definitions[1]. R is a record type and models a round. According to this declaration, every round has a SelectionMode (<Unselected>, <Recording>, and the two "main modes" <X1Guard> and <X2Guards>). In mode <X2Guards>, there are two guards on the round. R has two invariants. An invariant further restricts the possible values of a datatype. Here, a round consists of one station or more. Second, the first station is codable. Type R only contains rounds that satisfy these properties.

Station is another record type and models a single station that is part of a round. A station has an identifier s_adr. switches and iscodable have been explained above. ststate contains the state of the station, StState defines 10 possible values. For example, a station may be taken out of order temporarily (<disabled>), and before the guard has hit that station it is in state <normal>.

Fig. 2 defines three functions: R_Selected returns true if and only if the round has been selected. R_Mode_X1 checks whether the selection mode is executing with one guard. Finally, R_has_disabled_S determines if a round contains disabled stations or not.

Finally, an operation is shown. In contrast to a VDM-SL function, an operation may define local variables. OPselX1 is an *extended explicit* operation: it consists of an explicit algorithm, and a pre/post condition pair making up the implicit part of the operation. In the VDM-SL specification, there are 58 specialized operations similar to this one. OPselX1 is invoked when the operator (OP) has decided to select (sel) a round for executing with one guard (X1). The pre condition makes sure that the function is only invoked provided certain conditions hold: first, a local variable r0 is defined by fetching a round with identifier r_adr. The pre condition holds if and only if that round has been recorded and programmed, but not selected.

The post conditions first "binds" a local variable new_r to the RESULT that is returned by that operation. At any occurrence of new_r we could use RESULT instead. The new round is selected in mode <X1Guard>. The following two functions R_Waiting_Begin and Where_next_Hit_G1 are not defined in the present paper: they determine whether the round is currently waiting for the guard to hit the first station.

In the explicit part of the operation, first two local variables are defined: r0 is fetched from SSD-0E's internal round store. In case that round has been active before, it is prepared by Reset_R for a new run. Then, the two fields selmode and rstate are set such that the return value of that operation satisfies the post condition.

---

[1] In some cases, simplifications have been made with respect to [   ].

```
types
  R          :: selmode    : SelectionMode
                stations   : seq of Station
  inv r == len r.stations >= 1  and  r(1).codable   =  true;

  SelectionMode = <Unselected> | <Recording> | <X1Guard>  | <X2Guards>;

  Station :: s_adr      : S_Adr
             switches   : Assigned_Switches
             iscodable  : bool
             ststate    : StState ;

  StState =  <disabled> | <normal> | <toolate> | <tooearly> | <unknown>
  | <wrongorder> | <silentalarm> | <wrongcode> | <secgdtoolate> | <hit>;

functions
  R_Selected : R -> bool
  R_Selected (r) == r.selmode <> <Unselected>;

  R_Mode_X1 : R -> bool
  R_Mode_X1 (r) ==  r.selmode=<X1Guard>;

  R_has_disabled_S : R -> bool
  R_has_disabled_S (r) ==
      exists si in set inds r.stations & S_disabled(r,si);

operations
  OPselX1 : R_Adr   ==> R
  OPselX1 (r_adr) ==
  ( dcl r0:R := Get_R(r_adr);  dcl new_r:R :=Reset_R(r0);
    new_r.selmode:=<X1>;        new_r.rstate.waiting_begin:=true;
    return new_r )
  pre  let r0=Get_R(r_adr) in  R_Recorded(r0) and
        R_Programmed(r0) and not R_Selected(r0)
  post let new_r=RESULT in
        R_Selected(new_r)          and R_Mode_X1(new_r)
        and R_Waiting_Begin(new_r) and Where_next_Hit_G1(new_r)=1;
```

Fig. 2. Data Types, Functions, and Operations for SSD-0E

3   Formal Development

Choice of Notation, Method & Tool. There are a few formal methods that
have achieved a certain level of maturity, are applicable in a practical context
and cover a wide range of the software development life cycle (including code
generation!). These include VDM [   ], Z [   ], and B [   ]. Because of
previous positive experiences by the people involved in this project, VDM-SL

was selected as a notation, together with the light-weight development approach described in [   ], and the IFAD Toolbox [   ].

Specification Language. When choosing a formal method, the characteristics of the application need to be taken into account. In the present case, SSD-0E is complex with respect to data- *and* control aspects: it can be seen as a state-transformer changing its state depending on the kind of event that is received. Fig. 2 showed an operation which is invoked once the operator selects a round for executing with one guard. VDM-SL [   ] is a specification language that is well-suited for modeling data. It has been chosen, even though it might not be the first candidate for modeling event-based systems.

Development Method. When developing a specification based on an informal requirements document (and finally : executable code), usually the first step is to write an abstract specification. In the case of VDM-SL, such an abstract specification consists of implicit functions/operations which consist of pre/post condition pairs. Only in the second step, these functions/operations are complemented with explicit algorithms. The IFAD Toolbox can automatically generate C++ code from certain explicit specifications.

Tool Support. IFAD's VDM-SL Toolbox [   ] is a set of tools which supports formal development in ISO standard VDM-SL [   ]. VDM-SL specifications are entered in ASCII. Specifications may be parsed and type checked. An interpreter supports all of the executable constructs of VDM-SL allowing a form of animation and specification "testing". For each function/operation, test coverage information is automatically generated. A pretty-printer uses the ASCII input to generate VDM-SL specification in LATEX format. The IFAD Toolbox for VDM-SL has been used in a number of substantial projects[2]. There is a comprehensive list of publications related to VDM and VDM-SL called the *VDM bibliography*[3]. It provides links to many reports on projects in which the Toolbox has been used. These documents provide insights on how various kinds of problems have been solved.

A Comparative Case Study. In the present case study, the SSD-0E module was re-developed from the original informal requirements. One of the goals was to develop a program that could be compared with the original one.

---

[2] IFAD Web page. http://www.ifad.dk

[3] The VDM Bibliography. http://liinwww.ira.uka.de/bibliography/SE/vdm.html Maintained by Peter G. Larsen.

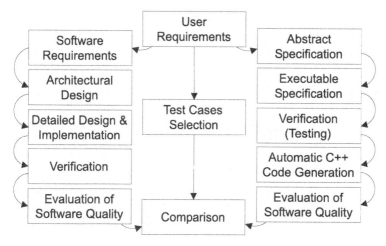

Fig. 3. Overview of Development Phases: Conventional Path and Formal Path

Conventional Path. SSD-0E has been developed at ARCS using conventional software development methods. As at spring 2000, ARCS, Philips and their customers have a decade of experience with CSS. From the beginning of the 1990's until 1997 there has only been a prototype version of SSD-0E. A second version has emerged in 1997: first, the requirements have been analyzed and put down to paper. Then, SSD-0E was designed using state diagrams and sketches of the system's architecture. In parallel to implementing the design, an environment was built that could be used to comfortably run test cases. It allows the simulation of hardware devices like the round station terminals. The original SSD-0E program consists of 12,000 lines of Pascal code.

Formal Path. The development of the formal methods version started in January 1998. In the first phase, about 70 A4 pages of abstract specification were written. About half of that document were extraneous – informal – text and documentation. The specification was abstract in the sense that, essentially, functions were defined implicitly. This specification was functional, meaning that the functions did not have side-effects on a state.

In the second phase, explicit algorithms and state declarations were added. At the same time, the structure of the document was changed. The final VDM-SL specification, including comments, contains more than 5,500 lines non-blank lines.

In the validation phase, test cases were applied to the executable specification. Test cases were developed partially automatically using a test case generator [   ]. Finally, the specification was submitted to the automatic C++ code generator of the IFAD Toolbox and the code was compiled on a Solaris platform.

For a more detailed discussion see [   ]. [   ] aims to bridge the gap between VDM and PVS by taking the design of SSD-0E into account. The interplay of VDM and PVS is also addressed in [   ]. [   ] presents a pragmatic approach to test case generation which proved to be of value in the validation process of SSD-0E.

4   Comparison

Quality. The quality of the two versions was estimated according to the degree of conformance with the requirements. For this purpose, a set of test cases was deduced from the requirements. Fig. 4 summarizes the results of the comparison. Altogether, 40 out of 58 requirements were considered to be testable, leading to 71 test cases. Thus, each one of the 40 requirements resulted in at least one test case. A requirement was considered to be implemented correctly if the specification satisfied all of its test cases.

The formal methods version was the clear winner. It satisfied 82.5% of the requirements, whereas the original version supported only 62.5%. A possible reason for the relatively moderate result of the conventional version is that the code may have been modified without keeping all of the requirements consistent. The formal version could also have achieved a better ranking without a number of extraneous assumptions which were made with respect to the requirements.

About half of the requirements (57.5%) were correctly implemented by both versions, while both failed to satisfy 12.5% of the requirements. These two groups of requirements can thus be interpreted as requirements which are easy to satisfy, and requirements which are difficult to satisfy, respectively. Essentially, the second group consists of requirements which are on a low operational level.

Formal modeling and analysis has revealed new, undesirable properties of the requirements: first, the guard may be unable to move on because the system may fail to unlock doors. Second, the requirements lack an important relationship expressing the relative physical location of an obstacle to be toggled after a given station has been hit. The latter deficiency is surprising because it is considered to be a potential source of important misunderstandings between developers and users of the system.

	Requirements	Test Cases
Size of Test Suite	40/58 Reqs. tested (68.9%)	71 Test Cases (1-6 per Req.)
Conventional Development	**25 Reqs. OK** **(62.5%)**	48 Test Cases OK (67.6%)
Formal Methods	**33 Reqs. OK** **(82.5%)**	61 Test Cases OK (85.9%)

Fig. 4. Comparison of Quality of the two Versions of SSD-0E

Effort. Fig. 5 gives an overview of the required efforts. The conventional version was developed in 28 weeks and wins by a narrow margin. Since the same engineer was involved in requirements elicitation and in design and implementation the two numbers were added.

The VDM development took 28.5 weeks. Writing an abstract VDM-SL specification took 18 weeks. An initial phase of 6 weeks to learn the syntax and tool were not considered. Writing a concrete specification and validating it took 5 weeks each. It shall be pointed out that half a week devoted to code generation deserve the attribute "automatic". This includes installation work and time spent reading manuals.

Finally, a few points shall be made concerning the efforts: First, the ARCS engineers had major prior experience and domain knowledge. Second, the formal path has produced much more documentation in addition the actual development work. Also, the specification is considered to be at a higher level of abstraction than the given Pascal program.

Activity	Conv. version	Activity	Formal version
Requirements elicitation	8 weeks	Abstract Spec.	18 weeks
		Executable Spec.	5 weeks
Design, Implementation	20 weeks	Validation	5 weeks
		C++ code	1/2 week
Total Effort	**28 weeks**	Total Effort	**28 1/2 weeks**

Fig. 5. Comparison of Efforts spent for the Development of two Versions of SSD-0E

5   Interpretation of Results

We feel that the real benefits of using VDM (even in its light-weight form) are in the improvement of the quality of the requirements (by formalizing them), and in the fact that it can be objectively demonstrated that a software satisfies these requirements. However, the testing approach for validation is considered not to provide sufficient evidence for high quality software: it seems that tests only cover the transition from an abstract specification to an executable specification, while the most critical step of formal development is probably the transition from natural language requirements to the abstract specification. Furthermore, automatic code generation has some disadvantages: as automatically generated code is hardly readable, it seems very difficult to improve its performance or to find coding errors, although they seem very unlikely here.

We were surprised by the comparatively low cost of the formal development in the experiment. Of course, having a well trained specialist within a project team is a prerequisite. In a different environment, (e.g. when code generation cannot be used), the cost could increase, but still, it is within comparable dimensions to traditional design methods.

We think that it is important to choose the right project or software component (within a project) for being successful with light-weight VDM. Particularly components with high quality needs (e.g. components, which should often be reused or components with initially identified high risks) seem to be appropriate candidates. Today the highly dynamic market of software components with its frequently discussed quality aspects opens a wide area of application. To begin using VDM we feel that one should either hire somebody already familiar with these methods and tools or spend something like half a person-year to train one of the group. Since one of the major benefits of VDM is in the detection of errors in the requirements, in practice the dialog with the customer is influenced by the method. We think that the customer should not be burdened with the formalism of formal methods - it will be the developer's task to translate any improvements back into natural language requirements for the customer.

Based on the experiment described above and our conclusions we are convinced of the usefulness on certain areas and therefore we are considering to use light-weight VDM for the development of critical modules (probably not for a whole project).

References

Abr96.   J.-R. Abrial. *The B-Book: Assigning Programs to Meanings*. Cambridge University Press, 1996. 188, 191

Abr99.   J.-R. Abrial. System study: Method and example. Unpublished, 1999. 188, 189

BBFM99. P. Behm, P. Benoit, A. Faivre, and J.-M. Meynadier. METEOR : A successful application of B in a large project. In J. M. Wing, J. Woodcock, and J. Davies, editors, *Proceedings of FM'99 – Formal Methods, World Congress on Formal Methods in the Development of Computing Systems, Toulouse, France*, number 1708/1709 in Lecture Notes in Computer Science, pages 369–387. Springer-Verlag, 1999. 188

BDW96.   J. Bicarregui, J. Dick, and E. Woods. Quantitative analysis of an application of formal methods. In M.-C. Gaudel and J. Woodcock, editors, *FME'96: Industrial Benefit and Advances in Formal Methods*, volume 1051 of *Lecture Notes in Computer Science*, pages 60–?? Springer-Verlag, 1996. 188

BFL96.   T. M. Brookes, J. S. Fitzgerald, and P. G. Larsen. Formal and informal specifications of a secure system component: Final results in a comparative study. volume 1051 of *Lecture Notes in Computer Science*, pages 214–?? Springer-Verlag, 1996. 188

BH95.   J. P. Bowen and M. G. Hinchey. Ten commandments of formal methods. *Computer*, 28(4):56–63, April 1995. 187

CGR94.   D. Craigen, S. Gerhart, and T. Ralston. Case study: Paris Metro signaling system. *IEEE Software*, 11(1):32–35, January 1994. 188

CTW99.   M. Chaudron, J. Tretmans, and K. Wijbrans. Lessons from the application of formal methods to the design of a storm surge barrier control system. In J. M. Wing, J. Woodcock, and J. Davies, editors, *Proceedings of FM'99 – Formal Methods, World Congress on Formal Methods in the Development of Computing Systems, Toulouse, France*, number 1708/1709 in Lecture Notes in Computer Science, pages 1511–1526. Springer-Verlag, 1999. 188

Del99.   S. Dellacherie. *The specification and verification of an access control system using the LPV technology.* PhD thesis, University of Caen, France, 1999. 188, 189

DLV97.   L. Devauchelle, P. G. Larsen, and H. Voss. PICGAL: Practical use of formal specification to develop a complex critical system. In J. Fitzgerald, C. B. Jones, and P. Lucas, editors, *FME'97: Industrial Applications and Strengthened Foundations of Formal Methods. Proc. 4th Intl. Symposium of Formal Methods Europe, Graz, Austria, September 1997*, volume 1313 of *Lecture Notes in Computer Science*, pages 221–?? Springer-Verlag, 1997. 188

DPdB95.   E. H. Dürr, N. Plat, and M. de Boer. CombiCom: Tracking and tracing rail traffic using VDM++. In M. G. Hinchey and J. P. Bowen, editors, *Applications of Formal Methods*, Series in Computer Science, pages 203–226. Prentice Hall, 1995. 188

Dro99a.   G. Droschl. Analyzing the requirements of an access control using VDM-Tools and PVS (abstract). In *Proceedings of FM'99*, number 1708/1709 in Lecture Notes in Computer Science. Springer-Verlag, September 1999. 194

Dro99b.   G. Droschl. Design and application of a test case generator for VDM-SL. In *Workshop Materials: VDM in Practice!, Part of FM'99*. Springer-Verlag, September 1999. 193, 194

Dro99c.   G. Droschl. Events and scenarios in VDM and PVS. In *3rd Irish Workshop in Formal Methods, Galway*, Electronic Workshops in Computing. Springer-Verlag, July 1999. 193

Dro99d.   G. Droschl. Using PVS for requirements analysis of an access control. *Australian Journal of Information Systems*, 7(1):146–157, September 1999. Special issue on Requirements Engineering. 189

Dro00.   G. Droschl. *Formal Specification and Analysis of Requirements in Software Development.* PhD thesis, Institute for Software Technology, TU-Graz, Austria, April 2000. Supervisor: Peter Lucas. 189, 190, 193

ELL94.   R. Elmström, P. G. Larsen, and P. B. Lassen. The IFAD VDM-SL toolbox: A practical approach to formal specifications. *ACM SIGPLAN Notices*, 29(9):77–80, September 1994. 192

FL98.   J. Fitzgerald and P. G. Larsen. *Modelling Systems – Practical Tools and Techniques in Software Development.* Cambridge University Press, 1998. 187, 191, 192

HK91.   I. Houston and S. King. CICS project report: Experiences and results from the use of Z in IBM. volume 551 of *Lecture Notes in Computer Science*, pages 588–?? Springer-Verlag, 1991. 188

Jon90.   C. B. Jones. *Systematic Software Development Using VDM.* Prentice-Hall International, second edition, 1990. 187

KS93.   W. Kuhn and E. Schoitsch. Dependability of scaleable, distributed systems: Communication strategies for redundant processes. In *Proceedings of Safecomp'93, Poznan, Poland*. Springer-Verlag, 1993. 187, 189

PL92.   N. Plat and P. G. Larsen. An overview of the ISO/VDM-SL standard. *Sigplan Notices*, 27(8):76–82, August 1992. 192

Spi88.   M. Spivey. *Introducing Z: A Specification Language and its Formal Semantics.* Cambridge University Press, 1988. 188, 191

Formal Methods: The Problem Is Education

Thierry Scheurer

Department of Computation, University of Manchester
Institute of Science and Technology, Manchester M60 1QD, UK
t.scheurer@co.umist.ac.uk

Abstract. One of the most important contributory factors of software correctness, hence reliability, is the application of Formal Methods. These methods should be widely used in practice, but their acceptance by industry is well below what it should be. The most commonly mentioned way of improving on this situation is to reform education. This must address two issues. The first is to establish an *appropriate* concept of Formal Methods, one which is both sound and practicable. The second is to establish the proper way of teaching the appropriate methods. This paper addresses these two issues. First, it proposes a concept of Formal Methods and examines various misconceptions about these methods. The main tenet of the paper is that Formal Methods should give priority to the *formalisation of specifications* of system components over the production of completely formal proofs. Second, the paper reports on the author's experience in teaching Formal Methods and related topics at introductory (MSc conversion) level over many years. Examples of simple specifications are given, their contribution to students' education discussed, and a number of teaching recommendations are proposed.

1 Introduction

One of the most important contributory factors of software correctness, hence reliability, is the application of Formal Methods. The reason is that every stage of the software development process involves a combination of deductive reasoning and other activities, such as empirical observation, empirical induction, conjecture or simply imagination. Digital computers are capable of extremely complex behaviour, but this behaviour is *entirely predictable* by deductive reasoning. Consequently, deductive reasoning plays a central role in software development, the more so at the stages closer to programming in machine-executable language. The *essence* of deductive reasoning is precisely that it can be *formalised*, i.e. expressed explicitly in a very accurate manner. (Symbolic logic, which is the root of formalisation, has been aptly defined as 'a model of deductive thought' [10].) This formalisation is fundamental: it appears to be the only way of demonstrating the validity of deductions. This view is supported by the totality of the mathematical experience acquired by mankind over the

F. Koornneef and M. van der Meulen (Eds.): SAFECOMP 2000, LNCS 1943, pp. 198–210, 2000.

centuries. Consequently, it is reasonable to conclude that formalisation is not simply a major factor of software quality, especially correctness: *it is its dominant factor*, well ahead of any other sources.

Formalisation is not a unique process: there are many different ways of formalising ideas, some more appropriate than others – to see this, simply consider the multiplicity of mathematical theories, calculi, programming languages, etc., all with their relative advantages and disadvantages. Another key question is the extent to which formalisation should be applied in software development. One option is to limit formalisation to the *specification* of system components, and to allow other aspects of deductive reasoning to be conducted informally or semi-formally. The other option is to insist on a complete formalisation of deductive reasoning, i.e. the production of completely formalised proofs of system components. Therefore a key question to resolve is what formalisation is *appropriate* for each aspect of software development.

The aims of this paper are twofold. The first is to examine the concept of Formal Methods, some key views about them and their status in IT. The conclusion will be that although these methods should play a central role in industry, this is far from being the case, and the primary remedy to this state of affairs must be a reform of education. The second aim of the paper is to present the author's experience in teaching Formal Methods and related topics at introductory (MSc conversion) level over many years, as a contribution to the two related questions: what Formal Methods are appropriate, and how they should be taught. The lessons that may be learnt from this experience concur largely in particular with the views presented by A. Hall in his seminal paper 'Seven Myths of Formal Methods' [15].

The plan of the paper is as follows. In Section 2 we discuss alternative concepts of Formal Methods. Then we expand this discussion by analysing three major misconceptions about them. Finally, we discuss the low acceptance of Formal Methods by industry and present the case for a reform of education to remedy this situation. In Section 3 we describe the basis of the author's teaching experience and present the lessons learnt from this experience. We conclude in Section 4.

2   A Concept of Formal Methods

2.1   Specifications versus Proofs

Many definitions of Formal Methods can be found in the literature, e.g. [9], [11], [17], [18], [19], [23], [28], [29], [33]. A common view regards as 'formal' only those methods involving the complete formalisation of *both specifications and proofs* of systems. For instance the emphasis on formal proofs is particularly strong in VDM [19], and it is the essence of higher-order logic and related systems, as described in [17] and [23] for instance. An alternative and more liberal definition, adopted in this paper, regards as formal any method that satisfies the following two main conditions. First, it must involve a special notation with at least a well-defined syntax. Second, it must explicitly *support deductive reasoning* in software development. However, the method is not required to construct completely formalised proofs. Its aim is primarily to formalise *specifications* and to encourage *informal* deductions; and only secondarily, to pave the way towards the progressive formalisation of proofs, where these are particularly critical. The proponents of the Z notation for instance incline towards this second definition [15], [20], [29], [33]. Its validity is argued in the author's textbook [26], and a main aim of this paper is to show that it is supported by the author's teaching experience. Next, we first expand on the conflicting views held on Formal Methods and their consequence; then we turn to teaching issues.

2.2   Some Misconceptions about Formal Methods

Many opposing views have been expressed about Formal Methods, their nature and potential [2], [15]. It is essential here to distinguish the views of experts from those of potential users: software engineers, analysts, programmers and, indirectly, managers; for our purpose, it is the latter that matter. Our aim now is not to reproduce the comprehensive lists of misconceptions that can be found in the literature; it is to discuss a selection of only three of them, which appear to form the main bar to the adoption of Formal Methods by practitioners.

Misconception 1: The sole purpose of Formal Methods is to produce complete formal proofs of programs

The complete formal proof of a program is an attractive ideal, and it must be stressed that proof methods have been brought to a high level of perfection; see [14] for instance. The reason for a complete formalisation of proofs is that it is a necessary condition for their automation, which in turn greatly reduces the chances of errors in the proofs themselves. Unfortunately this ideal has proved to be very difficult to attain in practice [15]. This then leads to the second question: can we settle for a compromise, i.e. methods involving only a limited formalisation of proofs? A key tenet of this paper is that this is indeed a valid objective, for the following reasons.

First, we must distinguish *two* definitions of 'proof' [26]. In the first sense, a proof is an argument, expressed in any form, and sufficiently rigorous to convince a competent person of the truth of some proposition. In the second sense, a proof is completely formal. This means that the proposition to prove is represented by a list of symbols in a syntactically well-defined notation, and this list has been generated by equally well-defined symbol manipulation rules (called rules of inference) from initial propositions taken as axioms. The question then is: is a proof in the first sense acceptable?

The answer is 'yes', by the following argument. We must accept that if the proof is partly informal, it cannot be automated, and there is no absolute guarantee that it is valid. But it lends at least a *very high degree of confidence* in the proposition proved, which is clearly a major gain over the mere acceptance of the proposition as 'obvious'. The empirical evidence of this fact is provided by all the achievements of mathematics over the centuries. The vast majority of proofs in this discipline are of the first type. It is well known that they are not immune to errors, but the totality of the results obtained shows the high degree of certainty that such proofs have provided.

Second, in the development of a system (which could be a component of a larger system), a proof generally involves three main elements: (a) a *specification* of the properties required of the system, (b) the system itself – typically, a module or program *text* in some notation – and (c) the demonstration that the latter satisfies the conditions stated in the former. Experience shows that specifications are often easier to establish than full proofs. Moreover, the formalisation of a specification on its own is a very useful step by its sheer precision, even if the rest of the proof is not completely formalised. This point is expanded below.

To sum up, our first tenet is this. The purpose of a Formal Method is not necessarily to produce complete formal proofs of systems. It is first to formalise the specifications of systems and their components, possibly selectively; second, to support the production of at least informal proofs; and third, to support the progressive formalisation of such proofs.

Misconception 2: Formal Methods are excessively complex

Another frequent belief is that Formal Methods require a high level of mathematical expertise, and that this difficulty is compounded by often arcane symbolism, putting them way beyond the grasp of 'ordinary practitioners' [15]. There are two likely reasons for such a belief. The first is the previous misconception that Formal Methods are necessarily about formally proving programs. As mentioned above, complete proofs are generally much more difficult to work out than just specifications, and it is true that the full proof of seemingly trivial programs may require considerable skills. A good example in the author's experience is the proof of the binary search algorithm: the system of loop invariants it requires is surprisingly complex by comparison with the conceptual simplicity of the algorithm and the shortness of its implementation (five Pascal lines for the loop).

The second reason is the nature of the vast academic research that may be classified under the name 'Formal Methods'. This is indeed often very advanced, if we are to judge by the underlying theories involved, e.g.: Algebraic Semantics, Denotational Semantics, Type Theory, Combinatory Logic, Category Theory, Universal Algebra, Process Calculi (CCS, CSP, etc.) and so on. It is not difficult to see why confusing Formal Methods with such academic research is bound to lead to the misconception stated.

The reality is quite different. First, if we allow Formal Methods to be concerned with formalising specifications only, then the difficulty of establishing full proofs is removed. For instance consider the formal expression of the property that a C array A of n integers is in ascending order (assuming the members of A are indexed from 0 to n−1):

```
for all i such that 0 <= i and i < n-1 (A[i] <= A[i+1])
```

This condition, which is part of the specification of a function to sort A in ascending order, is in itself already invaluable. Clearly, it is much more precise than the informal counterpart 'A is sorted in ascending order'; it is no more difficult to understand, and much shorter, than any sorting algorithm; and it already contains a good deal of information which may be used to question its suitability or guide the construction of the algorithm. Two examples illustrate this last point: (a) the fact that a given value may occur several times in A, shown by the second occurrence of '<=' instead of '<'; (b) the fact that any test 'A[i] <= A[i+1]' should not be performed for a value of i greater than n-2. These two facts are not 'immediately obvious' and may have important implications: The first may suggest that the *specification* should be strengthened to disallow multiple occurrences of a value in A, for whatever reason. The second should help prevent a classical programming error.

Second, Formal Methods need not be equated with the more advanced research carried out in universities and other research institutions. Many useful and practical specifications require no more than a knowledge of elementary logic and set theory. The special symbolism involved is much smaller than any popular imperative programming language, and our experience of many years demonstrates that this can be acquired in a one-semester module by students with *no* initial knowledge of mathematics beyond simple arithmetic. The above formal definition of an integer array in ascending order is a typical example of such specifications.

Misconception 3: Formal Methods are too expensive

This third misconception is the consequence of the previous two. A 'difficult' method is expensive for two reasons, which combine multiplicatively. First, it requires special knowledge and skills, which in general must be paid for. Second, it is likely to be relatively time-consuming to apply. Further hidden costs may be perceived, e.g. the risk of excessive dependence on specialists, culture clashes between old and new methods, etc.

From our answers to the first two misconceptions, this view too may be largely refuted. First, the *training* costs need not exceed those required by the methods of Software Engineering which are 'inevitable', such as programming or effective use of essential tools. Second, a formal specification of a system or system component is generally shorter than the system itself. Again, the above example of the formal specification of an array in ascending order is typical. Moreover, the very task of implementing the required component, as a problem-solving exercise, is generally bound to be *substantially more demanding* than that of producing its specification alone. Consequently, in many practical cases, the cost of additional Formal Methods is likely to be a fraction of the minimum cost of software development, particularly if the former is confined to formalising specifications.

Actually, this additional cost may well be more than outweighed by the savings that Formal Methods may entail. The measurement of such savings has proved to be very difficult in practice. But it is also widely accepted that the sooner errors are identified, the easier, i.e. cheaper, they are to rectify [32]. As the primary function of a formal specification of a system is to enable the proof of its correctness, this effect is certain to be significant. (The difficulty of measuring the benefits of a method does not imply they do not exist.) Thus, the likelihood of a *decrease* in the total cost of software development resulting from the introduction of 'well-targeted' Formal Methods is at least a tenable proposition. All these points are reported in [15]. See also Boehm's classical model Cocomo of software development time and cost, in particular his graph and comments on the relative cost of errors at each stage of the software life cycle [1].

2.3   Consequence: Formal Methods in Industry and the Role of Education

The above analysis suggests that *appropriate* Formal Methods are a major means of achieving high software reliability, in fact arguably the *primary means*. As Bowen and Hinchey argue [2], these methods must be recommended as a guarantee of software correctness not only for safety- and security-critical systems, but also for the much wider range of applications in which the consequences of failure might be catastrophic for any reason, including economic. A similar view is expressed in [4], in which such applications are referred to as 'enterprise-critical systems'. Furthermore, contrary to the misconceptions discussed, for 'reasonable goals', Formal Methods are practical, feasible, need not entail excessive additional costs, and are likely to result in actual substantial savings in the long term, even though evidence of this last point is hard to come by.

Accordingly, Formal Methods should have been adopted by industry with the same enthusiasm as the 'primary' tools of IT: computers, communication technology, programming languages and application packages; or as the popular programming paradigms such as Structured Programming in the seventies, and Object-Oriented Programming today. Yet the opposite is true: To date, these methods are far from having been taken up by industry on the scale they should have. Their low acceptance by industry is undeniable, and must be regarded as a major concern by the IT community.

This state of affairs can only be explained by the misconceptions stated, but this does not address its root causes. From several papers considering this issue, one conclusion emerges: The most commonly mentioned way of resolving this situation is *a reform of education*. For instance, Bowen and Stavridou state: "Currently, a major barrier to the acceptance of Formal Methods is the fact that many engineers and programmers do not have the appropriate training to make use of them, and many managers do not know when and how they may be applied" [3]. Garlan concurs: "A critical issue in the design of a professional Software Engineering degree program is the way in which Formal Methods are integrated into the curriculum" [13]. Cuadrado makes a plea for US firms to develop the teaching and use of Formal Methods in colleges [5]. Parnas is pessimistic about the influence of academic research on industrial practice [21], but stresses too the importance of education: "For Formal Methods technology transfer to succeed, we must do two things: (1) integrate Formal Methods into basic university programming courses, and (2) improve the methods until they are better suited for practical application" [22]. Ralston, Gerhart and Craigen report on surveys of education and training and the requirements for the successful transfer of Formal Methods to industry [25]. Further similar views are expressed in [6], [27], [30] and [31]. See also [8].

In conclusion, there is wide support for the view that a reform of education is necessary in order to secure the acceptance of Formal Methods by industry. The question then is: in which direction this reform, if the disappointments of the past must not be repeated? The remainder of this paper is devoted to the lessons that may be learnt from the author's experience in teaching these methods at an introductory level, by way of contribution to this debate.

3   The Author's Teaching Experience

3.1   Basis of the Author's Experience

The author's main relevant responsibilities have been the teaching of two parallel modules in the first semester of an MSc conversion course, the MSc in Computation at UMIST, Manchester, over a period of more than a decade. The course has grown in size regularly from an annual intake of about 15 in the seventies to about 60 in the second half of the nineties. It is open to all graduates of non-computing disciplines. There has always been a balance of graduates from engineering and scientific disciplines and from the humanities. Women are encouraged to join and the female-male ratio (25%-75% in recent years) is markedly higher than in undergraduate computing courses in British universities. Apart from a good first degree (normally 2.1) there are no prerequisites. Teaching is from first principles and in particular many applicants come with no knowledge of mathematics beyond elementary arithmetic. Thus the intake may be regarded as a fairly good cross-section of the graduate population, those who will form the backbone of tomorrow's IT. The course is vocational and demanding. Significantly, there is no marked difference between the performance distributions of Arts versus Science students, and of female versus male.

The two modules taught by the author are closely related. The first, called *Foundations of Computation*, covers set theory and propositional logic. The emphasis is on the practical applicability of the theory: A substantial part of the course is devoted to the construction of simple 'Z-like' information system models in set theory. The full notation of first-order logic is used in the presentation of set theory, in particular the logical quantifiers. However, full treatment of first-order logic, including structures, is not covered as it would be well beyond the scope of an introductory course. Propositional logic is treated rigorously, as a first example of a simple formal language with an inductively-defined syntax and recursively-defined semantics. The material taught represents about one third of [26].

The second module, called *High-level Programming*, is an introduction to program design principles and programming in C. (A move to Java is planned for 2000-2001.) A distinctive feature of this module is an introduction to Formal Methods at the program design stage, mainly through the systematic specification of functions by pre- and postconditions. Principles are illustrated through weekly programming exercises. These are highly specified in the manner indicated. In each case, much of the student's task consists of *reading* the formal specifications given and demonstrating an understanding of their implications through correct implementations. The practice of verification of the code produced by deductive reasoning is constantly emphasised. The close connection between the two modules is also regularly stressed.

3.2   Lessons Learnt

The experience of teaching these two modules over many years has led the author to a number of conclusions. The most relevant are as follows.

Formal specifications versus proofs

In both modules, the emphasis is put primarily on *specification*, i.e. *formalising* ideas, rather than *proving* facts systematically. This is based on three observations: First, the formalisation of an idea, i.e. its expression in a special notation, is already a serious difficulty in its own right which can only be overcome through repeated practice. Second, the formalisation of ideas is a necessary first step of any proof: a proposition can be proved only if its content is clear, i.e. if it has been properly formulated. Third, in general, the proof of a proposition, as a mechanism, is much more difficult to grasp than the proposition to prove on its own. To follow proofs of even seemingly simple facts requires intellectual discipline, which either dedication or long practice may bring about. (Recall the example of the binary search algorithm given above.) To insist on taking beginners through complete, formal proofs before they have even mastered the notation used is likely to be *most counterproductive*: They may well conclude, prematurely, that (a) the method is beyond their ability and (b) it is excessively complex (and tedious!) for the results achieved. (Students might benefit more from an introduction to such classics on problem solving in general, which subsumes the problem of constructing a proof, as Descartes's *Discourse on Method* [7] and Pólya's popular *How to Solve It* [24].)

Now the reader may well wonder whether on its own, the formalisation of ideas achieves anything? The answer is definitely 'yes'. First, the student is confronted with a general fact of capital importance: this is the great difficulty, in general, of expressing an idea *precisely* in natural language – English in our case. The whole point of resorting to formal notation is primarily to overcome the shortcomings of natural language where precision is essential: ambiguity, verbosity, irregularity, in general complexity due to the very richness of the language (all features which, in other contexts, may well be regarded as qualities rather than weaknesses). Learning to *see* the precision of formal notation, for instance set theory expressed in the language of first-order logic, is a first objective of major importance.

A second benefit of a specification on its own is that it acts as a *mental pivot*. It fixes key facts from which useful information may then be derived. In other words it naturally supports the reflective process involved in system development, both *ex-ante* by *guiding* the implementation of the component specified, and *ex-post* by providing a means of checking this implementation, even if informally. This is certainly the key lesson to be learnt from Floyd's seminal 1967 paper recommending the use of assertions in programs [12], [14]; these are no more than specifications in our sense.

A third benefit concerns the students' long-term education. The formal specification of a component *is* a first step in the direction of a complete formal proof of the component. As students learn to work with formal specifications, and to relate implementations to specifications, they may be expected to see progressively by themselves what a proof entails and how to construct it systematically. They will be better prepared and positively motivated to embrace this ultimate aim of Formal Methods.

Example

These three points may be illustrated by the following example, which naturally builds on the above formal definition of an array of numbers sorted in ascending order. Consider the specification of a function *Pos* taking as arguments (a) a list L of natural numbers in ascending order, (b) the number n of members of L and (c) a certain integer *key*, and returning the position of *key* in L if it occurs there. Using the notation of set theory for variety, *Pos* can be specified as follows. Let Nat denote the set of natural numbers i.e. Nat = {0, 1, 2, ...}, and assume that the list L is defined as a function from {0, 1, ..., n-1} to Nat for given n: Nat. Furthermore, extend Nat with a special value *Undef*. This is to be the result to be returned by *Pos* if *key* does not occur in L. *Pos* may now be specified as follows:

Given L, n and *key* as defined, $Pos(L, n, key) = p$: Nat + {*Undef*} satisfying the following property:

$$(\exists\, i: \text{Nat with } 0 \leq i \leq n\text{-}1 \cdot L(i) = key) \Rightarrow (p \in \text{Nat} \wedge L(p) = key)$$
$$(\forall\, i: \text{Nat with } 0 \leq i \leq n\text{-}1 \cdot L(i) \neq key) \Rightarrow (p = Undef)$$

In English, the definition of p (i.e. the postcondition of *Pos*) says quite naturally: if there is an index i such that *key* equals $L(i)$, i.e. if *key* occurs in L, then p is an index of L such that $L(p) = key$, i.e. p is *a* position of *key* within L. Otherwise, i.e. if every value of L is different from *key*, then p is undefined, which is represented by $p = Undef$. (The symbol '+' is used to denote the union of two *disjoint* sets; '*x*: *S*' means '*by definition* $x \in S$')

This is the level of formalism that is 'just achievable' on a beginners' course such as the Foundations module or the High-level programming module. To expect students systematically to derive or prove an implementation of *Pos* from it would be excessive at this level. But students may already learn a great deal from it. First, this specification clearly addresses a common problem of practical importance. Second, students can see how vague English statements such as '*key* occurs in *L*', its negation, or 'position of *key* in *L*' may be given a very precise form, using the existential and the universal quantifiers for the first two statements. Third, they may start reasoning about the specification itself. For instance they may ask: is this specification *consistent*? What if $n = 0$, does it still make sense? If they see that it does, as they should, will they see that in this case the formal specification does imply that *key* does not occur in L, in accordance with common sense? Likewise if *key* occurs in L, should we not state more precisely that p must be a member not just of Nat, but of its subset {0,..., n-1}? This can indeed be done, a definite improvement. A final question that may well be suggested by the specification is: what if $L(i) = key$ for *several* indexes i: {0, ..., n-1}? In that case, students should see that the specification says: *Pos* may return *any one* of these indexes, i.e. it is *underdetermined*. All these are questions of potentially vital importance. Fourth, students may well conclude that the specification is not adequate, for any reason. For instance, they may feel that the case $n = 0$ should not be allowed, and therefore add a further precondition $0 < n$. Or, they may think that the values of L should all be different, i.e. that L should be *injective* to be precise, and impose that as another precondition. Fifth, the students should now have an understanding of the problem – the implementation of *Pos* – in terms much closer to the solution than the initial English counterpart. For instance they may see that some repetition will be needed, and they are reminded that any test '$L(i) = key$' makes sense only if i is in the range $\{0, \ldots, n\text{-}1\}$. Clearly, they are now better equipped to solve the problem and check their solution against the specification.

Other priorities

Finally, a number of further priority goals appropriate for an introductory course were identified over the years. They may be summarised as follows:

(1)   Teach set theory and logic primarily as a notation with a minimum of symbols, and give priority to the simplest ways of formulating ideas. Encourage students to practise the *formulation* of simple concepts, and to translate ideas from English to set theory and vice-versa. Emphasise the simplicity and *naturalness*, i.e. closeness to English, of the special notation.

(2)   Give priority to *a few fundamental ideas*, but insist on students *mastering* them. In his popular book 'Naïve Set Theory', Halmos makes this recommendation to the reader: 'Read it, *absorb* it, and forget it' [16]. This is certainly sound advice. Three steps are required to achieve mastery of a theory: *understanding, memorising*, and *applying*. Students must be made to see that these are both essential and highly complementary. Understanding is an obvious requisite, and clearly facilitates memorising; but the opposite is equally true: it is a fact of experience, too often ignored nowadays, that *memorising is often a factor of understanding*. This is particularly true of formal subjects. Once memorised, an idea is instantly available in the mind of its owner, and this ability of quick recall often plays a key role in learning new ideas or following more complex lines of thought. As for applying, this is one of the major factors and safest tests of understanding. Thus, students should constantly be made to work out instances of general principles, to rediscover the latter from the former, and to establish the precise links between the two.

(3)   Start with the specification of simple information systems. Two examples used in the Foundations module are as follows:
   (a)   A model of an *evolving* set, which may be used to describe the evolution of a club, a library as a set of book copies, etc. The evolving object is modelled as an object going through successive states, each defined as a subset of some predefined set (set of people, book copies, etc.). The successive states are generated by three operations, namely Emp, which returns the empty set; Ins, which 'inserts' a new member into its main argument; and Rem, which 'removes' a member.
   (b)   A model of an evolving dictionary, which may be used to describe the evolution of a dictionary proper, a directory, an address book, etc. Here the evolving object is modelled as an object whose successive states are partial

functions D from a constant domain, *Words*, to a constant codomain, *Definitions*. State changes are modelled by operations similar to those of the set model.

These two examples are both simple and relevant. They already illustrate a number of important points, in particular: (a) the fundamental distinction between essentially 'static' objects (like pure sets and numbers) and *evolving* ones; (b) the alternatives open to the modeller in designing operations, in particular the adoption of appropriate preconditions; (c) the design decision illustrated by both models to use *basic* operations, i.e. making one elementary change at a time, rather than compound operations; (d) the need to reason about these alternatives and their consequences; and (e) the abstract nature of the models, which enables the modeller to focus on essential features separately from implementation concerns. All of these are major themes of Software Engineering.

4   Conclusion

The promotion of Formal Methods in industry is still one of the most important tasks of Software Engineering today. It is essential to find the proper way to do so in order to avoid repeating the errors of the past. That industry has been reluctant to adopt Formal Methods for so long must not be dismissed lightly. Failing to recognise the true reasons of this state of affairs may only lead to further disappointment, with perhaps even more negative consequences than has been the case in the past.

This task has two main aspects. The first is to establish the *appropriate* Formal Methods required at each stage of the software life cycle. This must allow for all relevant aspects in each case: nature and objectives of the project involved; level of training and competence of the system development team; culture and traditions of the host company; etc. The second is to establish the proper way of teaching these methods, i.e. the educational problem, either in institutions of education or as part of companies' own training programmes. In this second respect, perhaps the most important rule to remember is that ideas can only be learnt *progressively*, in the right order, at the right pace.

Therefore, it is always better to start with less ambitious but achievable objectives than with grand but unattainable ones. This strategy would be wrong if the pursuit of the former was detrimental to the latter. Happily, the opposite is true: a fortunate feature of Formal Methods is that they may be introduced progressively, specifications first and then formal proofs. Indeed this is their natural order of application; moreover each stage paves the way to the next.

Finally, do formal proofs have a place in education? The answer must be definitely 'yes', but *at the right stage* of the student's development, i.e. only when the notation has been fully mastered and applied extensively to the formulation and use of specifications. Then only will the student see the point of such methods and benefit from them. To introduce these methods too early may only lead to inadequate levels of achievement, disillusion and the perpetuation of prejudices against Formal Methods.

Acknowledgements

The author wishes to acknowledge with thanks the contributions made by the following: John Harris, for his assistance in the literature survey and comments on initial drafts of the paper; Mauricette Scheurer, for providing an excellent reference and URL management tool; the referees and colleagues of the Department of Computation, for their constructive criticisms of the paper.

References

1. Boehm, B. W. *Software Engineering Economics.*   Prentice Hall, Englewood Cliffs, N.J. (1981)
2. Bowen, J. P. and Hinchey, M. G. Seven more myths of formal methods. IEEE Software, July (1995)
3. Bowen, J. and Stavridou V. Safety-critical systems, formal methods and standards. Software Engineering Journal, Vol 8, No 4 (1993) 189-209
4. Clarke, E. M., Wing, J. M. et al. Formal Methods : State of the art and future directions. ACM Computing Surveys, Vol 28, No 4 (1996)
5. Cuadrado, J. Teach formal methods. Byte, Vol 19, No 12 (1994) 292
6. Dean, C. N. and Hinchey, M. G. (Eds). *Teaching and Learning Formal Methods.* Academic Press, San Diego, Calif. (1996)
7. Descartes, R. *Discours de la Méthode* (1637). English translation by F. E. Sutcliffe, *Discourse on Method and the Meditations.* Penguin Books, Harmondsworth, England (1968)
8. Dick, J. and Woods, E. Lessons learned from rigorous system software development. Information and Software Technology, Vol 39, No 8 (1997) 551-560
9. Dix, A. *Formal Methods for Interactive Systems.* Academic Press, San Diego, Calif. (1991)
10. Enderton, H. B. *A Mathematical Introduction to Logic.* Academic Press, New York (1972)
11. Feijs, L.M.G. and Jonkers, H.B.M. *Formal Specification and Design.* Cambridge University Press, Cambridge, England (1992)
12. Floyd, R. Assigning meaning to programs. In *Mathematical Aspects of Computer Science*, XIX American Mathematical Society (1967) 19-32
13. Garlan, D. Making formal methods education effective for professionals. Information and Software Technology, Vol 37, No 5-6 (1995) 261-268
14. Gries, D. *The Science of Programming.* Springer-Verlag, New York (1981)
15. Hall, A. Seven myths of Formal Methods. IEEE Software, September (1990)
16. Halmos, P. R. *Naïve Set Theory.* Springer-Verlag, New York (1974)
17. Hoare, C.A.R. and Shepherdson, J.C. *Mathematical Logic and Programming Languages.* Prentice-Hall International, London (1985)
18. Ince, D.C. *An Introduction to Discrete Mathematics and Formal System Specification.* Clarendon Press, Oxford (1988)

19. Jones, C.B. *Systematic Software Development Using VDM.* Prentice-Hall International, London (1986)
20. McDermid, J. A. (Ed). *The Theory and Practice of Refinement : Approaches to the Formal Development of Large-Scale Software Systems.* Butterworth & Co. (Publishers) Ltd (1989)
21. Parnas, D. L. On ICSE's "Most influential" papers. ACM SIGSOFT Software Engineering Notes, Vol 20, No 3 (1995) 29-32
22. Parnas, D. L. "Formal Methods" Technology Transfer Will Fail. Journal of Systems and Software, Vol 40, No 3 (1998) 195-198
23. Paulson, L. C. *Logic and Computation.* Cambridge University Press, Cambridge, England (1987)
24. Pólya G. *How to Solve It.* 2nd renewed edition, Penguin Books, London (1990)
25. Ralston, T., Gerhart, S., and Craigen, D. The role of education and training in the industrial application of formal methods. Algebraic methodology and software technology, Lecture Notes in Computer Science, Vol 936 (1995) 41-49
26. Scheurer, T. *Foundations of Computing.* Addison-Wesley, Wokingham, England (1994)
27. Sobel, A. E. K. Applying an operational formal method throughout software engineering education. Information and Software Technology, Vol 40, No 4 (1998) 233-238
28. Sommerville, I. *Software Engineering.* 3rd Ed., Addison-Wesley, Wokingham, England (1989)
29. Spivey, J.M. *The Z Notation: A Reference Manual.* Prentice-Hall International, London (1989)
30. Thimbleby, H. Computerised Parkinson's law. Computing & Control Engineering Journal, Vol 4, No 5 (1993) 197-198
31. Tse, T. H. Formal or informal, practical or impractical - towards integrating formal methods with informal practices in software engineering-education. Software Engineering Education, IFIP Transactions A - Computer Science and Technology, Vol 40, (1993) 189-197.
32. Woodcock, J. C. P. Calculating properties of Z specifications. ACM SIGSoft Software-Eng. Notes (1989) 43-54
33. Wordsworth, J. B. *Software Development with Z.* Addison-Wesley, Wokingham, England (1992)

Formal Methods Diffusion:
Past Lessons and Future Prospects

R. Bloomfield[1], D. Craigen[2], F. Koob[3], M. Ullmann[3], and S.Wittmann[3]

[1] Adelard, United Kingdom,
reb@adelard.co.uk
[2] ORA, Canada
dan@ora.on.ca
[3] Bundesamt fuer Sicherheit in der Informationstechnik, Germany
{koob,ullmann,wittmann}@bsi.de

Abstract. Based on a study by Adelard (UK) commissioned by the German Bundesamt fuer Sicherheit in der Informationstechnik this paper identifies crucial factors leading to the success or failure of the application of formal methods and provides ideas of improved technology adoption perspectives by analysing the formal methods market.

1   Introduction

The application of formal methods has a long history but they have not been substantially adopted by the software engineering community at large. To gain a perspective of what is working and what is not in the formal methods area we have reviewed their use by industry and the results of past R&D programmes. The objective is to identify crucial factors leading to the success or failure of the application of formal methods and in doing so provide a perspective on the current formal methods landscape. The overall aim is to inform future formal methods dissemination activities and other initiatives. An introduction to formal methods is the "Guidance on the use of Formal Methods in the Development and Assurance of High Integrity Industrial Computer Systems" (available at www.ewics.org).

2   The Formal Methods Landscape

In the report [1] we develop a picture of the formal methods landscape based on existing surveys (especially [2]), and:

- A survey of the conference circuit.
- A review of past R&D including the UK Alvey programme and its evaluation [3], the European ESPRIT programme, and other related part funded R&D.

F. Koornneef and M. van der Meulen (Eds.): SAFECOMP 2000, LNCS 1943, pp. 211-226, 2000.

- A survey of U.S. R&D programmes relating to security-critical and safety critical applications. The safety-critical formal methods research programme at NASA [4] was of particular interest.

This was augmented with interviews with formal methods practitioners, sponsors and other (past or present) technology stakeholders. Additionally, we reviewed formal methods applications in three key industrial areas: safety, security, and hardware and microcode verification.

2.1   Safety Systems

The use of formal methods with railway systems originated in about 1988 and since then has seen an increasing scope in their use, greater machine support achieved by the development of the B Method and the Atelier B toolset, and more recently the integration of the formal methods with the requirements engineering process. Formal methods have been applied to a number of train protection products (e.g. those used on the Cairo and Calcutta Metros and recently to the new Paris metro line [5]). The costs of applying formal methods have decreased by about two orders of magnitude from the early projects reported in [2] and from 0.5 to 2 lines per hour using B today [6]. We also looked at the use of special purpose theorem provers to model specifications [7], and some protocols have been analysed in detail with the HOL theorem prover as part of academic research [8]. The ability to model the railway signalling philosophy and demonstrate with high confidence that changes to it are consistent and safe may be an important tool in facing the future challenges of new and hybrid control regimes. There are examples of model checking using SPIN [9] and Prover [10]. There are also some significant applications of RAISE as reported in [11].

As for defence applications there is work stimulated by the UK. The Ministry of Defence standard Def Stan 00-55 sets out requirements for a formal methods based approach. The application of this standard has been progressive. One of the first applications is reported in [12]. There is also the verification of the safety critical software used in the Hercules C130J aircraft [13].

The avionics industry approach is represented by the requirements of DO-178B: formal methods are not mandated in DO-178B. Formal methods were applied to certain critical algorithms in the Boeing 777 Primary Flight Computer. Formal specification was beneficial in some of the simpler algorithms, and problems were identified and resolved. However, formal proof was less beneficial in the same algorithms and the task was labour intensive of the highest grade of effort. Attempts to apply formal methods to more complex algorithms also required high-grade effort and produced no useful result (as reported in [14]).

Much work on flight critical aspects has been sponsored by NASA and is described in [4], [15]. Rushby's work on formal methods and assurance is widely read in the safety critical community [16]. The parallel made between proof and calculation is an important insight underwriting the need for capable tools. The development of PVS and its associated application in requirements, hardware verification and fault tolerance is a significant step in demonstrating the potential of formal methods tools (PVS has been installed at over 1200 sites).

Earlier work in the aerospace sector [17] provides an example of over claiming, or at least a lesson in the care needed when presenting the results of this type of work. An independent investigation into the project provided some detailed criticism and later work showed flaws in the proofs that were undertaken.

There is considerable work in Europe on the development of drive by wire automotive systems and the use of deterministic time triggered architectures with formally verified hardware and protocols. The automotive industry has also sponsored the development of a verified compiler for PLCs [18]. There is also related work in the defence industry [19].

There are emerging new applications of model checking to operator procedures in aerospace, air traffic control and nuclear applications [20], [21]. Work is being carried out in both air traffic control and nuclear plant control in which the complex procedures that have to be followed by the operator are formally modelled and desirable properties proved.

While the process industry does not appear to be innovative in its use of formal methods the application of model checking to PLC programs seems a promising area and one that has been picked up by the SACRES project led by Siemens. There is also perhaps the world's only shrink-wrapped formally specified product, DUST-EXPERT™, an advisory system on avoiding dust explosions [22]. DUST-EXPERT™ was developed by Adelard and involved a 20k line VDM specification.

2.2   Security Applications

Since the 1970s there has been significant investment into formal methods by agencies concerned with national security. Investment by these agencies has helped to accelerate certain aspects of formal methods, but has also retarded evolution through, for example, restrictions on the dissemination of research results and on the distribution of leading-edge formal methods systems. Many of these restrictions have now been significantly eased.

In North America, early security-related formal methods research was aimed at tool-supported processes, with definite emphasis on relating formal security models, through top level specifications, to code. Systems such as the Gypsy Verification Environment, HDM, Ina Jo, and m-EVES all aimed at handling the above, with varying degrees of success. Early research emphasised processes and tools that led to "code verification." Some of these systems (or their ilk) were used, again with varying degrees of success, on security products of some importance to national governments. Deployed security-related systems exist that have benefited from these tool-supported analyses.

From a formal methods perspective, there appears to have been a change on the application of the technology from the 70s/80s to the current day. While much of the early focus (at least in North America) was on tools and processes that handled the entire development process (from security models to code), much of the current work appears to be at a security modelling level. A review of the literature suggests substantial work on cryptographic/security protocols and pointwise applications elsewhere. As an example of the current work with formal methods on security protocols, consider a July 1999 workshop on the subject [23].

It appears that most efforts at evaluating security products are occurring at the EAL4 Common Criteria level or below (ITSEC level E3 or below, respectively) and, consequently, limiting the application of formal methods technology. It also appears that there is a much improved understanding within the security community on how to make use of formal methods technology in a manner that is much more effective than the earlier efforts in the 70s/80s, when formal methods tools were prematurely applied to significantly complex tasks. The use of formal methods by the security community seems consistent with the use of the technology by other communities: formal modelling is used to improve understanding of the artefacts being developed, while formal analysis is used both to "formally debug" formal models and to provide assurance of consistency (e.g., between a security policy and a top level specification).

2.3   Hardware and Microcode Verification

There is an enormous amount of work on the application of formal methods to the design and verification of hardware designs. Formal methods appear to be having a (potentially) major impact in the hardware industry. Some of the large hardware vendors are either developing in-house capabilities in formal verification (e.g., Intel) or are adopting externally developed technologies (e.g., AMD with ACL2). The forthcoming Merced chip from Intel may be the first mass produced artefact to have formally verified parts of the hardware and microcode design (verified using HOL) although Intel have also retrospectively verified the floating point arithmetic of the Pentium Pro processor [24]. In doing so they have developed a framework that combines advanced model-checking technology, user-guided theorem-proving software, and decision procedures that facilitate arithmetic reasoning.

Model checking and related automatic decision procedures are the most widespread verification technology used in hardware verification. A significant amount of research work on Binary Decision Diagrams (BDDs), their optimisation and applications has been reported at FMCAD. Theorem proving, however, was not absent as indicated by papers on the application of PVS and ACL2. There were also research papers discussing how an industry standard hardware description language (VHDL) could be used formally.

At Siemens AG, Equivalence Checking (EC) is used to validate VHDL refinements and can routinely handle up to a million gates (see for example Chrysalis Symbolic Design who have "checked the formal equivalence of nine, extremely large, complex ASICs. Each of these ASICs comprises between one and two million gates. The equivalence checker typically takes between 10 minutes and 3 hours to formally verify each chip".). At least 800 Siemens engineers are required to use EC. Model Checking (MC) is used to validate circuits. However there are technical issues outstanding, in particular, while MC can handle a few hundred state bits, ASICs often have a few thousand state bits.

At higher levels of abstraction there are many examples of the application of theorem proving.[1] The work at Computational Logic, Inc. on the FM9001 is notable as part of their approach to developing a verified "stack" of products, and the verification of aspects of the Viper processor in HOL [25] resulted in a high profile for the claims for assurance that can be made following a proof of correctness. More recently the work with PVS at SRI and Rockwell Collins shows the continuing benefits of this form of semantic modelling and proof [4].

3   Analysis of the Formal Methods Market

3.1   Characteristics of the Market

The overall perception is that the formal methods landscape consists of a wide variety of techniques and tools. While the tools often tackle different problem areas their number would normally be taken for a sign of an immature market. However the formal methods market is not really a single market, more a particular technical viewpoint on a host of disparate activities.

The landscape primarily consists of smallish organisations (university research groups and commercial companies) with no widespread commercial adoption of core concepts and tools. There are a number of small service companies using formal methods as a leading edge service. They are generally technically motivated to grapple with new tools and put up with being the first to use the theories or tools on industrial scale projects.

Presently, the only places where formal methods appear to be having a (potentially) major impact is with the hardware industry and parts of the safety critical industry. Some of the large hardware vendors are either developing in-house capabilities in formal verification (e.g., Intel) or are adopting externally developed technologies (e.g., AMD with ACL2). There are indications that the telecommunications industry may also be adapting the technology. However, the areas of security critical systems show very little adoption although of course this work is not particularly visible even though security was originally one of the prime motivations for significant R&D funding.

It is also instructive to speculate on the extent of the formal methods activities world-wide. Taking the number of attendees at FM99 [31] as indicative of 10% of those involved in the software related activities, adding a similar number in the hardware fields and calculating the salaries and overheads of those involved we arrive at a figure of $1-1.5B per annum.

3.2   Economic and Other Drivers

Both the hardware and telecommunications industries have a compelling reason to adopt the technology. Intel's Pentium Flaw (FDIV) cost the company hundreds of

---

[1] Of the 386 papers in the HOL bibliography (http://www.dcs.glasgow.ac.uk/~tfm/hol-bib.html) about 30% relate to hardware verification.

millions of dollars and was a wake up call that the then existing process for developing increasingly complex chips was inadequate. With the only option being to recall the chips (unlike the software industry's general —but not ubiquitous— capability for releasing software patches), new scalable assurance arguments were necessary. Model checking was a good fit.

Both the hardware and telecommunication industries are spending substantial resources on simulation and testing to achieve (or approximate) relevant coverage criteria. On some projects, the cost is nearing 50% of overall project funding. Increasing the efficiency of the analysis (through either increased coverage or more efficient and cheaper exploration) is a compelling economic argument. This is also true in the avionics and parts of the safety critical industry where the direct costs and time of achieving test coverage is driving the adoption or investigation of formal methods.

There are similar economic drivers in the aerospace industry. Lucas Aerospace report in their justification for their ESSI project PCFM that V&V accounts for typically 41% of total software production costs and code corrections for typically 32% of total maintenance costs. The use of B reduced the need for module testing in a railway application.

3.3   The Impact of Development Process Failure

The Intel Pentium Flaw demonstrated that the complexity of contemporary chips was exceeding the engineering processes currently in place. The failure of Ariane 5, because of a software fault, indicated a failure in the software architecture and process. The failure of an U.S. Titan rocket was traced to a decimal placement error in its software.

Thomas Kuhn in his book "The Structure of Scientific Revolutions" [26] defines and discusses why paradigm shifts occur. In effect, a technical community will buy into (or start developing) a new theory/paradigm if the old theory is refuted or if the new theory extends scientific prediction in material ways. Often, the shift will occur when a significant infelicity with the current belief system is found. The Pentium Flaw was an indicator of such infelicities in the chip design processes.

The inability of hardware vendors and telecommunications companies to achieve an appropriate scope of validation with current technology may very well be another crisis point requiring a paradigm shift. Indeed the continual pressure on all companies to reduce costs and development times keeps new technologies under scrutiny. Companies are searching for order of magnitude improvements in cost and not just minor polishing of their processes: process improvement runs out of steam without a technology shift.

There also appears to be a lack of business models to assess impact of new technologies on process. There needs to be supporting, investment-oriented, risk type models of the engineering process that will allow the business case for new methods or techniques to be properly assessed.

3.4   The Impact of Communities

In the full report we consider the role that community belief systems play in the adoption of new technologies. The community viewpoint highlights a number of important points:

Self-referencing, who talks to whom, defines what we mean by a market in formal methods. E.g. avionics suppliers look towards other similar suppliers and to organisations like NASA for leadership. It is not just a case of everyone using the same technology is in the same market. There is a need to establish credentials within a community – entry costs can be expensive.

Another important aspect is the separation between the research communities. For example the self-appointed main formal methods conferences, even as late as 1998, had no representation from the model checkers. The communities of model checkers, theorem provers, abstract state machines, protocol verification are often too distinct.

Different communities tend to have different research agendas and this can lead to a self-perpetuating separation. For example the perception by NASA sponsored work in [16] that it is the front end of the lifecycle that is important influenced a large body of work and importantly the tools. Yet in the railway industry the emphasis has been on code verification which has led to a quite different toolset, Atelier B.

We also noted that research agendas can shift by external factors and that technology and companies must be sensitive to shifts in community values. As always there is a need to listen to the customer.

3.5   The Impact of Government and Standardisation Bodies

Government and other large organisations can influence the adoption of technology through their impact on the regulatory process, in regulated industries, and through shaping the market with their significant purchasing power. The development by the UK Ministry of Defence of a standard Def Stan 00-55 caused considerable international comment as a major purchaser of safety critical systems set out its requirements for a formal methods based approach. The standard was updated and issued as a full UK Defence Standard in 1996 and is notable for its emphasis on formal methods. One might also note that the emerging generic international standard for safety related systems, IEC 61508, requires the non-use of formal methods to be justified for the systems in the higher safety categories.

In the security area the agencies in the USA and the UK have had a far reaching influence on the development of formal methods. Although they have been significant sponsors of formal methods R&D and applications they have also distorted the market through the earlier US embargo on verification technology and their prescriptive approach to the methods and tools that should be used. The development of PVS was in part a response to the potential problems of the technology embargo. However the development of national and security requirements for different techniques for different security evaluation levels has had a stabilising effect on the market, and there is some evidence that this is now providing a driver to formal methods application as more higher level security evaluations are coming through. This is partly a result of the demands of electronic cash and e-commerce applications.

4   Technology Adoption Models

4.1   Introduction

Technology adoption models provide a systematic means of estimating the likely adoption trajectories of new formal methods technologies. Consideration of these models may suggest how various research programmes and projects could be altered to heighten the likelihood of success.

We have adapted the technology diffusion model of Everett Rogers [27] and a high technology model developed by Moore [28], [29]. For the Rogers model, we provide two examples of its application in the full report [1]. The first example demonstrates how the Rogers model was successfully used in ORA Canada's EVES project, resulting in substantially enhanced adoption of the EVES technology[2]. The second example concerns the Swedish company Prover Technology.

While the Rogers technology adoption model is useful it does not explain failures to market nor provide a strategy for successful adoption. Moore has taken the analysis further in two books [28], [29], where he discusses technology adoption of discontinuous innovations and, in particular, uses the model to discuss appropriate strategies and tactics for increasing the likelihood of success. While we do not envisage formal methods penetrating mass markets even their adoption in small niche markets can be informed by Moore's work. The additional perspectives provided by Moore include:

- describing a Technology Adoption Life Cycle (TALC) and particularly the chasm between two stages of this lifecycle
- introducing the importance of a complete product described in user terms and aimed at an identified and characterised buyer
- the need to define the market —this depends on communities of people not just on technical profile
- the extreme importance of referencing and word of mouth in developing sales
- the problems of selling $10–50k products
- the need to segment, segment and segment again until one is a significant player in the market

In Moore's model of the Technology Adoption Life Cycle (TALC), he defines a number of players: Innovators, Early Adopters, Early Majority, Late Majority and Laggards. Understanding these players is crucial for the successful marketing (technology transfer) of a new product.

Innovators pursue new technology products aggressively. They are crucial to any marketing campaign as their endorsement reassures the other marketplace players. *Early adopters* are not technologists, but individuals who find it easy to imagine, understand, and appreciate the benefits of a new technology and to relate the benefits to their concerns. They do not rely on well-established reference points to make their decisions, preferring their intuition and vision. The *Early Majority* shares the early

---

[2] The EVES technology, principally through Z/EVES, has been distributed to sites in over 40 countries.

adopter's ability to relate to technology, but are driven by a strong sense of practicality. They want well-established references before adopting. It is with these folks that substantial profits are available for the first time. The *Late Majority* has the same concerns as the early majority but are uncomfortable with technology products. They want a well-established standard, lots of support, and buy from large and well-established companies. *Laggards* don't want anything to do with new technology. It has to be buried deep inside another product.

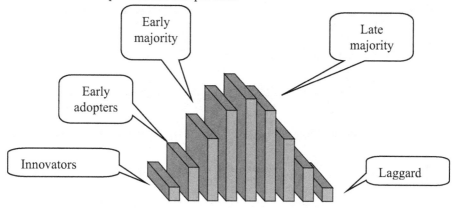

Fig. 1. Moore's Bell Curve

According to Moore, one can view the distribution of these players as a Bell Curve, with the early and late majority each consisting of one-third of the population (see Fig.1). However, Moore's Bell Curve is actually discontinuous, having three gaps of note: between innovators and early adopters; between the early majority and the late majority; and, most significantly, between the early adopters and the early majority. Moore goes on to argue that the basis for a sale between early adopters and the early majority is quite different. Early adopters are looking for a change agent while the early majority wants a productivity improvement for existing operations. Basically, when promoters of high-tech products try to make the transition from a market base made up of visionary early adopters to the pragmatist early majority, they are effectively operating without a reference base and without a support base within a market that is highly reference oriented and highly support oriented. In general, it is our view that formal methods are still in the early market (consisting of innovators and early adopters) and only to a highly limited extent has their been any effort to cross the chasm into niche-based adoption. The report [1] discusses some examples of market focus.

4.2 Adoption of the TALC Approach

Adopting the TALC approach will involve:

• Taking a "whole product" view, that is all the aspects of the product that the user may need to meets his or her goal.

- Characterising the buyer for these products and analysing the scenarios of use.
- Identifying the competition for the whole product and the reason for buying.

The characterisation of the buyer should include their place on the TALC (e.g., visionary or early majority) and the market. Bear in mind that technical similarity of problem and solution does not constitute a market. Community and self-referencing are defining aspects of a market.

Medium term strategies should seek to bring potential users together into a common market. This might include the stimulation of workshops, standards activities and general awareness and dissemination actions.

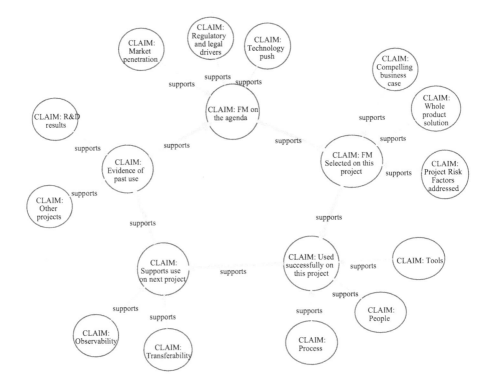

Fig. 2. Main classes of success and failure factors

4.3   Success and Failure Factors

We can summarise the technology diffusion and product marketing discussion into a five stage model: evidence of past use of formal methods, formal methods are on the agenda for a project, they are selected, used successfully, and that experience fed into the evidence for past use. The main classes of success and failure factors are shown in Figure 2:

If any one of these stages fails then formal methods will not be adopted or they might be adopted on one project but fail to diffuse. From each of these nodes questions can be generated to assess a project. The underlying questions will depend on the stage in the technology adoption lifecycle of the user.

The five stages of technology diffusion form a spiral of adoption when we consider the impact of the TALC of Moore. Not only has the technology to successfully

address these stages of diffusion but it has cross the chasm that separates different communities and groups of users. This is illustrated by Figure 3.

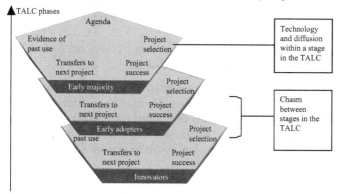

Fig. 3. Combined TALC and diffusion model

5   Recommendations and Conclusions

5.1   Past Failures

The application of formal methods has a long history but they have not been substantially adopted by the software engineering community at large. Failure to adopt has arisen for numerous reasons:

- Research that was successful but required heroic efforts to get results (e.g., from lack of theory base, tools not usable).
- Tools being developed but not transferred to other groups (e.g., due to a combination of platform and people issues).
- Large investments in tools without a corresponding advance in theory or method, premature attempts to increase rigour or increase scale.
- Results that did not scale from case studies: a common problem in the applied area.
- Not meeting customer requirements, e.g., sponsors' concerns shift but the research community not listening. There have been some notable shifts in emphasis by government agencies that in the past were the prime sponsors of formal methods.
- Over ambition and failure to meet expectations (e.g., from overselling by the research community or from failing to meet unreasonable expectations of the sponsors).

Yet in some respects these could be argued to be the normal turbulence in any area of technological research and deployment.

5.2   The Current Landscape

The overall perception of the current formal methods landscape is that it consists of:

- Techniques and tools mostly with a long history of usage and a community of use behind them. They have not been the product of relatively short term (3 year) R&D programmes.
- Smallish organisations (primarily university research groups and small commercial companies) with little in the way of widespread commercial adoption of core concepts and tools.
- Generally commercial companies making money from services, not tools.
- Stable core groups but no major break out, some fission.

However there is significant take up of formal methods in critical industries. Large hardware vendors are either developing in-house capabilities in formal verification (e.g. Intel, Siemens) or are adopting externally developed technologies and in the area of safety there is active research, case studies and serious application of formal methods throughout the safety lifecycle. The key points to emerge are:

- There are significant applications of formal verification in the railway and nuclear industry with variable degree of rigour. There is use of static analyses, interactive theorem proving and model checking with the use of domain specific solutions.
- There is some integration of formal methods with the existing system and software engineering processes. This has lead to the use of engineer friendly approach to notations – variants of table based notations, existing PLC notations — trading expressiveness with ease of analysis.
- There are examples of verified compilers for special purpose languages and rigorous back translation. There is significant work on verified hardware in flight and drive-critical applications.
- The use of model checking and equivalence checking has been adopted by hardware chip manufacturers. The forthcoming Merced chip from Intel may be the first mass produced artefact to have formally verified parts of the hardware and microcode design.

There are also examples of "over claiming", and the need for careful presentation of results – not an easy balance to maintain in commercially and academically competitive environments.

We calculated earlier that about $1-1.5B is spent annually on formal methods activities world-wide.

5.3   Present Limits

While not particularly scientific, it is instructive to identify the present limits of various FM-based technologies. Note that with judgement in abstraction and modularisation, larger systems could be piece-wise analysed. Furthermore, even small systems may have substantial intellectual depth and challenge technological limits. With these caveats the present limits appear to be:

- Equivalence checking of 1 Million gate ASICS.
- Model checking of 1000 latches at a time, using techniques for modularising and looking at components, e.g. there are claims of verifying large (10^{20}) state spaces.
- Software verification from design to code of ~80Kloc.
- Simple formally verified compilers for special purpose languages.
- Static analysis of >150Kloc.
- Specification and modelling of >30,000 lines of specification.

Theorem proving is a specialised activity, and there is some evidence of a skills shortage in hardware verification and proof techniques. Also despite some evidence that engineers can read and write formal specifications, mass uptake will be on derived partially automated solutions and the use and adaptation of familiar notations (e.g. tables, diagrams).

One should also note that investment in formal methods tools needs to be continual: they need to keep pace with the general industry rate of change in the implementation technology. While these changes often facilitate new functionality they also drive obsolescence. We have already mentioned hardware and operating systems but it also applies to databases, GUI builders, languages (Lisp, Smalltalk).

5.4   Increasing Adoption of Formal Methods

If the objective is to increase the use of formal methods in industry then this can be done in broadly two ways:

- increasing the use of formal methods based services (either external or as a part of large companies) that influence significant projects and products (i.e. not just a case study culture)
- increasing the use of formal methods based tools and products within software, hardware and systems engineering
  To achieve this it is necessary to address the following.

Apply Technology Adoption Models
Proven technology adoption models have not been comprehensively applied to formal methods technologies, by either sponsors or technology developers. The haphazard approach has reduced the adoption trajectory of formal methods and has resulted in unintended adoption barriers.

Therefor a major recommendation is that unlike other R&D and dissemination programmes we have investigated, the strategy of any future investment programme should adopt models such as the Moore TALC "chasm crossing" approach and take a more explicit view of how the market in high technology products actually develops. We consider this to be the single most likely factor to increases the chance of successful adoption. The adoption of the Moore TALC should take into account that formal methods are not a market as such but really a particular technical viewpoint on a host of disparate activities.

Sustained Investment in Tools

A realistic view is needed of the large investment required to develop and sustain tools, and the long time it may take for a tool and associated experience and theory base to develop. For specific projects this will involve the building on top of existing tools, and the importance and impact of freely available tools is immense (e.g., HOL, PVS, SMV, SPIN, Z/EVES). Also of importance is the extent to which APIs or source code is available.

However in critical applications there is a need to trust the authenticity of the tool and its correct operation. There is scope for intentional and unintentional flaws in the tools giving misleading results (e.g. hiding a subtle deadlock, not reporting dead code) and there is a need for innovation to see if the benefits of widespread use and scrutiny can be achieved without compromising trust.

The formal methods strategy should address pricing and the commercial viability of products, given the general problems posed by the investment needed to develop tools, the continuing investment needed to maintain their usability as platforms and operating system change, and the small size of the tools market.

Address Differences in Target Users

Most of the formal methods industrial work is done by service groups and small companies. The encouragement of this sector will be quite different from the larger market. This sector is more akin to Moore's visionaries, it can quickly apply new technical solutions and is not put off by the more intellectually challenging aspects of theorem proving or the heroism needed to grapple with immature tools and theories.

Increased formal methods uptake among other engineering disciplines will involve packing specific analyses into easier to use but more restricted components: the price of success is integration [30]. There is a need for guidance on how the existing tools and techniques can work together and how potential users should select those to invest in.

Focus on Critical Application Areas

The key drivers for adoption come from applications in areas with a large impact of development failure such as hardware (e.g., mass-market products, security or e-commerce products), telecommunications, safety and critical infrastructure. There are opportunities for formal methods throughout the system lifecycle. The strategy should take into account the increasing use of COTS in critical applications.

Continue R&D

A strong R&D agenda is needed to complement a comprehensive technology adoption agenda. To date the funding for formal methods has been a very small component in the overall IT R&D budget. While there appears a scientific consensus that the technical future is to combine model checking with theorem proving there is much work still to do.

There should be a clear distinction between R&D projects which are being pursued for pure knowledge purposes and those being pursued to have an impact on industry or governmental processes: both are necessary. In the former case, technology adoption criteria may be of limited concern. The "scientific market" will sift the importance and relevance of research results.

Acknowledgements

Numerous individuals have provided input into this report primarily through informal interviews or discussions. As many of these individuals provided commentary on a background basis, we will not specifically identify individuals. They know who they are and we thank them for their input.

References

1. Bundesamt fuer Sicherheit in der Informationstechnik, Formal Methods Diffusion: Past Lessons and Future Prospects, BSI report, 2000, available from: http://www.bsi.bund.de.
2. S. Gerhart, D. Craigen, T. Ralston, Experience with Formal Methods in Critical Systems. IEEE Software, January 1994. Reprinted in High-Integrity System Specification and Design, J.P. Bowen and M.G. Hinchey (eds.), Formal Approaches to Computing and Information Technology Series (FACIT), Springer-Verlag, April 1999.
3. Science Policy Research Unit, London HMSO, Evaluation of the Alvey Programme for Advanced Information Technology, 1991.
4. R. W. Butler et al., NASA Langley's Research and Technology-Transfer Program in Formal Methods, available from
    http://shemesh.larc.nasa.gov/fm.html.
5. P. Behm, P. Benoit, A. Faivre, J.-M. Meynadier, Meteor: A Successful Application of B in a Large Project, in [31].
6. P Chapront, Alstom: 10 years using B, interview in Lettre B, available from http://www.atelierb.societe.com/LETTRE_B/index_uk.html.
7. L.-H. Erikson Specifying railway interlocking requirements for practical use in 15th International Conference on Computer Safety, Reliability and Security (Safecomp 96), Springer, 1996.
8. M.J. Morley, Safety in Railway signalling data: a behavioural analysis, in Higher Order Logic Theorem Proving and its Applications, Springer, 1993.
9. A. Cimatti et al., Model Checking Safety Critical Software with SPIN: An Application to a Railway Interlocking System, in 17th International Conference on Computer Safety, Reliability and Security (Safecomp 98), Springer LNCS 1516.
10. G. Stalmarck, A System for Determining Propositional Logic Theorems by Applying Values and Rules to Triplets that are Generated from a Formula, 1989. Swedish Patent Number 467076. U.S. Patent Number 5276897, European Patent Number 0403454.
11. A. Haxthausen, J. Peleska, Formal Development and Verification of a Distributed Railway Control System, in [31].
12. S. King, J. Hammond, R. Chapman, A. Pryor, The Value of Verification: Positive Experience of Industrial Proof, in [31].

13. M. Croxford, J. Sutton, Breaking Through the V and V Bottleneck, Ada Europe 1995, Springer LNCS 1031, 1996.
14. The Safety of Operational Computer Systems, HMSO 1998.
15. S. Owre et al, PVS: An Experience Report, in Applied Formal Methods—FM Trends 98, Springer LNCS 1641, 1999.
16. J. Rushby, Formal Methods and Digital Systems Validation for Airborne Systems, NASA Contractor Report 4551, December 1993.
17. NASA Conference Publication 2377, Peer Review of a Formal Verification/Design Proof Methodology, July 1983.
18. G. Egger, A. Fett, P. Peppert, Formal Specification of a Safe PLC Language and its Compiler, in Proceedings Safecomp 94.
19. S. Stepney, Incremental Development of a High Integrity Compiler: experience from an industrial development, Third IEEE High-Assurance Systems Engineering Symposium (HASE'98), Washington DC, November 1998.
20. G. Lüttgen, V. Carreño, Analyzing Mode Confusion via Model Checking, in D. Dams et al.(eds.), Proceedings of the 5th and 6th SPIN Workshops., Springer LNCS 1680, 1999.
21. W. Zhang, Model Checking Operator Procedures, in D. Dams et al.(eds.), Proceedings of the 5th and 6th SPIN Workshops., Springer LNCS 1680, 1999.
22. T. Clement, I. Cottam, P. Froome, C. Jones, The Development of a Commercial 'Shrink-Wrapped Application' to Safety Integrity Level 2: The DUST-EXPERT(tm) Story, in M. Felici, K. Kanoun and A. Pasquini (eds.), Computer Safety, Reliability and Security (Safecomp 99), Springer LNCS 1698, 1999.
23. N. Heintze and E. Clarke (eds.). Proceedings of the Formal Methods and Security Protocols Workshop, Trento, Italy, July 1999.
24. J. O'Leary et al, Formally Verifying IEEE Compliance of Floating-Point Hardware, Intel Technology Journal, 1999.
25. A. Cohn, The Notion of Proof in Hardware Verification, in Journal of Automated Reasoning 5: 127-139, Kluwer Academic Publishers 1989.
26. T Kuhn, The Structure of Scientific Revolutions, University of Chicago Press, 1970.
27. E. Rogers, Diffusion of Innovations. Free Press, New York, 1983.
28. G. A. Moore. Crossing the Chasm. Harper Business, 1991. See also 2nd edition 1999.
29. G. A. Moore. Inside the Tornado: Marketing Strategies from Silicon Valley's Cutting Edge, Harper Business, 1995.
30. J Sifakis, Integration the price of success, in [31].
31. J. Wing, J. Woodcock and J. Davies (eds.), Proceedings of FM'99: World Congress on Formal Methods in the Development of Computing Systems, Toulouse, France, September 1999

Safe Tech:
A Control Oriented Viewpoint

Maarten Steinbuch

Eindhoven University of Technology,
P.O. Box 513, 5600 MB Eindhoven, The Netherlands
M.Steinbuch@tue.nl
http://www.wfw.wtb.tue.nl/control

Abstract. The interplay between processes and real-time software systems, together constitution a closed-loop system, is not trivial to investigate. For the 'low level' feedback loop much theory is available, however, for the supervisory level where discrete events may interfere with the dynamics of the system, no complete theory for analysis and synthesis exists. For controlled manipulator systems simulation examples show the effects of delay and start/stop scheduling for the controlled output variables. A common language for software development and dynamic systems is needed to be able to design embedded systems, in particular for safety critical applications.

1 Introduction

In many applications the use of *embedded control systems* is a necessity to cope with increased requirements on performance and economic operation. The addition of 'intelligence' into actuators, sensors and feedback, monitoring and safety systems is a fast growing field of real-time software implementation. It enables modification of the behaviour of hardware designs by addition of software algorithms. This provides important opportunities for flexible and adaptive operation of plants and processes. The issue of *safety* of operation of embedded control systems is becoming more profound as the number of lines of code increase fast.

The safety and reliability of embedded systems should play an important role during the design process of both hardware and software. However, the coupling between a (dynamic) system and real-time software, i.e. a closed-loop system, is not trivial to investigate. Although for the primary feedback loop much theory is available, the higher level where discrete events may interfere with the low level loop, poses major problems if considering structured design and analysis tools. In this paper we will discuss the problems and possible solution approaches of such embedded control systems.

From the wide range of embedded or computer control systems as being applied in automotive industry, process control, transportation, aerospace industry and many more, in this paper we will focus on manipulators. Mechanical positioning devices are widely present in industry for motion tasks such as pick-and-place, assembly tasks etc, but also in consumer electronics such as CDROM,

F. Koornneef and M. van der Meulen (Eds.): SAFECOMP 2000, LNCS 1943, pp. 227–239, 2000.

Hard Disc drives and VCRs. Also an important emerging field is telemanipulation and the application of manipulators in medical applications such as computer assisted surgery. The important role of software algorithms and safety and reliability requirements motivate the relevance of research within this area.

In Section 2 motion control systems are introduced. Section 3 discusses the problem field of embedded motion systems. In Section 4 some solution approaches will be sketched and roadblocks will be identified. Finally, Section 5 will summarize the main findings as concluding remarks.

2   Motion Control

The relevant disciplines for motion control systems are mechanics, electronic power supplies and electronics, electric motors, sensor and software technology and digital control. These areas have rapidly developed over the last decades. The field of *mechatronic* systems has emerged to emphasize the importance of a systems approach for design. However, the role of software engineering has not been emphasized much in the mechatronics and robotics literature.

In this section we will describe only a small, but basic part of mechatronic (motion) systems, namely the elementary positioning control loop. Consider a typical motion system as it is schematically depicted in Fig. 1.

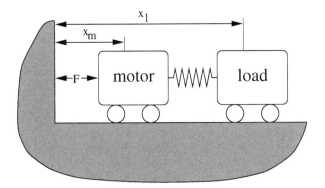

Fig. 1. Motion system

The driving force F is assumed to be generated by a current-controlled motor, such that the input of the system indeed can be seen as force. Either the motor position x_m or the load position x_l can be measured (in most cases unfortunately not both!). Both masses (or inertias for rotating machines) are assumed to be connected via a mechanical connection with finite stiffness and damping. From the equations of motion, a simple linear dynamic model can be derived. The model has a frequency response function (input/output map for sinusoidal signals) as depicted in Fig. 2, both for the motor position measurement case (F $\rightarrow x_m$) and for the load position measurement situation (F $\rightarrow x_l$). The frequency responses are elementary for many motion control and robotic systems seen in practice, although often more resonances occur at higher frequencies.

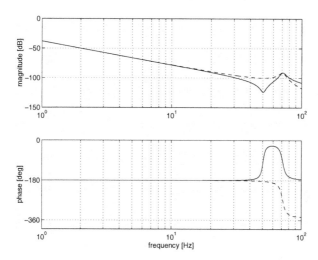

Fig. 2. Bode diagram of motion system, sensor on motor (–) or load (- -)

A block-diagram of the control loop is shown in Fig. 3, where PD represents the feedback controller and $Mass$ represents the plant. The output position y has to be controlled according to a reference trajectory r. The (feedback) controller PD for the above motion control system consists at least of a stabilizing Proportional/Derivative part mostly implemented in a computer coding sequence. The Digital/Analog conversion translates the binary information of the computer algorithm into continuous time voltage signals. The power amplifier is assumed to be contained in the system block 'Mass'. The Analog/Digital conversion transforms the analog voltage output of sensors (for instance speed or position) into digital information.

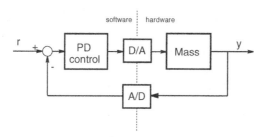

Fig. 3. Block-diagram of a motion control system

Notice that Fig. 3 is only a simplified diagram. In motion systems often setpoint filters and feedforward signals are being used as well. The controller algorithm itself often contains additional signal filtering and conditioning in addition to the Proportional and Derivative parts [ ].

A typical response of a motion system is given in Fig. 4 (no feedforward applied). In this case the setpoint is a low-pass filtered step function.

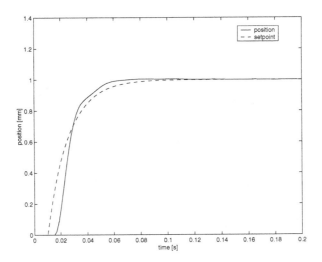

Fig. 4. Time response of a motion system

The choice of the *bandwidth*[1] normally depends on various (mixed) performance measures, such as disturbance rejection and settling behaviour under tracking conditions. Moreover, it is a well-known fact that disturbance dynamics should be accounted for in the controller tuning (and possibly in the controller structure) [ ].

3   Embedded Control Systems

The tuning of the basic feedback loop as described in the previous section is obviously key for the final performance of a feedback system. Nevertheless, it is a known fact from industry, that 95% of the development time (and hence cost!) of software for such systems is NOT dedicated to this tuning, but to the embedding of the basic feedback loop in an overall system. To further analyze embedded control systems we use a three level structure, consisting of the feedback loop (level 1), a supervisory system (level 2) and including plant wide economic optimization (level 3).

---

[1] speed of response of the closed-loop system

3.1   Level 1: Basic Feedback Loop

Level 1 is the basic feedback loop, as shown in Fig. 5. The design of this level concentrates on the hardware, and firmware dedicated to specific sensors/actuators. System type of requirements with respect to monitoring and safety functions may boil down to additional sensors or redundancy in actuators. Software concentrates within this level on coding the feedback and filter algorithms.

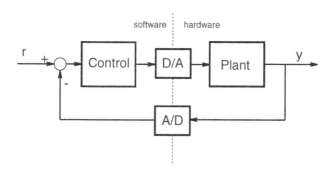

Fig. 5. Block diagram of feedback control system

In order to give an idea of this, consider again a motion system with a PD controller. Denote the sample instant as k, then the control error at time instant k is:

$$e_k = r_k - y_k$$

and the controller action then simply is:

$$u_k = Pe_k + D(e_k - e_{k-1})$$

in which the first part is the proportional part (with gain P) and the second part the derivative part (with gain D). Notice that for the second part a storage function is required.

To elucidate possible problems of interfacing software and hardware, consider as an example the situation for the motion system of Section 2 that within the software an additional delay of only one sampling instant occurs (in this case 5 ms)[2]. The block diagram is shown in Fig. 6.

Fig. 7 shows the resulting time response. Clearly, the system is not stable anymore. This points out the strong requirements on real-time behaviour of algorithms which are used within the level 1 feedback loop.

For the design and analysis of this level, theory of discrete time and continuous time systems is available and can be used, see for instance [ ]. A necessary

---

[2] in terms of the PD algorithm an additional delay can be written as $u_k = Pe_{k-1} + D(e_{k-1} - e_{k-2})$

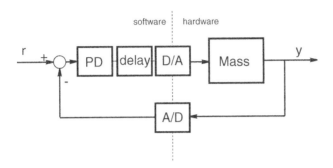

Fig. 6. Block diagram of motion control system with calculational delay

condition is that sampling and calculation is done with an exact and fixed period. For asynchronous operation, theory is not well developed yet, and this is equivalent with one of the key problems in the development of a thorough theory for embedded systems.

3.2   Level 2: Supervisory System

The first extension from the feedback loop level is the addition of a supervisory architecture, as shown in Fig. 8. The design of this level concentrates fully on the software design with respect to

- monitoring and safety functionality
- scheduling and setpoint generation
- adaptation
- quality control and exception handling
- start/stop procedures

This level (and also level 3) is what normally is addressed as 'embedded control systems'. Its characteristics are that it consists of asynchronous processes (discrete events) in combination with the continuous-time feedback loop[3]. This is also called a hybrid system, and such systems achieve a lot of attention in the recent literature, both from computer sciences and from the control community.

As an example of typical behaviour of a hybrid system, consider again the example motion system. Assume that the operator pushes the stop button at time 40 ms. (See also original the response Fig. 4). The supervisory software is programmed such that it immediately shuts down the controller output (i.e. the input signal to the motion system, which is normally a current resulting in a force). Then the response of Fig. 9 results.

Clearly, since the mass has a speed at t=0.04s (i.e. it has kinetic energy), the system will still move. A better supervisory action would be a smooth transition of the setpoint back to zero, as shown in Fig. 10.

---

[3] discrete-time systems with fixed period are also treated as 'continuous time', since the same system theoretic tools hold

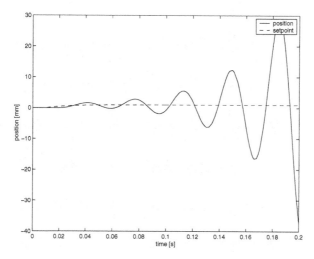

Fig. 7. Time response of a motion system with one step additional delay in the feedback loop

This simple example illustrates the influence of safety and supervisory systems can have on controlled dynamic systems. It is also relevant to notice that *there does not exist any structured way of analyzing and synthesizing such embedded systems!*

3.3   Level 3: Economic Optimization

Finally, in level 3 an optimizer is added, which is a trend seen in particular in process industry, where economic models are used to redefine new operating conditions for the plant to operate in. See also Fig. 11. This level may also infer maintenance models, driven by monitoring signals from level 2. The design of this level concentrates again on algorithms and software, but is less critical for the operation of the system, seen from a reliability and safety viewpoint.

In summary of this section, the rapid advances in computer and information technology are enabling a closer integration of the various decision and control tasks described within the three levels of hierarchy. The tendency to merge these levels and the increasing requirements on quality assessment (ISO, CMM) feed the need to develop a framework for modelling and analyzing such hybrid systems, and should lead to tools for structured synthesis. However, a necessity is that the various groups of engineers are able to understand one another and have some common language. In the next section we will give a short overview of current developments in this field.

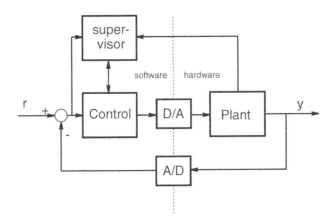

Fig. 8. Block diagram of embedded control system

4   Inventory of Problems and Approaches to Hybrid Systems

The previous section showed for a simple manipulator system how dynamics may interfere with software coding at different levels. In this section we will briefly point out in more depth the differences between continuous time system models and discrete event models. In Section 4.2 we will discuss some current approaches, and in Section 4.3 some statements will be made about safety and software in medical robotics.

4.1   Properties of Hybrid Systems

A definition of a hybrid system is a system that contains a continuous time part and a discrete event part. Although much is still to be done on hybrid systems, relatively much is known on the separate parts. In a comparison of characteristics of dynamic continuous time models and discrete event type of models we can observe the following [ ].

Continuous-time dynamic system models

– continuous time models of dynamic systems are used in studying mechanical, biological and other physical systems. Modelling is done using (partial) differential equations resulting from conservation laws, often via spatial discretization (Finite Element Modelling) leading to sets of ordinary differential equations
– the set of variables is invariant, i.e. the order of the model is fixed. Internal state variables do not disappear (although they can become irrelevant for the input/output behaviour).

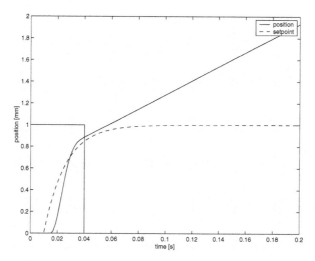

Fig. 9. Time response of a motion system with the control signal set to zero at t=0.04s

- most theory is developed for systems which have certain properties such as uniqueness of solutions and linearizability. This does exclude those physical systems where non-smooth nonlinear behaviour occurs (like dry friction).
- the modeller can decide about the size of the model, and can use well developed model reduction techniques to reduce the size of models [ ].

Discrete-event dynamic system models (DEDS)

- discrete-event models of dynamic systems are relevant in computer algorithms, descision making systems, queuing problems and to describe human operator effects. Modelling is done with procedural descriptions and state-transition diagrams. Typical description languages are petri nets, max algebra and finite state automata.
- the set of variables is variable, i.e. the 'order' of the model can change as a function of internal or external influences. Internal state variables can disappear.
- DEDS are a natural description for non-smooth nonlinear systems
- the modeller can decide about the size of the model, but can not relay on well developed model reduction techniques to reduce the size of models.

For the combination of the two, into a hybrid system, we need the notion of timing and continuous dynamics within discrete event operation. The development of analysis and synthesis for these kind of systems is by far from trivial and many researcher are working in (parts of) this area [ ].

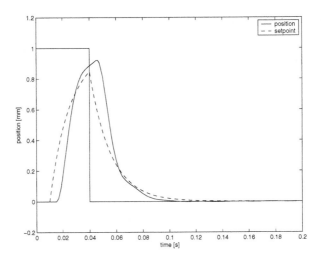

Fig. 10. Time response of a motion system with the setpoint signal set to zero at t=0.04s

4.2 Solution Approaches

Aspects of design methodology in increasing difficulty are (i) simulation, (ii) modelling tools, (iii) analysis and finally (iv) synthesis.

With respect to simulation much work has been done, and commercial packages are available, such as Simscript [ ], State Flow with Simulink [ ] or χ language [ ].

The modelling still does show a wide variety of approaches. To name a few: (timed) petri nets, complementarity systems [ ], max algebra, and mixed logic dynamical systems [ ]. Especially the latter development seems interesting, in particular, in combination with model based estimation and prediction. The method transforms logical decision variables into mixed-integer linear inequalities. Together with the time-continuous dynamics, tools are available for solving and analyzing such models. See [ ] for more details.

With respect to the third item analysis, much work is concentrating on stability and dead-lock prediction. As an example consider the work described in [ ]. It shows nicely how an industrial application needs to combine various analysis techniques from computer sciences and control engineering to assess safety and reliability of a hybrid system.

Finally, the *design* of hybrid systems is still underdeveloped, although structured design techniques from software engineering are common practice in industry. However, as mentioned in [   ] the use of tools for reliability *prediction* is needed, and we would like to extend this to overall system performance prediction.

From the control literature, recent developments also include *reconfigurable* control systems [   ], in which the structure of the feedback systems changes as a

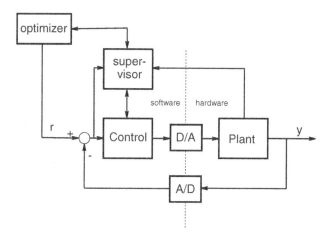

Fig. 11. Block diagram of embedded control system with plant optimizer

function of incidences or mode of operation. Another important development has been the advanced methods for uncertainty modelling, and the development of robust performance design methods [ ]. Although well-developed and useful for linear systems, it can be argued that extension of uncertainty modelling towards safety and integrity of control systems are possible also with application to hybrid systems.

4.3   Safety and Software in Medical Robotics

As a special application of motion systems, we will very briefly touch upon manipulators used in medical applications, in particular those use in operating rooms. The rapid developments in these robotic assisted surgery systems can be divided according to the distance of the surgeon to the patient. When the surgeon still is in contact with the patient, we speak about medical instruments which have added functionality like vision, tactile information or active actuators inside, see for instance [ ] for a recent overview. Such systems are being developed for instance for laparoscopic operations (*minimally invasive surgery*). When the surgeon is sitting behind a desk and is manipulating joysticks and looking to screens, but still sitting in the OR, we are dealing with remote (and more expensive) robotic manipulator systems. In the same way this surgeon can now be at a different locations, and we call this tele-operation. The group [ ] has an impressive experience within this area, and their website is very useful for its information. See also [ ],[ ] and [ ], and the conference [ ] showing the amount of recent attention for this field. As a motivation for further developments with respect to laparoscopic manipulators, we cite form [ ] the following:

"There is little question that laparoscopy represents a definite progress in patients' treatment. However, at present, there are a lot of drawbacks, some of which are not negligible. For instance, the surgeon has to perform operations with for only sensory input the two-dimensional picture on a video screen, and the procedure, performed with long instruments, is seldom done in a surgeon friendly position and has lost all tactile sensation. One of the first aims of new technology is to give back to the surgeon the input of three-dimensional vision and tactile sensation, and to restore the surgeon's dexterity with better adapted instruments, so as to permit him to perform surgery in ergonomically acceptable conditions."

The emergence of robotics in operating rooms clearly raise the question of safety, and it is obvious that this specific application is a safety critical one. Because of the technology involved, the issues raised in this paper are of concern. What never may occur is that due to failure, energy of motion is put via the manipulator into the patient, possibly damaging its interior tissue. However, the implication is that the use of active control filters should possibly be restricted, and this puts limitation of the achievable performance. Also sterility is of course putting severe requirements with respect to sealing and mechanical design. Nevertheless, the problem of safety and reliability is strongly coupled to the end-user, because of the strong coupling of the machine to the manipulating surgeon. In view of this, the development of robotics for medical applications like surgery, should be done with all disciplines working together, including the end-user, and from the very start of the project. This is the only way in which all these discipline start understand each others language and can work together in such a 'hybrid project'.

5   Conclusions

Starting from a fairly general and elementary description of motion systems, we have introduced a three level structure for analyzing embedded control system. For the low level feedback loop a delay is shown to be critical, as an example of coupling between software and hardware. The higher level comprises start/stop and other logical events, which can lead to very undesirable behaviour if not designed properly. Hybrid systems in general are very difficult to analyze, and in particular, safety critical applications such as robotic assisted surgery, motivate research in this area. For academia this means concentrating on developing a common modelling and simulation language with which analysis and synthesis is possible. In addition, to really realize progress within industrial environments, we should be aware of the multi-disciplinary nature of the problem area of hybrid systems. Its means that from the very start of development projects, project teams should have representatives of all relevant disciplines and one should aim for understanding the others languages. In practice this is by far a trivial statement!

References

1. Levine, W. S. (Ed.): The Control Handbook. IEEE/CRC Press (1996). 230, 231, 237

2. Steinbuch, M., Norg, M. L.: Advanced Motion Control: an industrial perspective. European Journal of Control (1998) 278–293. 230

3. Bosch, P. P. J. van den: Hybrid systems: modelling embedded controllers. Philips Conference on Applications of Control Technology PACT98, CTR595-98-0055 (1998), 8p. 234

4. Obinata, G., Anderson, B. D. O.: Model reduction for control system design. In preparation (2000). 235

5. Hybrid Control Systems. IEEE Control System Magazine **19** (1999), 12–64. 235

6. CACI International Inc., see also http://www.caciasl.com/. 236

7. The Mathworks Inc., see also http://www.mathworks.com/products/stateflow/. 236

8. Beek, D. A. van, Rooda, J. E. Rooda: Languages and applications in hybrid modelling and simulation: Positioning of Chi. Control Engineering Practice, **8** (2000) 81–91. 236

9. Heemels, M.: Linear complementarity systems, a study in hybrid dynamics. PhD thesis Eindhoven University of Technology, Delft (1999). 236

10. Morari, M., Bemporad, A., Mignone, D.: A framework for control, state estimation, fault detection and verfification of hybrid systems. AT-Automatisierungstechnik, **47** (1999) 374–381. 236

11. Beerthuizen, P. G., Kruidhof, W.: System and softwasre analysis for the ERA control computer. 18th International Conference SAFECOMP'99, Toulouse, France, In: Lecture Notes in Computer Science 1698, (1999) 164–176. 236

12. Musa, J. D.: Software reliability engineering in industry. 18th International Conference SAFECOMP'99, Toulouse, France, In: Lecture Notes in Computer Science 1698, (1999) 1–12. 236

13. Maciejowski, J. M.: Reconfigurable Control Using Constrained Optimization. Proc. 1997 European Control Conference ECC97, Brussels, July (1997). 236

14. Lazeroms, M.: Force reflection for telemanipulation, applied to minimally invasive surgery. PhD thesis Delft University of Technology, Delft (1999). 237

15. D'partement de Chirurgie, Service de Chirurgie Digestive., Brussels, see also www.LAP-surgery.com. 237

16. Sastry, S.: http://robotics.eecs.berkeley.edu/ mcenk/medical/ 237

17. Lueth, T. C.: http://www.srl-berlin.de/ 237

18. Computer Motion, see also http://www.computermotion.com/ 237

19. Third International Conference on Medical Robotics, Imaging And Computer Assisted Surgery Tools And Technologies For Clinical Practice, October 11-14, 2000, Pittsburgh, Pennsylvania USA, see also: http://www.miccai.org/ 237

Derivation of Safety Targets for the Random Failure of Programmable Vehicle Based Systems

Richard Evans[1] and Jonathan Moffett[2]

[1]Jaguar Cars Limited, W/1/014, Engineering Centre, Abbey Road,
Whitley, Coventry, CV3 4LF, United Kingdom.
revans52@jaguar.com
[2]Department of Computed Science, The University of York, Heslington,
York, YO10 5DD, United Kingdom.
jdm@cs.york.ac.uk

Abstract Increasingly, the dependability of vehicle based programmable systems is becoming a key feature in ensuring the safety of those in and around the vehicle. The goal of those responsible for the design and manufacture of such systems must be to control adequately the associated risks so that the potential of the technology may be exploited fully. The Motor Industry Software Reliability Association (MISRA) has provided guidance for the management of the safety risks associated with software, but there is no comparable guidance for the management of the risks associated with the random failure of electronic hardware. This paper describes the development of an automotive industry specific risk model and goes on to derive safety targets for the random failure of programmable vehicle based systems. In addition the work provides a basis for comparison between the MISRA Guidelines and related national and international standards.

1   Introduction

Safety engineering provides many processes, methods, and techniques for use during the design and development of safety related and safety critical systems - irrespective of application domain. However, most if not all approaches rely on there being some defined safety targets against which the system will be measured.

In 1994 the Motor Industry Software Reliability Association (MISRA) published the "Development Guidelines for Vehicle Based Software" [1] which addressed the management of the safety risks associated with vehicle based software. However, there is no comparable guidance for the management of the corresponding risks associated with random failure. The MISRA approach uses the concept of Safety Integrity Levels (SIL) but these are automotive industry specific and have no defined mapping to other industry specific or generic SILs.

F. Koornneef and M. van der Meulen (Eds.): SAFECOMP 2000, LNCS 1943, pp. 240-249, 2000.
© Springer-Verlag Berlin Heidelberg 2000

It is the belief of the authors that targets for the random failure of electronic systems are desirable in order to act as design drivers during system development. The purpose of these targets would be to provide a sound basis for decisions which affect the dependability of embedded systems, as for example, the introduction of redundancy.

This paper results from a project done as part of the MSc in Safety Critical Systems Engineering at the University of York, and sponsored by Rover Group Ltd [6]. It is structured as follows. Section 2 describes important characteristics of the automotive industry. Sections 3 & 4 describe the approach to deriving a safety target, with section 3 describing the method, section 4 creating a risk model. Section 5 & 6 derive safety targets, first for accidents and then for systems. Finally section 7 discusses the results and reaches some conclusions.

2   Characteristics of the Automotive Industry

2.1   Introduction

Historically there has been a trend to deploy programmable systems which enhance the functionality of existing mechanical systems e.g.

- engine control systems,
- gearbox control systems,
- chassis control systems.

The hazards associated with failure of these systems are largely independent of the introduction of programmable technology but the likelihood of the hazards occurring is very much dependent on the programmable system. The implication is that there is an existing level of safety performance by virtue of mechanical components which can be used as a baseline for risk.

In the future the programmable systems fitted to vehicles will perform more novel functions which to a greater or lesser extent can be characterised by automatic interaction between vehicles. As a result these will give rise to new hazards. Examples of these systems are:

- adaptive cruise control,
- road trains,
- collision avoidance.

Since these hazards are new there is no existing baseline against which to measure risk.

2.2   Hazard Classification

The concept of controllability was developed during the project DRIVE Safely [3]. Controllability is derived from the usual representation of risk i.e.:

$$R = P * E$$

Where R is the risk, P is the probability of a system failure which could result in an accident (not the probability of an accident given a failure) and E is the effect of the system failure given that the failure has occurred.

In the automotive context the environment in which vehicles are used is extremely variable due to the large number of factors that influence the safe passage of road users. A small subset of these variables are:

- Weather
- Traffic density
- Road type
- Driver behaviour
- Lighting levels

The consequence of this situation is that it is not possible to predict with any certainty the likely 'effect' of a system failure.

The DRIVE approach was to assign integrity levels based on the classification of the 'effect' in terms of five controllability categories. These categories had textual definitions which describe qualitatively the degree of control of the safety of the situation given that a failure has occurred.

3   Safety Target Derivation Method

In order to make a decision on which approach is most suitable it is necessary to bear in mind some general requirements for safety targets:

1. They should be justifiable and defensible.
2. They should be capable of adapting to changing perceptions of risk.
3. They should be reasonable.
4. They should cope with rapidly changing technology.

For automotive safety targets to be of most use they must be reviewed by all relevant parties and agreed as the definition of 'best practice'. If such targets can be agreed upon they could be used as a means to bridge the gap between industry specific standards (e.g. MISRA) and generic standards (e.g. IEC 61508).

In the light of these considerations the chosen solution was to:

1. Derive a model which enables a risk expressed in terms of transport accidents to be related to vehicle based systems.
2. Establish a level of risk, associated with accidents resulting from technological failure in vehicle based systems, that would be regarded as broadly acceptable in the sense used by the Health and Safety Executive [4].
3. Use the target risk in terms of accidents and the derived risk model to set safety targets for vehicle based systems.

4   Risk Model

4.1   Analysis of Accident Data

The analysis described in this section seeks to answer the questions:

1.   What kind of vehicle mode best determines the severity of an accident?
2.   What kind of vehicle mode best determines the probability of an accident?

The source of the data was the annual report from the UK Department of the Environment, Transport and the Regions. It is entitled "Road Accidents Great Britain: 1997 - The casualty report" (known as RAGB). The underlying data which provides the basis for this report is collected by the police, either as a result of an officer attending the scene of an accident, or through reports made to the police at a later time.

There are very many measures that can be used to describe the severity and probability characteristics of accidents. The Road Accidents Great Britain report employs a consistent approach to describing the severity of casualties and accidents:

*   Fatal (i.e. killed)
*   Serious (i.e. seriously injured)
*   Slight (i.e. slightly injured)

The data has been split into a number of modes. These modes have been grouped into classes as shown in Table 1.

Intuitively it was expected that the mode classes would influence both the probability and severity of an accident due to the differing factors involved.

A statistical analysis of a sample of the data shows that the severity distribution is largely independent of driving condition, their mean being: 1.52% fatal; 14.73% serious; 83.75% slight [6]. This is seen as an important result in this paper since it suggests that the overall distribution of outcomes is fixed and that the significant factor becomes the probability of an accident, independent of the level of uncontrollability of a hazard.

It should be noted that the accident data recorded in RAGB are only a subset of the relevant outcomes of accidents. This is because the accident data are only collected if the accident involves personal injury. However, the RAGB report states that the cost-benefit value of prevention of road accidents in 1997 was estimated to be £14,814 million, of which £10,453 million is attributable to personal injury accidents and the remainder being associated with damage only accidents. The report also states that the average cost per 'damage only' accident is £1,210 and, for all accidents involving casualties, the average cost was £43,550. Hence the number of damage only accidents, and personal injury accidents, can be estimated as:

$$1997 \text{ damage only accidents} = (£14.8 \times 10^9 - £10.4 \times 10^9) / £1,210 = 3.6 \times 10^6$$

$$1997 \text{ personal injury accidents} = £10.4 \times 10^9 / £43,550 = 2.4 \times 10^5$$

This means that the ratio between 'personal injury' accidents and 'damage only' accidents is approximately 15:1. Using this result we can scale the personal injury accident data with respect to the damage only accidents and hence derive the severity distribution in Table 2.

4.2   Resulting Risk Model

Table 3 defines terms used in the derived risk model, which itself is presented in **Fig. 1**. Relevant probabilities are defined as:

- $P(A|H_x)$ is the probability of an accident, given a hazard with classification denoted by H_x.
- $P(I|H_x)$ is the probability of an incident, given a hazard with classification denoted by H_x.
- $P(C|H_x)$ is the probability of control being maintained, given a hazard with classification denoted by H_x.
- $P(A_x|A)$ is the probability of an accident of severity denoted by A_x given that *an* accident has occurred.

In the absence of data generated from the results of an experiment such as the use of a driving simulator, we make the following intuitive assumptions:

- A hazard classified as uncontrollable will result in either an incident or an accident with a probability of 1.
- A hazard classified as nuisance only will not result in an accident or incident.
- There is likely to be a logarithmic relationship linking the likelihood of an accident for the remaining three categories of controllability.

If the above hold then we can derive a table which maps controllability categories to probability of an accident or incident. This is shown graphically in **Fig. 2**

5   Accident Safety Targets

In this section we derive accident safety targets that could reasonably be considered to represent a 'broadly acceptable' level of risk. The method used is to evaluate the overall level of risk to which drivers are exposed so as to act as a baseline. In addition, the HSE work on the definition of a broadly acceptable level of risk, and the MEM (Minimum Endogenous Mortality) criterion are evaluated. Finally an accident safety target is proposed.

The risk of death arising directly from travelling by car is approximately 10^{-4} per person. year based on the following data:

1. Total number of car road traffic fatalities in 1997 = 1,934 {[2] p54}.
2. Total car & taxi traffic in 1997 = 3,678 x 10^8 km {[2] p53}.
3. It is assumed that the average distance travelled per annum = 20,000 km.

The HSE (Heath and Safety Executive) ToR (Tolerability of Risk) framework involves the definition of the upper and lower limits of tolerable risk. The lower of the two limits corresponds to the point below which the risk is considered to be 'broadly acceptable'. The following quote from the HSE gives a definition of the limit between tolerable and broadly acceptable risk: "This level might be taken to be 1 in a million (1 in 10^6) per annum bearing in mind the very small addition this would involve to the ordinary risks of life… "{[4] p31}.

Endogenous mortality is the rate at which a particular age group of a population die due to technological causes. In central Europe and well developed countries in general, the Minimum Endogenous Mortality (MEM) rate corresponds to the age group 5 to 15 years and has a value of 2×10^{-4} fatalities/person.year [5]. A feature of the MEM criteria is that it is assumed that there is a maximum of 20 technological systems that affect an individual at any one time, therefore they each share a proportion of this failure rate with the result that the acceptable risk to an individual from a given system is 10^{-5} fatalities/person.year.

Therefore the target risk is defined by the MEM criteria at the upper limit and the HSE 'broadly acceptable' value for risk at the lower limit. Therefore the derived accident safety target becomes:

$$10^{-6} < P(A_3)_{target} < 10^{-5} \text{ per person.year}$$

Since there are approximately 10^4 hours in a year this target can be expressed as:

$$10^{-10} < P(A_3)_{target} < 10^{-9} \text{ per person.hour}$$

6   System Safety Targets

6.1   Single Vehicle Systems

The derivation of safety targets for the single vehicle context relies on the following characteristics:

1. Vehicles operate independently of each other.
2. The upper limit on the number of fatalities that could reasonably be expected to result from an accident is close to unity.
3. The severity ratios that were derived through an analysis of present day accidents is valid for these types of system.

Table 4 presents accident probability versus controllability category and suggests that an uncontrollable hazard is certain to result in a loss of control and hence either an incident (near miss) or an accident. Therefore, using the accident safety target derived in section 5, and since:

$$P(H_4)_{vehicle.target} = P(A_3)_{target} / P(A_3|A)$$

the safety target for all the uncontrollable hazards for an entire vehicle can be derived as:

$$10^{-7} < P(H_4)_{vehicle.target} < 10^{-6} \text{ per hour}$$

As each vehicle contains a number of systems it is necessary to reason about the collective influence that these systems can contribute to causing a hazard of a given controllability classification.

Assume that the various programmable systems on the vehicle are of similar designs, and use similar technology, and each have a probability of failure, P(F), per hour. If it is further assumed that these systems have high levels of reliability, then for N of these systems the probability of failure is N x P(F). At the current time there are very few systems fitted to vehicles that can cause the most severe hazards i.e. those which would be considered uncontrollable. For the purposes of deriving these safety targets it is conservatively estimated that there are 10 such systems fitted to the vehicle.

Based on the previous assumption the system safety target for an uncontrollable system hazard, $P(H_4)_{system.target}$ can be calculated as follows:

$$P(H_4)_{system.target} = P(H_4)_{vehicle.target} / 10$$

Giving the result:

$$10^{-8} < P(H_4)_{system.target} < 10^{-7} \text{ per hour}$$

The equivalent results for the remaining controllability categories may be calculated in the same way but with reference to Table 4 for the corresponding accident probability. These results have been calculated and are recorded in Table 5.

6.2   Multiple Vehicle Systems

The derivation of safety targets for the 'multiple vehicle' context relies on the following characteristics:

1. Vehicles operate in systems of more than one vehicle.
2. The upper limit on the number of fatalities that could reasonably be expected to result from an accident is of the order of 10.
3. The severity ratios that were derived through an analysis of present day accidents are valid for these types of system.

The concept of Differential Risk Aversion (DRA) [5] can be used to modify the safety target for single vehicle systems to be applicable in multiple vehicle systems. This results in an order of magnitude decrease in the allowable frequency of an accident for each order of magnitude increase in the upper limit of the number of fatalities per accident. Therefore, the system safety target for the 'multiple vehicle' scenario becomes:

$$10^{-9} < P(H_4)_{system.target} < 10^{-8} \text{ per hour}$$

This result is then used to derive the system safety targets for the remaining hazard classifications as in section 6.1, which are summarised in Table 7.

7   Conclusions and Discussion

The following is a summary of the main conclusions of the paper:

1. It is considered possible to define a reasoned approach to the definition of safety targets for automotive systems.

2. An analysis of UK road accident data suggests that the proportion of fatalities in road accidents is effectively independent of vehicle operating conditions and influencing factors. This fact resulted in the hypothesis that vehicle hazards have a bearing only on the probability of *an* accident and not the likely severity. This result has an impact on the definition of controllability and suggests that severity should be removed.

3. A safety target for automotive systems should be set to a level that gives rise to a negligible level of risk. This is despite the fact that vehicle users are exposed to a relatively high level of risk, due mainly, from human error rather than technological failures.

4. Safety targets based on a risk to an individual derived from the HSE definition of 'broadly acceptable' risk and the MEM criterion are considered appropriate and reasonable.

We observe that the conclusions are based on a number of assumptions, the most important of which are:

1. That the statistical analysis, which leads to the conclusion that accident severity is independent of the level of controllability of the hazard leading to the accident, is confirmed.

2. That the logarithmic relationship between the level of controllability and the probability of an incident or an accident is confirmed.

Further assumptions are detailed in [6], together with proposals of how to test them. In particular, the relationship between controllability and severity could be tested out by means of experiments in a driving simulator, which would enable realistic testing of driver behaviour, and its results, in the presence of hazards. Additionally, further investigation is needed into how the risk model can be affected by human factors, some of which could be addressed by experiments using a driving simulator. It is also uncertain how the structure and granularity of the data affect the risk model and the safety targets. If more detailed data were available, the results could change.

References

1. "Development Guidelines for Vehicle Based Software", MISRA, 1994
2. "Road Accidents Great Britain: 1997 The Casualty Report", Department of the Environment, Transport and the Regions, August 1998, ISBN 011 552068 6.
3. DRIVE Safely, Towards a European Standard: The development of Safe Road Transport Informatic Systems (Draft 2), DRIVE Project V1051, 1992.
4. "The Tolerability of Risk From Nuclear Power Stations", Health and Safety Executive, 1992, ISBN 0 11 886368 1.
5. "Generalised Assessment Method, Part 2:Guidelines", ESPRIT P9032, CASCADE, 1997.
6. "Derivation of Safety Targets for the Random Failure of Programmable Vehicle Based Systems", Richard Evans. MSc Thesis, Department of Computer Science, University of York. September 1999

Appendix: Tables

Table 1. Driving Modes Relevant to Accidents

Mode class	Modes
Infrastructure	Road type, Junction type, Street lighting
Driver	Sex, Age
Environment	Daylight/Darkness, Weather conditions, Road conditions
Temporal	Day of the week, Time of day
Other issues	Special conditions, Region, Object hit, Carriageway hazards

Table 2. Severity distribution for all accident severities

Fatal	Serious	Slight	Damage only
0.09%	0.92%	5.23%	93.76%

Table 3. Risk Model Definitions

Term	Definition	Classification
Accident	An unintended event or sequence of events that causes death, injury, environmental or material damage.	Slight, Serious, Fatal
Incident	An unintentional event or sequence of events that does not result in loss, but, under different circumstances, has the potential to do so.	Boolean
Hazard	A hazard is a situation in which there is actual or potential danger to people or the environment.	Nuisance, Distracting, Debilitating, Difficult to Control, Uncontrollable

Table 4. Probability of an incident/accident by controllability category

Controllability category	Probability of incident/accident
Uncontrollable	1
Difficult to control	1 in 10
Debilitating	1 in 100
Distracting	1 in 1000
Nuisance only	0

Table 5. Safety targets in single vehicle systems

Category of controllability	$P(A|H_x)$	$P(H_x)_{system.target} = P(H_4)_{system.target} \times P(A|H_x)$
Uncontrollable	1	$10^{-8} < P(H_4)_{system.target} < 10^{-7}$
Difficult to control	10^{-1}	$10^{-7} < P(H_3)_{system.target} < 10^{-6}$
Debilitating	10^{-2}	$10^{-6} < P(H_2)_{system.target} < 10^{-5}$
Distracting	10^{-3}	$10^{-5} < P(H_1)_{system.target} < 10^{-4}$
Nuisance only	0	N/A

Table 6. Safety targets for multiple vehicle systems

Category of controllability	$P(A|H_x)$	$P(H_x)_{system.target} = P(H_4)_{system.target} \times P(A|H_x)$
Uncontrollable	1	$10^{-9} < P(H_4)_{system.target} < 10^{-8}$
Difficult to control	10^{-1}	$10^{-8} < P(H_3)_{system.target} < 10^{-7}$
Debilitating	10^{-2}	$10^{-7} < P(H_2)_{system.target} < 10^{-6}$
Distracting	10^{-3}	$10^{-6} < P(H_1)_{system.target} < 10^{-5}$
Nuisance only	0	N/A

Appendix: Figures

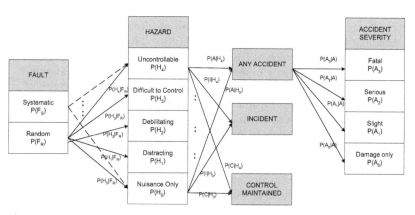

Fig. 1 Risk Model

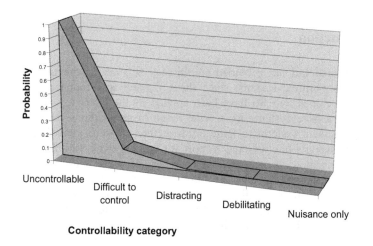

Fig. 2 Probability of incident/accident by controllability category

IEC 61508 – A Suitable Basis for the Certification of Safety-Critical Transport-Infrastructure Systems ??

Derek Fowler and Phil Bennett

CSE International Ltd
Glanford House, Bellwin Drive, Flixborough, N Lincs, DN15 8SN, UK
Tel. +44 1724 862169, Fax: +44 1724 846256
df@cse-euro.demon.co.uk
pab@cse-ltd.demon.co.uk

Abstract. IEC 61508 is widely viewed as the best available international generic standard for the management of functional safety in the development, operation and support of electrical, electronic and programmable electronic systems (EEPES). There is a danger, of course, that the existence of IEC 61508 will be seen as the solution to a wider range of problems in the development of safety-critical systems than such a standard could be capable of addressing. The suitability of IEC 61508 for the specification of relatively simple protection systems is not in doubt. However, in considering how effectively IEC 61508 could be used in the more complex environment of transport-infrastructure systems, the paper discusses the fundamental nature of, and means of deriving, safety requirements and considers how effectively compliance to the Standard may be used to provide assurance that a system is safe. From these discussions, the paper concludes on the feasibility and value of system certification against IEC 61508.

1   Introduction

CSE International Ltd has provided consultancy services in the field of software-intensive, safety-critical systems since the Company was founded in 1983. The techniques developed by CSE have been applied by the Company very successfully on software-intensive systems for a wide range of applications from safety-critical vehicle management systems to large infrastructure projects, including, the Channel Tunnel, Hong Kong's International Airport at Chek Lap Kok, Railtrack's West Coast Route Modernisation programme, a number of new European Air Traffic Management programmes, and Heathrow Airport's Terminal 5 project. The Company has also been heavily involved in the development of safety standards, especially IEC 61508, and in the design and delivery of safety training courses.

IEC 61508 [Ref 1] sets out a generic approach for all safety lifecycle activities for developments that involve the use of electrical, electronic and/or programmable

F. Koornneef and M. van der Meulen (Eds.): SAFECOMP 2000, LNCS 1943, pp. 250-263, 2000.
© Springer-Verlag Berlin Heidelberg 2000

electronic systems (EEPES) to perform safety functions. A key objective of the Standard is to facilitate the development of specific application-sector standards based on a rational and consistent technical policy.

The suitability of the Standard for use in relatively simple protection systems - typical of, say, the process and automotive industries – is fairly evident; indeed it is in such applications that the Standard has its origins.

Based on analysis first described in [Ref 2], this paper considers how IEC 61508 could be adapted to more complex, safety-related environments such as the development of transport-infrastructure systems. It examines two key areas: the derivation of safety requirements (including safety integrity levels (SILs), on which the application of most of IEC 61508 depends) and the relevance of the Standard to the *safety assurance* process (on which safety approval is usually based). It then outlines the evidence-based approach, adopted by the UK Civil Aviation Authority Safety Regulation Group, and proposes this as an improved way of applying the IEC 61508 to safety assurance. It concludes by considering whether system conformance and/or certification are meaningful concepts in the context of complex transport-infrastructure systems.

2   IEC 61508 Fundamentals

It is a fundamental requirement of IEC 61508 that, in the specification of any potential safety-related system, three key elements be identified:

- *equipment under control (EUC)* – "equipment, machinery, apparatus used for manufacturing, process, transportation, medical or other activities";
- *EUC control system* - "...responds to input signals from the process ... and generates output signals causing the EUC to operate in the desired manner";
- *safety-related system* - "system that ... implements the ... safety functions necessary to achieve or maintain a safe state for the EUC and is intended to achieve ... the necessary integrity for the ...safety functions".

The third point, that safety-related systems (SRS) are those systems whose primary purpose is to *reduce_*risk from the EUC / control system, is fundamental to understanding the nature of system safety requirements, as explained below.

3   System Safety Requirements

According to IEC 61508, safety requirements (ie the requirements of an SRS) need to be specified in two, complementary forms:

- a description of the functions to be performed by the SRS; *and*
- the integrity required of each of those functions;

as necessary to reduce to an acceptable level the risks originating in the EUC.

The relationship between risk reduction and safety requirements, as described in IEC 61508, is illustrated (logarithmically) in Figure 1, for a single-function SRS. R_u represents the level of risk from the EUC that would pertain in the absence of the SRS that we are attempting to specify, and (R_t) represents the tolerable level of risk as set by the safety policy for the application concerned. Part 1, para 7.5.2.2 of IEC 61508 suggests that the SIL of a safety function stems directly from the *necessary risk reduction* to be achieved by that function – ie (R_u -R_t) on Figure 1. That view might well be true in the specific case of a simple on/off protection system (ie an SRS which either works or doesn't) but is incomplete when considering an SRS whose performance is described as one or more continuous variables – eg a surveillance radar system. It is even less helpful in those applications for which it is difficult, if not impossible, to determine R_u. In both those situations, a more general interpretation is necessary.

Figure 1   IEC 61508 Risk/Requirements Model

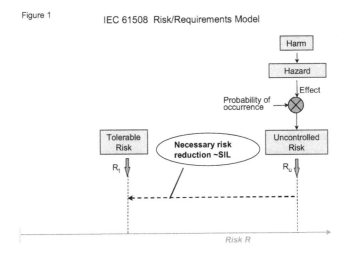

3.1   An Alternative Safety Requirements Model

An alternative view of the relationship between risk reduction and safety requirements is illustrated in Figure 2. As before, R_u represents the level of risk from the EUC in the absence of the SRS; but a new level of risk (R_m) is now introduced, representing the level of risk after adding a hypothetically *failure-free* SRS. [Ref 2] argues that:

- it is the *functionality and performance* of the SRS safety function(s) which determines the maximum theoretically possible risk reduction (R_u-R_m) - where performance includes all the desired attributes of the safety function - eg data attributes (accuracy, resolution, response time, update rate, latency etc) and human-machine interface (HMI) characteristics; and
- it is the *integrity* (ie SIL) of the SRS function(s) that determines the risk margin (R_t-R_m).

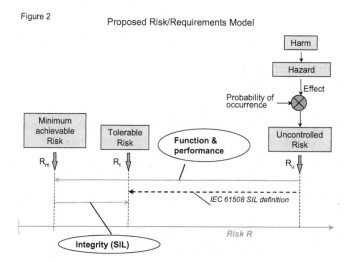

Figure 2   Proposed Risk/Requirements Model

It is suggested that Figure 2 indicates more clearly than Figure 1 that:

- safety should *not* be considered just as a matter of integrity (or reliability) – functionality and performance are at least as important, and must form an integral and explicit part of the system safety requirements; and
- the *lower* the performance of a safety function, the *greater* its integrity needs to be (and vice-versa) in order to achieve the same *net* level of risk reduction from the SRS.

3.2   Safety Requirements Determination

3.2.1   Practical Considerations

In specifying the safety requirements for, say, a new air traffic management or railway signalling system, designed to reduce the probability of collision between the vehicles concerned, some fundamental problems are immediately encountered:

- how to determine what the collision-risk probability would be without the system - ie R_u ;
- how to determine what an appropriate tolerable probability of collision (R_t) would be; and
- how to determine *how much* the system could contribute to the necessary reduction in risk ($R_u - R_t$).

Although an appropriate tolerable probability of collision is relatively easy to decide, the other two questions cannot be answered absolutely without the assistance of complex, validated collision risk models. In most instances, such models do not yet exist and, therefore, most transport safety cases have to be argued incrementally from a historical base, on the (often implicit) assumption that the means of delivering the service is not substantially different from that on which the historical evidence of a safe service is founded. However, even that apparently simple assumption can be difficult to validate, as will be shown below.

3.2.2   Specification of a Typical Transportation System

Function and Performance

A common solution to the problems of establishing absolutely what the level of risk *would* have been in the absence of the safety functions (R_u in Figure 2) and to quantifying the risk reduction (R_u-R_m) provided by the functions is to:

- require the new system to have at least as much functionality and performance as the system which it is intended to replace; and
- produce evidence to show that the service that was supported by the old system was itself tolerably safe.

This at least places R_m below R_t, albeit by an unknown amount, *provided* the system functionality and performance is specified as an explicit safety requirement.

Safety Integrity Requirements

Without knowing the risk margin (R_t-R_m), it is not possible to determine the integrity requirements for the safety functions by using the direct methods proposed in IEC 61508. A way around the problem is to use an inductive risk-analysis approach, which, working on the assumption that $R_m < R_t$, comprises two stages, as described in [Ref 3]:

- Functional Hazard Assessment (FHA) of every possible failure mode of each safety function, typically using an approach based on Failure Modes Effects and Criticality Analysis, involving skilled and experienced operational and technical staff; and
- determination of the maximum acceptable probability of occurrence of each function, using a Risk Classification Matrix (RCM).

To get around the problem of not being able to model the risk of collision, it is usual to base the approach on the risk of not being able to positively maintain the minimum required separation between aircraft – or trains in the case of railway systems.

A typical RCM (based on an ATM application) is shown in Figure 3, and is normally used by taking the assessed severity for the particular failure mode (severity category 1 being the worst case), and ascribing an allowed likelihood of occurrence of that failure mode, according to the Risk Class (ie risk tolerability) defined in the following table.

Figure 3   Illustrative Risk Classification Matrix

Likelihood		Risk Classification			
Frequency	**Probability** (per operating hour)	**Severity Category**			
		1	**2**	**3**	**4**
Frequent	$>10^{-3}$	A	A	A	C
Probable	10^{-3} to 10^{-4}	A	A	B	D
Occasional	10^{-4} to 10^{-5}	A	A	C	D
Remote	10^{-5} to 10^{-6}	A	B	D	D
Improbable	10^{-6} to 10^{-7}	B	C	D	D
Extremely improbable	$<10^{-7}$	C	D	D	D

Risk Class	Definition
A	Those risks which are not tolerable, save in the most extraordinary circumstances.
B	Those risks which are tolerable only if further risk reduction is impracticable or if its cost would be grossly disproportionate to the safety improvement gained.
C	Those risks which are tolerable if the cost of further reduction would exceed the improvement which would be gained.
D	Risk class D is allocated to those risks which are broadly acceptable. It is necessary only to maintain assurance that risks remain in this class.

A key feature of the table is that it embodies the ALARP principle - that risks shall be reduced to a level that is as low as reasonably practicable. Therefore, when specifying a system initially, the lowest risk level (Class D or, the case of a Category 1 failure, Class C) should be used.

Relationship with IEC 61508
It is worth considering at this point whether the above procedure is consistent with the safety-requirements determination process set out in Part 1 of IEC 61508. Reference back to section 3.1 above suggests this to be the case, on two counts:

• the safety functions required to achieve the necessary risk reduction have been identified; and

- given the alternative risk model presented in section 3.1, the values from IEC 61508 shown in the table below and the RCM values at Figure 3 are directly related – ie the allowed probability of failure of a safety function, as derived above, is synonymous with the IEC 61508–defined SIL of that function.

Probability of dangerous failure per operating hour	SIL
10^{-5} to 10^{-6}	1
10^{-6} to 10^{-7}	2
10^{-7} to 10^{-8}	3
10^{-8} to 10^{-9}	4

Therefore, the appropriate techniques prescribed in IEC 61508 can be applied to the development of the safety functions identified in the FHA.

Caution!
However, the use of the techniques described above comes with a number of "health warnings" which are often not clearly stated or are ignored:

- the risk of collision and the contribution of safety functions to risk reduction vary according the particular operational circumstances under consideration – eg the same set of RCM probability values would not be suitable for the approach and landing phase of flight, as used for the en-route phase;
- the RCM probability values are largely subjective and relate to risk of separation erosion not to risk of collision – the relationship between separation erosion and collision will change as traffic densities increase and/or the manner in which separation-maintenance function is implemented changes – eg the moves towards "free flight" in air transport and the introduction of moving-block separation on the railways;
- such methodologies typically treat the specification of equipment in isolation from human performance - the introduction of new technologies which change the balance in responsibility between man and machine could undermine the historical base;
- a given set of the RCM probability values are valid at only one level in the system hierarchy and include an assumption about the total number of system elements which could contribute to a particular failure in the service.

There is also a problem in the application of the SIL concept to complex systems which requires careful interpretation of IEC 61508. For example, it might be determined that a particular safety function should be SIL 2, and that the implementation of that function will comprise a number of essential, complex elements - including computer systems, people and procedures. Therefore, once the high-level integrity requirement for the SIL 2 safety function (a failure probability of $<10^{-6}$ per operating hour) has been allocated to the various system elements and then decomposed to software-component level, it is quite conceivable that the allowable failure probability of those components would need to be one or two orders of magnitude lower. In other words, the SIL 2 safety function in this example would require the corresponding software to be developed to a standard appropriate to SIL 3 or SIL 4.

4   Safety Assurance

4.1   Principles

The purpose of safety assurance is to ensure that the risks associated with the deployment of a system are tolerably low, and to provide positive evidence of that fact. For many projects, the task of demonstrating that a system is tolerably safe can involve a highly complex argument, each strand of which needs to be supported by adequate evidence. Furthermore, the degree of rigour required of the evidence should depend on the risks involved, and the assurance process therefore needs to focus on the higher-risk areas of the project. The need for basing assurance on a recognised standard stems from legal and technical issues:

- the safety environment is heavily governed by law, defining the roles and responsibilities of regulatory authorities, service providers and systems / component suppliers. The use of *best practice* through the adoption of relevant, recognised standards can be a valuable "defence".
- it is usually impracticable to prove the integrity levels of *any* high-integrity system by testing alone since the required time and effort to achieve a statistically meaningful result would be excessive;
- the systematic nature of software failures in particular makes the integrity of computer-based systems extremely difficult to predict by direct means, and it becomes necessary also to examine the processes used to develop the software as well as the intrinsic attributes of its design.

Therefore, the effective use of *appropriate* standards that govern, inter alia, the process of design and development of high-integrity systems is important in gaining the necessary assurance that the system will meet its safety requirements.

IEC 61508 was certainly produced as a standard for the development and deployment of safety-critical systems– the question now to be considered is how to ensure that its application is effective in the safety assurance process.

4.2   IEC 61508 and Safety Assurance

This section uses Goal Structuring Notation (GSN) to examine the scope and limitations of IEC 61508 as the basis for providing assurance that a system is tolerably safe for introduction into operational service. The basic notation, as applied to safety assurance, is shown in Figure 4.

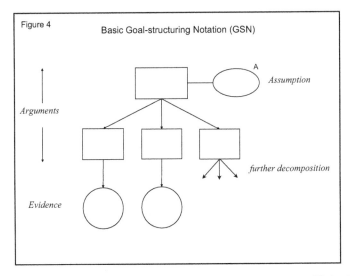

Figure 4   Basic Goal-structuring Notation (GSN)

Figure 5 starts with the (first-level) argument that the system will be [tolerably] safe. That argument can be said to be true if (and only if) the four second-level arguments can be shown to be true. For the purposes of this paper, installation and preparation for operational use are taken to be largely process arguments that are adequately covered by IEC 61508 and are not therefore further decomposed here.

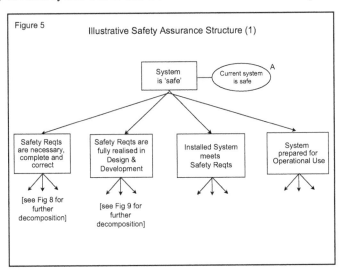

Figure 5   Illustrative Safety Assurance Structure (1)

Figure 6 decomposes the safety-requirements argument such that the next-level arguments map on to the first five phases of the IEC 61508 safety lifecycle, and shows the type of evidence (also determined from IEC 61508) which could be introduced to satisfy arguments at that level. It will be observed that the arguments relate only to the *process* of deriving the safety requirements and of course (because IEC 61508 is a generic standard) can say nothing about whether the requirements themselves are the *right* requirements.

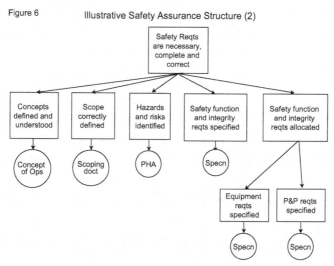

Figure 6   Illustrative Safety Assurance Structure (2)

The top-level argument on Figure 7 is complex and requires several layers of decomposition – for the purposes of this paper, only the equipment aspects are further decomposed, non-exhaustively.   Again IEC 61508 provides useful detail on the lifecycle aspects of hardware development but says little about the product which is required to emerge from those processes – except on matters such as hardware redundancy and proof test intervals.

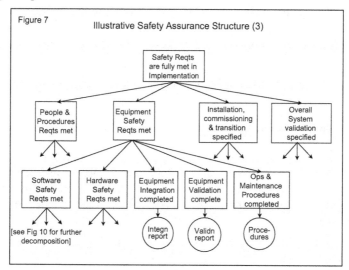

Figure 7   Illustrative Safety Assurance Structure (3)

A similar picture emerges in Figure 8, in which the software aspects of the equipment are further decomposed to the lower levels of the IEC 61508 software lifecycle. The Standard sets out very clear (but usually non-mandatory) requirements for each stage in the lifecycle (in many cases, depending on the SIL of the software) and specifies the type and quality of evidence necessary to demonstrate compliance with those requirements.   Clarity of the argument/evidence relationship can be enhanced by including the relevant IEC 61508 references on the GSN structure – an example is given, in Figure 8, for software code implementation.

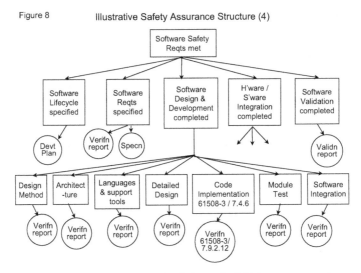

Figure 8   Illustrative Safety Assurance Structure (4)

However, the inevitable greater emphasis in IEC 61508 on process than on product leaves unresolved issues which are of growing concern to the procurers and developers of safety-critical, transportation systems, for example:

- the absence of requirements relating to issues specific to object-orientated design;
- the almost total lack of requirements concerning COTS / re-used software;
- the fact that the Standard treats each process within the lifecycle as being of equal importance.

The latter two points are discussed further in the following paragraph.

4.3   An Evidence-Based Approach

The requirements for the approval of software in safety-related systems specified by the UK Civil Aviation Authority, Safety Regulation Group in its manual CAP 670 [Ref 4] takes a different approach which is deliberately non-prescriptive in terms of the development process but rather demands evidence of achievement of four safety objectives, ie that:

1. the specified requirements are a necessary and sufficient for the development of a tolerably safe system;
2. the safety requirements are fully traceable to all levels of the design (and vice versa);
3. the safety requirements are fully met in implementation;
4. the developed software is based on a known and consistent configuration.

For each objective, evidence is specified under three categories, in descending order of weight:

- direct evidence, being the most direct and tangible way of showing that a particular objective had been achieved– for example, evidence from test results would be the most direct way in which satisfaction of safety requirements in a newly developed system could be demonstrated;
- backing evidence, which provides information about the quality of direct evidence, particularly the amount of confidence which can be placed on it - for example, evidence to show that a test regime was adequate and appropriate, and that tests had been properly conducted, would provide backing for test results which had been submitted as direct evidence;
- reinforcement evidence[1] is used where direct evidence (even with backing) would be inadequate to show that a particular objective had been achieved – for example, demonstration that new software met the requirements of a high-integrity application could never be achieved by testing alone, but evidence that the processes by which the software had been developed were appropriate to that application could be used to "extrapolate" results of the testing which had been submitted as direct evidence.

In most cases the rigour demanded of the evidence increases as the integrity required of the software increases. The requirements also contain detailed rules on testing and on the type and quality of evidence that can be used to support arguments of safety in COTS and re-used software.

The advantages of this approach over the simple lifecycle approach taken by IEC 61508 is that it is non-prescriptive in terms of the development standards used; it makes full provision for COTS; and re-used software and evidence is weighted according to its value in supporting a safety argument. Of course, it does *not* preclude the use of standards such as IEC 61508 – on the contrary it is possible (indeed highly desirable) to map the provisions of such standards on to the safety objectives and evidence categories, thereby improving the quality of the contribution of those standards to the safety assurance process.

5   Conformance and Certification

IEC 61508 is, by its generic nature, a process standard rather than a product specification – the basis of its approach is that by applying appropriately rigorous practices and techniques in the development of safety-related systems, the probability that a safe system would emerge will be greatly increased.

The Standard starts by specifying the processes by which the safety requirements for an SRS should be derived. Thus conformance with those aspects of IEC 61508 would provide only limited, *indirect* evidence concerning the adequacy of the system safety requirements – i.e. that the requirements were *right*, rather than that they were the *right* requirements.

---

[1] The current version of CAP 670, issued for consultation after this paper was written, no longer recognises the separate existence of 'reinforcement' evidence. It is acknowledged therefore that the specific interpretation set out in the paper may not reflect current UK CAA policy – however, it is asserted that the *principle* of the evidence-based approach is unaffected.

Most of the rest of IEC 61508 specifies (but usually does not mandate) design and development techniques and processes to be followed in the rest of the lifecycle, according to the target SIL. Again, because IEC 61508 necessarily focuses on process rather than product, conformance with the Standard can indicate at best only that the product is of a given *integrity* and not that it is the *right* product.

It follows, therefore, that attempts at specific *certification* (or type approval) of complex equipment against IEC 61508 face a number of difficulties, including the following:

- certification for use in a particular operational environment may not be valid for a different environment;
- equipment is only one element of the system – the safety requirements (ie function, performance and integrity) of the equipment depends on, inter alia, how those requirements are apportioned from the overall system requirements that itself is variable and likely to change with new technologies;
- because IEC 61508 deals only with system integrity and cannot, by virtue of its generic nature, specify the equally important system function and performance, any certification statement in relation to IEC 61508 would give an incomplete picture regarding the suitability of the system for the intended application;
- because most of the requirements in IEC 61508 are not mandatory it is left to the developer in consultation with the assessor to decide on how much to apply the recommendations given in the Standard (although the onus is on the developer to justify ignoring them!);

Therefore, a goal of equipment standardisation, however well intentioned, is unlikely to be achieved via attempts at *certification* against IEC 61508!

6   Conclusions

The paper argues that achievement of safety is as much dependent on the functionality and performance of an SRS as it is on its integrity, though IEC 61508 does distinguish between them as clearly as it might.

By means of a generalised risk/safety requirements model, the paper examines an inductive safety-analysis methodology commonly used in transportation-infrastructure applications and shows that, provided functionality and performance is included in the safety requirements, the results are consistent with the risk-reduction concepts of IEC 61508 and specifically that the integrity values thereby derived can be directly related to IEC 61508 SIL values. This is important since the application of IEC 61508 to the development process is largely SIL dependent.

However, frequently undeclared assumptions in safety analysis methodologies and lack of clarity in IEC 61508 about how SILs are applied down through the levels of decomposition of complex safety-related systems means that great care needs to be exercised in the specification of such systems.

In considering the relevance of certification to transport-infrastructure systems, the paper notes that the safety of such systems is heavily dependent on the environment in which they have to operate. Furthermore, because systems comprise not just equipment but also people and procedures, the apportionment of the requirements to the equipment element is somewhat arbitrary and likely to change with the introduction of greater automation. Therefore it is argued that the whole concepts is largely meaningless.

Conformance is a somewhat different issue and potentially less misleading than *certification*, if interpreted sensibly – ie if applied to the process of designing and developing a product, rather than directed at the product itself.   Whereas, demonstration of conformance of the development of a system to IEC 61508 would not addresses the fundamental issue as to whether the end-product would be safe for its intended use, it would give some assurance about the process which led to the product and indirectly something about the integrity of the product itself. The value of demonstrating conformance to IEC 61508 lies, therefore, not in a guarantee that a product will be safe, but rather in lessening of the likelihood that it will be unsafe!

A somewhat different, evidence-based approach is provided by the UK CAA's CAP 670 publication, which focuses on arguments and evidence concerning the system itself and relies on evidence of correct process when more direct evidence is incomplete. This approach has the added advantage of providing explicit requirements for the (commercially attractive) incorporation of COTS/re-used software in safety-related systems.

References

1   International Electrotechnical Commission, IEC 61508, Functional Safety of Electrical/Electronic/Programmable Electronic Safety Related Systems, 65A/254/FDIS, IEC:1999.

2   Fowler D. Application of IEC 61508 to Air Traffic Management and Similar, Complex, Critical Systems – *Proceedings of the 8th Safety-critical Systems Symposium, Southampton, UK, 2000*

3   Eurocontrol, Air Navigation System Safety Assessment Methodology, SAF.ET1.ST03.1000-MAN-01-00, edition 0.5, 30 April 1999

4   UK Civil Aviation Authority, CAP 670, Air Traffic Services Safety Requirements, Amendment 3, Sep 99.

An Approach to Software Assisted Recovery from Hardware Transient Faults for Real Time Systems

D. Basu and R. Paramasivam

Electronics Group, Vikram Sarabhai Space Centre,
Trivandrum, India.
d_basu@vssc.org

Abstract. Most of the mission critical real time systems are characterized by the cyclical execution of periodic processes with hard deadlines. Provision of fault tolerance for such systems, has been extensively studied. Most of these treat hardware faults as belonging to the permanent stuck-at category. In this paper we deal with hardware transient faults, which by their intrinsic nature manifest as software faults and thereby lend themselves to correction based on concepts used in the study of software fault tolerance. This scheme which has been proposed to be used in real time embedded computers used in India's satellite launch vehicle programs is simple to implement and uses an underlying process structure similar to the one proposed by Anderson and Knight [1]. It takes advantage of the natural synchronization existing in such processes and also the fact that the inertia of the physical systems in which these controllers are embedded absorb minor temporary deviations in their outputs so long as subsequent outputs are correct.

1   Introduction

The subject of providing fault tolerance for real time systems has attracted the attention of researchers over the years [1],[2],[3],[4]. However the requirements of fault tolerance vary from one application to another. For example an aircraft engine control may have less stringent requirements because of higher level redundancy i.e. multiple engines per plane as compared to digital flight control of an aircraft [3]. Similarly, the attitude control systems of a spacecraft in orbit can be less demanding from the point of view of fault tolerance than the avionics system deployed on board a satellite launch vehicle.

Historically the issue of hardware fault tolerance has received more attention from system designers in comparison to that paid to software fault tolerance. However software fault tolerance is becoming an increasingly important issue with many space missions having failed due to errors in the software design. The N-version programming (NVP) [5] uses voting on the outputs of different versions of the same

F. Koornneef and M. van der Meulen (Eds.): SAFECOMP 2000, LNCS 1943, pp. 264-274, 2000.

software and does not call for the establishment of recovery and rollback points. The recovery block (RB) approach [6] involves the use of "acceptance tests" and the establishment of recovery points for proper rollback and retry. Some researchers [2],[4] have suggested a unified approach to both hardware and software fault tolerance in real time systems using the underlying principles of both NVP and RB. However for many practical projects, implementation of NVP poses a problem from the point of view of cost. This method to be truly effective calls for the development of different versions of the same software application by independent development teams using different development tools [5]. The RB is a viable alternative but imposes time penalties, which may become unacceptable in hard real time systems. Fortunately many avionics applications share certain common characteristics [1] which can be used by the designers of such systems to impart a degree of fault tolerance which would otherwise be difficult to implement. These characteristics can be summarized below:-

a) Programs or processes are executed periodically and the periodicity of a process does not change for a given mission.
b) There can be several processes having different periodicities i.e. some programs are executed more frequently than others. Their synchronization points are defined to coincide with the end of a frame i.e. the end of the periodic execution of one of the processes.
c) For many of the outputs of embedded real time systems, the inertial characteristics of the environment in which the embedded system works permit temporary aberrations, so long as subsequent outputs are generated correctly and within a reasonable period of time. For example in the case of a satellite launch vehicle, the outputs are sent to the stage control actuators every 20 milliseconds. Simulation studies have established that even if one of these outputs is erroneous, no harm is done if correct outputs are generated within 100 milliseconds.

With the above realistic assumptions in mind, Anderson and Knight [1] have suggested a model for the software of a real time system that permits software fault tolerance using the RB technique. However, to take care of the well known "domino effect" for concurrently executing processes [6], they suggest a scheme known as an "exchange" which allows the establishment of proper recovery points for a set of interacting processes. The "exchange" is a restricted form of "conversation" as suggested by Randell [6].

Many intermittent hardware faults are very difficult to distinguish from software faults [2] and it is reasonable to expect that such hardware transient faults can be tackled in a manner similar to that of software faults. In this paper we propose a scheme which seeks to tackle hardware transient faults in real time systems using certain concepts borrowed from the study of software fault tolerance. This scheme is to be adopted in the future generation of on board computers used in India's satellite launch vehicle programs.

In the next section a description of the software model with essential modifications to meet the goals of our scheme is presented. The types of hardware transient faults and the requirements of the system to recover from such faults are discussed in section 3. In section 4, we establish that in certain situations, the restrictions imposed by the "exchange" can impair the recovery from hardware transients where there is no need to try out an alternate software block. Instead, a method of inter process communication of variables is suggested   such that separate recovery points are established for individual processes. Thus all processes in an "exchange" are not forced to roll back to a common recovery point which may otherwise be too far back in time. The variables are classified according to the requirements of inter process communication and the criteria for the selection of these variables to build appropriate recovery points are also discussed.

2   The Computational Model of a Real Time System

The computational model is characterized by the fact that there exists a set of processes, which repeat at fixed and predetermined iteration rates. The reciprocals of these iteration rates define the periodicities of these processes. There are in general multiple iteration rates depending on the bandwidth of the physical systems that the underlying processes service. For example, since the dominant natural frequencies of the stabilization and control systems of a launch vehicle are considerably higher than those of a guidance and navigation system, the processes, which support the control and autopilot algorithms have to be repeated more often than the processes which are a part of the ascent navigation and guidance algorithms. Each iteration cycle also defines the timing deadlines to be met for the processes executed in that iteration cycle. Moreover unlike in [1], we define a single deadline for a set of processes having the same periodicity. However the precedence relationships among processes within the same iteration cycle are maintained by the sequential execution of the processes. The set of processes having the highest periodicity defines a time period known as a "major frame". Thus the tasks having a lower periodicity will have to be repeated "n" times within one major frame. Obviously, for a feasible schedule "n" must be a positive integer i.e. the periodicities of the processes having the lowest iteration rate must be the least common multiple (LCM) of the periodicties of all other processes. Thus for a system having two iteration rates there are sub frames within a major frame. Without any loss of generality, we consider two iteration rates in this paper. Systems having multiple iteration rates can be built by considering two successive iteration rates at a time and applying our method recursively. An important characteristic of real time periodic processes is that the processes executed in one major frame are repeated till the objectives of the mission are met. For a satellite launch vehicle this happens with the injection of the satellite into orbit followed by post injection maneuver if any.

To describe the above concepts more elaborately, we define the following, $P_{i,j,k}$ depicts a process of periodicity 'i' in milliseconds and the jth process in the execution sequence of all processes having periodicity 'i'. 'k' denotes the kth iteration of a sub frame or a major frame in the in the overall execution sequence.

With the above background we can look at a typical synchronization graph for processes running in an on board computer of a satellite launch vehicle. As shown in Fig. 1, there are two iteration rates. One is every 10 milliseconds (msec) and the other every 100 msec. The 10 msec cycle is made up of three sequential processes $P_{10,1,k}$, $P_{10,2,k}$ and $P_{10,3,k}$ executed one after another and repeated cyclically. While the individual processes have to be executed in the given sequence in order to maintain a defined precedence relationship, they have to collectively meet deadlines every

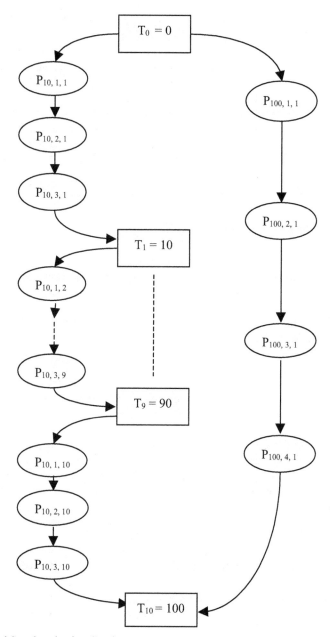

Fig. 1.   A Typical Synchronization Graph

10 msec as shown in the Fig. 1, by $T_1, T_2, \ldots T_{10}$. The 100 msec cycle consists of 4 processes $P_{100,1,k}$, $P_{100,2,k}$, $P_{100,3,k}$ and $P_{100,4,k}$ and executed in that order. As shown in Fig. 1, the deadline for these processes is at T_{10}, which corresponds to a time of 100 msec from the beginning of the major frame at T_0. The scheduling of the processes is based on the well known Rate Monotonic Scheduling (RMS) algorithm [7],[8], which permits the whole cycle shown in Fig. 1 to be repeated as the schedule has been achieved within a time frame of 100 msec given by the LCM of the periodicities of the processes. If the periods are relatively prime, then one may have to compute a fairly long schedule. But in reality there is often flexibility in adjusting the periods so that the LCM of all periods is not too long. An important point to be noted here is that T_{10} happens to be a synchronizing point, where the communication between the processes having different periodicities takes place. More detailed discussion on the synchronization graph can be found in [1]. Fig. 1 is only indicative of a typical system and does not describe the realization of an actual system. It is used to develop the concepts described in the next two sections.

3   Hardware Transient Faults

All commercially available microprocessor chips have the ability to detect various types of abnormalities during their operation [9],[10]. These are generally due to transient noise in the hardware and cause a temporary aberration in the system performance, which if left uncorrected could lead to a catastrophic failure of the mission. Examples of such transient faults are "invalid opcodes", "bad access", "spurious interrupt" etc. When the processor detects a fault it immediately responds in a manner similar to the servicing of interrupts. A fault is generally handled with a fault handling procedure, which the processor invokes by an implicit procedure call. Prior to making the call, the processor saves the state of the current process. It also saves information on the fault, which the fault handler can use to recover from the condition that caused the fault. This information is also useful in identifying whether the exception caused is due to hardware or software. If the information stored by the processor is sufficient to enable restoration of the state of the process to that existing prior to the occurrence of the fault, the fault handler can easily restart execution from that point and thus system recovery is complete. Any good real time system should be such that the minor timing overheads required for such recovery should not lead to a deadline being missed.

What we address in this paper is that there exists a large class of faults for which the only recovery possible is to shut down the system with as much debugging information as possible to carryout offline diagnostics. This is not acceptable for mission critical real time hardware and an attempt has to be made to recover from such faults as gracefully as possible. Clearly, whether a fault belongs to the recoverable category or not, depends on the type of state information that the processor can save before a fault handling procedure is invoked. Information on the nature of the faults is well documented in all the reference manuals provided by the chip manufacturers. For example the MC68000 stores enough information [9] to enable recovery from an "illegal opcode" or "spurious interrupt". But for faults such as "bus error" or "address error", it is not guaranteed that the process can be continued from the interrupted point where the fault occurs. In such cases, it may seem that recovery is not possible without resorting to rollback techniques as is done in the RB based software fault tolerance.

It is instructive to point out the subtle differences between the two approaches. In the RB scheme a process is declared to be faulty when it fails in its acceptance test before exiting from the process. An alternate process is then attempted for which the software should have a well-defined recovery point where it rolls back to, before trying out the alternate. When the goal is to recover from hardware transient faults, it is not necessary to try out an alternate software process. Instead recovery should be from the nearest in time recoverable point such that real time requirements are not compromised. How this can be done for the software model of Fig.1 is described in the next section.

4   Inter-Process Communication and Establishment of Recovery Points

A problem that arises when a high level recovery is attempted is the establishment of a proper recovery point. This is all the more important for a system which has inter-process communications, because it can cause the recovery of points of individual processes to roll back uncontrollably due to "domino effect" [6],[1]. The solution to this problem suggested by Randell [6] was to restrict the inter-process communication within a firewall known as "conversation". While this adequately addresses the requirements of sequential systems, difficulties arise when systems of communicating concurrent processes are considered, more so when real time constraints are imposed. An "exchange"[1] is a mechanism which is applicable to the process structure of real time system shown in Fig.1 and is depicted in Fig.2.

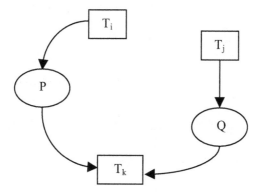

Fig. 2. An Exchange

It highlights the following,

1. P & Q are concurrently executing processes because their operations overlap. In the context of our model, two processes have overlapped operations when they have different periodicities.
2. They are allowed to exchange variables freely since they terminate together at time T_k.
3. Their recovery points are established when they are initiated i.e. at T_i for P and T_j for Q.
4. T_k is also the point where the exchange terminates and their recovery points are discarded.

The "exchange" is a clever extension of the "conversation" to suit the requirements of cyclic real time processes. It takes advantage of the fact that such systems are characterized by well-defined synchronization points, where all inter-process communications between two processes executing concurrently take place. The properties of an "exchange" suggest that the acceptance tests for all processes terminating at the synchronization points are carried out and should any of these acceptance tests fail, all processes roll back to their recovery points and start executing alternate versions of the processes. Thus, from Fig. 2 if P fails in its acceptance test at T_k, both P and Q restart from T_i and T_j respectively. Because of the iterative nature of these systems, the states of each process are similar at the beginning of every iteration cycle. Therefore restarting a process simply amounts to executing the alternate software block for the processes from the beginning of the corresponding iteration cycles, provided the frame dependent variables i.e. the variables whose values would change during that iteration have been preserved at the recovery points. How the overall scheme works in the larger context, is seen by examining Fig. 1. As can be seen, the processes with periodicities 10msec and 100msec have their synchronization points at T_{10}, which means the processes not only exchange their values but discard their recovery points at T_{10}. This imposes a very minor restriction that the variables communicated from $P_{10,j,k}(j=1,2,3$ and $k=1,2,....10)$ to $P_{100,j,1}(j=1,...4)$ are available to the latter for its next iteration i.e. $P_{100,j,2}$. Similarly, variables communicated from $P_{100,j,1}(j=1,..4)$ to $P_{10,j,k}(j=1,2,3$ and $k=1,2,....10)$ will be available to the latter for its next iteration i.e. $P_{10,j,k}(j=1,2,3$ and $k=11,12,....20)$. We call this restriction minor because as mentioned earlier the iteration rates are chosen keeping the bandwidth of the physical system in mind and no degradation is caused by this delayed but organized exchange of variables. All that is required is to store the frame and sub-frame dependent variables at the end of each iteration so that these can be reused as recovery point variables should there be a need to do so. Therefore, if an acceptance test for $P_{100,j,1}(j=1,...4)$ fails at T_{10}, all 4 processes in $P_{100,j,1}$ roll back to T_0 and the $P_{10,j,10}$ to T_9.

The goal of this paper is to extend the above concepts to achieve recovery from hardware transient faults. The significant differences between hardware transient faults and software faults are summarized by the following properties,

Property 1: Hardware transient faults can occur anytime during the execution of a process and not necessarily at the termination of an exchange i.e. for example at T_{10} in Fig. 1.

Property 2: For hardware transient faults there are no alternate software blocks to be retried as the failure is not due to software.

These two properties are used to develop a viable scheme for such faults. The second property allows forward recovery from errors, as the requirement is to try out the same software process using a set of variables, which have been preserved from the last correct execution of the process.

Hardware transient faults discussed in section 3 generate exceptions known as "faults" or "traps" which cause the microprocessor to branch to a fault handler routine. For the purpose of unambiguous explanation, the term "fault" shall be used henceforth in the paper to indicate that such a transient has been detected and the processor has branched to the execution of the corresponding fault handler. The process, which has been interrupted by the fault, will be termed the faulted process. Since faults can occur during the execution of individual processes, it is logical to conclude that only the faulted process needs recovery but with the following caveats.

Caveat 1: Processes, with which the faulted process interacts will have to use variables from the previous correct iteration of the faulted process.

Caveat 2: There does not have to be a retry of the faulted process from its entry point as envisioned by an "exchange" but it can be the next iteration of the same process. This follows from *Property 2*, which says that in the event of a fault there is no alternate software block to be retried. Thus the same faulted process can be retried which can as well be the next iteration of the same process.

All the above concepts can be best illustrated by an example. From *Property 1*, a fault can occur anywhere and not necessarily at the synchronization points. Let us assume that a hardware transient fault occurs during the execution of $P_{10,3,9}$. This does not cause the system to roll back in time to an earlier declared recovery point as in an "exchange". Instead, the progress is maintained through T_9 and $P_{10,1,10}$, $P_{10,2,10}$ etc. This can be done because re-execution of $P_{10,3,9}$ is the same as execution of $P_{10,3,10}$ but with a different but similar set of input variables. For a successful implementation, the output variables of $P_{10,3,9}$ which are to be used by any sequentially executing i.e. $P_{10,j,10}(j=1,2,3)$ or concurrently executing i.e. $P_{100,j,1}(j=1..4)$ have to be obtained from the last correct execution of $P_{10,3,9}$ i.e. $P_{10,3,8}$ as given in *Caveat 1*. This type of forward error recovery is most suited for hard real time systems. Any difference arising out of the use of the outputs of the previous iteration of the faulted process will cause minor deviations in the final outputs. As has been explained in section 1, such minor aberrations in the outputs are absorbed by the inertia of the physical system in which the software is embedded so long as subsequent outputs do not exhibit erroneous behavior. As our goal is to correct for transient faults, it is reasonable to expect that such occasional glitches in a system will make recovery possible without any significant time overheads that are associated with rollback and retry.

Another important aspect of the proposed system is that the processes which interact with the faulty process either sequentially or concurrently need not resort to roll back as in an "exchange", so long as "recovery buffer" with properly selected "recovery variables" are maintained for each process.

4.1   Choice of "Recovery Variables"

For the process structure of Fig. 1, the variables exchanged among processes can be broadly classified into the following four types,

a.   *Type 1:* Those variables which are the outputs of a process $P_{i1,j1,k1}$ and are inputs to process $P_{i1,j2,k1}$ ($j2 > j1$). These variables are characterized by the fact that they are used by processes, which follow a given process, in the same iteration cycle. They are not used in the next cycle but are recomputed from fresh data acquired through sensors in the next iteration of the same process. For example, $P_{10,2,1}$ generates outputs acquired instantaneously from some sensors and used by $P_{10,3,1}$.

b.   *Type 2:* Those variables which are the outputs of any process $P_{i1,j1,k1}$ and used in the next iteration by the same process $P_{i1,j1,k1+1}$ viz. $P_{10,1,1}$ generates outputs used as inputs by $P_{10,1,2}$.

c.   *Type 3:* Those variables which are outputs of any process $P_{i1,j1,k1}$ and are used in the next iteration by a process $P_{i1,j2,k1+1}$ such that $j2 < j1$ viz. $P_{100,4,1}$ generates an output used by $P_{100,2,2}$.

d.   *Type 4:* Those variables which are outputs of process executed with one periodicity and used by a process having a different periodicity viz. variables exchanged between $P_{10,1,10}$ and $P_{100,2,1}$ at T_{10} or more generally between $P_{i1,j1,k1}$ and $P_{i2,j2,k2}$.

From the above classification it is clear that for each process the variables of types 2, 3 & 4 need to be stored as "recovery variables" in a "recovery buffer". Type 1 variables are always generated afresh during every iteration cycle and need not be stored in a recovery buffer.

To summarize, the steps involved in the implementation of a scheme for the successful recovery from hardware transient faults are as follows,

1.   Each process before terminating its execution should create a "recovery buffer" consisting of "recovery variables" of types 2, 3 & 4.
2.   Any process that is affected by a hardware transient fault must terminate its execution and pass control back to the process scheduler.
3.   The scheduler should schedule the execution of all sequentially and concurrently executing processes as per the RMS algorithm as if nothing has happened.
4.   Subsequent execution of any process which includes the next iteration of the faulted process should use variables from the "recovery buffer" of the faulted process.

5   Conclusion

In this paper we have proposed a scheme which implements recovery from hardware transient faults for cyclic concurrently executing real time processes as in the on board computers of satellite launch vehicles. The basic system is of the forward recovery type and does not call for roll back and retry as in the case of RB based software fault tolerant approaches. Instead, variables are classified into four different types depending up on their usage and these are used to form a "recovery buffer" every iteration cycle. In case a hardware transient fault is detected in one cycle these variables are used in the next iteration cycle without attempting any alternate software block as suggested in [1]. A comparative summary of the different approaches is given in Table 1.

Table 1. Comparison of Different Approaches

Approach	Comments
Randell's Recovery Block [6]	First important paper on software fault tolerance. Not useful for real time systems. But introduced very important concepts used by subsequent researchers.
Avizienis' N-Version programming [5]	Requires N-different versions of software and a voter. Difficult to implement in real projects due to its complexity.
Anderson and Knight's model [1]	Useful for real time systems and an extension of the Recovery Block scheme. Uses alternate software block. Meant only for software faults.
Method proposed in this paper	Extension of the model used by Anderson and Knight to include hardware transient faults. Does not use alternate software blocks. Defines variable types used for creating "recovery buffer".

The approach has been explained for a system having two iteration rates. But the method can be extended to systems having more than two iteration rates by considering the two fastest iteration rates to start with and applying the logic to progressively slower iteration rates two at a time. For example for a system having the periodicities of 5 msec, 10 mec & 100 msec, the method can first be applied to all processes having periodicities of 5 & 10 msec and then to processes of periodicities 10 & 100 msec. This approach depends on the recognition of transient faults and then generation of traps by the processor. Any hardware transient fault, which does not cause a process to be interrupted through traps, will go undetected. But most commercially available processors for critical real time systems have exhaustive fault trapping mechanisms.

Acknowledgement

The authors would like to dedicate this paper to the memory of the late Dr. S. Srinivasan, Director, Vikram Sarabhai Space Centre (VSSC) at Trivandrum, India up to 1st September, 1999. It was his vision of a vibrant R&D culture which inspired us in many ways. The authors would also like to acknowledge the interest taken by Mr. G. Madhavan Nair, the present Director of VSSC in this research. Thanks are also due to Dr. B.N. Suresh, Deputy Director, VSSC for his encouragement to publish this work.

References

1. Thomas Anderson and John C. Knight: A Framework for Software Fault Tolerance in Real Time Systems, IEEE Trans. Software Eng., Vol. SE-9, No.3, (1983), 355-364.
2. K.H. Kim and Howard O. Welch: Distributed Execution of Recovery Blocks: An Approach for Uniform Treatment of Hardware and Software Faults in Real Time Applications, IEEE Trans. Computers, Vol. 38, No.5, (1989), 626-636.
3. Jaynarayan H. Lala and Richard E. Harper: Architectural Principles for Safety-Critical Real Time Applications, Proceedings of the IEEE, Vol. 82, No. 1, (1994), 25-40.
4. Krishna Kant: Performance Analysis of Real Time Software Supporting Fault-Tolerant Operation, IEEE Trans. Computers, Vol. 39, No. 7, (1990), 906-918.
5. A. Avizienis: The N-Version Approach to Fault-Tolerant Software, IEEE Trans. Software Eng., Vol. SE-11, No. 12, (1985), 1491-1501.
6. Brian Randell: System Structure for Software Fault Tolerance, IEEE Trans. Software Eng., Vol. SE-1, No. 2, (1975), 220-232.
7. Jia Xu and David Lorge Parnas: On Satisfying Timing Constraints in Hard-Real Time Systems, IEEE Trans. Software Eng., Vol. SE-19, No. 1, (1993), 70-84.
8. C.L. Liu and J.W. Layland: Scheduling Algorithms for Multiprogramming in a Hard Real Time Environment, J. Ass. Comput. Mach., Vol. 20, (1973), 46-61.
9. Gerry Kane, Doug Hawkins, Lance Leventhal: 68000 Assembly Language Programming, OSBORNE/McGraw Hill, (1986).
10. Intel Corporation: i960 MC Microprocessor Reference Manual, (1991).

Programmable Electronic System Design & Verification Utilizing DFM

Michel Houtermans[1,2], George Apostolakis[3],
Aarnout Brombacher[1], and Dimitrios Karydas[4]

[1] Eindhoven University of Technology, Faculty of Mechanical Engineering,
Reliability of Mechanical Equipment
PO Box 513, 5600 MB, Eindhoven, The Netherlands
a.c.Brombacher@wtb.tue.nl
[2] TÜV PRODUCT SERVICE, Automation, Software and Electronics – IQSE,
5 Cherry Hill Drive, Danvers MA 01923, USA
mhoutermans@tuvps.com
[3] Massachusetts Institute of Technology, Nuclear Engineering,
77 Massachusetts Avenue, Cambridge, MA 02139, USA
apostola@mit.edu
[4] Factory Mutual Insurance, Factory Mutual Engineering,
1151 Boston-Providence Tnpk, Norwood, MA 02062, USA
dmkarydas@aol.com

Abstract. The objective of this paper is to demonstrate the use of the Dynamic Flowgraph Methodology (DFM) during the design and verification of programmable electronic safety-related systems. The safety system consists of hardware as well as software. This paper explains and demonstrates the use of DFM to verify the hardware and application software design for safety issues. The outcome of the design verification is used to define the necessary diagnostic capabilities that are essential to guarantee the correct functioning of the safety system. The paper also demonstrates how DFM can be used as an application software test tool.

1 Introduction

It is generally recognized that safety is a property of the total system [1]. Addressing hardware and software safety issues independently assumes the correct behavior of software while analyzing hardware and vice versa. This is seldom the case. The objective of this paper is to demonstrate the use of a relatively new safety analysis technique called the Dynamic Flowgraph Methodology (DFM) during the design and verification of programmable electronic (PE) safety-related systems. DFM allows studying the system in an integrated manner.

F. Koornneef and M. van der Meulen (Eds.): SAFECOMP 2000, LNCS 1943, pp. 275-285, 2000.

2   Dynamic Flowgraph Methodology

The DFM approach is very general in nature and can model the logical and dynamic behavior of complex systems, including such elements as hardware, software and human actions. DFM models the relationships between important process parameters because of cause-and-effect and timing functions inherent to the system. If this system is a PES, i.e., a system where mechanical devices and physical parameters are controlled and operated by software, then both the physical system as well as the software controlling the system can be taking into account by the DFM system model. As such, DFM is a useful methodology capable to analyze and test hardware and/or software related systems [2,3,4].

A DFM model of a system is presented as a directed digraph representing the logical and dynamic behavior of the system in terms of important system parameters (physical, software, human interaction, or any other parameter). DFM uses a set of basic modeling elements to represent the system parameters and their relationships. The possible modeling elements are (Figure 1):

1. Process variable and condition nodes,
2. Causality and condition edges, and
3. Transfer and transition boxes and their associated decision tables.

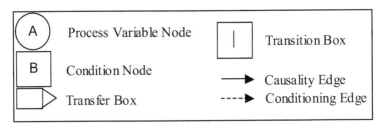

Fig. 1. DFM Modeling Elements

The nodes of the DFM system model represent important system components, parameters, or variables and their normal and abnormal functional conditions. Nodes are discretized into a finite number of states that represent the parameter best, and can thus represent much more then just success or failure, or on/off situations. They can represent, for example, a possible temperature range or the possible range of a software variable like an integer or a real. The two different edges are only used to visually represent the kind of relationships that exists between parameters, i.e., a cause-and-effect or conditioning relationship.

The transfer and transition boxes represent the relationship that exist between parameters. Each box has an associated decision table that is used to incorporate a multi-state representation of the cause-and-effect and timing relationships that can exists among the connecting parameters. For example, a decision table can be used to model the output of a software routine that compares the measured temperature in a tank with the limit programmed by the operator.

```
If (SLUI < STL) THEN ST = "OK" ELSE ST = "TO_HIGH"
```

The SLUI1 variable represents a temperature that is OK or TO_HIGH. The variable STL is the temperature limit programmed by the operator and can be LIMIT or HIGHER_LIMIT. The output variable ST has only two possible states, OK or TO_HIGH. The software routine can only be executed if the controller (CCNT), the clock (CCLK) and the ROM memory (CROM) function normal. It is assumed that any failure of these components will lead to the OK state for the ST variable, which is the worst-case assumption. The actual relationship, which exists between the parameters SLUI1, STL, ST, CNTL, CCLK and CROM, is represented by a mapping of the possible combination of states in the associated decision table (**Table 1**). In this way, it is possible to map any relationship. The accuracy or quality, in case of complex physical relationships, depends ultimately on the level of discretization.

Table 1. Decision table

INPUT					OUTPUT
SLUI1	STL	CROM	CCLK	CCNT	ST
OK	LIMIT	NORMAL	NORMAL	NORMAL	OK
OK	HIGHER_LIMIT	NORMAL	NORMAL	NORMAL	OK
TO_HIGH	LIMIT	NORMAL	NORMAL	NORMAL	LIMIT
TO_HIGH	HIGHER_LIMIT	NORMAL	NORMAL	NORMAL	OK
_1	-	-	-	NO EXEC	OK
-	-	-	-	WRONG CODING	OK
-	-	-	-	STUCK DATA	OK
-	-	-	-	STUCK ADDRESS	OK
-	-	-	SUB HARMONIC	-	OK
-	-	-	SUPER HARMONIC	-	OK
-	-	STUCK DATA	-	-	OK
-	-	STUCK ADDRESS	-	-	OK
SLUI1 = Software variable Logic Unit Input 1, STL= Software variable Temperature Limit, CROM = Condition ROM memory, CCLK = Condition Clock, CCNT = Condition Clock, ST = Software variable Temperature					

The DFM approach follows a 2-step process. First, a model is built of the system. The DFM model is created independently of the analyses of interest, which in practice means that once the DFM model is created it is possible to carry out a multitude of analyses based on this model. The DFM model contains every system feature that determines the possible desirable and undesirable behavior of the system. This is one of the key features that distinguish DFM from other analysis methods, which usually are only focused on modeling undesirable behavior.

Second, the model is analyzed. In the analysis phase two different approaches can be utilized, i.e., deductive analysis and inductive analysis. The deductive analysis

---

[1] The "-" represents "No matter what the state is". The other input variables, and not this one, determine the state of the output variable(s).

follows a top down approach, i.e., the objective it is to determine how combinations and sequences of parameter states can produce systems states, failure or success, or any other state or top event of interest. The deductive analysis acts as an automated dynamic fault tree generator. Inductive analysis follows a bottom-up approach by introducing a set of component states and analyzes how this particular set of interest propagates through the system and what the effect will be on a system state level of interest. Inductive analysis follows the principles of fault injection and can be used to examine the consequences of hazards on system level.

When deductive analysis is used, DFM generates so-called prime implicants [3]. A prime implicant consists of a set of variables of interest that are in a certain state at a certain time. Prime implicants are similar to minimum cut sets known from Fault Tree Analysis. They differ in the sense that they can hold normal or non-failed states and failed states. Each variable state is also associated with a time, stating when this prime implicant variable needs to be in this state. Each variable with its properties is called a literal. A typical prime implicant looks as follows:

Prime implicant[2]
At time -4 ,	LUI1	= High (Temp High)	AND	(Literal)
At time -4 ,	CCNT	= Stuck (No Execution)	AND	(Literal)
At time -3 ,	CBUS	= Normal (Operates normal)	AND	(Literal)
At time -2 ,	CCOMO	= Normal (Operates normal)	AND	(Literal)
At time -1 ,	COC	= Normal (Operates normal		

There are three properties of interest for each literal, i.e., the time "-4", the variable name "LUI1", the state of the variable "High" (meaning "Temp High"). The "AND" at the end of the line represents the Boolean relationship that exists between the literals. Each literal needs to be true in order for the prime implicant to be true and thus for the top event to happen. The number of prime implicants depends on the complexity, size, required level of detail of the system to be modeled and the total analysis time. The prime implicants can contain valuable information, especially if the interaction between hardware and software is modeled. A prime implicant with no hardware failures could indicate a mistake in the software and thus focus the analysis on a certain software module. This is one of the key improvements made by DFM.

DFM is introduced and used in this paper because it has major advantages over conventional safety and reliability methods. Only one DFM model is necessary to capture the complete behavior of a system. This model can be used to verify design requirements, to do failure analysis and to define test cases. It is an automated tool that represents the capabilities of FMEA, FTA, and HAZOP in one tool. When DFM is used as a deductive technique, it is possible to generate automatically as many (timed) fault trees as necessary. A major improvement made by DFM is that it is possible to analyze the interaction between hardware and software. This makes it possible analyze the software using the concept of an error-forcing context [5]. It is recognized that the software itself cannot fail. If it leads to an unexpected state, this means that it was not designed to handle that certain situation or environment (the

---

[2] LUI1 -= Logic Unit Input 1, CCNT = Condition Controller, CBUS = Condition Bus communication, CCOMO= Condition Common Circuitry Output Module, COC = Condition Output Channel

"context"). With DFM, it is possible to model the environment the software can be in and thus analyze the software for all possible circumstances, including its error-forcing context. The DFM methodology is implemented in a software tool to support the creation and analyses of the DFM model [6].

3 Practical Example

The system subject to the analysis is a PE safety-related system. The example is based on a real batch process protected by the PE safety-related system and presented as a case study in [7]. The batch process produces a product by mixing two basic materials in a tank. The mixing process itself needs to be carefully controlled. The critical parameter for this process is the temperature. Explosive fumes will be created, if the temperature during mixing gets too high. The temperature of the mixture can be controlled by the speed of the mixer, the feeding of the materials, and the water-cooling of the tank. The mixed material is dumped into a drowning tank, by opening a drain valve, if the temperature exceeds 35 °C. When this happens, it is necessary to guide the material to the drowning tank by a divider. The highly explosive material will be erroneously guided to the next step of the batch process, if the divider is pointing in the wrong direction while opening the drain valve. A Basic Process Control System (BPCS) carries out the necessary control functions of the batch process.

The PE safety system serves as last layer of defense against hazards that can arise from the operation of the process. This safety system carries out specific identified safety functions. It reads inputs from the field (process parameters) via sensors. The PE logic solver uses these inputs to execute the application software designed by the process safety engineers. The safety system is supposed to work autonomously and opens the drain valve, and, if necessary switches the divider to the drowning tank, if the temperature in the tank exceeds its limit. In this example, only the logic solver part is modeled by DFM. A simplified version of the logic solver is presented in Figure 2. It consists of three distinct modules, i.e., the input module, the main processor module, and the output module.

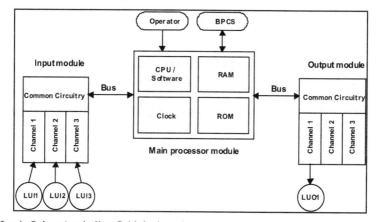

Fig. 2. Logic Solver (excluding field devices, i.e., sensors, actuators, and cabling)

Table 2. Description of safety system input and output signals in Figure 2

Signal	Description	Possible states
LUI1	Logic Unit Input signal 1: Temperature switch in the tank.	[Ok, To high]
LUI2	Logic Unit Input signal 2: Diverter drowning tank switch.	[Drowning Tank, Off]
LUI3	Logic Unit Input signal 3: Diverter filter switch	[Filter, Off]
LUO1	Logic Unit output signal 1: Drain valve	[Open, Close]

3.1   DFM Model

The DFM model of the PE safety system is shown in Figure 3. This model has been created taking into account the failure mode requirements of the IEC 61508 standard [8]. This standard addresses functional safety of electrical / electronic / programmable electronic safety-related systems and has strict requirements concerning the failure modes of electrical, electronic, and PE components. The level of detail in this model has been chosen in a way that it reflects identifiable functional blocks that, if they fail, will fail the complete safety systems or one safety function carried out by the safety system.

This model is still on a high level and does not address the lowest possible individual component failures, but it allows the verification of the system structure for safety issues before the design is worked out and verified in detail. The DFM model includes the complete functional behavior of the safety system, including the interaction between hardware and software. The application software design is as well modeled by DFM. In addition, the interaction with the BPCS and Operator is modeled in a simplistic way. It is assumed that the BPCS can fail and exchange the wrong information. The operator can change the critical values and thus enter the wrong values, for example setting the limit higher then the supposed 35 °C.

4   Analysis

The model in Figure 3 will be used to demonstrate the use of the DFM technique to verify the hardware and application software design for safety issues. The outcome of the design verification will be used to define the necessary diagnostic capabilities that are essential to guarantee the correct functioning of the safety system. The model will also be used to demonstrate how DFM can be used as an application software test tool.

4.1   Hardware and Software Analysis

The safety system carries out two safety functions. The main objective of the safety system is to open the drain valve when the temperature exceeds 35 °C. Before it is possible to open the drain valve, the safety system needs to verify, and change if

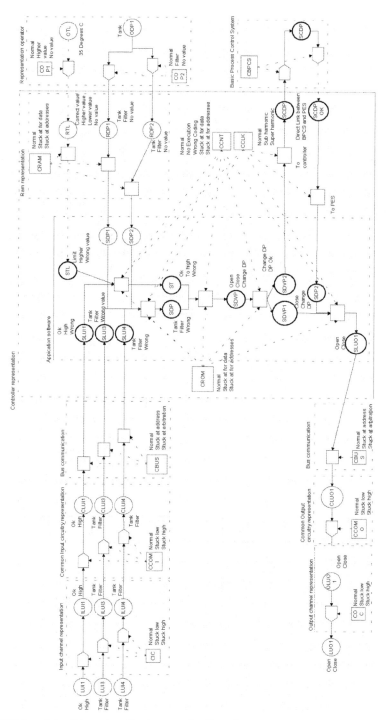

Fig. 3. DFM model safety system (hardware and software)

necessary, whether the position of the diverter is towards the drowning tank. Therefore, one of the first top events of interest would be to analyze what would prevent the logic solver from giving a signal to open the drain valve while the temperature in the tank was high. The top event would be specified as follows:

```
Top Event
At time 0 ,  LUO1 = Close (Close drain valve)      AND
At time -10,  LUI1 = High  (Temp high)
```

This top event verifies the condition of two variables at different time steps. The time steps are in this case chosen based on the time it takes for the signal to propagate through the system. In case of a PE, system the speed mainly depends on the clock cycle of the microcomputer. If the temperature goes high in the tank, it will take 10 time steps to initiate a close signal at the output. This is why the top event examines the output signal at time 0 and the input signal (LUI1) at time -10.

The top event was examined using the deductive analysis engine [6]. Back tracking through the model resulted in close to 30 different prime implicants that could cause this top event. Two of these prime implicants are presented below. These prime implicants demonstrate the strength of DFM. Prime implicant 11 shows that when the operator puts in a higher value for the temperature limit (COP1 = higher) and all other components are working the output signal will be close. Prime implicant 21 shows that if there is a stuck at failure in the common output circuitry (CCOMO = High) then the output signal will always be high, representing a closed drain valve. This example clearly shows that prime implicants can contain failed states as well as normal operating states.

```
Prime Implicant #11
At time -10,  LUI1 = High   (Temp high)              AND
At time -9 ,  COP1 = Higher (Higher value)           AND
At time -8 ,   CRAM = Normal (Operates normal)       AND
At time -6 ,   CROM = Normal (Operates normal)       AND
At time -6 ,   CCNT = Normal (Operates normal)       AND
At time -5 ,   CROM = Normal (Operates normal)       AND
At time -5 ,   CCNT = Normal (Operates normal)       AND
At time -4 ,   CCLK = Normal (Operates normal)       AND
At time -4 ,   CROM = Normal (Operates normal)       AND
At time -4 ,   CCNT = Normal (Operates normal)       AND
At time -3 ,   CBUS = Normal (Operates normal)       AND
At time -2 , CCOMO = Normal (Operates normal)        AND
At time -1 ,    COC = Normal (Operates normal)

Prime Implicant #21
At time -10,  LUI1 = High  (Temp high)        AND
At time -2 , CCOMO = High  (Stuck high)       AND
At time -1 ,    COC = Normal (Operates normal)
```

In addition, the intended design of the application software is part of the DFM model. The top event to the right is intended to test the software routine that interprets whether the diverter position is towards the drowning tank or towards the next step in the batch process. An interesting exercise would be to verify what could cause the software variable SDP (software representation of the diverter position) to point at the tank. The top event caused 12

```
Top event
At time 0  ,    SDP = Tank  (Drowning tank)
Prime Implicant #1
At time -1 , SLUI3 = Tank  (Drowning tank)   AND
At time -1 , SLUI4 = Off   (Off)             AND
At time -1 ,  SDP1 = Tank  (Drowning tank)   AND
At time -1 ,  SDP2 = Off   (Off)
Prime Implicant #2
At time -1 , SLUI3 = Tank   (Drowning tank)  AND
At time -1 , SLUI4 = Filter (Filter)         AND
At time -1 ,  SDP1 = Tank   (Drowning tank)  AND
At time -1 ,  SDP2 = Filter (Filter)
Prime Implicant #3
At time -1 , SLUI3 = Off    (Off)            AND
At time -1 , SLUI4 = Off    (Off)            AND
At time -1 ,  SDP1 = Off    (Off)            AND
At time -1 ,  SDP2 = Off    (Off)
Prime Implicant #4
At time -1 , SLUI3 = Off    (Off)            AND
At time -1 , SLUI4 = Filter (Filter)         AND
At time -1 ,  SDP1 = Off    (Off)            AND
At time -1 ,  SDP2 = Filter (Filter)
```

prime implicants by backtracking one time step. The first prime implicant is the only prime implicant that is truly wanted. The next three prime implicants clearly indicated a situation that should not lead to the tank position for the variable SDP. This is a sign that the design of the software routine is wrong and needs to be examined further. The intended software routine was stated as follows:

```
IF ((SLUI3 = SDP1) AND (SLUI4 = SDP2)) THEN (SDP =
TANK) ELSE (SDP = FILTER)
```

The initial design of the software routine is to simplistic as it only compares the input variables SLUI3 and SLUI4 with the stored values in the memory. This condition could easily occur if the operator would accidentally switch the values in the memory (see prime implicant 4). Please note that if the batch process and the safety system were modeled this software routine would have been found because at least one prime implicant would contain no hardware failures. This condition would also occur if a stuck at failure for the data would happen any were down the path. Both these situations were represented in prime implicants when the top event was traced back several time steps. A more sophisticated software interpretation routine then presented above is required to be on the safe side.

4.2   Diagnostic System Analysis

One of the reasons that the PES safety system market has grown so fast over the years is their excellent capability to build in on-line diagnostics. The main role of the diagnostics is to verify that the PES is capable of performing uninterruptedly the specified safety functions. The diagnostic functions monitor the performance of the PES within the context of its operating environment. In this example, only the logic solver has been modeled with DFM and therefore only the necessary diagnostics systems in terms of the logic solver can be determined.

The prime implicants contain valuable information that can be used to define the necessary diagnostic systems. The DFM model will produce all necessary diagnostics if at first a model is created without taking into account any diagnostic capabilities. The prime implicants can serve as checklist. Every prime implicant that represents an unwanted situation can be used to define a diagnostic. For example, prime implicant #21 reveals that a stuck at failure in the common circuitry of the output module is a reason not to open the drain valve. The diagnostic system handling this kind of failure mode could be a feed back loop in combination with a software test vector that would periodically test the correct functionality of the common output circuitry. The diagnostic systems can also go beyond the safety system. DFM can identify certain software parameters as being critical, and if an operator can change these parameters in the application program (like the temperature limit or the position of the diverter) then special procedures can be created that determine how, when and by whom these variables can changed.

4.3   Application Software Testing

Sometimes, the software can be too complex to model by hand or information about the software is just not available, e.g., in the case of COTS software. In these situations, it is possible to model the actual software as a black box and use DFM to generate test vectors for the input parameters to the software. The multi-state representation of the input parameters to the software is the basis for the test vectors. The actual software is executed using these test vectors and the output of the software is fed back into the DFM model. In addition, in this way, it possible to find conditions that would produce undesired output results. These conditions do not necessarily need to represent hardware failure conditions. See, for example, the case of the software routine that determines the diverter position. Because DFM would automatically produce all test vectors, and not only the obvious ones, also conditions where, for example, all four input variables to the diverter routine would equal OFF are found if the output condition of interest is what can cause the safety system to think that the diverter is pointing to the drowning tank. Utilizing test vectors like this and verifying desired and undesired outputs turns DFM into an automated fault injection tool. Fault injection is particularly useful in finding situations that where not "thought about" during the design specification phase, also referred to as the error-forcing context.

5   Conclusions

DFM is introduced and used in this paper because it has major advantages over conventional safety and reliability techniques and methods. Only one DFM model is necessary to capture the complete dynamic behavior of a system. This model can be used to verify design requirements, to do failure analysis and to define test cases. In this paper, DFM was used to model the hardware and software of a PE safety-related system. DFM was used as a deductive technique to generate automatically prime implicants. These prime implicants contain the necessary information (in terms hardware and software states, failure and non failure states and human interaction) to carry out safety design verification. Prime implicants make it easy to find mistakes made in the software. The list of prime implicants is used as a checklist to verify the required diagnostic capabilities of the programmable electronic system. DFM is also used to generate automatically test vectors that verify the effect on system states of interest. This is particularly useful to identify the error-forcing context of the software. In practice, this means that the software behavior is verified for unexpected and unanticipated situations in the context of the total hardware and software safety system.

Acknowledgement

The authors would like to thank Dr. Michael Yau of ASCA Inc. for the use of the DFM software tool and the support and advice during the modeling and analyses of safety system.

Reference

1. Leveson, N., 1995, *Safeware, System Safety and Computers*. Addison Wesley
2. Garrett, C.J., Guarro, S.B., Apostolakis G.E., The Dynamic Flowgraph Methodology for Assessing the Dependability of Embedded Software Systems. *IEEE Transactions on Systems, Man, and Cybernetics*, Vol. 25, No. 5, May 1995
3. Yau, M., Apostolakis, G., Guarro, S., 1998, The Use of Prime Implicants in Dependability Analysis of Software Controlled Systems. *Reliability Engineering and System Safety*, 62, 23-32
4. Milici, A., Yau, M., Guarro, S., Software Safety Analysis of the Space Shuttle Main Engine Control Software. *PSAM 4*, New York, September 1998
5. Garrett, C.J., Apostolakis, G., Context in the Risk Assessment of Digital Systems. *Risk Analysis*, 19, 23-32, 1999
6. ASCA, DFM software tool, ASCA Incorporated, 706 Silver Spur Road, Ste 203, Rolling Hill Estates, CA, 1999
7. Health and Safety Executive, Programmable electronic systems in safety related applications. Health and Safety Executive, ISBN 0 11 883906, Sheffield, United Kingdom, 1987
8. IEC 61508, Functional Safety of Electrical / Electronic / Programmable Electronic Safety-Related Systems. International Electrotechnical Committee, Part 1–7, Version 5.0, 1999

SIMATIC S7-400F/FH:
Safety-Related Programmable Logic Controller

Andreas Schenk

Siemens AG, Automation and Drives, Advanced Group Technologies, A&D GT 4,
P.O.Box 4848, D-90327 Nuremberg, Germany
andreas.schenk@nbgm.siemens.de

Abstract. SIMATIC S7-400F/FH is a fail-safe and fault-tolerant programmable logic controller which achieves safety integrity level 3 (SIL 3) with one standard SIMATIC CPU module and distributed fail-safe input and output (I/O) modules. This paper shows the underlying safety principles.

1   Introduction

Safety-related programmable logic controllers are used for risk reduction when a process or a machine endangers persons, environment or equipment. Generally they are fail-safe - in process industry even fault-tolerant.

The safety-related programmable logic controller SIMATIC S7-400F/FH deals with the following challenges:

1. *Standard* SIMATIC modules should be used where possible – especially in case of complex modules like CPU modules and the programming environment. The reasons for this are cost savings, profit from improvements of the standard modules and better integration into the automation system.
2. *Mixing* of safety-related and not safety-related functions and modules in the same automation system should be allowed.
3. *One* CPU module should already achieve safety integrity level 3 according to IEC 61508 [1]. SIMATIC S7-400FH uses a second CPU module for fault-tolerance.

The answer to this was concentrating safety functions in few hardware and software modules, the so called 'safety islands'. These safety islands contain measures to detect and control faults at the hardware level as well as at the safety function level. By the latter interference of standard modules on the safety function is controlled.

F. Koornneef and M. van der Meulen (Eds.): SAFECOMP 2000, LNCS 1943, pp. 286-293, 2000.
© Springer-Verlag Berlin Heidelberg 2000

2   Architecture of Safety Islands

Safety is achieved by few safety-related modules:

1. Fail-safe I/O modules (F-SMs)
2. Option package 'S7 F Systems'
3. Safety-related application program, built of safety-related function blocks (F-FBs)

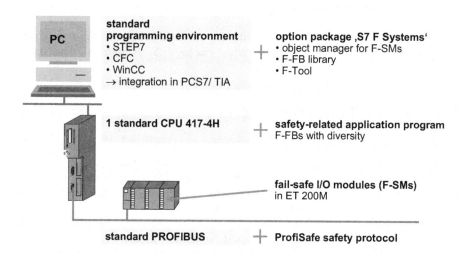

Fig. 1. Architecture of safety islands

2.1   Safety-Related Distributed I/O

Safety-related input from and output to the process are done with special *fail-safe I/O modules* that are inserted in distributed ET200M-cabinets at the PROFIBUS. The fail-safe I/O modules provide an internal 1oo2 structure with comparison, self-tests and external fault diagnostics.

2.2   Safety-Related Communication

For safety-related communication standard busses and protocols can be used together with a safety layer. Guidelines are given in prEN 50159 [2][3].

Safety-related communication between the safety-related application program and the fail-safe I/O modules via the PROFIBUS is done with the safety protocol *ProfiSafe* [4]. This safety protocol is transparent to the programmer as it is implemented in the fail-safe I/O modules and special safety-related function blocks.

Safety-related communication between safety-related application programs in different CPUs, e.g. via PROFIBUS or Industrial Ethernet, is done with special safety-related function blocks implementing a similar safety protocol.

2.3   Safety-Related Processing

Processing of the safety-related application program is done with a standard S7-400 CPU suitable for fault-tolerance. Processing is fail-safe by the use of special *safety-related function blocks* containing failure control measures that are specified in a separate chapter.

2.4   Safety-Related Programming

Safety-Related programming is done with the standard programming environment that is extended by installation of the *option package 'S7 F Systems'*. This option package contains:

- object manager for the fail-safe I/O modules
- library with safety-related function blocks
- F-Tool

The fail-safe I/O modules are configured with the standard hardware configuration tool that is extended by the object manager for the fail-safe I/O modules.

The safety-related application program is written with the standard continuous function chart (CFC) - a function block diagram language - by interconnecting and initializing special safety-related function blocks (F-FBs).

When compiling the CFC program at first the F-Tool is started. It includes special additional safety-related function blocks and initializes the safety-related application program before compilation. Without this the safety-related application program is not able to generate valid output telegrams. Afterwards the standard compiler is started.

3   Safety-Related Processing by one CPU

Processing of the safety-related application program by one standard CPU with a 1oo1 structure is fail-safe according to safety integrity level 3. This is achieved by the combination of fault control measures at the hardware level and the safety function level and external checking by the independent fail-safe output modules. The advantage of measures at the safety function level is that they are effective against hardware and software faults. This functional approach is similar to that of the vital coded microprocessor [5]. However inside the safety-related function blocks diverse operations are used instead of coded operations [6][7].

3.1   Code and Data Redundancy and Diversity with Internal and External Comparison

Data redundancy of at least 16 Bits is used. Diversity is achieved by using checksums in telegrams and inverse data in data blocks and parameters. Safety-related parameters are structures with a DATA element and a COMPLEM element.

Inside the safety-related function blocks code redundancy and diversity is used. First the DATA elements are processed, then the COMPLEM elements. Diverse operations are used to detect processing faults. Example: Boolean AND:

1. The boolean AND of the DATA elements (BOOL) of the input parameters is processed in the bit processing unit (BPU) of the SP7-ASIC of the CPU.
2. The word OR of the COMPLEM elements (WORD) of the input parameters is processed in the arithmetic and logic unit (ALU) of the SP7-ASIC of the CPU.

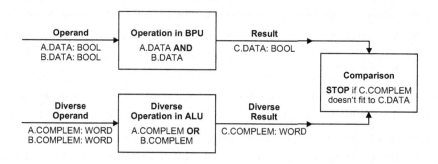

Fig. 2. Diversity in safety-related function blocks

Comparison of the diverse results of the safety-related application program and fault reaction is done

1. directly in the safety-related application program for better fault location as well as
2. indirectly by the recipients of the safety telegrams sent by the safety-related application program, i.e. fail-safe output modules and safety-related application programs in other CPUs, because the checksums of the safety telegrams are calculated on the basis of the data redundancy.

If there is no diverse operation, the operation is still processed twice to control transient faults and code violation and it is tested in each cycle. Test patterns with high effectiveness were available as the SP7-ASIC was developed by Siemens.

3.2   Program and Data Flow Monitoring

The safety-related application program is executed cyclically. Cycle time is checked directly by the safety-related application program itself and indirectly by the recipients of safety telegrams waiting for a new sequence number in the safety telegram.

The safety-related function blocks generate a signature of the program and data flow during execution. The signature is the diagonal checksum of:

1. Identifiers of the executed function blocks
2. Identifiers of the used data blocks
3. Identifiers of the used parameters
4. Identifiers of the initial state of the data blocks

This signature is precalculated by the F-Tool and checked by special safety-related function blocks that are included by the F-Tool and which are necessary for sending valid safety telegrams. In case of a signature difference, sending of safety telegrams is blocked and the CPU is stopped. If this fault detection and reaction to a signature difference fails, the checksums of the safety telegrams sent are invalid and fault detection and reaction is done by the recipients of safety telegrams, i.e. fail-safe output modules and safety-related application programs in other CPUs.

In a similar way it is checked whether all safety-related data blocks have the same logical time, i.e. whether all safety-related function block instances are in the same cycle.

3.3   Additional Measures in the CPU

In order to prevent fault accumulation additional self-tests are performed in the background by the CPU's operating system. Complete and successful execution in time is checked by the program and data flow monitoring. Self-tests include SP7-ASIC, RAM and CRC of code blocks and operating system.

For time functions the CPU provides redundant time bases. The redundant time values are handed to the safety-related application program. Comparison is done by a special safety-related function block.

Access to safety-related code and data is protected diversely in the CPU and the engineering station by a password.

4   Safety-Related Programming

In safety-related programmable electronic systems there are also safety requirements for the programming environment. E.g. according to IEC 61508-3 a translator/compiler has to be certificated, validated, assessed or proven-in-use. Another method is diverse reverse compilation. SIMATIC S7-400F/FH uses a method that is *independent* from the standard compiler:

1. The safety-related application program is written with the CFC editor.
2. The F-Tool calculates and initializes the signatures of the program and data flow monitoring.
3. The standard compiler generates the code that calls the safety-related function blocks and transfers parameters.
4. The program and data flow monitoring during execution in the CPU reveals compiler errors.
5. Modifications can be shown with a comparator at CFC level.

In calculating and initializing signatures of the program and data flow monitoring the F-Tool does a diverse forward compilation.

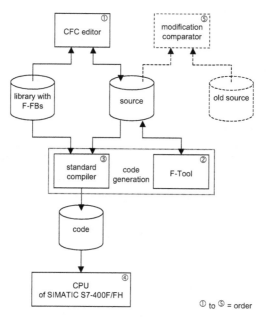

Fig. 3. Code generation

5   Flexibility

The architecture of 'safety islands' increases flexibility of the automation system:

1. The capsulation of the safety-related components and the control of dangerous interference enables *mixing* of safety-related and not safety-related components:

   - Fail-safe I/O modules and standard modules can be used at the same PROFIBUS.
   - Safety-related and not safety-related communication is possible via the same bus.
   - Safety-related and not safety-related application program can be processed by the same CPU.

2. Scaling of safety and availability is easy:

   - *Safety integrity level 3* is achieved without redundancy of CPU modules or I/O modules.
   - *Availability* of CPUs, busses and I/O modules can be increased independently by redundancy in 2oo2 structure, which is supported by the operating system of the fault-tolerant CPUs.

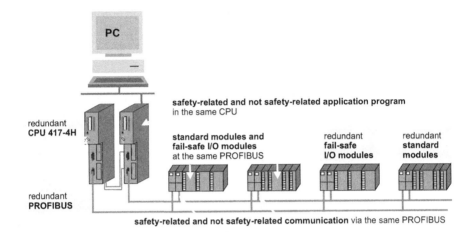

Fig. 4. Flexibility

6   Conclusion

The SIMATIC S7-400F/FH architecture of safety islands together with a highly effective combination of fault control measures enabled the use of standard modules even for the CPU and mixing of safety-related and not safety-related functions and modules in the same automation system.

SIMATIC S7-400F/FH is certificated by TÜV Product Service GmbH for requirement classes AK 1 to 6 in accordance with DIN V 19250, categories 2 to 4 in accordance with EN 954, and safety integrity levels SIL 1 to 3 in accordance with IEC 61508.

References

[1]   IEC 61508 - Functional safety of electrical/ electronic/ programmable electronic safety-related systems, 1999

[2]   prEN 50159-1: Railway Applications: Requirements for Safety-Related Communication in Closed Transmission Systems, 1996

[3]   prEN 50159-2: Railway Applications: Requirements for Safety-Related Communication in Open Transmission Systems, 1996

[4]   PROFIBUS-DP/PA, ProfiSafe, Profile for Failsafe Technology, V1.0, 30.03.99

[5]   Forin, P.: Vital coded microprocessor principles and application for various transit   systems; in Perrin, J.P.: Control, Computers, Communications in Transportation. Selected Papers from the IFAC/IFIP/IFORS Symposium, Pergamon, Oxford, UK, 1990, p.79-84.

[6]   Lovric, T.: Systematic and Design Diversity – Software Techniques for Hardware Fault Detection; First European Dependable Computing Conference, EDCC-1, Berlin, conf. proc., Springer, 1994, p. 309-326.

[7]   Lovric,   T.:   Fehlererkennung   durch   systematische   Diversität   in entwurfsdiversitären zeitredundanten Rechensystemen und ihre Bewertung mittels Fehlerinjektion, Berlin, Logos-Verl., 1997

Assessment of the Reliability of Fault-Tolerant Software: A Bayesian Approach

Bev Littlewood, Peter Popov, and Lorenzo Strigini

Centre for Software Reliability, City University,
Northampton Square, London, EC1V 0HB, UK
{b.littlewood,ptp,strigini}@csr.city.ac.uk

Abstract. Fault tolerant systems based on the use of software design diversity may be able to achieve high levels of reliability more cost-effectively than other approaches, such as heroic debugging. Earlier experiments have shown multi-version software systems to be more reliable than the individual versions. However, it is also clear that the reliability benefits are much worse than would be suggested by naive assumptions of failure independence between the versions. It follows that it is necessary to assess the reliability *actually achieved* in a fault tolerant system. The difficulty here mainly lies in acquiring knowledge of the degree of dependence between the failures processes of the versions. The paper addresses the problem using Byesian inference. In particular, it considers the problem of choosing a prior distribution to represent the beliefs of an expert assessor. It is shown that this is not easy, and some pitfalls for the unwary are identified.

1 Introduction

Achieving high reliability in software-based systems is not easy. *Assessing* the reliability of a software-based system - in particular, gaining high confidence that the required reliability has been achieved in the case of a critical system - is probably even more difficult.

The use of software design diversity in a fault tolerant architecture has been suggested as one solution to the problem of achieving very high reliability. Whilst the benefits of software diversity do not seem to be as high as those sometimes claimed for hardware redundancy [1], there is nevertheless evidence that fault tolerance can deliver levels of reliability higher than could be achieved with a single software version [2]. Indeed, there are several examples of apparently successful use of design diversity in engineered systems that are in operational use, e.g. [3], [4], [5].

The reason why software fault tolerance does not deliver dramatically high reliability is that the failures of different software versions in a fault tolerant system cannot be assumed to be independent [6], [1], [7]. One reason for this is that human designers and builders of software systems tend to make similar mistakes. This means that even two versions of a program that have been produced using 'independent' development teams will not fail dependently - instead there will be a greater tendency for the

F. Koornneef and M. van der Meulen (Eds.): SAFECOMP 2000, LNCS 1943, pp. 294-308, 2000.

versions to fail simultaneously, thus decreasing the reliability of a 1-out-of-2 system built from them.

This means that it is imperative that we *assess* the actual reliability that has been achieved in a fault tolerant system: we cannot simply assume that the probability of system failure is the product of the two version failure probabilities. In this paper we address this problem of assessment of reliability using a Bayesian approach. For simplicity we shall restrict ourselves to a demand-based 1-out-of-2 system architecture, i.e. one in which the system fails if and only if both versions of the software fail. Such an architecture has considerable practical interest: for example, it is the architecture employed in many safety systems, such as nuclear reactor protection systems.

The simplest way to assess the reliability of a system - fault tolerant or otherwise - is to observe its failure behaviour in (real or simulated) operation. Quite simple statistical techniques allow the reliability to be estimated from such data [8], [9]. However, it is well-known that such a 'black-box' approach to reliability estimation has severe limitations [10], [11]. Essentially, it is infeasible to assess very high levels of reliability this way because impracticably long periods of testing would be required. An important issue, then, is whether knowledge of the fault tolerant nature of a system aids its reliability assessment. Can we use the details of the version failures to obtain greater confidence in the system reliability than would come just from the black-box system data? In this paper we shall investigate a Bayesian approach to questions like this.

2   Bayesian Inference

We shall assume that the successive demands are independent, and that the probabilities of failure on demand (*pfd*s) for versions and for the system remain constant.

Consider the case where the system is being treated simply as a black box, so that only *system* failure or success is observed. Denoting the probability of failure on demand for the system as p, the posterior distribution of p after seeing r failures in n demands is:

$$f_p(x|r,n) = \frac{\binom{n}{r} x^r (1-x)^{n-r} f_p(x)}{\int_0^1 \binom{n}{r} x^r (1-x)^{n-r} f_p(x) dx} \tag{1}$$

Here $f_p(\bullet)$ is the prior distribution of p, which represents the assessor's *a priori* beliefs about p, i.e. before seeing the result of the test on n demands.

If we can observe the success/failure of the individual *versions* comprising the 1-out-of-2 system, there are four different possible outcomes for each demand as shown in Table 1:

Table 1. 1-out-of-2 on demand system. In the first column the possible outcomes of processing a demand by the system are listed, the second and the third columns show how each of the outcomes relates to the failures/successes of the individual channels. The forth column represents the number of occurences of each of the outcomes if n demands are processed by the system. Finally, in the fifth column we list the notations used in the rest of the paper to label the probabilities of all four possible outcomes

Event	Version A	Version B	Number of occurrence in n tests	Probability
α	fails	fails	r_1	P_{AB}
β	succeeds	fails	r_2	$P_{\overline{A}B}$
γ	fails	succeeds	r_3	$P_{A\overline{B}}$
δ	succeeds	succeeds	r_4	$P_{\overline{A}\,\overline{B}}$

There are now four parameters, given in the last column of the table, in the probability model. However, these four probabilities sum to unity, hence there are only three degrees of freedom: any three of these four parameters completely specify the model. If we choose to deal with the first three, the posterior distribution is:

$$f_{P_{AB},P_{\overline{A}B},P_{A\overline{B}}}(x,y,z|r_1,r_2,r_3,n) =$$

$$= \frac{L(r_1,r_2,r_3,n|P_{AB},P_{\overline{A}B},P_{A\overline{B}})f_{P_{AB},P_{\overline{A}B},P_{A\overline{B}}}(x,y,z|r_1,r_2,r_3,n)}{\underset{P_{AB},P_{\overline{A}B},P_{A\overline{B}}}{\iiint} L(r_1,r_2,r_3,n|P_{AB},P_{\overline{A}B},P_{A\overline{B}})f_{P_{AB},P_{\overline{A}B},P_{A\overline{B}}}(x,y,z|r_1,r_2,r_3,n)dP_{AB}dP_{\overline{A}B}dP_{A\overline{B}}} \qquad (2)$$

where

$$L(r_1,r_2,r_3,n|P_{AB},P_{A\overline{B}},P_{\overline{A}B}) =$$

$$\frac{n!}{r_1!r_2!r_3!(n-r_1-r_2-r_3)!}P_{AB}^{r_1}P_{A\overline{B}}^{r_2}P_{\overline{A}B}^{r_3}(1-P_{AB}-P_{A\overline{B}}-P_{\overline{A}B})^{n-r_1-r_2-r_3}. \qquad (3)$$

is the multinomial likelihood of seeing r_1 coincident failures of both versions, r_2 failures of version A only, r_3 failures of version B only, respectively, in n tests, and $f_{P_{AB},P_{A\overline{B}},P_{A\overline{B}}}(\bullet,\bullet,\bullet)$ is the prior distribution.

It may sometimes be convenient to use a different parameterisation. For example, we could use the triplet P_A, P_B and P_{AB}, denoting the probabilities of failure of both versions and the probability of coincident failure of the pair (i.e. failure of the system). Trivially,

$$P_A = P_{A\overline{B}} + P_{AB} \text{ and } P_B = P_{\overline{A}B} + P_{AB}$$

and a simple change of variables gives the posterior:

$$f_{P_{AB},P_A,P_B}(x,y,z|r_1,r_2,r_3,n) =$$

$$= \frac{L(r_1,r_2,r_3,n|P_{AB},P_A,P_B)f_{P_{AB},P_A,P_B}(x,y,z|r_1,r_2,r_3,n)}{\underset{P_{AB},P_A,P_B}{\iiint} L(r_1,r_2,r_3,n|P_{AB},P_A,P_B)f_{P_{AB},P_A,P_B}(x,y,z|r_1,r_2,r_3,n)dP_{AB}dP_AdP_B} \qquad (4)$$

where

$$L(r_1,r_2,r_3,n|P_{AB},P_A,P_B) =$$

$$= \frac{n!}{r_1!r_2!r_3!(n-r_1-r_2-r_3)!}P_{AB}^{r_1}(P_A - P_{AB})^{r_2}(P_B - P_{AB})^{r_3}(1+P_{AB}-P_A-P_B)^{n-r_1-r_2-r_3} \qquad (5)$$

is the likelihood of the same observation as above, and $f_{P_{AB},P_A,P_B}(\bullet,\bullet,\bullet)$ is the prior.

From either of (2) and (4) the posterior marginal distribution of the *system* probability of failure can be computed.

The practical advantage of these multivariate posterior distributions over the 'black-box' version, (1), is that they take account specifically of any information we might have concerning the individual version reliabilities and the failure dependence between versions. It might be expected that such extra information would provide greater confidence in the reliability (or, conversely, unreliability) of the system: i.e. that the fault tolerant architecture provides benefits in the *assessment* of reliability, as it does in its *achievement*.

Consider, for example, the situation where one or both of the versions have been operating for considerable time in other systems, and thus have built up extensive data on successful and failed demands. They are then bought in as commercial-off-the-shelf (COTS) software components to be used in a novel fault tolerant system. If the assessor believes that these earlier data come from operational environments that are sufficiently similar to that of the new application, they could be incorporated into the prior to express 'strong' beliefs about the version reliabilities. In contrast, such earlier individual version histories would tell the assessor little about the *system* reliability, and hence the prior for (1) would have to be a vague one.

In this scenario, the past operational experience of the versions allows the assessor to learn about their individual reliabilities, but not about the dependence between their failure behaviours. Information about this would have to come from testing the versions together on the n operationally representative demands.

Clearly, the role of the prior is crucial in the analysis. Eliciting from an expert assessor his or her prior beliefs can be very difficult, especially when these take the form of a multi-variate distribution. When safety-critical systems are being assessed, in particular, it would be useful to have an assurance that this elicited prior was in some sense a 'conservative' one. Unfortunately, it is not clear currently how to do this. In the next section we report on a preliminary study of some classes of prior distributions for this simple 1-out-of-2 model.

3 Prior Distributions

3.1 Dirichlet Distribution

It is common in Bayesian statistics to use a *conjugate family* of distributions to represent prior belief. This is a parametric family of distributions that has the property for a particular problem (i.e. likelihood function) that if the expert uses a member of the family to represent his/her prior beliefs, then the posterior will automatically also be a member of the family. It can be shown that, when a conjugate family exists (this is not always the case), it is unique.

For the simple example of the binomial likelihood used in (1), the conjugate family is the Beta distribution: if the prior is $B(x,\alpha,\beta)$, and r failures are observed in n demands, the posterior will be $B(x,\alpha+r,\beta+n-r)$.

This result generalises to deal with the case considered above in (2) and (4): when the likelihood is multinomial, the conjugate family is the Dirchlet distribution [12]. This takes the form:

$$Dirichlet(\theta_0,\theta_1,\theta_2,\theta_3) = f_{y_1,y_2,y_3}(y_1,y_2,y_3) = \frac{\Gamma\left(\sum_{j=0}^{3}\theta_j\right)}{\prod_{j=0}^{3}\Gamma(\theta_j)}\left(1-\sum_{j=1}^{3}y_j\right)^{\theta_0-1}\prod_{j=1}^{3}y_j^{\theta_j-1} \tag{6}$$

If this is used as the prior for the 1-out-of-2 system comprising versions A and B, and the observed data are r_1 coincident failures of both channels, r_2 failures of only version A and r_3 failures of only version B in n demands, the posterior distribution is again a Dirichlet distribution:

$Dirichlet(\theta_0 + n - r_1 - r_2 - r_3, \theta_1 + r_1, \theta_2 + r_2, \theta_3 + r_3)$.

A property of the Dirichlet distribution is that its marginal distributions are also Dirichlet distributions. In particular, its univariate marginals are Beta distributions; in this sense the Dirichlet can be seen as a multivariate generalisation of the Beta distribution.

Would the Dirichlet family of distributions be suitable to represent an expert assessor's prior beliefs about the joint failure behaviour of the software versions making up a 1-out-of-2 system? Certainly there is a great advantage to be gained by restricting the elicitation exercise within such a parametric family: the expert only has to find the four parameters of the distribution that capture his/her beliefs. Whilst this is by no means a trivial task, it is much easier than trying to describe in an unconstrained way a complete tri-variate distribution.

We now consider how, when the prior is a Dirichlet distribution, posterior beliefs about system reliability based on complete version failure data differ from those using only 'black-box' system data. We might expect there to be a benefit in taking account of the more extensive data of the former case.

To make the two cases comparable, we need to assume that the expert's prior belief about the *system reliability* are the same in the two cases. That is, the prior $f_{P_{AB}}(\bullet)$ to be used in the black-box inference is the marginal distribution obtained from the more general Dirichlet prior by integrating out two of the variables, $P_{A\overline{B}}$ and $P_{\overline{A}B}$:

$$f_{P_{AB}}(\bullet) = \iint\limits_{P_{A\overline{B}},P_{\overline{A}B}} f_{P_{AB},P_{A\overline{B}},P_{\overline{A}B}}(\bullet,P_{A\overline{B}},P_{\overline{A}B})dP_{A\overline{B}}dP_{\overline{A}B} = B(\bullet,\theta_1,\theta_0+\theta_2+\theta_3) \tag{7}$$

For testing results ($n:r_1$, r_2, r_3) the black-box approach takes account only of the number of *system* failures; the posterior distribution of the probability of system failure is thus:

$$f_{P_{AB}}(\bullet|n,r_1) = B(\bullet,\theta_1+r_1,\theta_0+\theta_2+\theta_3+n-r_1) \tag{8}$$

The white-box result, taking account of the joint version failure behaviour, is obtained from the joint posterior, $Dirichlet(\theta_0+n-r_1-r_2-r_3,\theta_1+r_1,\theta_2+r_2,\theta_3+r_3)$, by integrating out $P_{A\overline{B}}$ and $P_{\overline{A}B}$ to obtain the marginal posterior of the probability of system failure:

$$f_{P_{AB}}(\bullet|n,r_1,r_2,r_3) = \iint\limits_{P_{A\bar{B}},P_{\bar{A}\bar{B}}} Dirichlet(\theta_0,\theta_1,\theta_2,\theta_3|n,r_1,r_2,r_3)dP_{A\bar{B}}dP_{\bar{A}\bar{B}} =$$

$$= \iint\limits_{P_{A\bar{B}},P_{\bar{A}\bar{B}}} Dirichlet(\theta_0+n-r_1-r_2-r_3,\theta_1+r_1,\theta_2+r_2,\theta_3+r_3|n,r_1,r_2,r_3)dP_{A\bar{B}}dP_{\bar{A}\bar{B}} = \qquad (9)$$

$$= B(\bullet,\theta_1+r_1,\theta_0+n-r_1-r_2-r_3+\theta_2+r_2+\theta_3+r_3) =$$

$$= B(\bullet,\theta_1+r_1,\theta_0+\theta_2+\theta_3+n-r_1)$$

Somewhat surprisingly, this is completely identical to the 'black-box' result, (8). In other words, whatever the detailed failure behaviour of the versions, there is no benefit from taking this extra information into account in assessing the reliability of the system. The posterior belief about the system reliability will be exactly the same as if only the *system* failures and successes had been recorded.

This result is disappointing. Whilst fault tolerance based upon software design diversity may help in the *achievement* of high reliability, it brings no advantage for the *assessment* of the reliability that has actually been achieved.

Of course, the result depends crucially upon expressing prior beliefs in the form of the conjugate Dirichlet family of distributions. Whilst restricting an assessor's expression of belief to this family is a great convenience, for the reasons stated earlier, it could be that an assessor's actual beliefs do not fit into this family. For instance, Dirichlet distribution implies negative correlation between each pair of variates, P_{AB}, $P_{A\bar{B}}$ and

$P_{\bar{A}B}$, which may be against the assessor's intuition. Negative correlation between P_{AB}

and $P_{A\bar{B}}$, for instance, means that seeing A fail and B succeed makes the failure of

both channels a less likely event. The assessor, on the contrary, may see in the failure of channel A evidence of increased risk of system failure and, therefore, may wish to reduce his confidence in system reliability. This is impossible with Dirichlet distribution and in such cases Dirichlet distribution, despite its convenience, can not be recommended as a reasonable prior.

3.2   Prior with Known Failure Probabilities of Versions

Consider now the plausible situation in which there is a very great deal of data from past operational use for each version, so that each probability of failure on demand can be estimated with great accuracy. Here the uncertainty - or the ignorance of the assessor - almost entirely concerns the *joint* failure behaviour of the versions. In this section we shall approximate to this situation by assuming that version probabilities of failure on demand are known *with certainty*.

The prior in this case can be written:

$$f_{P_{AB},P_A,P_B}(\bullet,\bullet,\bullet) = f_{P_{AB}}(\bullet|P_A,P_B)f_{P_A,P_B}(P_A,P_B) \qquad (10)$$

where the second term on the right is a Dirac delta function at the point ($P_A = P_{Atrue}$, $P_B = P_{Btrue}$), representing the known version failure probabilities.

The prior marginal distribution of the system *pfd* is

$$f_{P_{AB}}(\bullet) = \iint_{P_A, P_B} f_{P_{AB}}(\bullet | P_A, P_B) f_{P_A, P_B}(P_A, P_B) dP_A dP_B =$$

$$= f_{P_{AB}}(\bullet | P_{Atrue}, P_{Btrue})$$

In other words, the uncertainty in the prior concerns only the (marginal) probability of system failure, as we would expect.

The posterior marginal distribution of system *pfd* is:

$$f_{P_{AB}}(\bullet | n, r_1, r_2, r_3) =$$

$$= \frac{\displaystyle\iint_{P_A P_B} L(n, r_1, r_2, r_3 | P_A, P_B, P_{AB}) f_{P_{AB}}(\bullet | P_A, P_B) f_{P_A, P_B}(P_A, P_B) dP_A dP_B}{\displaystyle\iiint_{P_{AB}, P_A, P_B} L(n, r_1, r_2, r_3 | P_A, P_B, P_{AB}) f_{P_{AB}}(\bullet | P_A, P_B) f_{P_A, P_B}(P_A, P_B) dP_{AB} dP_A dP_B} \tag{11}$$

where

$$L(n, r_1, r_2, r_3 | P_A, P_B, P_{AB}) = (P_{AB})^{r_1}(P_A - P_{AB})^{r_2}(P_B - P_{AB})^{r_3}(1 - P_A - P_B + P_{AB})^{n - r_1 - r_2 - r_3}.$$

After trivial manipulations (11) is transformed to:

$$f_{P_{AB}}(\bullet | n, r_1, r_2, r_3) = \frac{L(n, r_1, r_2, r_3 | P_{AB}, P_{Atrue}, P_{Btrue}) f_{P_{AB}}(\bullet | P_{Atrue}, P_{Btrue})}{\displaystyle\int_{P_{AB}} L(n, r_1, r_2, r_3 | P_{AB}, P_{Atrue}, P_{Btrue}) f_{P_{AB}}(\bullet | P_{Atrue}, P_{Btrue}) dP_{AB}},$$

where

$$L(n, r_1, r_2, r_3 | P_{AB}, P_{Atrue}, P_{Btrue}) =$$

$$(P_{AB})^{r_1}(P_{Atrue} - P_{AB})^{r_2}(P_{Btrue} - P_{AB})^{r_3}(1 - P_{Atrue} - P_{Btrue} + P_{AB})^{n - r_1 - r_2 - r_3}.$$

We illustrate this set-up with a few numerical examples as shown in Table 2. In each case we shall assume that $P_{Atrue} = 0.001$, $P_{Btrue} = 0.0005$. Clearly, a 1-out-of-2 system will be at least as reliable as the more reliable of the two versions, so the prior distribution of the probability of simultaneous version failure on demand is zero outside [0, 0.0005] in this case. We shall consider below two examples of this distribution: a uniform prior, *Beta(x, 1, 1)*, and a *Beta (x, 10, 10)* both constrained to lie on this interval.

We make no claims for 'plausibility' for these choices of prior. However, it should be noted that each is quite pessimistic: both priors, for example, have mean 0.00025, which suggests a prior belief that about half the channel *B* failures will also result in channel *A* failure.

We assume that $n=10,000$ demands are executed in an operational test environment. In each of the examples in Table 2, one case is that where the observed numbers of channel *A* and channel *B* failures take their (marginal) expected values, i.e. 10 and 5 respectively. The other case is the extreme one where there are no single channel failures.

In each case our main interest is in how our assessment of system reliability based upon the full information, r_1, r_2, r_3, differs from the assessment based only upon the black-box evidence, r_1, alone.

Table 2. Two groups of results are summarised: with uniform prior and non-uniform prior, $Pab|Pa,Pb=Beta(x,10,10)$ on the interval $[0, 0.0005]$. The percentiles illustrate the cumulative distribution $P(\theta \leq X) = Y$, where X are the values shown in the table and Y are the chosen percentiles, 10%, 50%, 75%, 90%, 95% and 99%. Rows labelled 'Black box' represent the percentiles, calculated with the black-box inference, those labelled 'White box' show the percentiles calculated for a posterior derived with (11). '(no version failures)' and '(version failures)' refer to two different observations, in which no individual failures of channels and individual channel failures were observed, respectively

Uniform prior Pab|Pa,Pb

		Percentiles					
		10%	50%	75%	90%	95%	99%
	Prior	0.00005	0.00025	0.000375	0.00045	0.000475	0.000495
$r_1=0$	Black Box	0.000011	0.00007	0.000137	0.000225	0.000286	0.00041
	White Box (version failures)	0.000008	0.00005	0.000095	0.000148	0.00018	0.000245
	White Box (no version failures)	0.000268	0.00042	0.000462	0.00048	0.000485	0.00049
$r_1 = 1$	Black Box	0.000045	0.000155	0.000246	0.000342	0.000396	0.000465
	White Box (version failures)	0.00004	0.00012	0.000179	0.000238	0.000271	0.00033
$r_1 = 3$	Black Box	0.00015	0.0003	0.000384	0.000443	0.000465	0.000485
	White Box (version failures)	0.000165	0.000283	0.000343	0.00039	0.000413	0.000448
$r_1 = 5$	Black Box	0.000235	0.000375	0.000435	0.00047	0.00048	0.00049
	White Box (version failures)	0.000345	0.00044	0.000469	0.000482	0.000485	0.000489

Non-uniform prior Pab|Pa,Pb

		Percentiles					
		10%	50%	75%	90%	95%	99%
	Prior	0.000175	0.000245	0.000283	0.000317	0.000335	0.000368
$r_1=0$	Black Box	0.000146	0.000215	0.000253	0.000286	0.000306	0.000343
	White Box (version failures)	0.00013	0.000188	0.00022	0.00025	0.000269	0.0003
	White Box (no version failures)	0.000205	0.000278	0.000313	0.000345	0.00036	0.00039
$r_1 = 1$	Black Box	0.000161	0.000228	0.000265	0.0003	0.000318	0.000353
	White Box (version failures)	0.00015	0.00021	0.000244	0.000275	0.000291	0.000325
$r_1 = 3$	Black Box	0.000185	0.000251	0.000287	0.00032	0.000336	0.00037
	White Box (version failures)	0.000195	0.000255	0.00029	0.00032	0.000335	0.000365
$r_1 = 5$	Black Box	0.000205	0.000271	0.000305	0.000335	0.000353	0.00038
	White Box (version failures)	0.00024	0.000304	0.000335	0.00036	0.000375	0.000402

Discussion

Table 2 ($r_1=0$) shows the increased confidence that comes when extensive testing reveals *no system failures*. The black-box posterior belief in the system *pfd* is everywhere better than the prior belief: the two distributions are stochastically ordered. More importantly, the posterior belief 'White box (version failures)' based on version failures, but no system failures, is better than the black-box posterior: these distributions are also stochastically ordered. Here the extra information of version failure behaviour has allowed greater confidence to be placed in the system reliability compared with what could be claimed merely from the system behaviour alone.

The result is in accord with intuition. Seeing no system failures in 10,000 demands, when there have been 10 channel *A* failures and 5 channel *B* failures suggests that there is some *negative correlation* between failures of the channels: even if the channels were failing *independently* we would expect to see some common failures (the expected number of coincident failures, conditional on 10 *A*s and 5 *B*s, is 2.5).

The rows where ($r_1 \neq 0$) show what happens when there are system failures (common version failures), with the same numbers of channel failures (10 *A*s, 5 *B*s). As would be expected, the more system failures there are on test, the more pessimistic are the posterior beliefs about system reliability. More interesting, however, is the relationship between the black-box and white-box results. Consider ($r_1=5$). These rows of Table 2 represent the most extreme case where all channel *B* failures are also channel *A* failures. This would suggest strongly that there is *positive correlation* between the version failures. Here the black-box posterior belief would give results that are too optimistic compared with those based on the complete failure data: the white-box and black-box distributions are stochastically ordered.

These results show that knowledge of the detailed version failure data can strongly influence belief about the reliability of a 1-out-of-2 fault tolerant system, compared with the case where only the results of system tests are known. In particular, it may be possible to exploit evidence of negative correlation of version failures from test to sustain stronger claims for reliability than could be made just from knowledge of system behaviour.

As a cautionary note, when $r_1=0$ the posterior 'White box (no version failures)', shows the posterior distribution of system *pfd* for the case where there have been no failures of either version (and hence no system failures) in 10,000 demands, we nevertheless believe the system reliability to be worse than it was *a priori*. How can the observation of such 'good news' make us lose confidence in the system?

The reason for this apparent paradox lies in the constraints on the parameters of the model that are imposed by assuming the versions reliabilities are known with certainty. Consider Table3:

Table 3

	A fails	A succeeds	Total
B fails	θ	$P_B-\theta$	P_B
B succeeds	$P_A-\theta$	$1-P_A-P_B+\theta$	$1-P_B$
Total	P_A	$1-P_A$	1

There is only one unknown parameter, θ, the system *pfd*, which appears in all the cells above representing the four possible outcomes of a test. If we observe no failures in the test, this makes us believe that the entry in the (*A* succeeds, *B* succeeds) cell, $1-P_A-P_B+\theta$, is large. Since P_A, P_B are known, this makes us believe that θ is large.

Of course, it could be argued that observing no version failures in 10,000 demands, with the known version *pfd*s 0.001, 0.0005, is extremely improbable - i.e. observing this result in practice is essentially impossible. This does not remove the difficulty, however: it can be shown that *whatever the value of n*, the 'no failures' posterior will be more pessimistic than the prior. In fact there is stochastic ordering here, both between the prior and the posteriors, and among the posteriors for different *n*.

The practical conclusion seems to be that if this model is to be used the number of demands in test should be great enough to ensure that at least some version failures are observed.

3.3   Other Plausible Priors

The previous two examples show some danger of using "simple" priors. What other "plausible" choices for priors do we have? Among the plethora of choices we will address only one - priors in which the uncertainties about P_A and P_B are independent. This formally can be expressed as:

$$f_{P_A,P_B}(\bullet,\bullet) = f_{P_A}(\bullet)f_{P_B}(\bullet) \tag{12}$$

The assumption we make can be spelled out as: "Even if I were told the value of P_A, this knowledge would not change my uncertainty about P_B (and vice versa)". This assumption is not necessarily the only one plausible. It may also be plausible to believe in some particular form of dependence between the uncertainties represented by $f_{P_A}(\bullet)$ and $f_{P_B}(\bullet)$. If this is the case, $f_{P_A,P_B}(\bullet,\bullet) \neq f_{P_A}(\bullet)f_{P_B}(\bullet)$, then the dependence should be quantified, which makes the definition of the prior much more difficult.

Notice that (12) is not equivalent to assuming independence between the failures of the two channels, which is well known to be unreasonable both empirically, e.g. [1], and theoretically, e.g. [6], [7]. In fact, (12) says *nothing* about the probability of coincident failure, P_{AB}. The uncertainty about the values of P_{AB} can be represented via the conditional distribution, $f_{P_{AB}}(\bullet | P_A = y, P_B = z)$. Certainty here can be expressed as:

$$f_{P_{AB}}(\bullet | P_A = y, P_B = z) = \delta(Kyz) \tag{13}$$

where $K \in [0, \max(y,z)]$. Independence of failures is represented by the special case *K=1*.

The assumption of certainty is extremely strong - it does not change whatever we observe from a system in operation, and is, therefore, implausible: we expect to *learn* something about the system from observing it in operation. Therefore, (13) should be avoided in defining a plausible prior.

Since, by definition, the system can not be less reliable than the more reliable channel, once the channel failure probabilities are known, $(P_A = y, P_B = z)$, P_{AB} can take non-zero values within $[0, \min(P_A, P_B)]$ only.

"Indifference" between the possible values of P_{AB} can be a plausible prior. In this case:

$$f_{P_{AB}}(\bullet | P_A = y, P_B = z) = \frac{1}{\min(y,z)} .$$

The expected value $E[P_{AB}|P_A, P_B] = \frac{1}{2}\min(y,z) > yz$ for realistically small y and z. In other words, "indifference" represents a (reasonable) belief that the system is worse than if the channels failed independently.

Plausible may be any other $f_{P_{AB}}(\bullet | P_A = y, P_B = z)$ defined on $[0, \min(P_A, P_B)]$, too.

Selecting a particular shape for this conditional distribution allows us to represent different beliefs about the probability of system failure including channels' failures being negatively correlated, in which case $f_{P_{AB}}(\bullet | P_A = y, P_B = z)$ should be parameterised in such a way that:

$E[P_{AB}|P_A = y, P_B = z] < yz$

Defining the prior through conditional distributions, $f_{P_{AB}}(\bullet | P_A, P_B)$, clearly poses difficulties, especially if we want to avoid "indifference". These come from the fact that a whole conditional distribution function should be defined for every possible pair of values of the channels probabilities of failure, (P_A, P_B), which may be difficult.

3.4   Priors Allowing Conservative Claims for System Reliability

Given the difficulty in specifying complete priors and also possible numerical difficulties with multiple integrals required for the inference it seems desirable to find approximate simpler inference procedures, provided they produce conservative predictions. This turns out to be quite difficult . In this section we give an example.

Since we showed in section 3.2 how to perform the inference if P_A and P_B were known, we explore here whether this assumption can be used as a conservative approximation in some practical cases.

Suppose that we know the full prior $f_{P_{AB},P_A,P_B}(\bullet,\bullet,\bullet)$ and upper confidence bounds, P_{Amax} and P_{Bmax}, on P_A and P_B. It is then tempting to use these bounds as supposedly known probabilities of channel failure for the procedure shown in 3.2[1]. We thus have an artificial joint prior distribution $f^*_{P_{AB},P_A,P_B}(\bullet,\bullet,\bullet)$, given by assuming that $P_A = P_{Amax}$ and $P_B = P_{Bmax}$ and the marginal prior distribution of the probability of system failure, $f_{P_{AB}}(\bullet)$:

$$f^*_{P_{AB},P_A,P_B}(\bullet,\bullet,\bullet) = f_{P_{AB}}(\bullet)\delta(P_{A\max}, P_{B\max})$$

Hence, $f_{P_{AB},P_A,P_B}(\bullet,\bullet,\bullet)$ and $f^*_{P_{AB},P_A,P_B}(\bullet,\bullet,\bullet)$ are *comparable* in the sense that the uncertainty about *system reliability* with both priors is the same, represented by $f_{P_{AB}}(\bullet)$.

---

[1] One should then account for the small probability of P_A and P_B exceeding the confidence bounds by some manipulation after the Bayesian inference

Now we want to compare the posterior marginal distributions, $f_{P_{AB}}(\bullet|n,r_1,r_2,r_3)$ and $f^*_{P_{AB}}(\bullet|n,r_1,r_2,r_3)$, derived with the comparable priors, $f_{P_{AB},P_A,P_B}(\bullet,\bullet,\bullet)$ and $f^*_{P_{AB},P_A,P_B}(\bullet,\bullet,\bullet)$, for the same observation (n : r_1, r_2, r_3). We illustrate the relationship between the two posterior distributions in Table 4 in which their percentiles are shown. The percentiles of the prior and the black-box posteriors are also included.

$f_{P_{AB},P_A,P_B}(\bullet,\bullet,\bullet)$ used in the examples was defined with the following additional assumptions:

- The marginal distributions $f_{P_A}(\bullet)$ and $f_{P_B}(\bullet)$ were assumed to be Beta distributions, $f_{P_A}(\bullet) = Beta(x,20,10)$ and $f_{P_B}(\bullet) = Beta(x, 20, 20)$ within the interval [0, 0.01], respectively. $P_{Amax} = P_{Bmax} = 0.01$.

- $f_{P_A,P_B}(\bullet,\bullet) = f_{P_A}(\bullet)f_{P_B}(\bullet)$.

- "indifference" between the possible values of P_{AB}, i.e.:

$$f_{P_{AB}}(\bullet|P_A,P_B) = \frac{1}{\min(P_A,P_B)} \text{ within } [0, \min(P_A, P_B)] \text{ and 0 elsewhere.}$$

The system was subjected to 4000 tests, and the number of failures of the system, of channel A and of channel B, represented by r_1, r_2 and r_3, respectively, are shown in the table. The selected examples cover a range of interesting testing results: no failure, no system failure but some one-channel failures, system failure only, a combination of system and one-channel failures.

Table 4. Percentiles of the prior marginal distribution $f_{P_{AB}}(\bullet)$ and the following three posterior distributions: $f_{P_{AB}}(\bullet|n,r_1,r_2,r_3)$, $f^*_{P_{AB}}(\bullet|n,r_1,r_2,r_3)$ and black-box posterior, are shown.

	Percentiles	10%	50%	75%	90%	95%	99%
	Prior	0.00025	0.00225	0.0035	0.00435	0.00485	0.0056
$r_1=0,r_2=0$	$f_{P_{AB}}(\bullet|n,r_1,r_2,r_3)$	0.00278	0.003525	0.00406	0.00445	0.00473	0.00124
$r_3 = 0$	$f^*_{P_{AB}}(\bullet|n,r_1,r_2,r_3)$	0.0055	0.00635	0.0067	0.00705	0.00725	0.0076
	Black-box posterior	0	0	0.000125	0.00035	0.0005	0.001
$r_1=1,r_2=0$	$f_{P_{AB}}(\bullet|n,r_1,r_2,r_3)$	0.0029	0.00372	0.0042	0.00455	0.0048	0.00525
$r_3=0$	$f^*_{P_{AB}}(\bullet|n,r_1,r_2,r_3)$	0.0055	0.00638	0.0067	0.00685	0.00735	0.00763
	Black-box posterior	0	0.00033	0.00058	0.00092	0.00115	0.00173
$r_1=1,r_2=24$	$f_{P_{AB}}(\bullet|n,r_1,r_2,r_3)$	0	0.0001	0.00035	0.00062	0.00076	0.001245
$r_3=20$	$f^*_{P_{AB}}(\bullet|n,r_1,r_2,r_3)$	0.00035	0.00123	0.00178	0.00235	0.00275	0.0033
$r_1=0,r_2=20$	$f_{P_{AB}}(\bullet|n,r_1,r_2,r_3)$	0	0	0.00022	0.00049	0.00067	0.00112
$r_3=15$	$f^*_{P_{AB}}(\bullet|n,r_1,r_2,r_3)$	0.00015	0.00135	0.00224	0.0029	0.00331	0.004

The percentiles reveal stochastic ordering of the posteriors, $f_{P_{AB}}(\bullet|data)$ and $f^*_{P_{AB}}(\bullet|data)$ whatever the observations. The ordering is in favour of $f_{P_{AB}}(\bullet|data)$: the probability of system reliability being better than any reliability target will be greater with $f_{P_{AB}}(\bullet|data)$ than with $f^*_{P_{AB}}(\bullet|data)$. In other words, if we use $f^*_{P_{AB},P_A,P_B}(\bullet,\bullet,\bullet)$ instead of $f_{P_{AB},P_A,P_B}(\bullet,\bullet,\bullet)$, the confidence that we will be prepared to place on a claim that system reliability is better than a predefined reliability target will be lower than if the claim would be based on using $f_{P_{AB},P_A,P_B}(\bullet,\bullet,\bullet)$, i.e. the predictions based on $f^*_{P_{AB},P_A,P_B}(\bullet,\bullet,\bullet)$ will be conservative.

The data presented in Table 4 illustrate only a small part of the experiments we carried out with different priors and testing results. The observations we had were consistent with those presented: when $f_{P_{AB},P_A,P_B}(\bullet,\bullet,\bullet)$ was used as a prior the posterior probability of system failure was stochastically smaller than the posterior obtained with $f^*_{P_{AB},P_A,P_B}(\bullet,\bullet,\bullet)$.

This observation, if universally true, is good news for everyone wishing to use Bayesian inference for conservative reliability assessment of a two-channel system. It suggests a relatively easy way of avoiding the difficulty in defining the full $f_{P_{AB},P_A,P_B}(\bullet,\bullet,\bullet)$. In order for us to be conservative, we need to define $f^*_{P_{AB},P_A,P_B}(\bullet,\bullet,\bullet)$ only which is not much more difficult than defining the marginal probability of system failure, $f_{P_{AB}}(\bullet)$. The only extra parameters it requires are the upper bounds P_{Amax} and P_{Bmax}, which, as stated above, seems feasible a task.

The usefulness of the conservative prior $f^*_{P_{AB},P_A,P_B}(\bullet,\bullet,\bullet)$ seems *limited*. Indeed, for the important special case of testing which does not reveal any failure ($r_1 = 0$, $r_2 = 0$, $r_3 = 0$), the conservative result is too conservative and hence not very useful: the posterior will be more pessimistic than the prior, which is due to the phenomenon explained in section 3.2. This fact reiterates the main point of this paper: elicitation of priors is difficult and there does not seem to exist easy ways out of this difficulty.

The results presented in Table 4 allow us to see the interplay between the black-box and the white-box predictions. Consider, for instance, the cases with observations ($r_1 = 1$, $r_2 = 24$, $r_3 = 20$) and ($r_1 = 0$, $r_2 = 20$, $r_3 = 15$), respectively. In both cases there is ordering between the full white-box and the black-box posteriors but the ordering is in reverse order. In the case with a single system failure the black-box posterior is more pessimistic that the full white-box posterior, while in the case with no system failure the black-box posterior gives more optimistic prediction about system reliability. In the case ($r_1 = 1$, $r_2 = 24$, $r_3 = 20$) we have evidence of negative correlation between the failures of the channels. The expected number of system failures under the assumption of independence is 1.4 in 4000 tests, while we only observed 1. In the case ($r_1 = 0$, $r_2 = 20$, $r_3 = 15$) even though no system failure is observed the evidence of negative correlation is weeker (lower number of individual failures is observed). In result, the white-box prediction is worse than the black-box one.

In summary, using the black-box inference for predicting system reliability may lead either to overestimating or to underestimating the system reliability.

4   Conclusions

1. We described the mathematically correct way of doing Bayesian inference of the reliability of a 1-out-of-2 on-demand system using the testing results. This development, hardly innovative, nevertheless is important because there exist attempts in the literature to use Bayesian inference with unjustified simplified priors. The interested community can be misled by such attempts to believe that Bayesian inference can be applied without due attention to the assumptions made. We showed that even plausible simplifying assumptions used in defining the prior can have counterintuitive consequences.
2. We analysed in depth some priors which are convenient for the inference in the case of a two-channel system, which may be of interest for safety assessors, and showed their limitations, which are new results.
3. We illustrated that a conservative prior for the two channel system can be defined with relative ease if upper bounds on channel probabilities of failure are known with certainty. The level of conservatism, however, can be too great, in particular in the important case when no failures are revealed by the testing.

Open problems:

1. The elicitation of a full prior which can be trusted is still an open problem. In practice, given the difficulties shown, an assessor may want to apply several alternative assumptions about the prior to clarify their effect on prediction and possibly to choose the more conservative predictions.
2. Formal proof of the conservatism of the prior of section 3.4 is needed.
3. For the case of no failures during the testing, *reducing the level of conservatism* to obtain a useful upper bound on system reliability will make Bayesian inference much more attractive for practical reliability/safety assessment.

Acknowledgement

This work was funded partially under the UK HSE Generic Nuclear Safety Research Programme under the 'Diverse Software PrOject' (DISPO) and by the UK Engineering and Physical Sciences Research Council (EPSRC) under the 'Diversity In Safety Critical Software' (DISCS) project and is published with the permission of the UK Nuclear Industry Management Committee (IMC). The authors want to thank Martin Newby for helpful discussions.

References

1. Knight, J.C. and N.G. Leveson, *An Experimental Evaluation of the Assumption of Independence in Multi-Version Programming.* IEEE Transactions on Software Engineering, 1986. **SE-12**(1): p. 96-109.

2. Knight, J.C. and N.G. Leveson. *An empirical study of failure probabilities in multi-version software.* in *16th International Symposium on Fault-Tolerant Computing (FTCS-16).* 1986. Vienna, Austria: IEEE Computer Society Press.

3. Voges, U., ed. *Software diversity in computerized control systems.* Dependable Computing and Fault-Tolerance series, ed. A. Avizienis, H. Kopetz, and J.C. Laprie. Vol. 2. 1988, Springer-Verlag: Wien.

4. Briere, D. and P. Traverse. *Airbus A320/A330/A340 Electrical Flight Controls - A Family Of Fault-Tolerant Systems.* in *23rd International Symposium on Fault-Tolerant Computing (FTCS-23).* 1993. Toulouse, France, 22 - 24: IEEE Computer Society Press.

5. Kantz, H. and C. Koza. *The ELEKTRA Railway Signalling-System: Field Experience with an Actively Replicated System with Diversity.* in *25th IEEE Annual International Symposium on Fault -Tolerant Computing (FTCS-25).* 1995. Pasadena, California: IEEE Computer Society Press.

6. Eckhardt, D.E. and L.D. Lee, *A theoretical basis for the analysis of multiversion software subject to coincident errors.* IEEE Transactions on Software Engineering, 1985. **SE-11**(12): p. 1511-1517.

7. Littlewood, B. and D.R. Miller, *Conceptual Modelling of Coincident Failures in Multi-Version Software.* IEEE Transactions on Software Engineering, 1989. **SE-15**(12): p. 1596-1614.

8. Musa, J.D., A. Iannino, and K. Okumoto, *Software Reliability: Measurement, Prediction, Application.* 1987: McGraw-Hill International Editions. 621.

9. Brocklehurst, S., *et al.*, *Recalibrating software reliability models.* IEEE Transactions on Software Engineering, 1990. **SE-16**(4): p. 458-470.

10. Littlewood, B. and L. Strigini, *Validation of Ultra-High Dependability for Software-based Systems.* Communications of the ACM, 1993. **36**(11): p. 69-80.

11. Butler, R.W. and G.B. Finelli. *The Infeasibility of Experimental Quantification of Life-Critical Software Reliability.* in *ACM SIGSOFT '91 Conference on Software for Critical Systems, in ACM SIGSOFT Software Eng. Notes, Vol. 16 (5).* 1991. New Orleans, Louisiana.

12. Johnson, N.L. and S. Kotz, *Distributions in Statistics: Continuous Multivariate Distributions.* Wiley Series in Probability and Mathematical Statistics, ed. R.A. Bradley, Hunter, J. S., Kendall, D. G., Watson, G. S. Vol. 4. 1972: John Weley and Sons, INc. 333.

13. Miller, K.W., *et al.*, *Estimating the Probability of Failure When Testing Reveals No Failures.* IEEE Transactions on Software Engineering, 1992. **18**(1): p. 33-43.

14. Littlewood, B. and D. Wright, *Some conservative stopping rules for the operational testing of safety-critical software.* IEEE Transactions on Software Engineering, 1997. **23**(11): p. 673-683.

Estimating Dependability of Programmable Systems Using BBNs *

Bjørn Axel Gran[1], Gustav Dahll[1], Siegfried Eisinger[2], Eivind J. Lund[3],
Jan Gerhard Norstrøm[3], Peter Strocka[3], and Britt J. Ystanes[3]

[1] OECD Halden Reactor Project
P.O.Box 173, N-1751 Halden, Norway
{bjorn.axel.gran, gustav.dahll}@hrp.no
[2] Det Norske Veritas
Veritasvn. 1, N-1322 Høvik, Norway
siegfried.eisinger@dnv.com
[3] Kongsberg Defence & Aerospace AS
P.O.Box 1003, N-3601 Kongsberg, Norway
{eivind.johan.lund,jan.norstroem,peter.strocka,
britt.jorunn.ystanes}@kongsberg.com

Abstract. This paper describes a project carried out by a consortium composed of Kongsberg Defence & Aerospace AS, Det Norske Veritas, and OECD Halden Reactor Project. First of all the project goal is to research the use of Bayesian Belief Nets to investigate the implementation of the DO-178B standard for software approval in the comercial world. To reach our objectives a computerized system for atomized transmission of graphical position information from helicopters to land based control stations was selected and studied. This paper describes the Bayesian Belief Nets used, and sumarises some of the findings in this study.

1   Introduction

The last decades shows that one is more dependent on, programmable digital equipment, also in safety critical systems. Therefore there is focus to make international standards for the development of programmable systems for safety related applications. The most important generic standard is IEC 61508 "Functional safety of electronic safety-related systems" [1]. This standard will constitute a framework for other, more specific standards. An existing branch specific standard is the guideline for safety relevant software in civil aviation, DO-178B [2].

Applying Bayesian Belief Nets (BBN) is a method to make reliability estimates based on information of disparate nature, to combine quantitative observations and

---

* Please note that this paper represents by no mean any official policy of KDA.

F. Koornneef and M. van der Meulen (Eds.): SAFECOMP 2000, LNCS 1943, pp. 309-320, 2000.

human judgments. The objective of using BBNs in software safety assessment is to show the link between observable properties and the confidence one can have in a system. The theory about BBNs is well established, and the method has been applied with success in various areas, including medical diagnosis and geological exploration. There has also been an activity to apply this method for safety assessment of programmable systems [4, 5, 9, 11, 12], and there are smart tools to perform computations with BBNs. We will particularly refer to the HUGIN tool [3, 6, 10] and the SERENE methodology [5].

In the project described in this paper the BBNs were applied on a real, safety related programmable system, *viz.* a computerized system (M-ADS) for atomized transmission of graphical position information from helicopters to land based control stations, and the standard for safety critical software in civil aviation, DO-178B [2] was applied. The main purpose of the system is to aid in a rescue operation if the helicopter has made an emergency landing on the sea. A correct localization is necessary for a successful rescue operation, the system is therefore safety critical, and the system had to be approved by the Norwegian Civil Aviation Authority.

This paper describes the methods used, and emphasizes the practical evaluation of the proposed methodology, based on the application on the test case.

2   Overview of M-ADS, DO-178B and the BBN-Methodology

2.1   The M-ADS Airborne Equipment

The M-ADS airborne equipment is designed by KDA for installation in helicopter aircraft. The system provides air traffic services with aircraft parameters upon request from the air traffic control where personnel will request positioning data. The M-ADS system is designed to automatically transmit flight information via data link to one or more requesting air control centers. M-ADS uses existing avionics on board the aircraft to provide aircraft position, speed and additional optional data. Most important are the aircraft position, position accuracy, altitude and time stamp for the data validity. The work described below uses parts of the M-ADS system to exemplify the software development process according to DO-178B standard.

2.2   The DO-178B Guideline

The purpose of the DO-178B standard [2] is to provide a required guideline for the production of safety critical software for airborne systems. This guideline was chosen for the study since the M-ADS system is applied in civil aviation, and was previously qualified on the basis of this standard. DO-178B discusses aspects of airworthiness certification that pertain to the production of software for airborne systems and equipment used in aircraft. To aid in understanding the certification process the system life cycle is briefly discussed to show relationship to the software life cycle process. It does not provide guidelines concerning the structure of the applicant's organization, relations to suppliers and personnel qualification criteria.

DO-178B defines, similar to IEC 61508 [1], a set of five software levels (A, B, to E), based on the contribution from software to potential failure conditions as determined by the system safety assessment process. The main recommendations in DO-178B are given in a set of 10 tables, see description in the Appendix. Each table relates to a certain stage in the development and validation process, and contains a set of objectives. A difference between the two standards is that most of the requirements are mandatory in IEC 61508, while the requirements are guidelines in DO-178B, [13].

2.3   Bayesian Belief Net and Basic Methodology

A Bayesian Belief Net (BBN) is a connected and directed graph, consisting of a set of nodes and a set of directed arcs between them. Uncertain variables (both events and singular propositions) are associated to each node where the uncertainty is expressed by a probability density. The probability density expresses our or confidence to the various variable outcomes. This probability depends conditionally on the status of other nodes at the incoming edges to the node (the parent nodes). Some nodes are denoted as "observables". They represent the different observable properties about the software system and its development. Network edges model relations between adjacent nodes, and the "strength" of these relations is represented as conditional probability distributions. The computation of our belief about a specific node (target node) is based on the rules for conditional probability calculations backward and forward along the edges, from the observable nodes, through the intermediate nodes to the target node [7, 8, 14].

The construction of the BBN is normally made gradually. Information about the software system and the DO-178B standard is collected and expressed via the nodes. The nodes are connected together to a directed graph that expresses the conditional relationship between the variables. The aim is to combine information in the net. One way is to start from a target node and draw edges to influencing nodes. To decide the direction of an edge, one follows the causal direction. However, this direction is not always obvious, in particular between nodes representing qualitative variables. In these cases the direction of the arrow often goes from higher abstraction to lower abstraction, or from the more general concept to the more detailed. For computations of a realistic BBN computer tools are necessary. We have applied the SERENE methodology [5] and the HUGIN tool [3].

3   Construction of the BBN for M-ADS

3.1   The Construction Process

A basic philosophy for the proposed process is to relate the safety of the system to the fulfillment of the requirements in an internationally accepted safety standard. This philosophy can of course be questioned, but such standards are based on consensus among experts in the area relevant for an actual safety critical system. Even if conformance to a safety standard does not imply safety, it is a strong indication of the effort put into making the system safe. This indication can also be used as prior probability in a Bayesian model for a further safety assessment based on safety testing.

Recall that one want to achieve a way of stating how well the development of a safety critical system conforms to the requirements of the standard. However, such standards do not contain any measures of conformity, but rather a large number of requirements of rather disparate nature, which should be fulfilled. Our objective is to use BBN methodology to construct such a measure.

The first action in the construction is to identify the main aspects that may influence the dependability of a system. One can distinguish between aspects that are related to the system itself and aspects that are related to the interaction between the system and its environment (usage of the system, potential hazards etc.).

The former includes quality aspects, which were divided into four types:

- *Quality of the producer.* (*Qproducer*) This includes the reputation and experience of the producer, quality assurance policy, quality of staff etc.
- *Quality of the production process.* (*Qprocess*) A high quality implies that the system is developed according to guidelines for good software engineering, that all phases are well documented, and that the documentation shows that the system at all development phases possesses desirable quality attributes as completeness, consistency, traceability etc.
- *Quality of the product.* (*Qproduct*) This includes quality attributes for the final product, as reliability, simplicity, verifiability etc.
- *Quality of the analysis.* (*Qanalysis*) This includes all activities performed to validate the correctness of the system during all stages of the system development. Such activities may include model checking of the specifications, inspections and walkthroughs of the documentation, static analysis of code and testing of the system.

The BBN was constructed in two levels. The higher level shows how nodes representing the four aspects above are combined with other nodes in the net and lead to nodes representing the reliability and safety of the system. At the lower level there are four BBNs, where the four aspects are represented as top nodes. These nodes are connected to observations that are expressed as edges going from these nodes, via intermediate nodes to the observable nodes. The procedure in our project has been to associate the recommendations of a standard with the observable nodes. This is made in the form of questions that are formulated in a way that makes it possible to transfer the answer into a quantitative measurement. One should also notice that many of the observables/questions are linked to more than one top node. This expresses the fact that there are clear correlations between the four quality aspects mentioned above. At both levels the edges between the nodes are associated with conditional probability tables. In this project these were estimated based on judgments in a brainstorming activity among the project participants.

3.2   The Higher Level BBN

The higher level network, see Figure 1, consists of two parts. The first upper part represents all aspects relevant for the quality of the development of the final system prior to final testing. It leads to a node "P(failed state)", representing the "probability of finding the system in a failed state". This node is the connection to the lower part, which consists of the connections between the node "P(failed state)" and the node representing "the system safety".

The upper part consists of the four quality nodes listed in the above section. In addition it includes the nodes "problem complexity" and "solution complexity". The initial nodes or top nodes are the nodes: "Qproducer" and "problem complexity", where the latter is an attribute of the system to be developed, and can be measured. It is assumed that the "Qproducer" directly influences the "Qprocess", ant that the "solution complexity" is influenced by the initial "problem complexity" and the "Qprocess". The same dependencies are assumed for the "Qproduct". The product quality depends upon how difficult it is to fulfill the requirements (the complexity of the problem), and upon how good the development process handle complex systems. The "Qanalysis" is assumed to be influenced by the "Qproducer", how well prepared the organization is to perform an analysis, and the "solution complexity", how difficult it is to analyze. All these assumptions are in accordance with BBNs presented in the SERENE project [5] and networks presented by HRP-project [9].

Based on the assessment of the "Qanalysis", the "Qproduct" and the "solution complexity" it is possible to combine these factors into an assessment of the node representing the "P(failed state)". This is not to be viewed as a failure rate representing a specific usage or safety function, but rather as a deterministic property of the system expressing fault content. One interpretation is the fraction of the total input space that leads to failure. Assuming that no failures are found or modifications are made during later testing of the system, this true failure rate is not changed; only the confidence in the reliability of the program is enhanced.

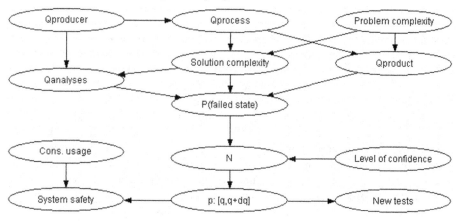

Fig. 1. The BBN for the higher level

The nodes in this network can be viewed as a quality aspect representing all the activities that has been made previous to final testing of the system with the aim of minimizing this true failure rate. There is no unique way to construct this dependency. It is to a large degree based on experience and judgments, and was in this project made as a brainstorming exercise among the project participants.

The lower part of this BBN reflects a statistical reliability model based on failure free testing. This model is an expression for the confidence (c) in that the true failure rate (p) is lower than a certain low level (q), given that n tests of the system have been executed with no failures:

$$c=P(p<q|\ n\ failure\ free\ tests) = 1-(1-q)^{n+1} \tag{1}$$

This model is based on frequentistic probability theory. It can, however, be refined by using Bayesian theory. With this theory one can incorporate in the model all additional previous information expressed in the upper part of the BBN. This is made in the form of a prior probability density function:

$$pdf_{prior}(q)= P(q<p<q+dq\,|\,all\ previous\ information) \tag{2}$$

An objective is now to get an expression for a probability density function that considers both all previous information and n additional failure free tests. If one express $pdf_{prior}(q)$ in the form $(1-q)^N$, which can be interpreted so that all previous information is equivalent to N failure free tests, this expression could be simplified to:

$$(N+n+1)*(1-q)^{N+n} \tag{3}$$

This is expressed in the node "N" and the edge from the node "P(failed state)" to this node. The intention is to translate the information in the upper node to an expression representing N hypothetical failure free tests. However, the $pdf_{prior}(q)$ is only a probability distribution, whereas the node "P(failed state)" represents a confidence in the reliability of the system. In order to transfer the value of this node into the node "N", one also needs to state the confidence level (c). Thus one can express the node "P(failed state)" in the form: "we state with confidence c that the true failure probability, p, is not greater than Q". This means that the node "N" contains the information of the node "P(failed state)", given an optional confidence level. That is, given a certain confidence level (c) and a probability distribution on "the probability of finding the system in a failed state", one can express the previous measurements as a "number of hypothetic failure free tests".

Another aspect occurs if the safety test is not failure free, but that a failure occurred after m failure free tests. One can, of course, argue that if a failure occurs in a safety related system, a safety assessor would reject this system and hand it back to the system developer for correction. The correction of the system may introduce new faults in the system, and from the assessor's point of view this is a new system with a new prior distribution. However, the failed test may have influence on the prior belief in the reliability of the system. If the failure occurs very much earlier than expected from the prior distribution, one may be lead to the conclusion that this distribution was too optimistic, and should be corrected. Thus, a test that leads to a failure after m tests may be used as a way to evaluate and eventually modify the prior assumptions made for the BBNs. This aspect is addressed in section 4.3.3.

3.3   The Lower Level BBN Identification Based on DO-178B

The lower level BBNs are constructed by identifying the quality aspects with top-nodes in four BBNs. Each top node is linked to intermediate nodes representing the 10 process tables of DO-178B (A1, A2... A10). Each of these nodes was again linked to other intermediate nodes; representing the objectives of the tables, see Figure 2. Finally some additional objectives to be considered in the networks were identified

The further step was to identify a list of questions to each objective. These questions are based of the understanding of the text in the main part of DO-178B, and they are in general formulated so that the answer can be given by a "yes" or a "no". However, as the questions often are of a qualitative nature, it may be difficult to give a straight answer. It is therefore possible to answer the question with a number between 0 and 1 as an expression of the strength in the belief that the answer is "yes" (1) or "no" (0). This number is then used as input to the computation of the BBN.

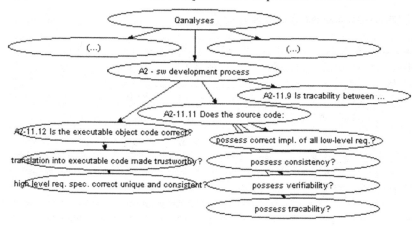

Fig. 2. A part of the BBN for the *"Quality of the analysis"*

4   Computation on the M-ADS BBN

4.1   Description of Assumptions, Restrictions and Scenarios

As described in section 3.3, no modeling of the dependencies with respect to the node "system safety" was made in this pre-study. Of this reason there was therefore not put any observations, or done any calculations on this node. Another restriction is given for the node "level of confidence". Instead of stating a specific level of confidence, as intended and discussed in section 3.2, a uniform distribution over the variable outcomes was assumed. Taking the expectation resulted in a value equal 0.87. Besides, no observations were placed on the node representing "problem complexity".

Another set of assumptions is discussed at the end of sections 3.1. As the project created a rather complex BBN (or system of BBNs), there were a large number of conditional probability tables to be assessed. In this project these were estimated based on judgments in a brainstorming activity among the project participants. Of course, this opens for some subjectivity. On the other hand, some of the project members were considered as experts within their field.

After observing the results of four initial (no observations, KDA observations, best case, worst case) scenarios some additional scenarios were defined. For all scenarios observations have been made with respect to the four quality aspects and the node "$p \in [q,q+dq]$". In this paper some results from these scenarios are presented:

- "Partial": the effect of observations during only one stage in the development and validation process, such as A1, A2... A10 (see description in the Appendix).
- "Incremental": the effect of first observing during the stage A1, then A2, and so on, representing the fact that the processes can be viewed as subsequently.
- Sensitivity analysis for the node "$p \in [q,q+dq]$" given observations on the node "New tests".

4.2   Observations on the End Nodes

The observations were produced by KDA through several interview sessions with experts involved in the project. Totally, experts representing the software design and coding role, as well as project management role, where involved. In each session the questions associated with the end nodes in the network were used to assess the module in the view of the scope defined by the node.

The answers were, as discussed in section 3.3, given as weighted values in the scale from zero to one. In general the value zero means objective achieved with poor quality, while the value one means objective achieved at highest level of quality. We also have a few cases where a score, say 0.95, indicates objective achieved at highest level of quality for 95% of the modules. As an example refer to a question for the BBN for "Qanalysis"; "is the software quality assurance process properly performed and recorded?" The answer, 0.95, means that the expert board judged that software quality assurance process is properly performed and recorded for 95% of the modules.

4.3   Results

4.3.1   The Partial Scenarios

The effect of the observations during only one stage in the development and validation process showed that with respect to the "Qproducer" that the processes with largest effect were "the sw planning process (A1)", "the sw development process (A2)" and "verification of verification process results (A7)". Remark, however, that the effects were approximately the same for the other processes. With respect to the "Qprocess" the processes with largest effect were "verification of outputs of sw requirements process (A3)", "sw configuration management process (A8)" and "certification liaison process (A10)", while "other aspects" had lowest effect. With respect to the "Qproduct" the processes with largest effect were the process A7 and "other aspects" including aspects such as e.g. human machine interfaces. Quite low effect was observed for the processes: "verification of outputs of sw design processes (A4)" and the process A10. With respect to the "Qanalysis" the process "other aspects" had largest effect, but also all the other processes had a large effect. For the node "$p\in[q,q+dq]$" the largest effects were for the processes A3, A7 and "other aspects", while the lowest effects were for the processes A4 and A10. These results are in accordance with the dependency between the node "$p\in[q,q+dq]$" and the nodes "Qproduct" and "Qanalysis".

4.3.2   The Incremental Scenarios

The observations could also be added subsequently, first during process A1, then A2 and so on. This illustrates how the posterior pdfs change from the initial prior values towards a scenario given by "all the KDA observations". For the "Qproducer" the expected value came up to the "top level" already after made observations during process A1 and A2. This does not mean that the quality of the producer will remain on this level independent of what more to observe, but means that making additional "good" observations do not change our posterior results. With respect to the nodes "Qprocess", "Qproduct", and "Qanalysis" we had to make positive observations on all the processes A1 towards A8 before the posterior pdfs achieved the "top level". For the node "$p\in[q,q+dq]$", the posterior pdf was on its "top level" after observations were made during process A1 up to A3. This is the similar effect as for the "Qproducer". Remark that, although there is no direct link between these two nodes, they behave in the same manner due to the propagation of positive measurements.

4.3.3   Sensitivity Cases

A sensitivity analysis was performed for the node "$p\in[q,q+dq]$" given future observations on the node "New tests". That is, with all the observations on the quality aspects, represented in the node "N", different measurements were made on the node "New tests". Remark that making a measurement equal to m, assumes that a failure occurred after m failure free tests (see section 3.2). The posterior pdfs for "$p\in[q,q+dq]$" are shown in Figure 3. Compared to testing alone, these results shows that observing m failure free tests, where m is higher than the hypothetical N failure free tests, will increase our belief in a shift left of the pdf for "$p\in[q,q+dq]$". In the same way, observing m lower than N, will shift the pdf right, due to the situation that our prior belief is not in accordance with the real measurements.

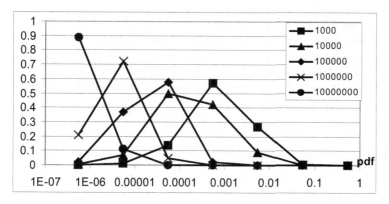

Fig. 3. The posterior pdfs for "$p\in[q,q+dq]$" for different number of new tests

5   Experiences from the Evaluation

The BBN methodology was mainly developed and applied in the AI society, but more recently there have been attempts to apply it for estimation of the dependability of programmable safety relevant systems. From the experiences from applying the methodology on the M-ADS system, including a BBN modeling of the DO-178B guideline, we can conclude that the BBN methodology offers a systematic way to combine quantitative and qualitative evidences of relevance for the safety assessment of programmable systems.

Conceptually, estimation of the dependability of programmable systems is nearly impossible to compute, since many of the aspects to be considered are of qualitative nature and not directly measurable, but have to be estimated. The most difficult activity was to perform the expert judgment, in particular in the assignment of values to the conditional pdfs. Even if some of the project members can be considered as experts within their fields, it is highly recommendable to make use of some expert judgment tools or expert judgment expertise.

Another observation is that the establishment of the BBNs and prior pdfs was rather time consuming. However, the process of building up the network, e.g. by making questionnaires, and the elicitation of the prior pdfs were related to DO-178B, and not to the actual system. This implies that these have a general nature, and can be reused in many applications. They can also be gradually improved based on experience. Furthermore, it may be feasible to transfer this knowledge to other safety related software engineering standards. It should also be remarked, that the project provided an improved understanding of the DO-178B.

The experiences from collecting the different observable properties to be used in the calculations, and performing the calculations, are that these tasks are fairly easy and not so time consuming. Since tool support is necessary, we applied the HUGIN tool and the SERENE methodology (Demo 1.0), and found it satisfactory.

Knowledge within BBN and probabilistic theory is to a great advantage in the construction of the networks and the assessing of the pdfs. This knowledge is also an advantage in the evaluation of the results from the computations.

Another finding from the project is that the BBN methodology is not only applicable in the final assessment of a system, but could be used at all stages throughout the whole software lifecycle. The network could e.g. in this specific project be used to evaluate the difference between two different safety levels before any other measurements are collected. In this way it is possible to make assessments about the system before it is even designed or implemented. In such a way corrections to e.g. the development process can be made early in the project, in order to be able to reach specific objectives of the final product.

6   Further Work

The following list presents the main objectives or tasks that should be considered for further work:

- The sub networks based upon DO-178B should be revised and clearer defined. That is, one should control that each selected node belongs to the network, and one should check for missing nodes. On should also clearer define the meaning of each node state. Related to this is also a possibility to apply expert judgment tools in order to obtain better expert judgments on the pdfs.
- The upper network, describing the connection between the quality aspects and the node representing the "probability of finding the system in a failed state" should be reviewed and perhaps be redrawn.
- To evaluate the possibility of validate the BBNs or a sub network including the topology (which node is connected to which node), and the pdfs (the probability of observing a certain state given that the parent node is in a certain state).

Acknowledgement

The project participants want to acknowledge Martin Neil for advice and interest with respect to the use of SERENE (Demo 1.0). The project participants also want to acknowledge Hugin Expert A/S for allowing Gran the use of the HUGIN tool for his Ph.D. work, and for supporting help.

References

1   IEC 61508: "Functional safety of electrical/electronic/programmable electronic safety-related systems", (1995).
2   RTCA/DO-178B: "Software Considerations in Airborne Systems and Equipment Certifications", (1992).
3   HUGIN. Tool made by Hugin Expert a/s, Aalborg, (http://www.hugin.dk)
4   IMPRESS: "Improving the software process using bayesian nets". EPSRC project nr. GR/L06683, (1999).
     (http://www.csr.city.ac.uk/csr_city/projects/impress.html)
5   SERENE: "Safety and Risk Evaluation using Bayesian Nets". ESPRIT Framework IV nr. 22187, (1999). (http://www.hugin.dk/serene/)
6   Aldenryd, S. H., Jensen, K. B., Nielsen L. B.: "Hugin Runtime for MS-Windows", (1993).
7   Casella, G., Berger, R. L., *Statistical Inference*, Wadsworth & Brooks/Cole Advanced Books & Software, (1990).
8   Cowell, R. G., Dawid, A. P., Lauritzen, S. L., Spiegelhalter, D. J.: *Probabilistic Networks and Expert Systems*, Springer-Verlag, (1999).
9   Dahll, G. & Gran, B.A.: "The Use of Bayesian Belief Nets in Safety Assessment of Software Based Systems". *Int. J. General Systems*, Vol. 29(2), (2000) 205-229.
10   Jensen, F.: *An Introduction to Bayesian Networks*, London: UCL Press, University College London. (1993).

11   Neil, M., Littlewod, B., Fenton, N.: "Applying Bayesian Belief Nets to Systems Dependability Assessment". In: Proceedings of 4th Safety Critical Systems Symposium, Springer-Verlag, (1996) 71-93.

12   Neil, M., Fenton, N.: "Predicting Software Quality using Bayesian Belief Networks". In: Proceedings of 21st. Annual Software Engineering Workshop, NASA Goddard Space Flight Centre, (1996) 217-230.

13   Fenton, N., Neil, M.: "A Strategy for Improving Safety Related Software Engineering Standards". *IEEE Transactions on Software Engineering*, Vol. 24(11), (1998) 1002-1013.

14   Welsh, A. H.: *Aspects of Statistical Inference*, Wiley & Sons, (1996).

Appendix: The Main Recommendations in DO-178B

	Stage in the development and validation process
A1	Software planning process.
A2	Software development process.
A3	Verification of outputs of software requirements process.
A4	Verification of outputs of software design process.
A5	Verification of outputs of software coding & integration process.
A6	Testing of outputs of integration process.
A7	Verification of verification process results.
A8	Software configuration management process.
A9	Software quality assurance process.
A10	Certification liaison process.

Improvements in Process Control Dependability through Internet Security Technology

Ferdinand J. Dafelmair

TÜV Süddeutschland Bau und Betrieb
Westend Street 199, 80686 Munich, Germany
Ferdinand.Dafelmair@tuevs.de

Abstract. The increasing use of the internet as a global communication media drives the development of new methods to cope with the deficiencies in reliability and security, inherently associated with the internet in its current form. Thus data integrity and confidentiality, as well as peer-to-peer authentication and non repudiation of transactions, are considered fundamental for a wide success of electronic commerce. As an answer to this demands, application of Public Key Infrastructures (PKI) gains momentum. This paper shows how this internet security technology may be successfully transferred into the process industry sector to provide valuable support for many of the current issues in dependable process control. The applications addressed reach from improvements in safe process control to reliability of communication and even commercial efficiency of operation, showing that a PKI is a valuable instrument to maintain the staff's confidence in procedures and communication, that migrate from paper to computer screens.

1   Introduction

Computer based communication changes the process of information and data exchange between people in such a fundamental way, that well known properties of the different traditional communication means may no longer be considered ensured in the way, we learned from long experience. We know the properties of a signed document instantiated as letter, a contract or just a simple memo. In verbal communication situations we know how to identify each other and how to protect confidentiality of our communication and we also know what to do to ensure that a partner cannot repudiate for example a given commitment. The Basis of our certainty are techniques of identification and authentication we developed in centuries and continuously improved and adapted to changing environments. Examples are seals, insignia, mechanical keys, handwritten signatures or the hologram on a credit card. With the Information Age we again need to adapt these techniques of identification and authentication. One promising solution is to use a technology called Public Key-Infrastructure (PKI) which provides a new basis for personal identification called a certificate and associated electronic keys. The next section shows how this set allows even more than just identification and authentication.

F. Koornneef and M. van der Meulen (Eds.): SAFECOMP 2000, LNCS 1943, pp. 321-332, 2000.
© Springer-Verlag Berlin Heidelberg 2000

2   PKI Basics

2.1   Certificates and Certification Authorities

All the functionality provided by a PKI relies on the fact, that it is based on a so-called public key cryptosystem with the fundamental characteristics that the key for encryption is different from the key for decryption, and one key cannot be calculated from the other[1]. Both keys are associated to one owner. The encryption key can be made public whereas the decryption key is kept secret[2]. Using the public key anyone can encrypt a document that only the owner of the private key can decrypt and any document signed by the owner using his secret key can be verified by everybody with the help the owners public key, which may be retrieved from directories [1][10].

The basic identification object in a PKI is the public key certificate or just certificate. It contains the public key of it's subject[3] whether this is a person, a hardware device or a software process [2]. It also contains some other information about the subject[4], and information on which certification authority (CA) issued the certificate. Upon issuing a certificate the CA renders the data of the certificate unforgeable by encipherment with it's own private key [3][6][8].

In a process called registration, the CA acquires personal data of the PKI-user and future certificate owner, checks correctness of that data, generates the key-pair for the user, hands over the secret key protected by a Personal Security Environment (PSE)[5] to the user, and generates the certificate for the user which it publishes on a directory server. In a similar way, certificates are generated for devices or other non human subjects. A certificate thus may be considered a subject's unforgeable universal electronic identification (Electronic ID). The next chapter will show what basic structured environment is necessary to use such certificates.

2.2   Generic PKI Structure

A PKI structure is similar to a client-server architecture with central and distributed elements. Fig. 1 outlines this structure. There are several core elements of a PKI that require highly reliable and trustworthy operation. Those are concentrated in a physically secured Trust-Center holding also the items that require the utmost protection of the whole PKI – the secret signature keys of the CA.

Core PKI-elements are the systems of the CA which generate the key pairs and the certificates (KG&CA). Data for this generation comes in from Registration Authori-

---

[1] Asymmetric Encryption Algorithm [9]

[2] The secret key is a synonym for the private key and it is used as encryption key for enciphering operations and as decryption key for verifying digital signature operations.

[3] The abstract subject may be understood as owner as it is implicitly obvious if the certificate belongs to a person.

[4] This data describes the subject more precisely, e.g. name, address etc. and may contain attributes e.g. special authorizations, memberships etc.

[5] Usually a smart card with provisions against any attempts to retrieve the secret key from it.

ties (RA) which may be decentralized to be closer to the customer. Protection and integrity of the registered data is accomplished by protection of the RA itself, together with strict authentication of the Registration Officers and application of strong cryptography during data registration and transmission processes. Several RAs may be connected to one CA. To avoid eavesdropping or jeopardizing user keys during personalization of smart cards, it is beneficial to centralize this activity in a trusted environment (PERS[6]). The same is mandatory for the timestamping (TS) and verification service (Verify), which both use secret CA keys to sign their response to the user (U, UCA, UCB[7]). The former delivers a proof, that a given document existed at the stated time, the latter reports the certificate status indicating whether the certificate data hasn't been invalidated i.e. caused by changes of personal attributes after registration, loss of the PSE[8], expiration etc. Another central element of a PKI is the Directory (DIR) which allows every user to obtain a peer's certificate. It's advisable to replicate the directory to local directories of user groups (LDIR A or LDIR B), which allow central administration and configuration of the client software of the PKI (see below). The entire PKI relies on stable communication from when the user applies for registration throughout certificate use until he requires certificate revocation. The next section will give a brief overview of what to use a PKI for.

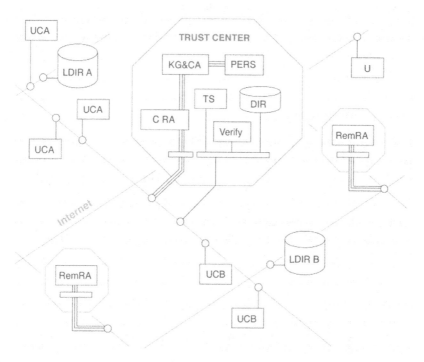

Fig. 1 Generic PKI Structure

---

[6] PERS = Electrical Personalization of SmartCards
[7] UCA = User Company A, UCB = User Company B
[8] usually a smart card

2.3   Basic Operations

The PKI's functionality is based on a handful of basic operations. It is helpful to distinguish roughly between two major groups of them, the one dealing with the task of concealing sensitive information the other with ensuring authenticity, non-repudiation and integrity of data and associated transactions. Operations of both groups may be combined to achieve for example protection against information disclosure and guarantee for authenticity.

Members of the first group are the basic operations of enciphering and deciphering of files (e.g. email and their attachments, source code files, sensitive records etc.) or stream data, like video or audio data-streams in real time communication scenarios (cellular phone or internet audio communication, video conferences etc.). The most important basic operations of the second group are signing electronic documents. They are applicable in most areas where we traditionally use handwritten signatures (email, electronic order forms, contracts etc.)

Two other basic operations are of great importance for a PKI. The first is key generation and exchange the other is timestamp creation and verification. The former is essential for generating symmetric one time session keys (e.g. 3DES [5], IDEA [7] keys), necessary for enciphering high volume data, and exchanging these keys between the partners participating in an enciphered communication session[9]. The latter introduces a time reference. Also methods need to be provided to revoke keys respectively their associated certificates. Based on its basic operations a PKI usually offers a set of generic applications to its users.

2.4   Generic Applications

Based on a few generic applications within a PKI, even complex information handling processes can be efficiently protected. Fig. 2 shows the "PKI Enabled Workstation" with its generic applications. The secure web access application, which must be understood as a standard browser ideally enhanced with modules for high level cryptography or certain authentication protocols or signing functions, protects the entire data communication between user and server against disclosure, and provides reliable peer-to-peer authentication and even non-repudiation, such that the user can trust the server and vice versa.

---

[9] In it's most primitive form a key exchange protocol could be like this: The local peer generates a random symmetric session key, enciphers it with the public key of the remote peer and transfers it to him. Only the remote peer can decipher the session key with his private key. Now both parties have a private session key to encipher data communication between them using fast symmetric algorithms without the need to transfer the symmetric key separately as it would be necessary with sole application of a symmetric encryption algorithm. Practical key exchange protocols are more complex to avoid weaknesses of the simple scheme e.g. replay attacks [8] [4].

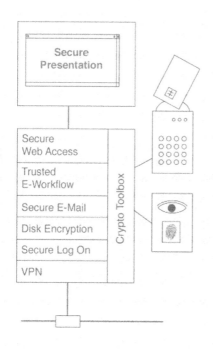

The secure email application adds encryption and signatures, eventually even timestamps, to mail messages and their attachments. Thus email messages can reach validity, similar to manually signed letters, and even much better protection against disclosure. Volume encryption is another helping application to ensure, that the data is sufficiently protected not only during transmission on networks but also on the workstation's disk volume.

The secure user authentication/system log-on application is the basis for introducing the user to the system, making sure that only the well-known individual has access to his resources their. With certificates and smart cards instead of usernames and passwords it reaches the level of reliability overdue for years. The ideal solution to secure communication over insecure networks is an application called Virtual Private Network (VPN), that encrypts the entire communication among it's participants on network layer 3 or below, meaning that really the contents of every IP packet despite

Fig. 2 PKI Enabled Workstation

of it's affiliation to particular applications, like file transfer or WWW-Server Access, gets protected. With sophisticated PKIs the functions of the above mentioned applications are available as modules with Application Programmers Interfaces (API) to be integrated into already existing groupware or specialized electronic workflow applications which benefit substantially from new dependability qualities and become Secure Electronic Workflow systems.

It is important to mention that configuration and management of user applications within a PKI shall be done centrally based on a directory application. For this purpose clients of powerful PKIs support the ldap protocol for receiving configuration data from a directory which is usually operated enterprise specific, with more than one directory easily coexisting within a PKI. Directory based solutions provide the advantage of centralized security policy management making sure that every client is configured correctly at any time and as such avoiding security breaches.

3   PKI Support in Process Control Environments

This section shows, how a PKI is well suited to support the complex operations in a process control environment with its high demands on safety and security. It addresses each support function as indicated in Fig. 3 and finally introduces an implementation example according to Fig. 4.

3.1   Network Infrastructure Protection

The network infrastructure is the backbone of communication not only within commercial companies but also in process control environments as process control nowadays is vastly computer based. Using certificates not only for individuals, but also for the components of the infrastructure, access to the components as well as peer-to-peer authentication between components may be controlled much better than with traditional authentication schemes. Encryption of configuration and management traffic in networks eliminates security weakpoints through exploiting management protocol weaknesses. Certificate based authentication of external users already at the firewall increases the threshold for successful break-ins. Application of VPN technologies provides reliable remote access. For critical internal communication it's advisable to even apply VPN technology with internal networks to protect against insider attacks.

3.2   Supervision and Control Authorization

The operators of the technical process bare a huge portion of responsibility for safe process operation. The information they get needs to be genuine, the decisions they make shall be traceable and the actions they carry shall not be forgeable. A PKI could assist in assuring this by providing process information from process computers e.g. across secure SSL links or VPN channels. This becomes more and more important with increasing network connectivity of control systems with other systems like information, communication or management systems or centralization of process control with process control data traveling across the enterprise intranet rather than a special process-net. In cases where the decisions of the staff need to be justified, it protects all parties if trusted logs exist, and the human operator decision may be clearly distinguished from effects caused by machinery faults or even sabotage. Digitally signed logs provide this certainty. The PKI's strong authorization functions ensure that only authorized staff has access to the process's command interface, independent from where this interface is located, and therefore certificate and smartcard based authentication is a consequent extension of security policies already relying on strong physical access control. With a PKI it could even be realized that process computers or PLCs accept digitally signed commands only, making it extremely difficult to control such systems without permission.

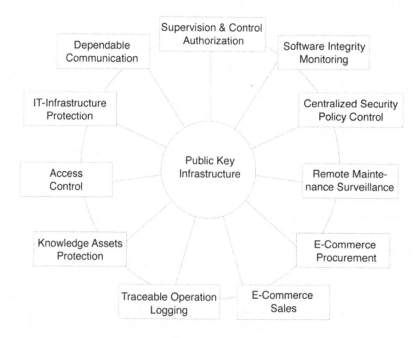

Fig.3 Areas that benefit from a PKI

3.3   Dependable Communication

Optimized operation of a process depends on communication. This communication is in a process of being transferred from traditional means of phone and paper to e-mail, shared databases, workflow management systems etc. This happens for interaction with management as well as coworkers as is not only associated with delegation of actions but even more important for coordination of safety critical operations. The recipient of a message must be able to definitely rely on the correctness of its contents, and that it really came from the indicated originator, because it may cause severe damage, injury or even death if for example the wrong valve was taken into mainte-nance mode and opened. Unforgeable digital signatures associated with email, data-base entries or granting statements for sequencing critical operations, as well as signed forms in database or workflow management systems, provide the level of trustworthi-ness required without any need of additional handwritten memos or orders. Even voice and image based communication over data networks may be protected in a PKI envi-ronment using strong authentication and data-stream encryption.

3.4   Traceable Operations Logging

Logs are important to trace process history whether to improve process quality, learn from problems in the past or even investigate accidents. Therefore information in logs shall not be modifiable after entry. Logs also contain valuable information about the strength and weaknesses of the process that may require protection against disclosure. Signed and timestamped log entries and optionally encrypted logfiles solve both problems and work for personal log entries as well as automatic log entries created by the system autonomously. In the first case the operator signs a log entry using his smart card, in the latter case the systems uses its device certificate to sign log entries before delivering them to the log server. In both cases timestamps are requested from the timestamp service, which could be a local one or an external public one.

3.5   Physical Access Control

More and more physical access control systems that control individual's access to restricted areas of firms premises use electronic identification tokens or biometric characteristics to identify and authenticate people. With a PKI in place, where every user carries his own personalized smart card, this smart card may contain a separate certificate for physical access control which will be presented to card readers at checkpoints. Thus the need for additional tokens is eliminated and human resource administration as well as security administration and staff members benefit from having a single multifunctional smart card. The central PKI directory provides one personal account for each staff member holding all personal information and access-rights. The access controllers at the checkpoints look up the status of the presented certificates in the smart cards against the corresponding directory entry to be always up to date about the certificate status and e.g. refuse passage if a user's access certificate or specific rights have been revoked.

3.6   Software Integrity Monitoring

To ensure process control dependability, the process control software always has to be in a well known state. This is usually achieved through on-site Quality Management (QM) activities based on manufacturer's quality documents. The problem with this approach is that accidental or deliberate software modifications during transmission from the developer to the installation site, as well as during operation, may hardly be detected through classical methods of testing or inspection. With the help of digital signatures code may be clearly and unambiguously identified to be of the correct version and unmodified. This testing may be carried out even on-line at the target system which reduces QM efforts drastically and improves quality assurance at the same time [4].

3.7   Remote Maintenance Surveillance

The dramatic increase of complexity and variations in operating systems and process control software often requires remote system maintenance assistance by manufacturer's specialists. Due to many reasons remote maintenance is desired but introduces a high potential of risk for malicious software modifications or even direct influence on process control. As mentioned above, strong user authentication for the remote user is mandatory, together with data transmission protection, preferably through a VPN connection and extensive data logging. In addition to that, a high level PKI could provide legal evidence in case of legal disputes associated with remote maintenance, if the remote user is required to sign the logs of the session and thus taking over legal responsibility for the actions he executed. Going without such provision means, that the risk is nearly completely on the plant's site.

3.8   Centralized Security Policy Control

A powerful PKI is directory centered, meaning that not only certificates are kept in a directory, but also other user related data and especially the configuration of the user's PKI software clients is managed through the directory. Thus the user may not accidentally or deliberately for example switch off encryption and mail company critical data without protection, or create logs without signature. In case of staff change, these changes become immediately effective within the PKI once the user entry in the directory has been updated. This avoids dangling user accounts on systems' local user databases for staff members already off the payroll. It's obvious that centralized PKI management not only reduces the costs of managing security policies but also strengthens the effectiveness of their implementation.

3.9   Intellectual Property Asset Protection

Operating complex processes is a challenging task requiring a lot of experience. More and more interconnectivity puts up the risk not only for manipulations or sabotage but also pin-pointed industrial espionage. Security policies need to consider this fact for engineering departments and also for process control. The encryption technology coming with a carefully selected PKI providing high grade encryption algorithms difficult to break, provides protection even for such sorts of high tech attacks.

3.10   E-Commerce Sales and E-Commerce Procurement

Being an internet driven technology the PKI is of course ideally suited for modern e-commerce whether at the sales or at the procurement side. It provides the infrastructure to establish a secure web-order server as well as the basis for data exchange within closed user groups or selected customers. Furthermore it allows efficient and secure ordering with suppliers or reliable internet banking.

4   Implementation Example

Implementation of a PKI for a company in the process sector with the whole variety of PKI based applications needs careful planning and selection of the right PKI. Such a PKI needs to provide standard off-the-shelf solutions for basic operations e.g. VPN or secure e-mail or applications for the e-commerce side as well as toolboxes and modules that allow integration of basic PKI based operations like signatures, timestamps or data encryption into customized control or communication software. Fig. 4 shows a sample implementation of a PKI in a process company. The company operates its own in-house trust center to be all the time in full control of the PKI. From a networking viewpoint there are two different internal networking domains, the one is the general intranet the other is the process-net which is separated from the former by a process-net firewall gateway (PNGW). The intranet is protected against the internet through another firewall gateway (INGW). The process-net is considered to be at a higher security level than the intranet. The PNGW and INGW both feature VPN gateway technology thus allowing VPN connections from internal or external sources, e.g. the supervision and control stations or external maintenance workstations.

To reach sufficient performance VPN firewall gateways may be equipped with a hardware crypto module. Note also that from an external user's viewpoint a VPN connection either may end at the INGW in case that the external user needs to access general intranet resources or even be routed through to the PNGW if it is required to connect to resources on the process-net. This may be considered a sort of defense in depth strategy with multiple barriers protecting the process-net against the internet. Interconnections to process-net segments at dislocated external facilities may also be secured through VPN gateways not necessarily providing firewall functionality. The process computers as well as the PLCs may be equipped with device certificates which is more and more easy to accomplish with standard internet protocols like http spreading into embedded control systems.

The central enterprise directory is situated in the intranet and shall be reachable from any system within the company to retrieve configuration information and user-related data. Every workstation with a user interface is equipped with a smart card reader such that the user may use his personal smart card for all interaction with the PKI. Thus workstations may really be person-independent without deficiencies in confidentiality for all data considered to be office-personal to the user. This is possible because the workstation interacts with the users smart card and only the one who holds the correct keys in his smart card has access to restricted information or may issue restricted functions.

The workstation gets additional information about what the user needs in terms of functionality from looking up the user's directory entry when he inserts his smart card to start a workstation session.

Note that all Servers that provide information carry a server certificate to identify the server as well as a crypto-module if multiple encrypted user interaction is required, e.g. with the sales server that handles a whole bunch of encrypted connections at a time.

Springer
Berlin
Heidelberg
New York
Barcelona
Hong Kong
London
Milan
Paris
Singapore
Tokyo

References

[1]   Bruce Schneier, Applied Cryptography, Wiley, New York 1996

[2]   Jalal Feghhi, Jalil Feghhi, Peter Williams, Digital Certificates, Addison Wesley, Reading 1999

[3]   ISO/IEC 9594-8 (X.509): OSI – The Directory – Authentication Framework

[4]   Whitfield Diffie, Martin E. Hellman: New Directions in Cryptography, IEEE Transactions on Information Theory, 22 (1976), 644-654

[5]   Data Encryption Standard, Federal Information Processing Standards Publication 46, U.S. Department of Commerce/National Bureau of Standards, National Technical Information Service, Springfield, Virginia, 1977 (revised as FIPS 46-1:1988; FIPS 46-2:1993)

[6]   ISO/IEC 14888-3: Information technology – Security techniques - Digital signatures with appendix – Part 3: Certificate-based mechanisms, 1999

[7]   X. Lai: On the design and security of block ciphers, ETH Series in Information Processing, J.L. Massey (editor), vol. 1, Hartung-Gorre Verlag Konstanz, Technische Hochschule (Zürich), 1992

[8]   Alfred J. Menezes, Paul C. van Oorschot, Scott A. Vanstone: Handbook of Applied Cryptography, CRC Press, Boca Raton 1996

[9]   Ronald L. Rivest, Adi Shamir, Leonard M. Adleman: A method for obtaining digital signatures and public-key cryptosystems, Communications of the ACM, 21 (1978), 120-126

[10]   F.J.Dafelmair, Model and Implementation of a Secure SW-Development Process for Mission Critical Software, Lecture Notes in Computer Science Vol. 1516, Springer Heidelberg, 1998

A Survey on Safety-Critical Multicast Networking

James S. Pascoe and R. J. Loader

Department of Computer Science
The University of Reading, UK
{J.S.Pascoe,Roger.Loader}@reading.ac.uk
http://www.cs.reading.ac.uk/

Abstract. This paper presents the results of an in-depth survey [ ] into
the concept of a generic safety-critical network technology. We identify a
need for an architecture that would provide a number of distributed services (such as membership, clock synchronization etc.) generically. Such
a technology would not only exploit the benefits of software reuse, but
would also eliminate a substantial part of the complexity (including the
scope for error) from the design process. We first discuss the main results
of this survey, namely the requisite properties of such a technology before giving a detailed definition of an arbitrary "safety-critical network".
This section also considers the OSI reference model and gives reasons as
to why it is not suitable for use in a hard real-time system. As exemplars, we describe a number of related networking technologies, namely,
TTP, PROFIBUS and CAN. The paper is concluded with a discussion
concerning the future direction of this research.

1 Introduction

The field of distributed safety-critical systems is evolving evermore rapidly. In
the first instance, this can be attributed to a greater trust being placed on technology to monitor, control and co-ordinate applications which were traditionally
managed by humans [,]. At present, designing, verifying and implementing
such systems is a costly exercise that often results in bespoke solutions. Furthermore, it is usually impractical to modify or reuse parts of such solutions in
future work; only a small amount of intangible skill is transferable. Because of
this, we conducted a detailed study into the field of distributed safety-critical
systems and from this we postulate that there exists a need for a generic safety-
critical network technology. This would not only reduce the duration and cost of
development (through the exploitation of software reuse), but a well-engineered
solution would also eliminate design faults.

The remainder of this paper is structured as follows. Section 2 presents the
fundamental results of an extensive survey into this idea, namely, the requirements that such an architecture must exhibit. The next section (i.e. section 3)
gives an explanation of the structure of an arbitrary safety-critical network by
considering communication at the field bus, real-time network and backbone

F. Koornneef and M. van der Meulen (Eds.): SAFECOMP 2000, LNCS 1943, pp. 333–343, 2000.
© Springer-Verlag Berlin Heidelberg 2000

levels. This section also considers the OSI reference model and gives reasons as to why it is not suitable for use in a hard real-time system. In section 4 we present three exemplars of safety-critical networking technologies, namely, TTP, PROFIBUS and CAN. Finally, section 5 concludes the paper.

2   Survey Results: Requisite Properties

This section summarises the results of an extensive survey, namely, the requisite properties that a generic safety-critical network technology must exhibit. Each of these requirements stem from a necessity for a small and predictable real-time *latency* of real-time transactions.

2.1   Composability

Support for *composability* is arguably the most important requirement in the context of real-time systems [ ]. In many disciplines, large systems are constructed from a number of well specified and well tested subsystems. It is important to maintain the known properties of these subsystems as they exist in *isolation* when the overall system integration is performed. If a component exhibits this property, then it is said to be *composable*.

Let us consider composability from the perspective of verification and validation in a railway. The development of a *safety case* (see section 2.2) for such an application can only be achieved by reasoning about each subsystem in isolation. Thus, composability is a fundamental requirement since properties established in isolation must not change when viewed in conjunction. Evidentally, verifying and validating the mechanism employed to guarentee composability is a fundamental part of the safety case.

In a distributed safety-critical real-time system, the integration is achieved by the interactions between different nodes. Thus, the communication system has a fundamental role in determining the composability of an architecture.

Flexibility. Over time, it is likely that a real-time communication system will be altered. A composable real-time protocol is flexible enough to accommodate these changes without requiring a software modification and re-testing of unaffected nodes.

2.2   Support for Verification and Validation

In most cases, the design of a distributed safety-critical system must be approved by an independent certification body. The judgement of such a body is based on the analysis of a *safety case* presented by the designer. A safety case is the evidence that convinces the certification body of whether the system is fit for its purpose. For brevity, we do not discuss safety cases in depth here; the intention is to acknowledge the necessity of producing such a case and the inclusion of a support mechanism.

2.3   Protocol Latency

The *protocol latency* is the time interval between the start of transmission for a given message, and the reception of that message at the receiving node.

Latency Jitter. A real-time network protocol should have a small and predictable maximum protocol latency with a minimum amount of jitter[1]. This is because application programs often rely on an *a priori* known latency.

Simultaneous Delivery. The *de facto* communication method in distributed real-time systems is multicast and not point-to-point. The same data is often required simultaneously by more than one node. As an example, consider a node in a railway system that is transmitting the speed of a train wheel. This data can then be simultaneously read by a number of other devices (e.g. dashboard display, engine management, braking system).

2.4   Error Detection

Communication Errors. The communication system must provide a reliable and predictable service even in the light of communication errors. Errors that occur during message transmission must be detected and should be corrected without increasing the jitter of the protocol latency. If an error can not be corrected, all of the communicating partners must be informed of the occurrence of the error with low latency. The detection of message loss by the *receiver* is of particular concern.

Detection of Node Errors (Membership Service). The failure of a node must be detected by the communication protocol, and must be reported consistently to all the remaining nodes of the ensemble. In a real-time system, the detection of node failures at both the receiver and the sender is important. This is the function of the membership service.

As an example, let us return to the railway system introduced in above. Consider the trains braking system that intelligently monitors the brake-force distribution to the wheels. Let us now assume that this is facilitated by a computer node situated at each wheel. If a wheel computer (or its communication link) fails, then the affected brake automatically relinquishes any hold (allowing free movement). If the other nodes learn about this failure within a short latency, then the brake force can be redistributed to the operational wheels thus maintaining control of the train. Otherwise the braking system may erroneously consider all four wheels to be functional thus placing the train in danger.

---

[1] The jitter is the difference between the minimum and the maximum duration of an action.

End-to-End Acknowledgment. In a real-time system, the end-to-end acknowledgment about the success or failure of a communication action can arise
from a node that is different from the receiver of the actuation message. An
output message to an actuator could cause an action which is monitored by an
independent sensor. The results observed by this sensor ensure that the desired
action has been executed. A wrong end-to-end protocol can have serious consequences, as seen in the following quote regarding the Three Mile Island Nuclear
Reactor accident on March 28, 1979:

> *Perhaps the single most important and damaging failure in the relatively
> long chain of failures during this accident was that of the Pressure Oper-
> ated Relief Valve (PORV) on the pressuriser. The PORV did not close;
> yet its monitoring light was signaling green (meaning closed).*
>
> *–F Sevcik*
> Reliability and Maintainability Symposium

In this system, the designers had assumed that once an actuation signal
had been sent to a device, then the requested action was indivisibly executed.
However, due to a faulty valve, this was not the case and the fault contributed
to the catastrophe. A less naive end-to-end protocol would have detected this
problem and possibly avoided the disaster.

2.5   Physical Structure

The physical structure of a real-time network is often governed by technical
and economic reasoning. The multicast requirement suggests the use of a shared
medium e.g. a bus or ring network. A fully connected point-to-point network that
provides single-hop broadcasting requires N-1 communication ports at each node
for an ensemble of N nodes. For many requirements, the high cost of multiple
communication ports, physical drivers, and the cabling are prohibitive in a point-
to-point network.

3   The Structure of a Safety-Critical Network

In this section we clarify the concept of a safety-critical network and how it
relates to other communication systems, namely, those that conform to the OSI
reference model [ ].

Communication Architecture. In many real-time applications, three types of
communication networks are distinguished: the field bus, the real-time network
and the backbone network. Two of these architectures, namely, the field bus and
the real-time network must provide temporal performance.

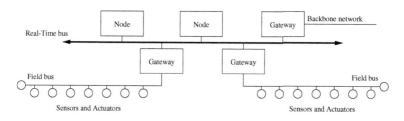

Fig. 1. Real-Time Communication Architecture

Field Bus. The term *field bus* is used to describe a generic serial communications network arrangement between controlling processors and instrumentation, in the field. The purpose of the field bus is to provide a means of interconnecting the computer system to the sensors and actuators of the controlling system. Sensors and actuators are often controlled by local single-chip microcontrollers that use a standard UART (Universal Asynchronous Receiver Transmitter) interface. The type of messages transmitted on a field bus carry state information and are typically small (e.g. 2 bytes in length). They are transmitted with strict requirements for latency and latency jitter which also means that clock synchronization is an issue. The main concern at this level is low cost, both for the controllers and the cabling. Standard unshielded twisted pair is often used as a physical medium.

Real-Time Network. The real-time network is the core of the nodes in a *cluster*[2], and must provide the following services:

– Reliable and temporally predictable message transmission
– Support for fault tolerance
– Clock synchronization (in the order of microseconds)
– Membership service (detection of node failures)

The real-time network must use replicated communication channels. Furthermore, the system should be designed to eliminate *single points of failure* and care must be taken to contain the effects of a *babbling idiot failure*[3]. Periodic state messages with implicit flow control are predominantly exchanged on the real-time network.

Backbone Network. The purpose of the backbone network is to provide connectivity to other systems (e.g. an organisations network). This allows non critical information (e.g. statistics) to be exchanged. Table 1 compares the service characteristics of the three types of networks [ ].

---

[2] A cluster is a subsystem of a real-time system.
[3] This is the name given to a node that sends messages at the wrong moment.

Table 1. Comparison of field bus, real-time and backbone networks

Service Characteristic	Field Bus	Real-time	Backbone
Message semantics	state	states	event
Latency/jitter control	yes	yes	no
Typical data field length	1–6 bytes	6–12 bytes	> 100 bytes
Clock synchronization	yes	yes	optional
Fault-tolerance	limited	yes	limited
Membership service	maybe	yes	maybe
Topology	multicast	multicast	point-to-point
Communication control	multi-master	distributed	arbitrary
Flow control	implicit	implicit	explicit
Low cost	very important	important	not important

3.1   The OSI Reference Model

The OSI reference model [ ] was developed to provide a standard conceptual reference architecture so that any two computers in the world can communicate with each other through one or more diverse interconnection networks. Due to the models level of acceptance, it is worthwhile to investigate if a real-time system can be built upon a communication structure that conforms to the OSI architecture.

Although the OSI reference model was developed primarily as a *conceptual reference architecture*, it has been widely used as an *implementation architecture*, resulting in implementations where a stack of *event triggered protocols*, one per layer, must be executed before a message is delivered to the application process. These implementations are characterized by high latency jitter and low data efficiency. The following assumptions underlly many OSI protocol implementations:

1. The two communicating partners maintain a point-to-point connection.
2. The messages are event triggered.
3. The communication protocol uses explicit flow control and retransmission in cases of error.
4. Real-time performance, i.e. latency and jitter, is not an issue.

These assumptions do not match with the requirements above for a safety-critical real-time system [ ].

4   Current Safety-Critical Network Technologies

4.1   Time Triggered Protocol (TTP)

The Time Triggered Protocol family was developed by Dr H. Kopetz at the Technical University of Wien and contains two distinct sub-protocols (TTP/A and TTP/C)[4]. TTP/A (or *The Fireworks Protocol* [ ]) is the low end member of the TTP family and is a character oriented time triggered protocol for the design of low cost distributed real-time systems, particularly in automotive body electronics. TTP/A is designed to operate with standard UART hardware so that the utmost compatibility with single chip micro-controllers can be attained. The novel features of TTP/A over other protocols proposed for this industry are the support for composability in the temporal domain and the short error detection latency. TTP/C is orientated towards safety-critical distributed real-time control systems. Its intended application domains are automotive control systems, aircraft, industrial and power plants, or air traffic control.

4.2 TTP/C System Overview

A computer control system built around the TTP/C protocol consists of at least one *computational cluster*. Such a computational cluster comprises a set of self-contained computers (nodes), which communicate via a field bus using the TTP protocol. An approximate global time base is established throughout the cluster by synchronizing the clocks located within the nodes. Each node is considered to be fail-silent (i.e. only crash failures and omission failures can occur). At the cluster level, node failures and communication failures can be masked by replicating the nodes and grouping them into *Fault-Tolerant Units* (FTUs). Message transmission is replicated in both the space domain, by using two busses, and the time domain, by sending the messages twice on each bus. Babbling idiot failure is eliminated by the prescience of two independent *bus guardians* that do not allow untimely communications.

Within a computational cluster, the *communication subsystem* manages the global concern of providing reliable real-time message transmission. The *host subsystem* comprises of the host CPUs of each node computer which execute the local real-time application. The interface between these two subsystems is called the *Communication Network Interface (CNI)*. It provides the host CPUs with a memory area for submitting and receiving messages and for obtaining status and control information about the real-time network.

4.3 Field Buses

At present, there are several field buses in commercial use; a good summary can be found in [ ]. In addition to these, there are other proprietary standards available; for a more in-depth discussion see [ ] or [ ]. Let us now present a brief introduction to two field buses, namely, PROFIBUS [,] and CAN [,].

---

[4] The suffix corresponds to the classification of computer network applications issued by the Society for Automotive Engineers. Class A and B networks are for signal multiplexing and parameter sharing in the field of body electronics, such as power windows control or the transport of information to the dashboard. A class C network, on the other hand, is safety-critical and may control the operation of brake-by-wire systems or the operation of an engine. In short, class A and B networks can always enter a safe state (e.g by halting the current activity) whereas class C networks must continue operation, even in the presence of failures.

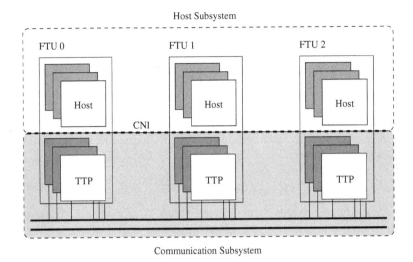

Fig. 2. Diagrammatic overview of TTP/C

PROFIBUS. PROFIBUS is a vendor-independent, open field bus standard for a wide range of applications in manufacturing and process automation. Vendor independence and openess are ensured by the international standards EN 50170 and EN 50254. PROF-IBUS allows communication between generic devices without any special interface adjustment and can be utilised for both high-speed time critical applications and complex communications tasks. PROFIBUS offers two functionally graduated communication protocols (or *Communication Profiles*): DP and FMS. DP is the most frequently used communication profile. It is optimised for speed, efficiency and low connection costs and has been designed for communication between automation systems and distributed peripherals. DP is suitable as a replacement for conventional, parallel signal transmission with 24 volts in manufacturing automation as well as for analog signal transmission. On the other hand, FMS is the universal communication protocol for demanding communication tasks that offers many sophisticated application functions for communication between intelligent devices. PROFIBUS as a whole defines the technical characteristics of a serial field bus system with which distributed digital programmable controllers can be networked, from field to cell level. PROFIBUS is a multi-master system which allows the joint operation of several automation, engineering or visualisation systems with their distributed peripherals on one bus. PROFIBUS distinguishes between the following types of devices:

- *Master devices* – These determine the data communication on the bus. A master can send messages without an external request when it holds the bus access rights (the token). Masters are also called *active stations*.
- *Slave devices* – This category of devices are peripherals such as I/O units, valves, drives and measuring transducers. They do not have bus access rights

and can only acknowledge received messages or send messages to the master when requested to do so. Slaves are also known as *passive stations*.

PROFISafe. PROFISafe [ ] is an extension to PROFIBUS that offers the prerequisites for the coexistence between safety and standard applications for PROFIBUS. PROFISafe does not offer any form of failure management, moreover, its functionality is restricted to the timely delivery of failure indication messages from slave devices to masters. The development and certification of error handling code then becomes the responsibility of the user. However, PROFISafe has already been certified by the BIA and the TÜV (in a composable context) drastically reducing the complexity associated with certifying the users code.

Controller Area Network (CAN). The Controller Area Network (CAN) is a mature, robust field bus designed for hard real-time distributed control systems in harsh environments [,]. CAN is an open standard (and is the subject of ISO 11898) with the backing of several silicon vendors. CAN is particularly suitable for use in 8, 16 and 32 bit microcontroller systems since it has a low implementation cost and a scalable performance. Other highlights are listed below:

- *Data transfer* – CAN is adept at passing simple commands or small amounts of data quickly since it uses packets with a maximum data payload of 8 bytes. Several higher layer protocols are available to transfer larger messages by fragmenting them into smaller packets. However, CAN is not well suited to moving large files; Ethernet is more efficient for this.
- *Sophisticated hardware* – CAN hardware is typically intelligent as it automatically handles most of the data link layer functionality. As the host controller does not need to constantly manage the CAN interface, a controller of moderate performance can be used to reduce costs. If a high performance controller is used, most of the networks bandwidth will remain available for time-critical non-network tasks.
- *Resistance to noise* – Although baud rates can reach 1 Mbit/s, CAN systems most commonly operate at 250 Kbits/s or 125 Kbits/s. This offers an increased resistance to noise. Slower traffic also allows the use of lower-cost cabling and slower, lower-cost host controllers. Media is typically twisted-pair or fiber-optic based cabling.

The CAN bus was designed as a multi-master architecture with a maximum transfer rate of 1 Mbit/s. As highlighted in section 2.5, CAN does not send messages point-to-point. In a CAN message, it is the data, as opposed to the node, which is given an identifier. The message is then broadcast to the entire network, and any "interested" node can listen (see section 2.3 for an example). The CAN protocol implements five methods of error detection and correction, so that if a message is corrupted, this will be detected and the message is ignored by all nodes on the network.

5   Conclusion

This paper has presented a preliminary study into the concept of a generic safety-critical network technology. Through this survey, we have presented the requirements of a safety-critical network. These are: *composability, support for verification and validation, small protocol latency, treatment of communication errors* and *end-to-end acknowledgement*.

To this list, we postulate that there exists one more requirement; the ability to interconnect a safety-critical network to a non real-time network. In [ ], Kopetz states that substantial benefits can be attained in connecting a hard real-time system to the Internet; these include: remote control, remote monitoring and remote failure diagnosis. Furthermore, Kopetz argues that there are two major problems in achieving this aim: *security* and *unpredictable temporal performance*. It is forseeable that the problem of security will be solved in the near future since huge emphasis is currently being placed on e-commerce. However, stabilising the temporal unpredictability of the Internet is a deep problem that will require a significant effort to solve. One approach may be to investigate current technologies such as TCP/IP to determine whether or not they can be applied in a safety-critical sense (e.g. by identifying a "safe" subset of a protocol). Another interesting approach may lie in the use of mobile agents. Indeed, *Chess et al.* discuss the relative advantages and disadvantages in [ ].

To the authors knowledge, there is little research that is addressing these ideas. Kopetz has made some progress (see [,]) in connecting a TTP system to the Internet, but has yet been unable to provide complete real-time control. Furthermore, in this work, Kopetz also dispels the notion that this problem is simply a different perspective on those already addressed by Quality of Service.

We outlined two related technologies (i.e., PROFIBUS and CAN) and from this, we can observe that neither comprehensively satisfy all of the above requirements. Another prominent project that offers a similar lack of interconnectivity is that of GUARDS [,]. The GUARDS[5] project aims to provide a generic fault-tolerant architecture in a manner that will reduce the lifecycle costs of developing fault-tolerant systems. It is a mature and comprehensive piece of work that has been applied to three application domains (i.e., nuclear power, railways and space travel).

The future direction of our work will consider these ideas and extend them further. Other interesting challenges will be uncovered when the above ideas are considered in the context of verification, validation and certification.

Acknowledgments

The authors would like to thank Geoff Hodgkinson of PROFIBUS UK for his kind help and support in obtaining the PROFIBUS references used throughout this paper. We would also like to thank Dr. N. Nissanke of South Bank University and the anonymous reviewers for their constructive remarks and guidance.

---

[5] Generic Upgradable Architectures for Real-Time Dependable Systems

References

1. B. Boyes. Hard real-time connectivity: It's in the CAN. Computer Design, January 1997. Editorial. 339, 341

2. D. Chess, C. Harrison, and A. Kershenbaum. Mobile Agents: Are They a Good Idea? In *Mobile Object Systems, Towards the Programmable Internet*, Lecture Notes In Computer Science. Springer–Verlag, July 1996. 342

3. H. Kopetz. TTP/A - The Fireworks Protocol. Technical report, Technical University Wien, September 1994. 339

4. H. Kopetz. *Real-Time Systems: Design Principles for Distributed Embedded Applications*. Kluwer Academic Publishers, 1997. 334, 337, 338

5. H. Kopetz, M. Kucera, and D. Millinger et al. Interfacing Time-Triggered Embedded Systems to the INTERNET. In *International Symposium on Internet Technology*, April 1998. Pp. 180 – 186. 342

6. M. Kucera and C. Sikula. Application Monitoring in the Time-Triggered Architecture. In *Ninth European Workshop on Dependable Computing*, May 1998. Pp. 137 – 143. 342

7. N. Leveson. *Safeware, System safety and computers*. Addison Wesley, 1995. 333

8. Hitex (UK) Ltd. Controller Area Networking - The Future Of Industrial Microprocessor Communications?, 1994.
   URL: *http://www.hitex.co.uk/CAN/canarticle.html*. 339, 341

9. J. S. Pascoe, N. Nissanke, and R. J. Loader. A Generic Safety-Critical Network Technology – Preliminary Study. Technical Report RUCS/2000/TR/001/A, The University of Reading, January 2000. 333

10. D. Powell, J. Arlat, L. BEUS-DUKIC, A. Bondavalli, P. Coppola, A. Fantechi, E. Jenn, C. Rabejac, and A. Wellings. Guards: Overview. Technical Report 99276, CNRS-LAAS, June 1999. 342

11. D. Powell, J. Arlat, L. BEUS-DUKIC, A. Bondavalli, P. Coppola, A. Fantechi, E. Jenn, C. Rabejac, and A. Wellings. GUARDS: A Generic Upgradable Architecture For Real-Time Dependable Systems. In *IEEE Transactions on Parallel and Distributed Systems*, volume 10, June 1999. 342

12. PROFIBUS UK. PROFIBUS, Technical Desription. 1 West Street, Titchfield, PO14 4DH, UK, 1999. 339

13. PROFIBUS UK. PROFIBUS UK, the plantwide worldwide field bus. 1 West Street, Titchfield, PO14 4DH, UK, 1999. 339

14. PROFIBUS UK. PROFISafe...in order to protect people, machine and nature. 1 West Street, Titchfield, PO14 4DH, UK, 1999. 341

15. F. Redmill and T. Anderson. *Safety-critical Systems, Current issues, techniques and standards*. Chapman and Hall, 1993. 333

16. A. Tanenbaum. *Computer Networks*. Prentice Hall, 1996. 336, 338

17. D. Wenn, N. Glover, and G. Foster. Flexible Distributed Control of Manufacturing System Using Local Operating Networks.
    URL: *http://www.cyber.reading.ac.uk/people/denw/WWW/*, 1996. 339

18. D. Wenn, N. Glover, and G. Foster. The Use of LONWorks in a Production Environment. URL: *http://www.cyber.reading.ac.uk/people/denw/WWW/*, 1996. 339

Causal Reasoning about Aircraft Accidents

Peter B. Ladkin

Faculty of Technology
University of Bielefeld, Germany
ladkin@rvs.uni-bielefeld.de
www.rvs.uni-bielefeld.de

Abstract. We show how objective, rigorous causal reasoning in the analysis of air transportation accidents can improve our understanding of the factors involved in those accidents, by considering two high-profile digital-automation-related air transport accidents.

1 Why Investigate Accidents?

Let us consider *safety* as *freedom from accidents*, where an accident is *an unwanted (but not necessarily unexpected) event that results in a specified level of loss* [ ]. Suppose one wants to improve safety. Then one must increase the relative freedom from accidents. One cannot undo accidents that have already happened, so one cannot improve safety by attempting to undo past accidents. Yet detailed accident investigation is widely regarded as a significant tool for improving safety. Why? Why not just say *"Oh dear, we regret very much ...... but we must move on with life"*, and ignore the whole event?

When one is trying to ensure safety, one is oriented to the future. Future events have not happened yet; one is trying to avoid those that would be accidents. We must think about the system we have, and we must attempt to assess what could happen and what could not, and if necessary reconfigure the system or its environment of operation or both in order to change what we believe to be the behavioral possibilities.

An accident is a concrete, irrefutable example of system and environment behavior. It is thus a guide to the possibilities. By comparing what we think we knew about the system with what we know from a detailed investigation of the accident, we may be able to correct and improve our reasoning about and our knowledge of possible system behavior.

Further, suppose one makes a general presumption that system and subsystem behaviors have some statistical distribution. We won't know what that distribution might be. However, the presumption entails that, in normal system use, specific states and events occur with a particular although unknown expected frequency. Events about which we may be very concerned are those events which are or can be involved in accidents. By investigating accidents in detail, one obtains information about which events and states are involved, and may focus on these events and states in this and other recorded instances to

F. Koornneef and M. van der Meulen (Eds.): SAFECOMP 2000, LNCS 1943, pp. 344–360, 2000.
© Springer-Verlag Berlin Heidelberg 2000

obtain information about their actual frequency of occurrence. One may then consider mitigating measures.

There can be no guarantee that one has thereby enumerated *all* events or states that may be involved in accidents. However, if all have some expected frequency, then some of those expected frequencies will be higher than others, and those events are those which we are likely to see – or to have seen – more often. In particular, when we mitigate accident contributors with high expected frequency of occurrence, we attempt to reduce their frequency of occurrence or eliminate it altogether. By mitigating the occurrence of contributing events and states that one has seen in accidents, one can expect to reduce the frequency of occurrence of the most frequent contributors, thereby reducing the overall frequency of likely occurrence of all accident contributors taken together, even if one does not know them all.

These, then, I take to be the general reasons for investigating accidents. Investigation is the art of discovering facts. Some of these discoveries are made "in the field" by finding things, by reading data recorders and listening to cockpit conversation. Others are discovered by reasoning, by inference from facts one has already determined, and enumerating behavior possibilities constrained by the facts one has already determined. Both sharp eyes and sharp minds are essential components of investigation. Both can be improved by methods: methodical ways of searching rubble fields, and methodical reasoning.

2   What-If Reasoning

I want to focus on the reasoning. General procedures have been known for over a century for how to add method to reasoning, and to check for one's mistakes. This is the science of formal logic. One way to become more methodical is to look closely at the features of the reasoning as practiced, identify general principles, justify these principles, and build them in to a formal logic. Then anyone can check whether the reasoning is sound by reproducing it – or failing to – in the formal logic.

What kinds of reasoning are involved in safety, and in accident investigation? One is reasoning about system behavior, and because one is trying to avoid certain kinds of behavior deemed to be accidents, one must engage in so-called *what-if* reasoning. What if this-and-this were to occur in a behavior? What if that-and-that were to occur? HAZOP is an example of this kind of reasoning. Other kinds of reasoning attempt to reason from problem behaviors of the system to contributory problem behaviors of subsystems by using the architecture of the system. Suppose this-and-this were to happen. It would happen if and only if that-and-that were to happen with that part. Fault tree analysis is an example of this kind of part-whole reasoning.

When investigating accidents, one engages also in what-if reasoning. This is what the U.S. Air Force says about accident explanations [ ]:

3-11. Findings, Causes, and Recommendations. The most important part of mishap investigation is developing findings, causes and recommendations. The goal is to decide on the best preventive actions to preclude mishap recurrence. To accomplish this purpose, the investigator must list the significant events and circumstances of the mishap sequence (findings). Then they [*sic*] must select from among these the events and conditions that were causal (causes). Finally, they suggest courses of action to prevent recurrence (recommendations).

3-12. Findings:
a. Definition. The findings ..... are statements of significant events of conditions leading to the mishap. They are arranged in the order in which they occurred. Though each finding is an essential step in the mishap sequence, each is not necessaily a cause factor......

3-13. Causes:
a. Definition. Causes are those findings which, singly or in combination with other causes, resulted in the damage or injury that occurred. A cause is a deficiency the correction, elimination, or avoidance of which would likely have prevented or mitigated the mishap damage or significant injuries. A cause is an act, an omission, a condition, or a circumstance, and it either starts or sustains the mishap sequence.....

The phrase "*... would have prevented ....*" talks about something that could have happened, but did in fact not. The correction, elimination or avoidance of feature X would have prevented the accident. But in fact X occurred, and so did the accident. The supposition, that had X not occurred as it did, the accident would not have happened, is known as a *counterfactual*. So reasoning about causes of accidents in the USAF is reasoning with counterfactuals.

The USAF was not the first to think this way. David Hume gave two definitions of causality over 200 years ago.

....we may define a cause to be *an object, followed by another, and where all the objects similar to the first are followed by objects similar to the second. Or, in other words where, if the first object had not been, the second never had existed.*

[, Section VII, Part II, paragraph 60].

We may consider the word '*object*' to refer also to events, maybe states, as noted in the work of John Stuart Mill [ ].

David Lewis notes [ ] that of the two definitions given by Hume, over the course of the intervening couple of hundred years, the second has been more neglected by Humean commentators. Hume's second definition is *counterfactual*. Like the U.S. Air Force, it talks of what might have been but was not.

Lewis's Formal Definition of Causal Factor In *op. cit.*, Lewis gives a formal definition of *necessary causal factor*, based on the counterfactual definition of Hume. Suppose A and B are state descriptions or events. Then A *is a (necessary) causal factor of B* just in case, had A not occurred, B would not have occurred either. This definition is obviously counterfactual. Lewis [ ] had already defined a formal semantics, and a complete logic, for counterfactuals, based on the formal-semantical notion of possible worlds, used ubiquitously by formal logicians, with an additional notion of *comparative nearness*: a behavior, or a history, is said to be *nearer* to a reference behavior than another behavior is to that reference behavior. Comparative nearness is a ternary relation - it has three arguments – and Lewis also required that it have certain formal mathematical properties for whose reasonableness he argued (for those interested in more detail, the properties are listed in [ ]).

An Example Consider a system in which there is a programmable digital component which contains a bit, stored in a variable named X. With systematic ambiguity, we shall refer to this bit as X. Suppose the electronics is wired such that, when X is set, a mechanism (say, an interlock) is thereby set in motion. Suppose the interlock has been well enough designed so that it can only be set in motion by setting X. Then X is a causal factor in any setting in motion of the interlock according to the Lewis definition: *had X not been set, the interlock would not have moved.* Furthermore, let us suppose that the digital component is well-designed, so that X can only be set by a specific operation O of a processor to set it, and that this operation is performed by executing a specific program instruction I. Then,

- *had the operation O not been performed, X would not have been set*, and
- *had the instruction I not been executed, the operation O would not have been performed.*

It follows that

- Performance of O is a necessary causal factor in setting X, and
- Executing I is a necessary causal factor in performing O

The Meaning of A Counterfactual Lewis's formal meaning for a counterfactual proceeds as follows. We interpret the counterfactual *had A not occurred, B would not have occurred.* The real world history is some behavior. We have a relation of comparative nearness amongst behaviors. In the real world, B occurred, as did A. But we want to know about behaviors in which A did not occur. Did B occur in them? We do not consider all these counterfactual behaviors – Lewis proposes we consider only the *very nearest behaviors* to the real world in which A did not occur. The counterfactual *had A not occurred, B would not have occurred* is defined to be true (in the real world) just in case, in all these nearest behaviors in which A did not occur, B did not occur either. Lewis's formal requirements on the notion of comparative nearness ensure that there are always very nearest behaviors.

The Semantics Applied to the Example We can consider behaviors near enough to the real world such that I was not executed. We may presume that the more properties of the system and environment that are the same, the nearer the states of the alternative behavior are to the real world. It follows that in

the nearest behaviors the design and intended operation of the system can be
assumed to be identical to its design and intended operation in the real world.
For these behaviors, then, in which I was not executed, O was not performed.
And in these behaviors in which O was not performed, X was not set. And in
these behaviors in which X was not set, the interlock was not set in motion.
So consideration of the nearest behaviors shows that the counterfactuals are
to be evaluated as true. Consequently, the assertions of causality (or, rather,
causal-factorality) are true.

Causal-Factorality and Causality It turns out that Lewis's formal notion of
causal factor is not transitive, that is

- If A is a causal factor of B, and B is a causal factor of C, this does not
  necessarily mean that A is a causal factor of C.

Since the intuitive idea of a cause is something that propagates through a
"chain" of causal factors, Lewis proposes to define "cause" as the "transitive
closure" of the relation of causal factor. The *transitive closure* of a relation R is
the smallest (or "tightest", most narrowly defined) relation R^* which, roughly
speaking, is transitive and contains R.

An Aside on Causality and Computers

Relation Between Instruction and Execution is Causal This example also illustrates that, according to the formal definition, the design of a digital system
ensures that the relation between the form of an instruction and and its execution is causal. The instruction I says to increment register R. I is executed; R
is incremented. Had the instruction not been to increment register R, then R
would not have been incremented. Therefore, the form of I, that I is an instruction to increment R, is a causal factor in incrementing R when the instruction
is executed.

Debugging is Causal Analysis This observation entails that debugging computer
programs is a form of causal analysis. One can consider it akin to 'debugging'
complex systems. Not only by analogy, but formally.

3   Where Does This Get Us?

So the first observation is that counterfactual, or what-if, reasoning is essential
not only for reasoning about safety but also for reasoning about causes of accidents. The second observation is that there is a mathematically satisfactory
formalisation of counterfactual reasoning. In principle, we can check our safety
reasoning and our reasoning about the causes of accidents against objective,
rigorous criteria.

In practice, however, one has to put it all together. Karsten Loer and I took
a formal logic sufficient for describing formal properties of distributed systems,

the temporal logic TLA [ ], and combined it with the causal/counterfactual logic of Lewis, adding in some inference rules which we observed were commonly used when arguing for sufficiency of causal explanations. The resulting logic, *Explanatory Logic* or EL, could be used for formal causal reasoning about complex system behavior. We developed a method, *Why-Because Analysis* or WBA, for causally analysing complex system accidents and applying EL to check the reasoning. WBA is described in [ ], along with applications to a number of high-profile aviation accidents.

Do we really need all this machinery to help us analyse systems and design safer ones? Or is this just an exercise for academics? I don't want to introduce the details of WBA here. For one thing, there are a lot of technical details, and for another thing, readers might prefer to use a different formalism. My goal here is to persuade that rigorous, counterfactual reasoning is needed for accident analysis.

Thus I would like to provide two examples to persuade readers of the necessity for objective, rigorous reasoning such as proposed in WBA. These examples employ the preliminary part of a WB-Analysis, which we call the WB-Graph method.

Our approach is very simple. For the 1993 Lufthansa Warsaw accident and the 1988 Air France Habsheim accident, Michael Höhl and I took the factual findings in the official accident reports at face value. We listed them all, and then for each pair of facts, say A and B, we applied Lewis's possible world semantical reasoning informally to determine whether A was a causal factor in B or not. We drew the results in a graph, called the *Why-Because Graph* or WB-Graph. I want to comment on what the graphs show.

4   The Warsaw Lufthansa A320 Accident [ ]

On 14 September 1993, a Lufthansa Airbus A320 landed at Warsaw airport in a thunderstorm. Upon landing, none of the braking systems (air brakes, thrust reverse, wheel brakes) functioned for about nine seconds: the wheel brakes only started to function after about thirteen seconds. The aircraft ran off the end of the runway, collided with an earth bank and started to burn. Primarily because of the superb behavior of the crew, only two people died: one pilot, who died when the aircraft hit the bank, and one passenger, who was unconscious in the front corner and unnoticed in the evacuation as the cabin filled with smoke, and was asphyxiated. It became clear that the logic of the braking systems was indeed a reason why the braking systems hadn't functioned as expected. However, many commentators focused upon this factor as *the* main cause of the accident, which as we shall see is probably incorrect. There were, as is usually the case, many other necessary causal factors.

The WB-Graph

Figure 1 shows the WB-Graph derived from the report by considering all the mentioned states and events and assessing their causal relations to each other using the Lewis semantics. An edge passing from a lower node N to a higher node M means that N is a necessary causal factor in M. No attempt was made to identify features of the accident that were not explicitly mentioned somewhere in the report. It is not easy to read all the node labels, so I divide the graph into three parts: the lower part in Figure 2, the middle part in Figure 3, and the upper part in Figure 4. This division also coheres with the statement of probable cause in the final report, and emphasises a missing feature.

The statement of probable cause from the report is as follows:

> Cause of the accident were incorrect decisions and actions of the flight crew taken in situation when the information about windshear at the approach to the runway was received. Windshear was produced by the front just passing the aerodrome; the front was accompanied by intensive variation of wind parameters as well as by heavy rain on the aerodrome itself.
>
> Actions of the flight crew were also affected by design features of the aircraft which limited the feasibility of applying available braking systems as well as by insufficient information in the aircraft operations manual (AOM) relating to the increase of the landing distance.

Decisions and Actions of the Flight Crew The first sentence of the probable cause statement coheres with what one sees in the lower portion of the graph in Figure 2. The events and states in this portion contribute to the "key" node *Decisions and actions of the flight crew in anticipation of wind shear.*

Weather The weather phenomenon plays a role in the middle portion of the WB-Graph, as may be seen in Figure 3. Also in this portion appear the "*design features of the aircraft*" adduced in the second paragraph of the statement of probable cause.

The Destruction Sequence Most of the upper portion of the graph, in Figure 4, enumerates the parameters of the accident. In order to be classified as an accident, people must be killed or severely injured, and/or the aircraft must be significantly damaged. Both occurred in this accident (although, thankfully, only two people lost their lives and other injuries were minor). One can see these factors appearing in this portion of the graph. But what caused all this?

Focusing In on Factors Let us now focus on the upper portion of the graph where it narrows down to one node. It is rare that a WBA of an accident results in a graph with a width of one. What is this single node?

```
AC hits earth bank
```

Take away this node, and you've avoided the accident. What are its immediate precursors?

```
AC overruns RWY
Earth bank in overrun path
```

The report's attribution of probable cause focused entirely on causal factors contributing to the first of these two events. What about the second? Why was there an earth bank in the overrun path? Because

```
Bank built by airport authority for radio equipment
```

Prophylaxis: Don't Overrun Or Don't Build So there is clearly something to consider. Don't build earth banks for radio equipment at the ends of runways in the overrun area. Or don't overrun runways. Well, measures are taken to minimise cases of the latter, but most authorities consider that no matter what one does, aircraft will still overrun runways once in a while. So if you want to prevent or minimise such catastrophic overrun accidents, one had better take the other option and not build in the overrun area.

In fact, leaving a clear overrun area at the end of runways is regarded not only as good practice but as essential practice by most Western European and US authorities and by practically all pilots.

Rigorous Causal Reasoning Helps The report's conclusions about probable cause and contributing factors said nothing about building earth banks in overrun areas.

The WBA of the accident shows clearly that this omission is a mistake in causal reasoning that the report made. The information necessary to infer that it was a contributing cause was contained in the body of the report - that is where we obtained the factors in the WB-Graph in Figure 1. The WBA shows it to be a causal factor.

This is not the only causal reasoning mistake in the Warsaw report, neither is it the only report in which significant causal reasoning mistakes may be demonstrated by WBA. Another, the report on the 1995 American Airlines B757 accident on approach to Cali, Colombia is one, which also omits demonstrably causal factors in its statement of probable cause. The omitted factors in that report were, however, taken into account by the U.S. National Transportation Safety Board in their letter to the U.S. Federal Aviation Administration containing their safety recommendations based on their analysis.

Using rigorous methods of causal reasoning such as WBA would thus help considerably in ensuring correctness of these important reports. Prophylactic measures are based on the reports' analyses. It is important to reduce future accidents that resources be pointed in the appropriate directions, and one can only do this if a report's reasoning is correct.

5   The 1988 Habsheim Accident [ ]

On 26 June, 1988, an Air France A320, new into service with the airline, took off from Basle-Mulhouse airport with sightseeing passengers, intending enroute to put in an appearance at an airshow at the small airport Mulhouse-Habsheim, just a few miles and minutes flying time away. The pilot had planned for a "low-speed pass", a manoeuver in which the aircraft is configured for landing, flies low along the line of the runway very slowly without landing, and then accelerates up and away. This manoeuver was believed to show off the automatic slow-speed flight protection capabilities of the autopilot, and thereby how the performance of the airplane is enhanced. The manoeuver had been practiced at altitude by the pilot, from a more-or-less level entry.

The pilots had not surveyed the display airport before appearing, and had submitted incomplete flight planning to the Air France administration on Friday. The incomplete planning was approved, although some of it contravened French aviation-legal restrictions on airshow performances by commercial aircraft.

Upon takeoff, the aircraft climbed to an intermediate altitude of 1000 feet above the ground while the pilots identified the airshow airport, which should have been visible almost immediately upon takeoff. A descent was commenced towards the Habsheim airport, which reached a rate of 600 feet per minute with the engines in flight idle. The power setting at flight idle is 29% N1 (a measure correlating with the thrust produced) although the Commission noted that the manoeuver been planned starting from a high power setting.

As the aircraft approached for the low pass and passed through 100 feet above ground level (the planned fly-by altitude), the aircraft was still descending at a rate of 600 feet per minute with the engines in flight idle. The aircraft reached a low altitude of about 30 feet above the runway while attempting to perform the manoeuver. Beyond the end of the runway was a forest, with tree tops considerably higher. "Take-off/go-around" (TOGA) thrust was applied, but the aircraft continued level as the engines accelerated up to TOGA thrust, and the aircraft settled into the trees as the engines ingested tree parts.

Despite a jammed exit door, most passengers were able to leave the aircraft before it was consumed by fire from the burning fuel. Two young children and an adult (presumed to have gone back to help) died from smoke inhalation.

Figure 5 shows a WB-Graph causally relating the major features of the accident flight, including preparation, from the official report.

Controversy The accident became controversial when the captain, who was piloting the aircraft during the accident flight, publically asserted

- that the engines did not respond as designed to his TOGA thrust request;
- that about 4 seconds of recording data were missing from the flight data recorder (FDR) trace;
- that there were at least two different FDR boxes presented to the public as "the" FDR, and/or visible at the accident site
- that some of the data ostensibly from the FDR did not fit some of the facts about the flight;
- that required legal procedures for securing the FDR and taking it for analysis were not followed; insecure procedures were followed.

The captain wrote a book containing his version of the events, published a short while after the accident, and other books suggesting official miscreance have appeared. A decade later, another book about the events is planned to be published.

We may take it as uncontroversial that, had the engines reached TOGA thrust, say, some two seconds earlier, the aircraft would likely have avoided settling into the trees, and thus avoided the crash altogether.

Further Evidence There was a private video made of the accident fly-by by a spectator at the airshow. This video corroborated the altitude at various points of the fly-by, the timing of events, including (through sound-spectral analysis) the % N1 levels of the engines, the start of thrust increase on the engines, and the settling into trees.

The engines as certificated require up to about 8 seconds to increase from 29% N1 up to TOGA thrust. The official FDR data showed that they performed better than their certification parameters.

Evaluation of the Two Versions Our concern in evaluating the accident is to identify causes and other contributing factors in order to increase knowledge about safety-related aircraft and crew performance and to mitigate undesirable or unsafe features in future operations.

Thus the sole significant assertion for our purposes amongst those made by the captain is that the engines did not perform according to specification when TOGA thrust was commanded.

What difference would this make to the WB-Graph in Figure 5? Indeed, none at all. At the level of detail at which the major factors are stated, the only factor under dispute would be Factor 1.1, "*Very low TOGA performance.* Both versions agree this was so, although for different reasons. Both versions agree that the manoeuver was commenced at commanded thrust equivalent to 29% N1, and that the manoeuver had been practiced, and was usually conducted, commencing at much higher N1 levels. Both versions agree on the descent profile, and that the flight-idle power setting was a result of that. Both versions agree that the aircraft was piloted to within 30 feet of the runway, although the captain planned to overfly at 100 feet. The incomplete and partially legally unsuitable planning, and the lack of oversight, are likewise uncontroversial.

The Political Controversy As far as our interest goes, then, any dispute is about the exact level of TOGA performance, which disappears into the details when we are looking at the major factors contributing to the accident.

However, the high-visibility political controversy at the time was concerned not just with how the authorities may or may not have acted in the aftermath of the accident, but whether this "wonder aircraft", the A320, in fact could perform according to its manufacturer's and operator's claims. We can see clearly from the WB-Graph that this latter dispute is a matter of mere technical detail as far as the accident is concerned; it does not affect the causal relations of the major factors at all. The asserted performance difference, while passing the Lewis semantic test for a causal factor, is a question of a finer difference that is subsumed within one of the major factors: it is undisputed that the TOGA performance of the aircraft did not suffice to avoid the trees. According to the official evaluation, it could not have been better. The captain thinks it could have been. That is all.

Had the status of this technical dispute been available and appreciated at the time, we can speculate that the major political controversy over the introduction of the A320 into service, following the accident, might have taken a much different form.

6   Conclusions

The two examples show that objective reasoning methods, had they been used during the investigation and ensuing controversy in these two cases, might have cast a very different light on things. If the methods of reasoning are not generally accepted and open to independent checking, then it is open to anyone to criticise and query for any reason they wish, and if two parties to a discussion reach significantly different conclusions, then there are no further ways of deciding the issues than deciding whom one believes. This is a highly unsatisfactory situation, and gives grounds for introducing objective reasoning methods. If reasoning methods are agreed to be rigorous and objective, then all parties to a discussion are bound to abide by the results.

Two questions: Do such methods exist, and how severe are the problems that stem from lack of rigor? Our use of the Lewis semantics for causality, and the related method WBA, show that the answer to the first question is yes.

The second question can be answered by considering what might have happened had a WB-Graph been available.

In the case of Warsaw, had a WB-Graph been constructed by the report writers based on the content of their report, they would have identified omissions in their statement of probable cause, and attention would have been brought to bear on the presence of an airport construction which adversely affected safety. Anecdotes say the mound is still there.

In the case of Habsheim, the heated political debate about the safety of the design of a new aircraft, and its consequences for public acceptance of the aircraft, might have evaporated, in favor of a technical performance debate and review of the sort which goes on every day at aircraft design and manufacturing plants.

Two anecdotes cannot prove a general hypothesis, but they may persuade. My purpose has been to persuade that objective methods of reasoning in accident evaluations are not just an exercise for academics. I believe they would have significant benefits, not only for accident investigation and the safety of air travel, but also for public debate as a whole.

There is another point worth remarking, again while taking care not to draw general conclusions from two individual cases. Both were publically high-profile accidents in which the digital automation on the aircraft was considered by many to have played a major contributory role. It is interesting to observe, when the causal reasoning is finally laid out, how few of the many factors involved in either of these accidents directly concerned the digital automation.

References

1. David Hume. *An Enquiry Concerning Human Understanding*. Oxford University Press, third edition, 1777/1975. Ed. L. A. Selby-Bigge and P. H. Nidditch. 346
2. Peter Ladkin and RVS Group.   RVS Group Publications.   RVS Group, Faculty of Technology, University of Bielefeld. Available through www.rvs.uni-bielefeld.de. 355
3. Peter B. Ladkin. Notes on the foundations of system safety analysis. Technical Report RVS-Bk-00-01, Networks and distributed Systems Group, Faculty of Technology, Bielefeld University, Bielefeld, Germany, 2000. Available through [ ]. 347
4. Peter B. Ladkin and Karsten Loer. Why-Because Analysis: Formal Reasoning About Incidents. Technical Report RVS-Bk-98-01, Networks and distributed Systems Group, Faculty of Technology, Bielefeld University, Bielefeld, Germany, 1998. Available through [ ]. 349
5. Peter B. Ladkin et al. Computer-related incidents with commercial aircraft. Technical Report RVS-Comp-01, RVS Group, Faculty of Technology, University of Bielefeld. Compendium of digitised accident reports and commentary, available through [ ]. 355
6. Leslie Lamport. The temporal logic of actions. *ACM Transactions on Programming Languages and Systems*, 16(3):872–923, May 1994. 349
7. Nancy G. Leveson. *Safeware: System Safety and Computers*. Addison-Wesley, 1995. 344
8. David Lewis. Causation. *Journal of Philosophy*, 70:556–567, 1973. Also in [,]. 346
9. David Lewis. *Counterfactuals*. Oxford University Press, Inc., Blackwell, 1973. 346
10. David Lewis. *Philosophical papers, Vol.II*. Oxford University Press, Inc., 200 Maddison Avenue, New York, New York 10016, 1986. 355
11. Main Commission Aircraft Investigation Warsaw. Report on the Accident to Airbus A320-211 Aircraft in Warsaw on 14 September 1993. Available through [ ], March 1994. 349
12. John Stuart Mill. *A System of Logic, Books I-III*, volume VII of *Collected Works*. University of Toronto Press, London: Routledge & Kegan Paul, 1973. 346
13. Ministry of Planning, Housing, Transport and Maritime Affairs (France). Investigation Commission concerning the accidents which occurred on June 26th 1988 at Mulhouse-Habsheim (68) to the Airbus A320, registered F-GFKC. Final Report, November 29th 1989. 351
14. Ernest Sosa and Michael Tooley, editors. *Causation*. Oxford Readings in Philosophy. Oxford University Press, Oxford, 1993. 355
15. United States Air Force. *Air Force Instruction 91-204*. Author, July 1994. 345

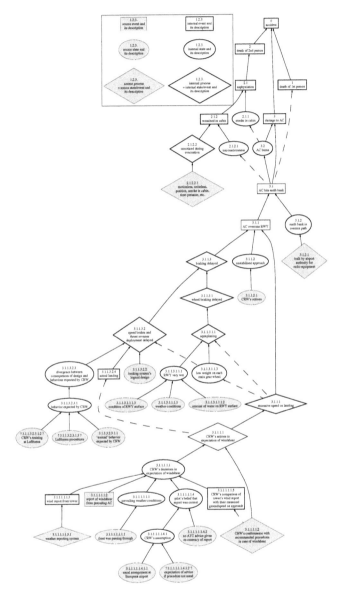

Fig. 1. The Warsaw WB-Graph: overall pattern

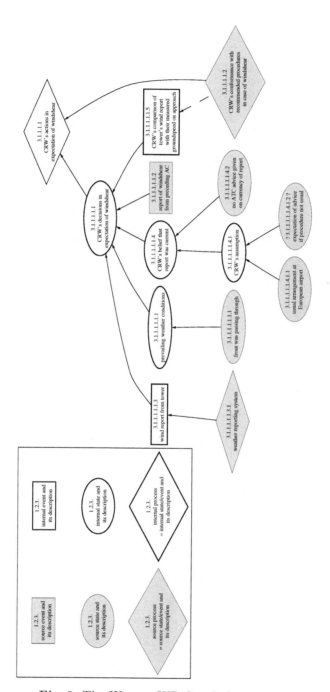

Fig. 2. The Warsaw WB-Graph, lower part

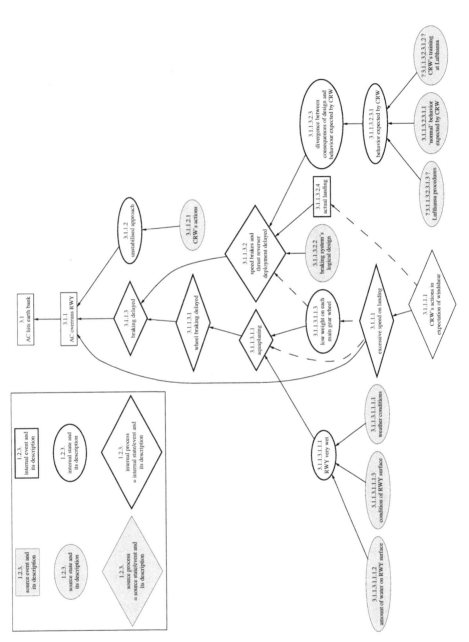

Fig. 3. The Warsaw WB-Graph, middle part

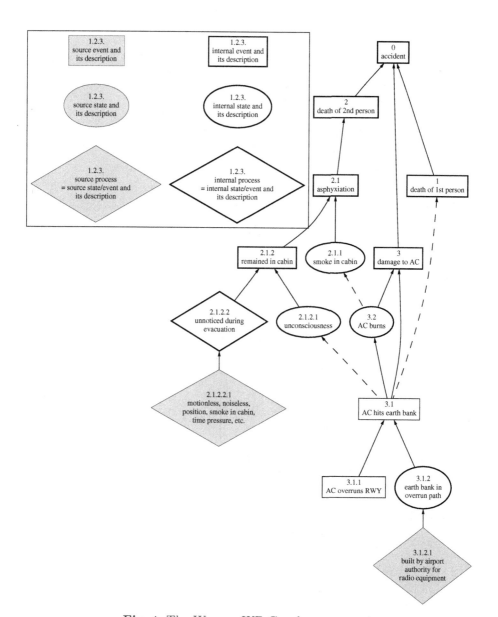

Fig. 4. The Warsaw WB-Graph, upper part

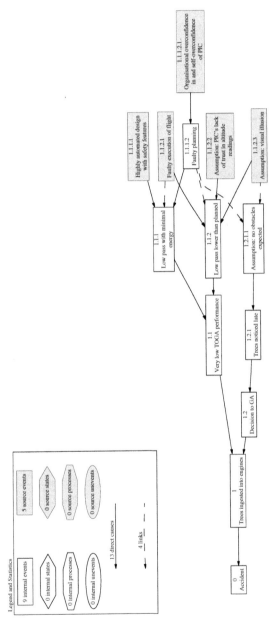

Fig. 5. The Habsheim WB-Graph

Controlling Requirements Evolution: An Avionics Case Study

Stuart Anderson and Massimo Felici

LFCS, Division of Informatics, The University of Edinburgh
Mayfield Road, Edinburgh EH9 3JZ, United Kingdom
{soa,mas}@dcs.ed.ac.uk

Abstract. This paper presents an empirical investigation of the control of requirements evolution in an avionics safety-critical system. Metrics can be used to manage (e.g., control and predict) requirements evolution. The results point out issues in the use of metrics for controlling requirements evolution in the case study. Moreover, they provide new evidence, which suggests a product line oriented management method for requirements. The empirical analysis supports a number of remarks that are described through the paper.

1 Introduction

Current practice in Software Engineering [, ,] emphasises the need for iterative development processes refining the software product in all its related representations (e.g., software requirements specification, design specification, testing activities, source code, etc.). Even small software projects require subsequent releases in order to fulfil changing user expectation and environmental constraints. Researchers and practitioners in Software Engineering have recognised the important role of requirements [, ,] leading to the development of the field of Requirements Engineering [,].

Recent research [ ] in Requirements Engineering identifies the origins of requirements change in the development environment. Changing requirements are classified according to five types, which are related to the development environments, stakeholders, development processes, requirements understanding and requirements relations. Requirements change raise problems that affect all aspects of software production [ ], i.e., processes as well as deliverables (e.g., software). Thus, software development environments from an external viewpoint look like a collection of processes, stakeholders and deliverables giving rise to instability in the product. The extremes of this turbulence are requirements evolution and software evolution. Previous studies [ ] have identified a set of laws of software evolution, but understanding the relationship between requirements evolution and software evolution still remains a challenge for researchers and practitioners [,]. This relationship is very important. Confirmation of its importance can be found in reported accidents in safety-critical systems, which have emphasis the relationship between requirements evolution, software evolution and system safety [ ].

F. Koornneef and M. van der Meulen (Eds.): SAFECOMP 2000, LNCS 1943, pp. 361–370, 2000.
© Springer-Verlag Berlin Heidelberg 2000

Metrics [ ] can be used as a means to manage (e.g., control and predict) requirements evolution. They have been used to investigate software evolution [,], but there is still little evidence how similar metrics can be effectively applied at the requirements level as well. The effective use of metrics requires a careful plan and a deep analysis of the specific problems for which a measurement program is developed [ ]. Previous analyses [,] emphasise the need for domain specific approaches in requirements engineering. The use of general measurement approaches could be misleading and could lead to misunderstanding. It is strongly recommended to develop specific measurement programs for each context. Only experience within a specific context can improve our level of confidence in a measurement approach.

The work reported in this paper aims to assess how metrics can be used to give quantitative evidence of the effectiveness of the management of requirements evolution. The empirical investigation aims to relate requirements features to the specific product line. The paper is organised as follows. Section 2 describes the avionics safety-critical case study. Section 3 summarises the empirical investigation. The empirical analysis supports a set of remarks that are reported in the Section 3. Section 4 summarises the work and identifies possible areas of future work.

2   An Avionics Case Study

The case study consists of software for an avionics system. There are stringent safety requirements for the software, which has been certified according to the standard used in the avionics context [ ]. The software project has been developed as part of a sub-contract. There are 22 successive releases of the software requirements specification each corresponding to a software release. The evolution of these requirements specifications is analysed in the empirical investigation summarised in the next section.

Figure 1 shows a representation of the phases of the development process and its deliverables (i.e., system requirements, software functional requirements, etc.). The *System Requirements* cover the whole system, that is, they are specified in terms of system and not software functions. Then the *System Process* translates the requirements and allocates them into the *Software Functional Requirements*. The software functional requirements are organised in terms of the software functions identified in the system requirements. These software functions will be integrated further in the development process. After the definition of the software functional requirements, the development process travels through design and coding. All the anomalies (e.g., faults, failures, misbehaviours, etc.) encountered during the development are reported by a *Fault Report*. Fault reports consist of a document reporting all the information useful to the development team in order to assess the possible faults. When a fault has been recognised actions are taken to fix it and the needed changes are allocated to a specific software release. The scope of these actions ranges from requirements to software code. Thus continuous feedback is provided by the fault reports. Notice that certification requires that all the changes are traced. This data is the basis for the empirical investigation described in the next section.

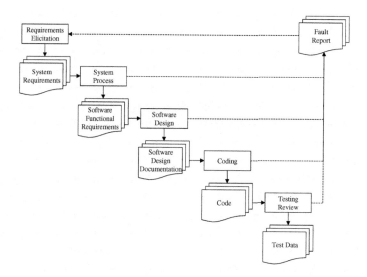

Fig. 1. Development activities and deliverables

3   Measures and Trends

This section summarises an empirical investigation aiming to identify quantitative features of requirements evolution. The empirical results are summarised in a number of remarks.

Figure 2 shows the total number of requirements changes (i.e., added, deleted and modified requirements) over the 22 software releases[1]. The trend of requirements changes does not give enough information about evolution features, but it emphasises the problem of changing requirements. Figure 3 shows the trend of the total number of requirements over the software releases. The view given by the total number of requirements is more interesting than that one by the total number of changes. The total number of requirements increases over the software releases.

Remark 1 (Size of Requirements). The number of requirements tends to grow over the software releases.

This is probably then because the requirements become clearer to the stakeholders, who split complex requirements into smaller, more precisely stated,

---

[1] There is a correspondence one-to-one between versions of the requirements specification and software releases. We will refer only to software releases along the rest of the paper to avoid any confusion.

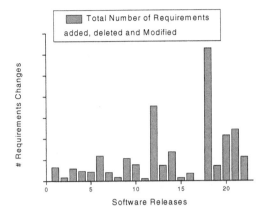

Fig. 2. Number of requirements changes per software releases

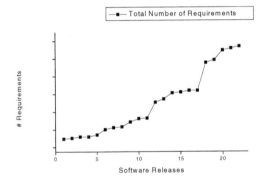

Fig. 3. Number of requirements per software releases

requirements. Another reason could be that new requirements arise during the progress of the project, in other words, there could be requirements which cannot be defined at the beginning for the lack of information. Finally, design, implementation and testing provide additional feedback to the requirements.

A question arises from the trend of the number of requirements. What is a suitable metric to assess the readiness of requirements? The stability of requirements [ ] can be assessed by (1).

$$Requirements\ Stability\ =\ \frac{Number\ of\ initial\ requirements}{Total\ Number\ of\ requirements}\ . \tag{1}$$

Equation (1) is not sufficiently expressive, because it does not take into account modified requirements. Hence, it is not adequate in cases where there are many modified requirements or there are roughly the same number of added and deleted requirements. The standard IEEE 982 [,] suggests a Software

Maturity Index to quantify the readiness of a software product. Hence, the idea of using a similar Requirements Maturity Index (RMI) to quantify the readiness of requirements. Equation (2) defines the RMI[2].

$$RMI = \frac{R_T - R_C}{R_T} \ .$$

(2)

Figure 4 shows the RMI calculated for all the software functional requirements. In this case the RMI results to be misleading to assess the readiness of the software functional requirements. The RMI does not have an increasing regular shape. Hence any assessment based only on the RMI could be misleading and risky, see Remark 2.

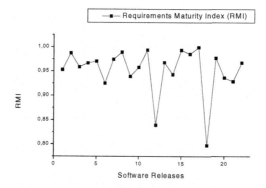

Fig. 4. Requirements Maturity index

Remark 2 (Requirements Maturity Index). The Requirements Maturity Index can be misleading in assessing the readiness of requirements. The metrics user should always asses its applicability in the specific context.

This result points out that it is not obvious how to apply even widely used software metrics. Metrics that are suitable at the software level can became unusable for the requirements. Metrics are context sensitive, therefore an aware metrics user should always assess their applicability for the specific case.

To provide a more detailed analysis our focus moves from the total number of requirements changes to the total number of requirements changes in each function that forms the software functional requirements. The software functional requirements fall into 8 functions for which separate documents are maintained. Figure 5 shows the trend of the cumulative number of requirements changes for each function. The figure points out that the likelihood that changes can occur into specific functions is not constant over the software releases.

---

[2] R_T = number of software requirements in the current delivery ; R_C = number of software requirements in the current delivery that are added, deleted or modified from a previous delivery.

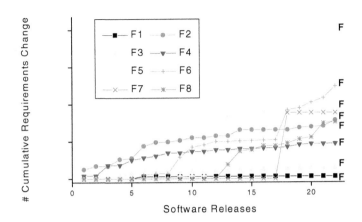

Fig. 5. Cumulative number of requirements changes for each function

The first outcome of this new viewpoint is that the function F1 is not likely to change, therefore it could be considered a stable part of the system. This aspect becomes interesting, because the specific function describes the hardware architecture of the system onto which the software architecture is mapped. Hence, Remark 3, the software architecture is a stable part of the requirements.

Remark 3 (Architecture). The software requirements of the system architecture represent a stable part of the requirements. The likelihood of architecture changes is low and changes usually occur in early releases of the software, when they can still be accommodated with affordable costs.

Another outcome, Remark 4, of this functions oriented view is that functions that are likely to change during early software releases change less during later releases, and vice versa. This aspect helps to relate requirements changes identified in the functions with the software life cycle. Moreover, the trends show an interesting switching feature that needs further investigation to clarify its consistency. The assumption is that there could be possible dependencies between subsets of the requirements, that is, the requirements identified by those functions which change later in the development process depend on those functions containing early changing requirements. Thus, there are requirements that are dependent upon others. It is not possible to define all the requirements at once due to these dependencies over requirements. At this level of granularity the empirical investigation does not allow easy analysis of these dependencies between requirements. We intend to validate Remark 4 by replicating the experiment in other case studies and in different industrial contexts.

Remark 4 (Requirements Dependencies). Functions that are likely to change during early software releases change less during later releases, and vice versa. The evolution trends show some dependencies between requirements.

Figure 6 shows a scatter plot relating the cumulative number of requirements changes for each function and the respective size in terms of number of requirements in the last release[3]. For most of the functions there exists a linear relation between these two measures. Figure 6 identifies the functions that have a non-linear relation upon these measures (i.e., F2, F5 and F8). Thus, the graph helps to identify those functions which are most likely to change (i.e., F5, F6 and F7) and those which are not. Questions arise from this result. In particular, can a product oriented approach to allocate changes help in managing requirements changes? In other words, can a product oriented requirements management be useful in obtaining a cost-effective allocation of requirements changes? Remark 5 summarises the last result of the empirical investigation.

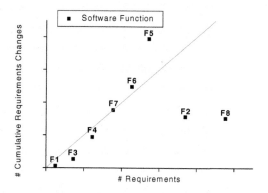

Fig. 6. Scatter plot of number of changes against number of requirements

Remark 5 (Product Oriented Perspective). Some functions are more likely to experience requirements change than others. For most of the functions there exists a linear relation between cumulative number of requirements changes and final number of requirements. The management of requirements changes could be improved by a product oriented perspective.

4   Conclusions and Further Work

The paper shows an empirical investigation of an avionics safety-critical case study. The empirical investigation points out interesting aspects of changing requirements. The results identify requirements features, which suggest product oriented management of requirements changes. Effective integration of current management processes together with a product oriented view offers the potential to improve our ability to bound the scope of change in order to guarantee continuous process improvement. Moreover, a product oriented view can provide a useful baseline to devise new tools for assessing the risk of requirements changes. The main remarks are summarised in what follows.

---

[3] The number of requirements in the 22nd release.

Size of Requirements. The number of requirements tends to grow over the software releases.

Requirements Maturity Index. The Requirements Maturity Index can be misleading in assessing the readiness of requirements. The metrics user should always asses its applicability in the specific context.

Architecture. The software requirements of the system architecture represent a stable part of the requirements. The likelihood of architecture changes is low and changes usually occur in early releases of the software, when they can still be accommodated with affordable costs.

Requirements Dependencies. Functions that are likely to change during early software releases change less during later releases, and vice versa. The evolution trends show some dependencies between requirements.

Product Oriented Perspective. Some functions are more likely to experience requirements change than others. For most of the function there exists a linear relation between cumulative number of requirements changes and final number of requirements. The management of requirements changes could be improved by a product oriented perspective.

The above results suggest further work aiming to

- validate the results in different case studies
- validate the results in different product line and industrial contexts
- extend the results by specific analyses of the features identified through the paper
- investigate relationships with other product aspects (e.g., reliability, safety, dependability, etc.)
- devise product oriented requirements engineering tools.

In conclusion, the paper shows a detailed quantitative analysis, which points out product oriented features that may improve the specification of requirements as well as their management. The results identify some research directions defining a work plan to understand requirements evolution.

Acknowledgements

The authors wish to thank the industrial partner, who has provided the case study. Due to the high safety level of the case study, the agreement with the industrial partner does not allow to show any numerical information. Despite this the analysis remains still valid and the results are clearly expressed.

References

1. Lowell Jay Arthur, Rapid Evolutionary Development: Requirements, Prototyping & Software Creation, John Wiley & Sons, 1992 361
2. Daniel M. Berry and Brian Lawrence,Requirements Engineering, IEEE Software, 1998, March, 26-29 361

3. Barry W. Boehm, Software Engineering Economics, Prentice-Hall, 1981
4. Barry W. Boehm, Software Engineering Economics, IEEE Transaction on Software Engineering, 1984, Vol.**101**, Januari, 4-21
5. Alan M. Davis and Pei Hsia, Giving Voice to Requirements Engineering, IEEE Software,1994, March, 12-16   361
6. Giorgio De Michelis and others, A Three-Faceted View of Information Systems, Communications of the ACM, 1998, December, Vol.**41**12, 64-70
7. DO-178B Software Considerations in Airborne Systems and Equipment Certification, RTCA, 1992   362
8. Ralf Dömges and Klaus Pohl, Adapting Traceability Environments to Project-Specific Needs, Communications of the ACM, 1998, December, Vol.**41**12, 54-62
9. Norman E. Fenton and Shari Lawrence Pfleeger, Software Metrics: A Rigorous and Practical Approach, Second edition, International Thomson Computer Press, 1996   362, 364
10. S. D.Harker and K. D. Eason, The Change and Evolution of Requirements as a Challenge to the Practice of Software Engineering, Proceedings of the IEEE International Symposium on Requirements Engineering, 1993, San Diego, California, USA, Januari, IEEE Computer Society Press, 266-272   361
11. IEEE Std 982.1 - IEEE Standard Dictionary of Measures to Produce Reliable Software, IEEE, 1988   364
12. IEEE Std 982.2 - IEEE Guide for the Use of IEEE Standard Dictionary of Measures to Produce Reliable Software, IEEE, 1988   364
13. Matthias Jarke, Requirements Tracing, Communications of the ACM, 1998, December, Vol.**41**12, 32-36
14. Matthias Jarke and others, Theories Underlying Requirements Engineering: An Overview of NATURE at Genesis, bookProceedings of the IEEE International Symposium on Requirements Engineering, 1993, San Diego, California, USA, Januari, IEEE Computer Society Press, 19-31
15. Chris F. Kemerer and Sandra Slaughter, An Empirical Approach to Studying Software Evolution, IEEE Transactions on Software Engineering, Vol.**25**4, July/August, 1999, 493-509   362
16. Gerald Kotonya and Ian Sommerville, Requirements engineering with viewpoints, Software Engineering Journal, Vol.**11**1, Januari, 1996, 5-18
17. W. Lam, Achieving Requirements Reuse: A Domain-Specific Approach from Avionics, The Journal of Systems and Software, Vol.**38**3, September, 1997, 197-209   362
18. W. Lam and J. A. McDermid and A. J. Vickers, Ten Steps Towards Systematic Requirements Reuse, Proceedings of the Third IEEE International Symposium on Requirements Engineering, 1997, Annapolis, Maryland, USA, Januari, IEEE Computer Society Press, 6-15   362
19. Mingjune Lee and Barry W. Boehm, The WinWin Requirements Negotiation System: A Model-Driven Approach, University of Southern California, 1996, USC-CSE p.96-502
20. M. M. Lehman and D. E. Perry and J. F. Ramil, On Evidence Supporting the FEAST Hypothesis and the Laws of Software Evolution, Proceedings of Metrics '98, 1998, November, Bethesda, Maryland   361, 362
21. SAFEWARE: System Safety and Computer, Nancy G. Leveson, Addison-Wesley, 1995   361

22. Mitch Lubars, Colin Potts and Charles Richter, A Review of the State of the Practice in Requirements Modeling, bookProceedings of the IEEE International Symposium on Requirements Engineering, 1993, San Diego, California, USA, Januari, IEEE Computer Society Press, 2-14

23. Saeko Matsuura and Hironobu Kuruma and Shinichi Honiden, EVA: A Flexible Programming Method for Evolving Systems, IEEE Transactions on Software Engineering, Vol.**23**5, May, 1997, 296-313

24. , Anneliese von Mayrhauser, Testing and Evolutionary Development, ACM SIGSOFT Software Engineering Notes, Vol.**16**4, October, 1991, 31-36

25. Bashar Nuseibeh and Jeff Kramer and Anthony Finkelstein, A Framework for Expressing the Relationships Between Multiple Views in Requirements Specification, IEEE Transactions on Software Engineering, Vol.**20**10, October, 1994, 760-773

26. James D. Palmer, Traceability, jSoftware Engineering, 266-276, 1996

27. Shari Lawrence Pfleeger, Software Engineering: Theory and Practice, Prentice-Hall, 1998 361

28. PROTEUS Project, Meeting the challenge of chainging requirements, Centre for Software Reliability, University of Newcastle upon Tyne, 1996, June, Strens, M. R. (eds,), Deliverable, 1.3 361

29. Balasubramaniam Ramesh, Factors Influencing Requirements Traceability Practice, Communications of the ACM, 1998, December, Vol.**41**12, 37-44

30. Carolyn B. Seaman, Qualitative Methods in Empirical Studies of Software Engineering, IEEE Transactions on Software Engineering, Vol.**25**4, July/August, 1999, 557-572

31. J. Siddiqi and M. C. Shekaran, Requirements Engineering: The Emerging Wisdom, IEEE Software, 1996, March, 15-19 361

32. Ian Sommerville, Software Engineering, Fifth edition, Addison-Wesley, 1995 361

33. Ian Sommerville, Gerald Kotonya, Steve Viller and Pete Sawyer, Process Viewpoints, Lancaster University, 1995, CSEG/1/1995

34. Ian Sommerville and Pete Sawyer, Requirements Engineering: A Good Practice Guide, John Wiley & Sons, 1997 361

35. Ian Sommerville and Pete Sawyer, Viewpoints: principles, problems and a practical approach to requirments engineering, Annals of Software Engineering, numero = 3, 101-130, 1997

36. Ian Sommerville, Pete Sawyer and Stephen Viller, Viewpoints for requirements elicitation: a practical approach, Proceedings of the IEEE International Conference on Requirements Engineering, 1998, Colorado Springs, Colorado, April

37. Stephen Viller and Ian Sommerville, Social analysis in the requirements engineering process: from ethnography to method, Lancaster University, 1998, CSEG/14/1998

38. George Stark and Al Skillicorn and Ryan Ameele, An Examination of the Effects of Requirements Changes on Software Releases, CROSSTALK The Journal of Defence Software Engineering, 1998, December, 11-16 361

39. Didar Zowghi and Ray Offen, A Logical Framework for Modeling and Reasoning about the Evolution of Requirements, Proceedings of the Third IEEE International Symposium on Requirements Engineering, 1997, Annapolis, Maryland, USA, Januari, IEEE Computer Society Press, 247-257

40. Karl Eugene Wiegers, Software Requirements, Microsoft Press, 1999 361

HAZOP Analysis of Formal Models of Safety-Critical Interactive Systems

Andrew Hussey

Software Verification Research Centre, The University of Queensland
Brisbane, Qld, 4072, Australia
ahussey@svrc.uq.edu.au

Abstract. We consider methods for analysing interactive systems for operator errors leading to hazards. We model an industrial case study using formal methods and show how a HAZOP-based approach can be used to determine hazardous operator errors. The analysis can be used to motivate and guide redesign of the system to reduce the likelihood of such errors. The technique is amenable to automation, which we demonstrate using the Possum specification animation tool.

1   Introduction

Defects in safety-critical computer-based systems may ultimately be responsible for injury or loss of life. The user-interface of a safety-critical computer-based system can be a source of operator error leading to such high consequence accidents. By removing deficiencies in the design of the user-interface, the safety of the system can be enhanced. In the safety-critical context, we are primarily concerned with robustness of the system; the designer of a safety-critical interactive system should strive to reduce operator error. Categories of operator error include omissions, substitutions and repetitions (the latter two are commission errors) [ ].

This paper is concerned with providing methods for analysing safety-critical interactive systems to detect design defects that would diminish system safety. The approach presented is essentially a variant of the HAZOP (Hazard and Operability) method, described for example in MOD 00-58 [ ]. HAZOP is the predominant technique for analysing human error (e.g., [, ,]). Because HAZOP has been described in detail in [ ] and elsewhere, here we mainly discuss those features that distinguish our approach. In this paper, we focus on the hazard analysis activities in HAZOP rather than on operability concerns.

The HAZOP process was originally conceived for the petrochemical industry. The purpose of HAZOP is to identify potential faults that may give rise to hazards in petrochemical plants by considering the flow of product in a piping and instrumentation diagram of the plant. In a computer system HAZOP, a similar process is followed, but the model considered is a data-flow diagram, or similar analysis of a data-processing system. For a user-interface, the model is usually a form of task analysis. The successful application of a HAZOP depends on the intuition of the designer applying the HAZOP.

F. Koornneef and M. van der Meulen (Eds.): SAFECOMP 2000, LNCS 1943, pp. 371–381, 2000.

Task analyses are commonly used as a means of capturing system requirements. The task analysis must describe both the logical sequence of actions that
the operator engages in, and the detailed physical executions that the operator
must perform in order to effect each step in the procedure.

State-based specification notations are well-suited to capturing abstract system requirements in terms of the effect of user actions on the objects comprising
the "functional core" of the system. The effect of a sequence of user actions must
satisfy the goal state for that task procedure.

In this paper, Sum [ ] is used for specification of task procedures, actions
and objects. Sum is used to express both state changes and behaviours, rather
than using a process-based notation for behaviour (e.g., [ ]), because separating
the specification into state and behavioural parts diminishes the readability of
the specification.

Section 2 considers an approach to detection of design defects based on HA-
ZOP. In section 3 we describe a case study that we have analysed using our
methods, while Section 4 gives the outcomes of the analysis. Section 5 discusses
our use of the Possum animation tool to partially automate the analysis process.
In Section 6, we discuss future directions for our work and conclude.

2   Interactive System HAZOP Studies

In this paper, we sketch a HAZOP approach to identify aspects of the user-
interface that can contribute to producing an accident.

1. Using operational scenarios for the system as a guide, we identify user goals.
   Our use of scenarios to drive the process is similar to THEA (Technique for
   Human Error Analysis) [ ] in which the designer considers scenarios as a
   tool for identifying accidents with which the user-interface may be involved.
2. For each user goal we determine possible action sequences (tasks). The process of formulating goals, tasks, objects and actions may occur in conjunction
   with scenario-based design of the user-interface with the aim of enhancing
   usability (e.g., as discussed by Rosson et al. in [ ]). Based on the tasks, it
   is possible to construct a model of the interactive system for the purpose of
   the hazard analysis.
3. To determine user-interface features that may result in accidents, we examine tasks using HAZOP-style keywords as a guide. For the purpose of this
   analysis (for brevity), we only consider a subset of the keywords discussed
   by Kirwan [, p.197]. Interconnections are defined by transitions from one
   state to the next. The *interconnections* are explicit in an action sequence,
   while the states that they connect are implicit. The *attribute* under consideration for each interconnection is the action itself. The keywords examined
   are shown in Table 1.

By analysing task structure the developer can reject structures that are fault-
prone prior to the expense of design and can more readily "design in" protections

Table 1. Example HAZOP keywords interpreted

Keyword	Meaning
No	Operation removed from scenario
Other	Other operation substituted in scenario
More	Input parameter "increased"
Less	Input parameter "decreased"
Repeated	Operation repeated in scenario

against such faults. The specification may be modified to include additional operation preconditions that help avoid undesirable action sequences. An operation precondition is a predicate that *must* be satisfied for the operation to proceed. Preconditions define modes of operation of the system. An analysis at the execution/perception level of abstraction is necessary to determine the residual risk following task level analysis and design.

3   Railway Control System Case Study

The Railway Control system is an Australian system, currently under development, for controlling the movement of trains on inland freight and passenger lines, preventing collisions between trains and maximising usage. The system is similar to an ATC system (with rail-traffic controllers and train drivers in lieu of air-traffic controllers and pilots) but is concerned with train movement, for which traffic movement and hence collision risk is more restricted. Figure 1 shows the controllers' screen for the system.

The controller and driver are in communication via a mobile phone or radio. For example, controllers may request drivers to move their trains from one location to another.

Commands to move a train to a new location are formulated by the train controller double-clicking on the train that is the subject of the command and then on the location that the train is to move to. In Figure 1, the train is at Torrens Creek station and has been cleared through to the "block-limit board" just to the left of Warreah station. Once a train has been instructed to move to a new location, all the track that the train must occupy in the course of executing that command becomes unavailable for use by any other trains. As the train moves along the track, the driver of the train contacts the controller to release sections of the track, so that other trains may move onto those track sections.

3.1   Scenario

We consider the scenario shown in Figure 2. The goal state is for train "A" to reserve the section of track between block-limit boards 0 and 2, and for train "B" to reserve the sections of track between block-limit boards 3 and 4. Train "A" is at block-limit board 1 and train "B" is at block-limit board 2.

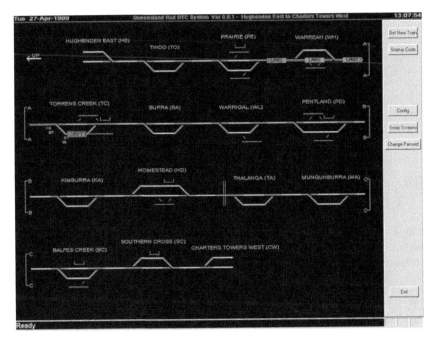

Fig. 1. Controller's screen for the Railway Control system

Fig. 2. Scenario for analysis

To achieve this goal, the following task sequence must occur:

1. train "B" reserves from block-limit board 3 to block-limit board 4.
2. the driver of train "B" releases the section of track between block-limit board 2 and 3.
3. train "A" reserves from block-limit board 1 to block-limit board 2.

3.2   Formal Object-Oriented Specification

In this section, we describe the objects and actions to perform the task steps using the railway control system, to achieve the goal. The formal specification is given using Sum.

Sum is a variant of the Z specification language [ ] devised primarily to facilitate the production of modular specifications and ease specification readability. Unique features of the Sum language relevant to this case study are:

1. A collection of declarations and definitions may be grouped into a module. Modules may be imported, giving visibility to the referenced entities.

2. State machines are easily represented by modules through the use of predefined *state*, *init* and *op* schemas. State schemas represent the state encapsulated by the module through a collection of typed variables. The state is initialised by the *init* schema. State transitions are captured by *op* schemas that specify the relationship between the state variables before and after a transition. The modified state variables are identified by an appended dash. The scope of variables that can be referenced by the *init* and *op* schemas is restricted to the variables in the *state* schema by default but can be extended arbitrarily. The *changes_only* expression in a schema specifies which part of the state may be changed by an operation.

3. Preconditions can be explicitly associated with *op* schemas in order to convey more information about the intended specification. A precondition is identified with the prefix *pre* and represents assumptions about the state prior to invocation of an operation.

Objects are modelled as schemas, while actions are modelled as Op schemas in the Sum notation. We only specify the system from the perspective of reserving and releasing sections of track, and moving trains between block-limit boards, because this is sufficient to enable analysis of that aspect of the system. Movement of trains is modelled as units (block-limit boards) in either the left or right direction. Note that the state of our model is only loosely constrained by the state invariant to admit the failure states that we wish to analyse. For example, a more tightly constrained model might include the predicate $\forall t : \mathrm{dom}\ trainPosn \bullet track(trainPosn(t)) \in \mathrm{ran}\ trainResv(t)$, but this would preclude the possibility of the hazard arising whereby a train was occupying a section of track that it had not reserved. However, note that the system *does* prevent trains from reserving overlapping sections of track.

TrainSystem $[BLB;\ TrainID]$

$Direction\ ::=\ forward\ |\ reverse$

state
$track : iseq\ BLB$
$trainResv : TrainID \nrightarrow iseq\ \mathbb{N}$
$trainPosn : TrainID \nrightarrow \mathbb{N}$
$trains : \mathbb{P}\ TrainID$

init
$track' = \langle\rangle$
$trainResv' = \{\}$
$trainPosn' = \{\}$
$trains' = \{\}$

$\mathrm{dom}\ trainResv = \mathrm{dom}\ trainPosn$
$\mathrm{dom}\ trainPosn \subseteq trains$
$\mathrm{ran}\ trainPosn \subseteq \mathrm{dom}\ track$
$\forall t_1, t_2 : trainID \bullet t_1 \neq t_2 \Rightarrow \mathrm{ran}\ trainResv(t_1) \cap \mathrm{ran}\ trainResv(t_2) = \varnothing$

$\_op\ AddTrain\_$
$train? : TrainID$
$posn? : \mathbb{N}$

$trains' = trains \cup \{train?\}$
$trainPosn' = trainPosn \oplus \{train? \mapsto posn?\}$
$trainResv' = trainResv \oplus \{train? \mapsto \langle posn? \rangle\}$
$changes\_only\{trains, trainPosn, trainResv\}$

$\_segment\_$
$s, f : \mathbb{N}$

$seg : iseq\ \mathbb{N}$

$seg = \{d : 1 .. (f - s + 1) \bullet$
$\quad d \mapsto (s + d)\}$
$s + 1 = min(\mathrm{ran}\ seg)$
$\#seg = f - s + 1$

$\_op\ SetTrack\_$
$tr? : iseq\ BLB$

$track' = tr?$
$changes\_only\{track\}$

$\_op\ Reserve\_$
$train? : TrainID$
$units? : \mathbb{Z}$
$direction? : Direction$

$[\ s\_in, s\_out : segment\ |$
$s\_in.seg = trainResv(train?)\ \wedge$
$if\ direction? = forward$
$\quad then\ (if\ s\_in.f + units? \leq \#track$
$\qquad\qquad then\ (s\_out.s = s\_in.s \wedge s\_out.f = s\_in.f + units?)$
$\qquad\qquad else\ (s\_out.s = s\_in.s \wedge s\_out.f = \#track)\ fi\ )$
$\quad else\ (direction? = reverse\ \wedge$
$\qquad\quad if\ s\_in.s - units? \geq 1$
$\qquad\qquad then\ (s\_out.s = s\_in.s - units? \wedge s\_out.f = s\_in.f)$
$\qquad\qquad else\ (s\_out.s = 1 \wedge s\_out.f = s\_in.f)\ fi\ )\ fi\ \wedge$
$trainResv' = trainResv \oplus \{train? \mapsto s\_out.seg\}\ ] \setminus (s\_in, s\_out)$
$changes\_only\{trainResv\}$

$\_$ op Move $\_$

train? : TrainID
units? : $\mathbb{N}$
direction? : Direction

$trainPosn' = trainPosn \oplus \{train? \mapsto$
(if direction? = forward
  then (if trainPosn(train?) + units? $\leq$ #track
     then trainPosn(train?) + units?
     else #track fi)
  else (direction? = reverse $\wedge$
if trainPosn(train?) $-$ units? ≥ 1
 then trainPosn(train?) $-$ units?
 else 1 fi) fi)\}
changes_only\{trainPosn\}

$\_$ op Release $\_$

train? : TrainID
units? : $\mathbb{N}$
direction? : Direction

$\exists s, s\_plus, s\_minus$: segment $\bullet$
$s.seg = trainResv(train?) \wedge$
$s\_plus.s = s.s + units? \wedge s\_plus.f = s.f \wedge$
$s\_minus.s = s.s \wedge s\_minus.f = s.f - units? \wedge$
if direction? = forward
 then if $s.s + units? \leq s.f$
    then $(trainResv' = trainResv \oplus \{train? \mapsto s\_plus.seg\})$
    else $(trainResv' = trainResv \oplus \{train? \mapsto \langle\rangle\})$ fi
 else if $s.f - units? \geq s.s$
    then $(trainResv' = trainResv \oplus \{train? \mapsto s\_minus.seg\})$
    else $(trainResv' = trainResv \oplus \{train? \mapsto \langle\rangle\})$ fi fi
changes_only\{trainResv\}

---

4   Analysis

To generate a HAZOP analysis of the train case study, we need to interpret each
of the HAZOP keywords in the context of the Sum specification of the system.
Table 1 gives example interpretations for several example HAZOP keywords.

We model the scenario, using Sum, and using each keyword in turn examine
the effect of each type of deviation. For each such deviation, we generate a
corresponding Sum operation which is substituted in the trace to produce the
failure trace for that keyword. In this paper, we do not describe a complete
analysis of the train case study. Instead we examine one operation in one scenario,

for one of the keywords in Table 1. The scenario we choose to examine involves reserving a new section of track for one train, followed by a release of the formerly occupied section of track, and then reserving the formerly occupied track for a second (following) train. The scenario is depicted in Figure 2. Train "B" reserves from block-limit board 3 to board 4, releasing the section of track between 2 and 3, then train "A" reserves from board 1 to board 2. Formally, the scenario is as follows (we assume initialisation of the system according to the *init* schema, and suitable invocations of *AddTrain*, *Move* and *Reserve* to place the system in the state shown in Figure 2):

$$Reserve \mathbin{\substack{\circ\\\circ}} Release \mathbin{\substack{\circ\\\circ}} Reserve$$

Note that for the train positions shown in Figure 2, this sequence of operations will not be permitted to complete, since otherwise overlapping track reservations will result. To analyse failures for this scenario that lead to hazards, we need to determine failure operations corresponding to each of the keywords in Table 1 for each operation. The operation we examine in this example is the *Release* operation. These failure operations are defined in the *TrainSystem* module. For the "No" operation, we substitute the empty operation *Skip*.

For the "Other" operation, we substitute *Reserve*. For the "More" and "Less" operations, we substitute for the *units* input (u?) of *Release* (the t? input parameter is dimensionless and therefore cannot be analysed for deviation using the "More" and "Less" keywords). The u? input of *Release* defines the number of segments of track (between block-limit boards) that the train releases. The "Repeated" operation is modelled as a repetition of *Release* in the scenario.

For example, for the "More" keyword, we can model a failure of the *Release* operation in which the driver releases too much track (i.e., including some track which they are currently travelling over).

$$
\begin{aligned}
ReleaseMore == Release \wedge \big[\exists\, p : \mathbb{N};\ s : segment\ \bullet \\
s.seg = trainResv(train?) \wedge trainPosn(train?) = p\ \wedge \\
((direction? = forward \wedge s.s + units? > p)\ \vee \\
(direction? = reverse \wedge s.s - units? < p)) \big]
\end{aligned}
$$

Further, we need to formulate hazard conditions. Two conditions are formulated, the second ($trainPosn(t_1) \in \operatorname{ran} trainResv(t_2)$) defines the hazard which arises from the failure operation *ReleaseMore*.

```
┌─ Hazard ──────────────────────────────────────────────────────
│  ∃ t₁, t₂ : trainId • t₁ ≠ t₂ ∧ ran trainResv(t₁) ∩ ran trainResv(t₂) ≠ ∅ ∨
│     trainPosn(t₁) ∈ ran trainResv(t₂)
└───────────────────────────────────────────────────────────────
```

It is straight-forward to demonstrate that the post-condition of *ReleaseMore* produces an overall goal state for the scenario that is a hazard condition. For example, taking the example shown in Figure 2, the state on the left holds at the commencement of the scenario while following the completion of the scenario the state on the right holds:

$$trainPosn(A) = 2 \qquad\qquad trainPosn'(A) = 2$$
$$trainPosn(B) = 3 \qquad\qquad trainPosn'(B) = 3$$
$$trainResv(A) = \langle 1, 2 \rangle \qquad\qquad trainResv'(A) = \langle 1, 2, 3 \rangle$$
$$trainResv(B) = \langle 3, 4 \rangle \qquad\qquad trainResv'(B) = \langle 4, 5 \rangle$$

Then the following predicate holds, and hence there is a hazard:

$$trainPosn(B) \in \mathrm{ran}\ trainResv(A)$$

5   Animation

We have used the Possum specification animation tool to explore behaviours of the system that incorporate failure operations. The Possum animator enables a sequence of operations of the specification to be invoked and the resultant system state to be explored. We have designed a proof-of-concept prototype that generates the appropriate input for the Possum animation tool based on supplied lists of keywords and operations for analysis. The tool has been coded as a "plug-in" to the Possum animator, so that it can directly interface with the animation engine. The use of the Possum animator as a model-checking tool has been previously explored by Atchison, Lindsay and Tombs in [ ]. The user-interface for our tool is depicted in Figure 3. The user of our tool selects the keywords for

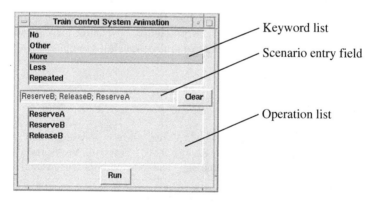

Fig. 3. User-interface of the analysis tool "plug-in" for Possum

analysis from a keyword list and defines the sequence of operations comprising the scenario under consideration by clicking on operation names in the operation list. For the prototype, operations must be parameterless, but in a complete implementation, operations could accept parameters and the system would check each possible interpretation of the "More" and "Less" keywords accordingly. We only consider simple sequential tasks, but the method could be readily extended to consider alternate, non-deterministic and concurrent tasks. The tool relies on the failure operations having names of the form #Opname#Failure, e.g., if #Opname is "ReleaseB" (i.e., a parameterisation of *Release* for Train "B" in the scenario under consideration) and #Failure is "More", then the generated operation name is "ReleaseBMore". The specification must contain operations corresponding to "ReleaseB" and "ReleaseBMore".

The tool calls the Possum animator to invoke the generated operation sequences. To simplify analysis of the resultant system state, we add a boolean attribute *hazard* to the module specification for the system. The value of *hazard* is recomputed each time an operation is invoked, and the result of the invocation of an operation sequence is recorded by the tool, along with the corresponding keyword and operation in the sequence.

6   Conclusions

We have shown how a simple safety-critical system, drawn from an industrial case study, can be modelled formally, and how the formal model and task analysis can be used as the basis of a HAZOP analysis. Our method produces a formal model, based on a task analysis of the system, in terms of objects, actions, tasks and goals. Our analysis uses scenarios as a mechanism for exploring the behaviour of the system when failures occur. For each action of the specification, corresponding failure actions are defined. There is one failure action for each keyword from the HAZOP analysis. The failure action can be substituted for the original action in the scenario, and the outcomes compared to formal definitions of hazard conditions. By using formal models, the identification of failures as constituting hazards is more precise. In particular, by using formal models, we are able to automate the process of hazard analysis, using specification animation tools.

References

1. B. Atchison, P. Lindsay, and D. Tombs. A case study in software safety assurance using formal methods. Technical Report 99-31, Software Verification Research Centre, School of Information Technology, The University of Queensland, Brisbane 4072, Australia. 379
2. M. F. Chudleigh and J. N. Clare. The benefits of SUSI: Safety Analysis of User System Interaction. In *SAFECOMP'93: Proceedings of the 12th International Conference on Computer Safety, Reliability and Security*. Springer-Verlag, 1993. 371
3. B. Fields, M. Harrison, and P. Wright. THEA: Human Error Analysis for Requirements Definition. Technical Report YCS-294, The University of York, 1997. 372
4. W. Johnston and L. Wildman. The Sum Reference Manual. Software Verification Research Centre TR99-21, The University of Queensland, November 1999. 372
5. B. Kirwan. Human reliability assessment. In *Evaluation of Human Work*, chapter 28. Taylor and Francis, 1990. 372

6. B. Kirwan, editor. *A Guide to Practical Human Reliability Assessment.* Taylor and Francis, 1994. 371

7. B. A. Leathley. HAZOP Approach to Allocation of Function in Safety Critical Systems. In *Proc. ALLFN'97: Revisiting the Allocation of Functions Issue - New Perspectives: Vol 1*, pages 331–343. IEA Press, 1997. 371

8. I. MacColl and D. Carrington. Specifying interactive systems in Object-Z and CSP. In *Integrated Formal Methods (IFM'99)*, pages 335–352. Springer, 1999. 372

9. Ministry of Defence. Draft Interim Defence Standard 00-58/1: A Guideline for HAZOP Studies on Systems which include a Programmable Electronic System. Directorate of Standardization, 1995. 371

10. M. B. Rosson and J. M. Carroll. Extending the Task-Artifact Framework: Scenario-Based Design of Smalltalk Applications. In H. R. Hartson and D. Hix, editors, *Advances in human-computer interaction*, volume 9, chapter 2, pages 31–57. Norwood, 1993. 372

11. J. W. Senders and N. P. Moray, editors. *Human Error: Cause, Prediction and Reduction.* Lawrence Erlbaum Associates, 1991. 371

12. J. M. Spivey. *The Z notation: a Reference Manual.* Prentice-Hall, 2nd edition, 1992. 374

Failure Mode and Effect Analysis for Safety-Critical Systems with Software Components

Tadeusz Cichocki [1] and Janusz Górski [2]

[1] Adtranz Zwus
Modelarska 12, 40-142 Katowice, Poland
tadeusz.cichocki@pl.adtranz.com
[2] Technical University of Gdańsk
Narutowicza 11/12, 80-952 Gdańsk, Poland
jango@pg.gda.pl

Abstract. One of possible ways to achieve a very high level of confidence in a system is to develop its adequate model and then to analyse the properties of this model. The paper presents how object oriented modelling extended with formal specifications is used to support FMEA of software intensive systems. The paper refers to the case study of a computerised railway signalling system.

1   Introduction

As a result of the progress in technology development an increasing number of applications include a software component which can directly affect risks associated with the system. In some applications, e.g. rail and air transportation, medical, nuclear, a very high level of confidence that the system will not do any harm has to be achieved before the system is commissioned to use. The criteria to be fulfilled and the guidance how to do this are provided by numerous national, international and sectoral standards and regulations, e.g. [5], [6], [4].

One of possible ways of achieving a very high level of confidence in the system is to develop its adequate model and then to analyse the properties of this model. If the model is a valid representation of the problem under consideration, the properties of the model can be understood as the properties of the real system. To increase confidence in the analytical results, the model and the associated analytical framework are often formal, i.e. are represented in terms of mathematical objects.

In this paper we demonstrate how object oriented modelling extended with formal notations, namely Z [20] and CSP [17] are used to model a problem related to computer based railway signalling in order to support FMEA (*Failure Mode and Effect Analysis*) [2], [3] of this system. Section 2 refers to the related works. Section 3 gives a rationale for the presented approach. Sections 4 and 5 demonstrate how object-oriented modelling was used to our case study system. Section 6 give more detail on performing FMEA on this system. The conclusions are given in section 7.

F. Koornneef and M. van der Meulen (Eds.): SAFECOMP 2000, LNCS 1943, pp. 382-394, 2000.

2   Related Works

Identification of the system architecture, modelling of functional dependencies between identified components, developing the inventory of their potential faults, and identification of error propagation scenarios initiated by those faults are the basic activities of FMEA [11]. The technique is commonly used for mechanical and/or electrical equipment. Its direct application to software encountered some difficulties, however, and required some extensions and modifications. Present standards, e.g. IEC 812 [11] and EN 50128 [5] recommend application of FMEA to software. When applied to software, FMEA is often known under the name SEEA - *Software Error Effect Analysis*. IEC 812 stresses limits in the scope of the analyses while including software. FMEA is also recommended for hardware parts of systems to extend requirements for the embedded software [14], [12]. A general approach of performing SEEA was presented in [15] where software was specified by data flows. The method aims at introducing safety constraints early in software development. Data paths are checked, potential errors are systematically searched for in the specifications, and when discovered, are eliminated or mitigated by applying proper fault avoidance or fault tolerance approaches. In [16] and [7] some further extensions of SEEA were proposed as well as suggestions on how SEEA can be integrated with other safety techniques.

Our approach differs from the previous works in two respects. Firstly, we choose object oriented modelling as the base for system description on the assumption that this provides for including both, software and hardware aspects in a common modelling framework. Secondly, we investigate a possibility to apply formal methods in order to support a systematic search for failure modes and to analyse the impact of failures.

3   Overview of the Approach

We have chosen the object-oriented framework to represent the system architecture. The advantages of the object orientation in the context of FMEA analysis include:

- provision of a common framework within which various system components can be represented (software, hardware, people),
- stress on univocal system decomposition and component independence (precisely written 'contracts' for object interfaces),
- covering static, dynamic and functional aspects of the system (e.g. [19], [18]),
- flexibility and stability: the models relatively easily can be modified, and modifications are usually localised in a limited number of objects,
- "smooth" transition from analysis to design and code: the objects identified during the analysis stage have their direct representation in implementation.

To provide for precision and unambiguity we extended the object-oriented model with its formal specification. Following [8] and [10] we have represented the object structure, object states, object operations and system state invariants in terms of Z schemas [20] and the dynamic aspects of object co-operation by using the CSP [17] notation. Within this framework we model faults and then analyse the consequences of those faults. By a *fault* we mean any deviation from desired properties of objects or their interaction, including disturbances of event timing and precedence. Faults may manifest themselves as *failures* of components, represented as a negation of the component function's desired result (its post-condition) or negation of any other assumption made while specifying the desired behaviour of the component (e.g. the pre-condition of the function or the state invariant of the component). In the CSP-based specification we represent them as additional *fault events*. Consequently the specification is extended by the cases handling the fault events occurrences.

Like in the standard FMEA, we develop *complete* lists of component failures. Two *domains of failure* are analysed and, respectively, two tables are constructed, consistent with the usual classification of defects in software [1], [13]:

- *Data Table,* involving communication failures and input deviations, used to analyse data dependencies and software interface errors, and
- *Event Table,* involving process failures and constraints on software states, used to analyze the effects of failures and deviations in outputs, possibly caused by software that fails to function correctly.

The general procedure of FMEA, based on the formal specifications, includes the activities to:

- develop an object-oriented model of the system,
- formalise the components of the model and its structure,
- develop an inventory of possible component failures,
- argue on the completeness of the list of failures,
- relate the effects of anticipated lower level faults to the higher level assumptions and failure lists.

In the subsequent sections we demonstrate some of those steps in reference to the Line Block System case study.

4   Line Block System – Object Model

The Line Block System (LBS) is supposed to control railway traffic on a rail track between two stations. It uses light signals shown on semaphores, each protecting a line segment of the rail track. Each segment is continuously tested in order to determine its occupation or its availability to move a train toward the next segment. The main goal is then to maintain separation of trains on the track while maintaining smooth passing of trains in the required direction.

An object-oriented model of LBS is shown in Fig.1. At the highest abstraction level, the LBS system is composed of the *operator*, rail track *sectors* and *trains*. Rail track sectors are further specialised from the point of view of an arbitrary sector (called *block*) and divided into sectors which are before (*units_before*) and after (*units_next*) the block. The block is further decomposed into train *detecting* device, train *signalling* device and *Line Block Controller* (LBC). The association *Line_Block_Control_Rules* describes the dependencies between the objects, reflecting the basic rules defined by the Polish State Railways (PKP) regulations. For instance, one of them requires that:

Safety Requirement	Each occupied line block must be protected by the 'STOP' signal displayed on its protecting SIGNALLING_DEVICE

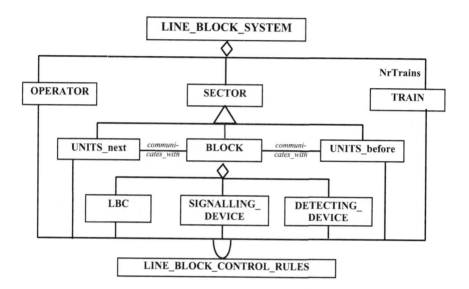

Fig.1. LINE_BLOCK_SYSTEM object structure

The above rules and the properties of objects of Fig.1 are expressed using the Z notation. Because of the space limitations we just recall a sample of it.

∪ **Safety_Requirement**
→ LB_Traffic_direction : {-1, 0, 1}   -- '1' corresponds to the traffic
→ DETECTING_DEVICE   -- direction *'from right to left'*,
→ SIGNALLING_DEVICE   -- '-1' to the opposite direction,
→   -- and '0' denotes *'no traffic direction defined'*
∩ _____
→ (DETECTING_DEVICE.Detection = YES & LB_Traffic_direction = 1) ⇒
→ SIGNALLING_DEVICE.Signalisation_1 ∈ {S0, S1}
∠ _____

Safety_Requirement schema defines a state invariant of the object BLOCK.

Comment. The attribute *DETECTING_DEVICE.Detection* indicates if a block is occupied by a train. *LB_Traffic_direction = 1* means that the traffic direction is set to *'from right to left'* and the attribute *SIGNALLING_DEVICE.Signalisation_1* restricts possible signals that can be displayed to trains in such situation.

5   Line Block System – Dynamic Model

Each object is specified as a CSP process. As a train is passing through subsequent rail track sectors, the system state changes in response to the signals from train detectors. Fig.2 shows the event channels between rail track sectors and the channels from and to train detectors and semaphores.

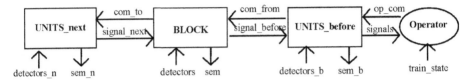

Fig. 2. Communication channels between objects

A formal specification of the behaviour of the BLOCK object of Fig.2 is given below. The text prefixed by '--' is a comment.

```
-- BLOCK process Specification
channel signal_before : {S0, S1, S2, S3, S4, S5}
channel signal_next : {S0, S1, S2, S3, S4, S5}
   -- Signals {S0, S1}, called 'STOP' signals, refuse the
   -- permission to move a train into the considered block
   -- ('S0' means 'dark' and 'S1' means 'red' ),
   -- and signals of {S2, S3, S4, S5} grant this permission.
channel sem : {S0, S1, S2, S3, S4, S5}
   -- shows signals on the semaphore protecting the block.
channel com_from, com_to
   -- carry the operator's commands (not developed here).
channel detectors : {IN, OUT}
   -- signals from train detectors

   -- The BLOCK process' alphabet is:
B = { |signal_before, signal_next, sem, detectors| }

BLOCK =
   detectors.IN →
       ( sem.S1 → signal_before.S1 → BLOCK
         [] sem.S0 → signal_before.S1 → BLOCK )
   [] detectors.OUT → BLOCK_not_occupied

BLOCK_not_occupied =
   signal_next.S0 → sem.S1 → signal_before.S1 → BLOCK
   []   signal_next.S1 → sem.S5 → signal_before.S5 → BLOCK
   []   signal_next.S2 → sem.S2 → signal_before.S2 → BLOCK
   []   signal_next.S3 → sem.S2 → signal_before.S2 → BLOCK
   []   signal_next.S4 → sem.S3 → signal_before.S3 → BLOCK
   []   signal_next.S5 → sem.S3 → signal_before.S3 → BLOCK
```

If the detector indicate the presence of a train in a block, the block's semaphore should signal S1 ('red light'). Otherwise the block considers the situation in the following unit (detected through the *signal_next* channel). The sequence: *detectors.IN* → *sem.S1* represents the BLOCK's desired (perfect) behaviour. We model *deviations* from this behaviour as visible events, offered by the object and activated by the environment. For instance, the specification includes the case for *sem.S0* (the 'dark' signal instead of the 'red' one). This specific case is classified by the railway regulations as a non-critical failure.

As it is shown in Fig.1, BLOCK is decomposed into its composite objects: LBC, SIGNALLING_DEVICE and DETECTING_DEVICE. In Fig.3 we show the communication structure that results from this decomposition.

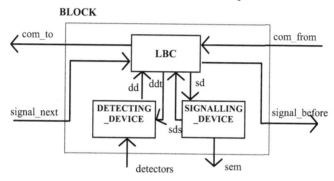

Fig. 3. Communication structure of the BLOCK component

The formal specification of the components of BLOCK follows.

```
-- LBC process Specification
channel signal_before : {S0, S1, S2, S3, S4, S5}
channel signal_next : {S0, S1, S2, S3, S4, S5}
channel com_from, com_to
   -- carry the operator's commands (not developed here).
channel dd : {IN, OUT}
   -- detecting device's output
channel ddt : {IN}
   -- DETECTING_DEVICE state test
channel sd : {S0, S1, S2, S3, S4, S5}
   -- setting the signalling device view
channel sds : {S0, S1, S2, S3, S4, S5}
   -- the signalling device state confirmation

   -- The LBC process' alphabet is:
L = {|signal_before, signal_next, dd, ddt, sd, sds|}

LBC = ddt.IN →
   ( dd.IN → sd.S1 → sds.S1 → signal_before.S1 → LBC
   [] dd.OUT → LBC_not_occupied )

LBC_not_occupied =
signal_next.S0 → sd.S0 → sds.S0 → signal_before.S1 → LBC
[] signal_next.S1 → sd.S5 → sds.S5 → signal_before.S5 → LBC
```

```
[] signal_next.S2 → sd.S2 → sds.S2 → signal_before.S2 → LBC
[] signal_next.S3 → sd.S2 → sds.S2 → signal_before.S2 → LBC
[] signal_next.S4 → sd.S3 → sds.S3 → signal_before.S3 → LBC
[] signal_next.S5 → sd.S3 → sds.S3 → signal_before.S3 → LBC
```

-- DETECTING_DEVICE process Specification
```
channel detectors : {IN, OUT}
channel dd : {IN, OUT}
channel ddt : {IN}

   -- The DETECTING_DEVICE process' alphabet is:
D = { |detectors, dd, ddt| }

DETECTING_DEVICE =
    detectors.IN → ddt.IN → dd.IN → DETECTING_DEVICE
    [] detectors.OUT → ddt.IN → dd.OUT → DETECTING_DEVICE
```

-- SIGNALLING_DEVICE process Specification
```
channel sem : {S0, S1, S2, S3, S4, S5}
   -- the signals shown by the signalling device
   -- (on the semaphore protecting the block)
channel sd : {S0, S1, S2, S3, S4, S5}
channel sds : {S0, S1, S2, S3, S4, S5}

   -- The SIGNALLING_DEVICE process' alphabet is:
S = { |sem, sd, sds| }

SIGNALLING_DEVICE =
    sd.S0 → sem.S0 → sds.S0 → SIGNALLING_DEVICE
    [] sd.S1 →
        ( sem.S1 → sds.S1 → SIGNALLING_DEVICE
        []
        sem.S0 → sds.S1 → SIGNALLING_DEVICE )
        -- failure of the sinchronisation on sem.S1
        -- by environmental choice
    [] sd.S2 → sem.S2 → sds.S2 → SIGNALLING_DEVICE
    [] sd.S3 → sem.S3 → sds.S3 → SIGNALLING_DEVICE
    [] sd.S4 → sem.S4 → sds.S4 → SIGNALLING_DEVICE
    [] sd.S5 → sem.S5 → sds.S5 → SIGNALLING_DEVICE
```

The BLOCK' composed of LBC, DETECTING_DEVICE and SIGNALLING_DEVICE processes is modelled as follows:

```
BLOCK' = DETECTING_DEVICE
                    | [D∩L] | LBC
                        | [L∩S] | SIGNALLING_DEVICE
```

The desired relation between the BLOCK specification (more abstract) and BLOCK' specification (more detailed), expressed in terms of the usual trace semantics of CSP processes [17] is as follows:

```
BLOCK  ⊑  BLOCK' \ {dd, ddt, sd, sds}
```

i.e. the more detailed specification should be consistent with the more abstract one. This verification step is to be performed with the help of tools.

6   Performing FMEA

6.1   Analysing Data Failures

Systematic review of component failures is supported by a checklist of generic component faults. From the data modelling point of view we distinguish:

- a change of an attribute value outside its type range,
- a change of an object invariant.

To illustrate the first case, let us consider the following Z specification of BLOCK.

∪ **BLOCK**_____

→ Traffic_direction : {-1, 0, 1}
→ Occupation : {YES, NO}
→ Signalisation_1: {S0, S1, S2, S3, S4, S5}
→ Signalisation_-1: {S0, S1, S2, S3, S4, S5}
∩ _____
→ Traffic_direction = 1 ⇒
→ ((Occupation = YES ⇒ Signalisation_1 ∈ {S0, S1})
→ & (Occupation = NO ⇒ Signalisation_1 ∈ {S2, S3, S4, S5}))
→ & Signalisation_-1 ∈ {S0, S1}
∠ _____

While analysing possible deviations of attribute values we refer to the interpretation of the attribute in the real world. For instance, for the attribute *Occupation,* its expected range of values is {YES, NO}. However the experience shows that we should also consider a value 'Y/N' corresponding to the train detection problems. Similarly, knowing that the attribute *Signalisation_1* represents possible 'legal' combinations of semaphore lights, from the physical implementation we can realise that also other, not 'legal' combinations, e.g. 'red+green', are possible and therefore should be considered. Those extensions of attribute range that are assessed as being likely (although undesired) should be then included in further analyses.

The second case is concerned with state invariants. Below we show the failure condition resulting from contradicting the *Safety_Requirement* (a state invariant) given in Section 5. By definition, a violation of such property (being a part of the top level *Safety specification*) constitutes a hazardous state of the system. For instance, the contradiction of the *Safety_Requirement* of Section 5 means that a train occupies a given rail track segment (*DETECTING_DEVICE.Detection = YES*) and at the same time the protecting semaphore's state is different than 'STOP' (compare Table 1). Protection against such situation has to be implemented in the LBC,

DETECTING_DEVICE and SIGNALLING_DEVICE objects. Violation of properties of components can impact safety requirements in indirect ways. Systematic search of the specification aims at discovering the impact the violating a property of a component has on fulfilment of the specified safety requirements of the system (note that contradicting a component invariant does not necessarily implies that a safety requirement is contradicted; some components are mission oriented and can have no impact on safety). The next step is to consider possible modifications of the specification that can decrease/remove this impact.

Table 1. State invariant failure condition

Condition	Consequence
DETECTING_DEVICE.Detection = YES & LB_Traffic_direction = 1 & SIGNALLING_DEVICE.Signalisation_1 ∉ {S0, S1}	**Hazard:** signals other then S0 or S1 could be interpreted as *permission* signals

6.2   Analysing Communication Failures

An occurrence of a communication between two objects (e.g. one object invokes an operation of another object) is the result of simultaneous execution by the CSP processes representing those objects of the matching communication commands. From the point of view of BLOCK, the train detectors read the state of 'reality' (the rail track state, in this case) and invoke a BLOCK operation associated with the *detectors* channel. This operation, let us call it *Monitor* (as it monitors the state of the rail track) assumes that the signals received from the environment consistently represent the situation on the rail track (the operations' *precondition*). It also assumes that the events signalled through the channel belong to the predefined domain (the *guard* condition of the operation). Finally, as the result of the execution of the operation, some visible effects are observed on the interface of BLOCK (this is specified by the *post-condition* associated with the operation).

The specification of the *Monitor* operation is given below. The operation is invoked through the *detectors* channel and its effects are visible through the *sem* channel.

```
pre Monitor =
      ('occupied rail track generates detectors.IN event and
       non-occupied, detectors.OUT event')
-- This condition is not formalised here.
guard Monitor = ( detectors : {IN, OUT} )
post Monitor = ( ( detectors.IN  ⇒ sem.[S0, S1] )
             & ( detectors.OUT  ⇒ sem.[S2, S3, S4, S5] ) )
```

Successful communication requires the conjunction of three conditions:

```
post op_sending  &  guard op_receiving  &  pre op_receiving.
```

The list of component failures (together with the impact of the failures) is represented in the following FMEA table:

Table 2. The structure of FMEA table

PROCESS: *name*			
Case	**Channel**	**Fault assumption**	**Corresponding deviations of ...**
(1)	(2)	(3)	(4)
INPUT Channels		¬ **guard** *op* ∨ ¬ **pre** *op* (*Data Table support*)	*availability and correctness of operation's input data*
OUTPUT Channels		¬ **post** *op* (*Event Table support*)	*correctness of operation's performance and data transformation*

In the case of *Monitor* operation the input conditions to be considered include:

```
¬ pre Monitor =    ('non-occupied rail track          (case 1a)
                   generates detectors.IN event or
                   occupied, detectors.OUT event')    (case 1b)
¬ guard Monitor =  ¬ ( detectors : {IN, OUT} )
                   = detectors.I/O                    (case 1c)
```

The results of the analysis are shown in Table 3.

Table 3. FMEA table for the BLOCK object (an extract)

PROCESS: **BLOCK**			
Case	**Channel**	**Fault assumption**	**Corresponding deviations of ...**
(1)	(2)	(3)	(4)
1a	detectors	detectors.IN - *failed interpretation of the rail segment non-occupation state*	sem.[S0, S1] - 'STOP' signals, according to the *perfect* specification - **system availability lost.**
1b		detectors.OUT - *failed interpretation of the rail segment occupation state*	sem.[S2, S3, S4, S5] - one of the *permission* signals - **hazard state.**
1c		detectors.I/O - *nonidentified rail track state* (*new environment offer*)	**design decision**: to extend specification by *detectors.I/O* occurrence and consequences.
2a	sem	*successful* detectors.IN *and failed output on* **sem**	sem.[S2, S3, S4, S5] - one of the *permission* signals - **hazard state.**

Using the information included in the above table we can modify the specification of BLOCK in order to prevent or reduce the risk associated with identified hazardous situations. An example modification follows (the extensions are shown in bold):

```
channel detectors : { IN, OUT, I/O }
BLOCK = detectors.IN →
            ( sem.S1 → signal_before.S1 → BLOCK
            []
            sem.S0 → signal_before.S1 → BLOCK )
        []
        detectors.OUT → BLOCK_not_occupied
        []
        detectors.I/O → sem.S1 → signal_before.S1 → BLOCK
```

On a more detailed level (shown in Fig.3) this extension also requires an extension of the specification of BLOCK's components, to resolve the *detectors.I/O* event acceptance in DETECTING_DEVICE and to show how LBC handles the event *dd.I/O*.

7   Conclusions

The paper presents application of FMEA to a software intensive safety related system. One of our objectives was to extend FMEA in such a way that it can be applied to software without significant changes in the overall method. The core of the proposed extension is to base the FMEA process on formalised object oriented specifications. This way we can better handle the problems that are software specific. Another objective is to fit the proposed method into present engineering practice in the company, the railway signalling systems developer. The project is still in progress and presently is performed in parallel to the traditional forms of analysis and documentation practised in the company. What can be already concluded about the proposed approach is:

- at the first stages of the project we achieved a significant concentration on relevant details and a strong developer guidance to the problems and solutions,
- the formal notation forces designers to concentrate on system structure and properties at the same time focusing attention on a proper abstraction level,
- the formal specifications support systematic search for possible deviations and inconsistencies, and support the analysis of their consequences,
- the proposed notations significantly improve precision, completeness and compactness of the specifications. Although it needed some training in formal notations, the approach could be used in an everyday engineering practice.

As the specifications grow in size a tool support is unavoidable. This is presently one of our concerns and we are examining various possibilities of choosing from the existing tools (e.g. the FDR tool of Formal Systems (Europe) Ltd. [17], [9]).

References

1. Barbacci, B. R., Klein, M. H., Weinstock, C. B.: Principles for Evaluating the Quality Attributes of a Software Architecture, Software Engineering Institute, Carnegie Mellon University. Technical Report, CMU/SEI-96-TR-036, March 1997
2. Cichocki, T., Górski, J.: Safety assessment of computerized railway signalling equipment. Proc. of CENELEC SC9XA/WGA10 Workshop, Münich (Germany), May 11, 1999
3. Cichocki, T., Górski, J.: Safety assessment of computerized railway signalling equipment supported by formal techniques. Proc. of FMERail Workshop #5, Toulouse (France), September, 22-24, 1999
4. Defence Standard 00-55: Requirements for Safety Related Software in Defence Equipment (Part 1&2), Issue 1, UK Ministry of Defence, 1997
5. EN 50128: Railway applications. Software for Railway Control and Protection Systems, CENELEC, Final Draft version, July 1998
6. ENV 50129: Railway applications. Safety Related Electronic Systems for Signalling, CENELEC, May 1998
7. Fenelon P., McDermid J. A., Nicholson M., Pumfrey D. J., Towards Integrated Safety Analysis and Design. ACM Applied Computing Review, 2(1), pp. 21-32, 1994
8. Fischer, C.: Combining CSP and Z, Univ. of Oldenburg. Technical Report, TRCF-97-1
9. Formal Systems (Europe) Ltd.: *Failures-Divergence Refinement, FDR2 User Manual*, 24 October 1997
10. Heisel, M.: Methodology and Machine Support for the Application of Formal Techniques in Software Engineering, Habilitation Thesis, Technische Universität Berlin, Berlin, 1997
11. IEC 812 (1985): Procedure for failure mode and effects analysis (FMEA), TC56
12. J-C. Laprie, B. Littlewood, Quantitative Assessment of Safety-Critical Software: Why and How? Predictably Dependable Computing Systems (PDCS) Technical Report no. 45, ESPRIT BRA Project 3092, February 1991
13. Lutz, R. R., Woodhouse, R. M.: Requirements Analysis Using Forward and Backward Search. (Annals of Software Engineering, 1997) JPL California Institute of Technology Technical Report, May 2, 1997
14. NASA-GB-A201, NASA Software Assurance Guidebook, September 1989
15. E. Noe-Gonzales, The Software Error Effect Analysis and the Synchronous Data Flow Approach to Safety Software: Method, Results, Operational Lessons. Proc. of SAFECOMP'94, pp. 163-171
16. Papadopoulos Y., McDermid J., Sasse R., Heiner G., Analysis and Synthesis of the Behaviour of Complex Programmable Electronic Systems in conditions of Failure. Reliability Engineering and System Safety Journal (forthcoming, 2000), Elsevier Science Limited (*an extension of SAFECOMP'99 paper*)
17. Roscoe, A. W.: The Theory and Practice of Concurrency, Prentice Hall, 1998, ISBN 0-13-674409-5, pp. xv + 565
18. Rumbaugh, J., Blaha, M., Premerlani, W., Eddy, F., Lorensen, W.: *Object-Oriented Modelling and Design*, Prentice-Hall Int., 1991

19. D'Souza, D., Wills, A. C.: Objects, Components, and Frameworks with UML. The Catalysis Approach, Addison Wesley Longman, Inc. 1998
20. Spivey, J. M.: The Z Notation: A Reference Manual, First published by Prentice Hall International (UK) Ltd., 1992 (Second edition), ISBN 0-13-629312-3

Risk Ordering of States in Safecharts

Nimal Nissanke and Hamdan Dammag

School of Computing, Information Systems and Mathematics, South Bank University
103 Borough Road, London SE1, 0AA
nissanke@sbu.ac.uk

Abstract. *Safecharts* [ ] are a variant of Statecharts developed exclusively for use in safety critical systems design. Its distinctive features include a safety oriented characterisation of transitions, restriction of default states to safe states, resolution of any nondeterminism in favour of safe transitions and representation of failures of items of equipment. These are achieved through ordering of system states according to risk levels. As a matter of principle, Safecharts permit transitions only between states with known risk levels. As a result, the effectiveness of Safecharts depends largely on the extent of coverage of the state space by the risk ordering relation. *Risk band* is a new concept used for default interpretation of risk levels of such states, both to alert the designer to the implications of any inadequacies in hazard analysis and to reduce nondeterministic behaviour. An example drawn from nuclear industry demonstrates the application of Safecharts.

Keywords: Safety, Statecharts, risk ordering, risk assessment, failures, nuclear safety

1   Introduction

Safecharts [ ] are a variant of Statecharts [,] specialising in safety critical systems. It exploits fully the traditional virtues of Statecharts: visual appeal, ease of abstraction, modular and hierarchical representation of systems, mathematical rigour, etc. However, it further recognises some of the imperatives of safety critical systems design: the ability to focus on safety matters without being distracted by functional issues, the ability to evaluate implications of function on safety, ensuring safety provisions for each and every unsafe function, etc. These are obviously attributes of any systematic approach to design.

In achieving the above goals, main strategy of Safecharts is to separate function and safety, but in such a way that each can be reviewed independently but without losing sight of the system as whole. In terms of the representation, this amounts to maintaining two separate 'layers', one layer depicting the system purely from a functional point of view while the other addressing the requirements and features required on safety grounds. The role of the former is fulfilled by conventional Statecharts, whereas the role of the latter is the exclusive domain of Safecharts. Obviously, the two layers must be consistent with

F. Koornneef and M. van der Meulen (Eds.): SAFECOMP 2000, LNCS 1943, pp. 395–405, 2000.
© Springer-Verlag Berlin Heidelberg 2000

each other, spatially in terms of states and temporally with respect to transitions and their execution. The objective of this separation is to provide a sharper focus on safety issues and to force a disciplined approach to design through a clear prescription of what is required. In practical terms, on the one hand, the approach prevents inadvertent omission of design obligations and, on the other, conveys requirements of every safety feature fully and unambiguously. The most characteristic feature of Safecharts is the ordering of system states according to relative risk levels. The resulting risk ordering relation (risk graph) characterises transitions according to the nature of risk, either as a low-to-high risk transition or a high-to-low risk transition. As a matter of prudence, Safecharts do not permit transitions between states with unknown relative risk levels. As a result, many transitions, including those which can be functionally useful, could be potentially excluded between states lying in sparsely covered areas of the risk graph. Among the possible reasons for this are gaps in the hazard analysis and the lack of information, both questioning the adequacy of the risk ordering relation as a representation of actual requirements. This anomaly, whereby certain transitions could be barred unduly purely on the grounds of inadequacy of available knowledge, is overcome here by using the concept of *risk band*, giving a default interpretation of risk levels to states not covered by the risk ordering relation. A disagreement with this thus obliges the designer to clarify the relative risk levels of the states concerned.

2   Statecharts

A state in Statecharts is made up from simpler states as a hierarchy of their conjunctions or disjunctions. Thus, the simpler states can be (logically) AND-ed, or OR-ed, to form more complex states in a tree–structured manner. As a result, there are three kinds of state, AND, OR and BASIC. Both OR-state and AND-state consist of a number of substates; being in an OR-state means being in exactly one of its substate, while being in an AND-state means being in all of its substates simultaneously. A BASIC state is a state with no substates. Statecharts thus extend conventional finite state machines by AND/OR decomposition of states, resulting in a concept of 'depth' and a superstate-substate relation.

In diagrams, substates of an AND-state are indicated by a dashed line, while those of an OR-state by solid lines. For example, the superstate S in Figure 1 is an AND-state which has to be in both substates S_1 and S_2 simultaneously. However, S_1 is an OR-state and, hence, it must be either in G, H or K. S_2 is also an OR-state and it must be either in M or in N, where being in N means being in P and Q simultaneously.

Given any OR-state, it is possible to bring about a change in its current state by moving from its currently active substate to another substate. This is achieved by transitions. An OR-state, taken together with all transitions among its substates, thus form a directed graph, nodes representing states and arrows labelled transitions. The most general form of a transition label is a triple shown as $e[c]/a$, e being an event that triggers the transition, c a condition that guards the transition when e occurs, and a an action that is carried out precisely if and when the transition takes place. Once generated, the action a is broadcast to the whole Statechart, triggering, if applicable, other transitions in the system. Referring to Figure 1, the transition from G to H (in substate S_1) takes place only if G is active, the event e has taken place and the condition c is satisfied. Consequently, the action part a is generated and, hence, the transition from M to N in S_2. On the other hand, if it is the substate H which is active then the realisation of the condition c is enough to trigger the transition from H to G. The default state, pointed by an arrow, is a substate of an OR-state that is to be entered if any transition arriving at the OR-state does not have an explicitly specified substate for entry. For example, both G and M in Figure 1 are default states for S_1 and S_2 respectively.

Given an AND-state, no transitions are allowed between its substates. This is because an AND-state is in all its substates simultaneously; the latter being known as *parallel* states. However, such substates themselves may be OR-states, giving rise to the possibility of events being shared by some of them and the possibility of events exclusive to a particular substate. These two possibilities correspond respectively to synchronisation and independence of events and arise from the property of *orthogonality* of AND-states. For example, the occurrence of event m in Figure 1 causes the transformation from H to K in S_1 and the transformation from N to M in S_2 to occur simultaneously.

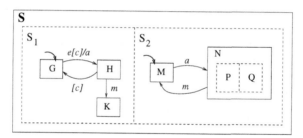

Fig. 1. Example of AND/OR decomposition of states

3   Safecharts

Safecharts maintain two separate layers of representation: *functional layer* capturing system's transformational behaviour purely from a functional point of view (using Statecharts in the conventional sense), and a *safety layer*. The latter consists of a *risk graph* (risk ordering relation $\sqsubseteq$ on system states) and a *safety clause* (an annotation of a condition or a constraint) against each transition between system states that differ in risk levels. There are two kinds of safety clause: a) a condition inhibiting transitions from low to high risk states, b) a timing constraint in the form of a mandatory deadline on transitions from high to low risk states. The latter kind of transition signifies the delivery of a service and is intended as a precautionary failure preventive measure or as a safety mechanism to avoid an imminent failure.

The meaning of the *risk ordering* relation $\sqsubseteq$ is such that for any two states s_1 and s_2, $s_1 \sqsubseteq s_2$ is true if and only if the risk level of s_1 is known to be less than, or equal to, the risk level of s_2. This assumes that risk levels are comparable, either quantitatively or qualitatively. The relation $\sqsubseteq$ can be decomposed into two relations: a partial order relation $\preccurlyeq$ (the risk level of s_1 being strictly lower than, or being the same as, that of s_2) and an equivalence relation $\approx$ (risk levels of s_1 and s_2 are known, or are assumed, to be identical). In order to facilitate integration of layers, by convention Safecharts maintain the positions of a given state in both layers of the diagram at the same level.

Safety is an issue because of the possibility of failures and, therefore, it is important that our formalism has the means to represent them. Failure modes themselves differ from one another in many different ways. The simplest form of abstraction would be to adopt two special OR-states for each component: IN (meaning a state of correct functioning) and OUT (meaning a failed state). The nature of these two states are such that IN $\preccurlyeq$ OUT. Associated with the states IN and OUT are two generic events: a nondeterministic internal event ε signifying a failure, and an external event μ signifying a maintenance or repair action which returns the component back to service. It follows from the above that ε is a low-to-high risk event, while μ is a high-to-low risk event.

Transitions in the functional layer are meaningful only within the IN state, whereas both IN and OUT states are important substates of the corresponding safety layer. Similarly, the generic events ε and μ have no relevance in the functional layer but only in the safety layer. However, the broadcasting property of Statecharts remain applicable to these generic events ε and μ in both layers, potentially having other effects elsewhere in the system. It is in this sense that the functional and safety layers are expected to be consistent with each other. The representation can be extended to include different failure modes by having a set of labelled OUT states and a corresponding set of ε and μ events.

Based on the risk ordering relation, Safecharts classify transitions into three categories: *safe* (high-to-low risk), *unsafe* (low-to-high risk) and *neutral* (between states of the same risk level). Relative to the specific relation used for comparing risk levels of states, $\sqsubseteq$ being the only such relation used so far, the above is an exhaustive classification and, thus, excludes transitions between states which are non-comparable by the chosen relation. The intention of such a strong restriction is to force the designer to resolve, as a matter of discipline, the risk levels of any non-comparable states, prior to introducing transitions between them. The reasoning behind this principle is prudence, because the presence of non-comparable states is likely to be a sign of an incomplete hazard and risk assessment and, hence, the introduction of transitions between such states also carries a certain risk, albeit a design risk.

Safecharts extend the general form of transition labelling $e[c]/a$ of Statecharts to $e\,[c]/a\,[l, u)\,\Psi[G]$, where e, c, a remain as in Section 2, $[l, u)$ is a right-open time interval from time l to time u, Ψ is a safety enforcement pattern specified using two alternative symbols: ⌐ and ⌐, and $[G]$ is a safety clause. Some of these fields are optional. $[l, u)$ is such that the transition concerned does not execute for at least l time units since its most recent enabling time. $t ⌐ [G]$ means that the transition t is forbidden to execute as long as G holds. $[l, u) ⌐ [G]$ means that the transition t is forced to execute within $[l, u)$ from whenever G begins to hold.

4   Risk Bands

The nature of the risk graph has certain implications. Consider a risk assessment process giving less attention to one part of the risk graph compared to the rest. Assuming that this is done on the basis of a risk ordering relation of the form ⊑, this could result, in extreme cases, in a few states being non-comparable with a large number of others, but themselves being mutually comparable. Figure 2(a) gives an example, where the state H happens to be non-comparable with the states D, G, I and J, and the state D with the states G and H. Consequently, if reliance is placed solely on ⊑, the principle of barring transitions between non-comparable states will exclude transitions in either direction between the state H, on the one hand, and the states D, G, I, J, on the other, and between other states.

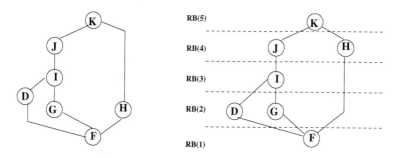

a) Before introducing risk bands   b) After introducing risk bands

Fig. 2. Non-comparable states in the risk graph

If such an extensive exclusion of transitions is undesirable, it might be worth questioning the appropriateness of the risk ordering relation ⊑. With this in mind, we introduce the concept of *risk band* as a way of enhancing the risk ordering relation. By definition, each state belongs to a unique risk band such that any states belonging to the same risk band are there precisely because, when taken pairwise, they are all either comparable by ≈ (explicitly stated to have an identical risk level) or non-comparable by ⊑. The intended use of risk bands is to allow only transitions between pairs of states either belonging to different risk bands, or belonging to the same risk band but comparable by $\approx$. By the same token, no transitions are allowed between states of the same risk band, unless they are comparable by $\approx$. Risk bands are thus a default scheme for ranking states according to risk levels when $\sqsubseteq$ is inadequate on its own. Obviously, unacceptability of such a default interpretation of risks should prompt the designer to establish the risk levels of the states concerned more accurately.

Given the risk ordering relation $\sqsubseteq$, and assuming that risk bands are indexed numerically from 1 to some n, risk bands of states may defined according to the following set of rules:

(i) Maximal elements in the partial order relation $\preccurlyeq$, and states related by $\approx$ but with no succeeding states according to $\prec$, are in the highest risk band n.

(ii) Any state s with just a single immediate successor state in risk band i according to $\prec$ is in risk band $i - 1$. However, if a state s has more than one immediate successor state, then it has a risk band one less than the lowest of the risk bands of its immediately successor states.

(iii) For any states s_1 and s_2, if $s_1 \approx s_2$ then both states s_1 and s_2 are in the same risk band.

Figure 2(b) illustrates the above rules using the risk graph given in Figure 2(a). As a result, transitions between H and D can now be introduced. The number of prohibited transitions can thus be reduced significantly, in this case, to transitions just between H and J, and D and G.

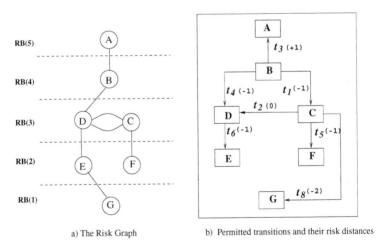

a) The Risk Graph   b) Permitted transitions and their risk distances

Fig. 3. Risk bands

The concept of risk band, together with the resulting numerical indexing scheme, allows a different basis for classifying transitions into *safe, unsafe* and *neutral* transitions, namely, depending on the risk bands of the source and target states of the transition concerned. For instance, a transition from state s_2 to s_1 is said to be *safe* if s_1 resides in a lower risk band compared to s_2.

A further advantage of risk bands is the possibility of extending the scope of rules in [ ] for resolution of nondeterminism, where transitions are prioritised according to the risk level of their target states so that lower the risk level of its target state, higher is the priority enjoyed by a given transition. This approach is thus different from other approaches such as that in [ ], based on the scope of transitions, and that in [ ], based on the hierarchy of their source state.

A deficiency of the approach in [ ] is that two conflicting transitions with a common source state enjoy the same priority if their target states are non-comparable by $\sqsubseteq$, irrespective of the relative positions of the latter states in the risk graph. This is overcome using the concept of *risk distance* of transitions, defined as the number of band boundaries between the source and target states of each transition and calculated by subtracting the risk band index of the source state from that of the target state. Thus, safe transitions have negative risk distances, unsafe transitions positive risk distances and neutral transitions zero risk distances. In Figure 3 risk distances are given in parentheses beside the transition labels.

Transitions can now be prioritised according to risk distances so that smaller the risk distance higher is the priority of a given transition. Thus, referring to Figure 3, the transition t_8 enjoys a higher priority over t_5. However, as in the case of transitions t_1 and t_4, comparison of risk distances of conflicting transitions alone cannot always resolve any nondeterminism. Such non-deterministic behaviour can be resolved by considering the cumulative risk distances of future transitions of conflicting transitions. Note that t_4 has only one future transition, namely t_6, whereas t_1 has two future transitions, namely t_5 and t_8. Therefore, cumulative risk distances of future transitions of t_1 and t_4 are -2 and -3, although the latter assumes a more optimistic outcome of the execution of t_8. Arguably, it is therefore better to resolve the nondeterminism between t_1 and t_4 in favour of t_1 based on cumulative risk distances of their future transitions. Cumulative risk distances of future transition paths thus provide us with a more sensible way to resolve any nondeterminism which cannot be resolved otherwise. It is possible that nondeterminism will continue to persist even when future transition paths are considered, but this kind of non-determinism is considered a *safe non-determinism* because all outcomes are identical in terms of safety or risks.

5   An Example from Nuclear Industry

This section illustrates the use of Safecharts by modelling certain aspects of a nuclear power plant. The reactor of the plant is a thick steel vessel housing the *core*, a bundle of large number of fuel rods, the site of the nuclear reaction. The intensity of the nuclear reaction is controlled by the lowering, or retraction, of cadmium *control rods*. These rods are held above the core by magnetic clamps, which in emergencies release the control rods into the core, bringing the nuclear reaction to a halt in an action called *scram*. In pressurised water reactors, the heat from the nuclear fission is extracted by means of water circulating through the core, which at the same time plays the role of a coolant that prevents fuel rods from overheating. The water is maintained under an appropriate pressure so that it does not boil under the extreme temperatures prevailing inside the reactor. Because of the risks involved through possible release of radioactivity into the surrounding environment, the moderating water is circulated in a closed loop called the *primary circuit*. The primary circuit runs through a heat exchanger and, in the process, passes its heat on to water circulating through another loop called the *secondary circuit* situated outside the reactor giving rise to steam used for creating electricity. A possible accident is the so–called *loss of coolant accident* (LOCA) in the primary circuit, leading progressively to extreme temperatures and pressures, cracks in the reactor and, eventually, to explosion and large scale release of radiation. In the case of such an event, operation of a *relief valve* in the vessel can relieve the pressure, by letting the coolant to flow out into a safe drainage system.

A chain of events that developed in the course of the Three Mile Island (TMI) accident in 1979 [,] involved the above components. As a consequence of an unexpected closure of a valve in the secondary circuit, a state of rampant temperature was reached in the coolant of the primary circuit. This has prompted the relief valve to open and, subsequently, to lower the control rods. Although these actions have helped to bring down the pressure, the relief valve malfunctioned and remained stuck–opened, while a sensor mistakenly confirmed that the valve has closed, for the sensor has been attached not to the valve directly but to the solenoid operating the valve.

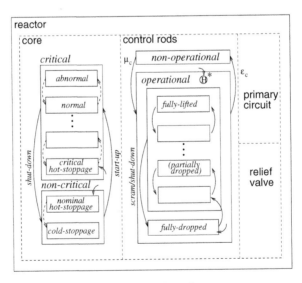

Fig. 4. Safechart model of reactor core

Figures 4, 5 and 6 present a simplified Safechart model of such a reactor. For reasons of space, functional and safety layers have been integrated. For clarity labelling of transitions are minimal and just indicative. Arrows shown in dashed lines are internal transitions that cannot be controlled directly but are observable after their occurrence through the monitoring equipment, whereas arrows shown in solid lines are controllable system transitions.

The overall system, reactor, consists of several AND-ed components: core, control rods, relief valve and primary circuit. The core consists of two OR-substates: *critical* and *non-critical*, each decomposed further into finer OR-substates. Transitions *start-up* and *shut-down*, brought about by the movements of control rods, enable alternations between the *critical* and *non-critical* substates. By having an OR-substate *non-operational*, our abstraction of the AND-substate control rods allows for a failure in control rods. Its *operational* substate has a safe state for initialisation and a default entry H^* by history, to be taken at the repair event μ_c, into the lowest level substate where the subsystem was last prior to leaving the substate *operational* when the failure signified by the generic event ϵ_c occurred.

The AND-substate primary circuit, expanded in Figure 5, is another component with several attributes such as *pressure* and *temperature* that cannot be directly controlled. Obviously, a proper modelling of its behaviour requires consideration of valves and pumps affecting the substates *flow* and *coolant content* in its representation.

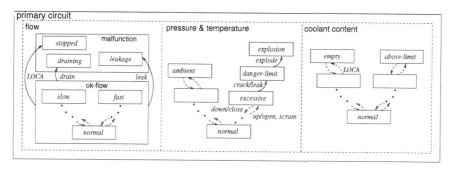

Fig. 5. Safechart model of primary circuit

The failure of the relief valve, shown in Figure 6, is modelled in a manner similar to control rods, except for the decomposition of the failure state *stuck* into two specific OR-substates *stuck-closed* and *stuck-opened*, which are entered depending on the generic events ϵ_{v1} and ϵ_{v2} respectively. The representation corresponds to the sensor being part of the relief valve.

In tracing the chain of events that led to the TMI accident in our model, the time when the high temperature in the coolant of the primary circuit triggered the opening of the relief valve corresponds to reaching the state *excessive* in the AND-substate *pressure & temperature* of primary circuit. The occurrence of the relevant transition *up* (and *down*) is established by the monitoring equipment. It triggers *open* in relief valve and *scram* in control rods. Although according to the

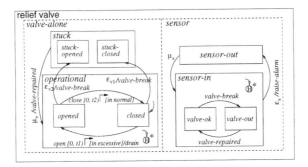

Fig. 6. Safechart model of relief valve

diagram the states *opened* and *closed* in relief valve have an identical risk level, this is generally not the case; their risk levels alternate depending on the actual circumstances. Dynamic fluctuation of risk levels in this manner is an issue under current research. The event *open*, therefore, is a high-to-low risk transition with a mandatory time limit $[0, t_1)$ and triggers the event *drain* in primary circuit.

Following the event *drain* in primary circuit and *scram* in control rods, the event *down* in primary circuit should have taken place, triggering the event *close* in relief valve. However, another possible event is the occurrence of the generic event ϵ_{v2}, an event not bound by the rules on prioritisation of non-deterministic transitions. In the TMI accident, this was indeed the case. In our model, this event would have triggered *valve-break*, letting the operators take an appropriate action to avert, or mitigate, any accident. In the TMI case, the sensor was attached to the solenoid, leaving the failure of the valve undetected. Furthermore, our model also caters for the failure of the sensor itself, in which case an alarm is raised.

6   Conclusions

The main objective of this paper has been to extend the treatment of risk ordering of states in Safecharts, a novel variant of Statecharts proposed in [ ] for specification and design of safety critical systems. Although it is fundamental to Safecharts, this kind of ordering has wider relevance for similar work in other state–based formalisms such as Petri nets. Despite being a precise mathematical concept, there can be deficiencies in the risk ordering relation $\sqsubseteq$. This is because $\sqsubseteq$ is the outcome of a human activity prone to omissions and inaccuracies of subjective judgement. A particular deficiency being addressed is the possible non-uniformity of states comparable by $\sqsubseteq$ in different areas of its (risk) graph. In this respect, the concept of risk band serves as a scheme to classify states not covered by the relation $\sqsubseteq$. Risk bands extend the extent of transitions permitted by Safecharts and prompt the designer to reassess the risk levels of states not covered by the initial risk ordering relation, should the default risk band based scheme turns out to be unsuitable. Risk bands also extend ways of resolving nondeterminism between any simultaneously enabled conflicting, or competing, transitions using risk distances of conflicting transitions themselves or cumulative risk distances of their future transitions.

References

1. V. Bignell and J. Fortune. *Understanding Systems Failures*. Manchester University Press, 1984. 402
2. H. Dammag and N. Nissanke. Safecharts for specifying and designing safety critical systems. In *18th IEEE Symposium on Reliable Distributed Systems, Lausanne*. IEEE, October 1999. 395, 401, 404
3. N. Day. A model checker for statecharts. Technical report, University of British Colombia, Vancouver, Canada, 1993. 401
4. D. Harel. *Statecharts:* a visual formalism for complex systems. volume 8 of *Science of Computer Programming*, pages 231–274. North-Holland, 1987. 395
5. D. Harel, J. P. Schmidt, and R. Sherman. On the formal semantics of statecharts. In *2nd IEEE Symposium on Logic in Computer Science*, pages 54–64, 1985. 395
6. N. G. Leveson. *Safeware – System Safety and Computers*. Addison-Wesley Publishing Company, 1995. 402
7. A. Pnueli and A. Shalev. What is in a step: On the semantics of statecharts. In *Symposium on Theoretical Aspects of Computer Software*, volume 526 of *LNCS*. Springer-Verlag, 1991. 401

Dependability Evaluation:
Model and Method Based on Activity Theory

Mark-Alexander Sujan[1], Antonio Rizzo[2], and Alberto Pasquini[3]

[1] Institute for Computer Design and Fault-Tolerance
University of Karlsruhe, Germany
sujan@ira.uka.de
[2] Multimedia Communication Lab, University of Siena, Italy
rizzo@unisi.it
[3] Innovation Department, ENEA, Italy
pasquini@casaccia.enea.it

Abstract. Dependability Evaluation employs techniques for hardware and software assessment, and derived from these corresponding techniques for the assessment of human reliability. The most prominent shortcoming of such an approach is the lack of a sound psychological basis, and the restriction to operator actions, mostly disregarding organisational and communicational aspects. In this paper the activity-theoretic framework is used as a psychological basis, which allows to model complex systems in such a way that many aspects, which have formerly been studied separately, can be united. The derived method for dependability evaluation can be combined with and complemented by traditional approaches. The theory is illustrated with examples from an industrial case study in the railways sector.

Keywords: Activity Theory, Dependability Evaluation, Distributed Cognition, Human Reliability Analysis

1   Introduction

Information technology can contribute substantially to the dependability and operation of complex systems such as train traffic control, air traffic control, aircraft cockpits, or chemical process control. Yet, we have seen some severe accidents throughout the last years. Tragic examples are the nuclear accidents of Three Mile Island in 1979 [ ] and Chernobyl in 1986 [ ], which had consequences of a global extent. In medical treatment the radiation therapy machine Therac-25 [ ] caused injuries and deaths of patients through severe overdoses between 1985 and 1987. Most recently a series of railways accidents led to an increasing concern about the safety of this transportation mode, e.g. the 1997 accidents of Piacenza and Southall, the accident at Paddington station in 1999, or the accident at Brühl in 2000.

All of these accidents occurred within systems, which were dependent on the interaction of people with complex technologies or among themselves during

F. Koornneef and M. van der Meulen (Eds.): SAFECOMP 2000, LNCS 1943, pp. 406–419, 2000.
© Springer-Verlag Berlin Heidelberg 2000

operation, maintenance and management. This is a characteristic of complex systems, which rely on the adequate and effective integration of all the available resources, including hardware and software artefacts, the people within the system, the rules and procedures used to support the activities of the humans. For many years, and even now, the investigations of accidents like the above, concluded with the identification of "human error" as the major contributing factor. In aviation industry, for example, we frequently find statistics, which attribute 70% of the incidents at least partially to pilot error [ ]. Similar figures hold for other industries like railways or the nuclear sector [ ].

"Human error" (see also [ ]) is seen to be an ontological entity, a cause as such, the removal of which through the automation of functions is expected to increase the dependability of systems. In reality, however, accidents are rarely the result of a single cause such as an operator action (or the absence thereof). Most accidents involving complex technology are caused by a combination of organisational, managerial, technical, social and political factors. In all of these we can, of course, identify human involvement, and it is therefore necessary to develop a conceptual framework, which adequately describes the complex system in its entirety, provides richer representations and descriptions of human behaviour, and emphasises the unique role of the human actors. Such a framework will necessarily need to describe a complex system in terms of human interaction with the available artefacts in a given environment and culture, and as a co-operative problem-solving process, where communication is a central issue.

In spite of this evidence, both current design practice and dependability evaluation are based mostly on a separation of the individual resources. Often the focus during design is on the efficient realisation of new technological artefacts, and system dependability is evaluated accordingly using a collection of methodologies and techniques (such as Fault-Tree Analysis, Failure-Modes-Effects Analysis, and Reliability Growth Modelling; for an overview see [ ], [ ]), which have proved to be successful in predicting the behaviour of technical components. These do not explicitely include human behaviour in their analysis, and they are therefore frequently complemented by techniques for Human Reliability Analysis (HRA; for an overview see [ ], [ ]), which are generally derived from methodologies for hardware and software reliability assessment (e.g. THERP [ ]), in order to allow an easy integration into existing approaches (like Probabilistic Safety Assessement). Most of the HRA approaches employ empirical estimations of human error probabilities (HEP), and are not supported by a sound psychological description of human behaviour.

In this paper we provide a principled critique of the theoretical assumptions underlying popular methods for Human Reliability Analysis (Section 2). Section 3 introduces the activity-theoretic conception of human behaviour which we use to analyse and describe complex systems. This emphasises that human reliability, or generally system dependability, cannot be evaluated without considering the material and social environment within which an activity takes place. This is the basis for the proposed approach to modelling complex systems and to assessing their dependability, which is outlined in section 4. We discuss the findings together with a brief summary in Section 5.

2   Human Reliability Analysis

Traditionally, dependability evaluation has focused on assessing the reliability of hardware and software components. With the continuing advances in technology and fault-tolerant design of components, there has been an increasing trend to the attribution of incidents to "human error" (see Section 1). This has raised the need for methods for assessing the reliability of human actions. A common approach to dependability evaluation, especially in the nuclear sector is the Probabilistic Safety Assessment (PSA). In order to perform a PSA, event-trees and fault-trees are constructed, which are graphical representations of accident scenarios. HRA approaches were thus derived to extend PSA to include human aspects. Therefore, to suit the needs of PSA, methods for HRA typically try to assess whether humans will perform an action correctly or not, and to assign a probability to the success (or failure) of an action.

A popular representative of HRA approaches is the Technique for Human Error Rate Prediction THERP ([ ]). THERP starts off by performing a task analysis, and representing the task model in an HRA event tree. At each node of the event tree there is a binary decision point, which represents the success or failure of an action. The probability of failure is derived from a database containing the Human Error Probabilities (HEP). HEPs are context-free failure probabilities for human actions derived from expert judgement. The HEPs are modified by Performance Shaping Factors (PSF) such as the time available. The findings thus derived can be integrated easily into the PSA study (see Fig. 1).

The most fundamental criticism is that there is a lack of an adequate underlying psychological theory. Driven by the needs of the engineering approaches, human behaviour is modelled according to the behaviour of hardware and software artefacts. This cannot be defended on psychological grounds, however, since human behaviour cannot be understood in the binary, context-free fashion proposed by such approaches. Human activity is a complex construct, shaped by things like the artefacts supporting the activity, and the community within which the activity takes place (e.g. organisation).

Secondly, most HRA approaches assume a static model of the system, neglecting the evolutionary characteristics of complex systems. For example, human work practices are changing continuously as the people working within the system create new knowledge, and adopt new, often improved ways of doing the job in response to breakdowns in the interaction with artefacts.

What is needed is a psychologically motivated approach to dependability evaluation, capable of modelling the complex system in terms of human activity mediated by resources like hardware artefacts, rules, norms and procedures. Such a model can be used to support and improve existing methods (e.g. estimating HEPs) if so desired, or it can be used together with new methods like the one

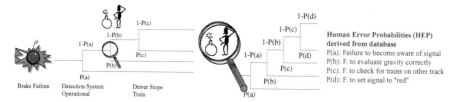

Fig. 1. Probabilistic Safety Assessment Event Tree (left) and Human Reliability Analysis Event Tree (right). Starting from an initiating event (e.g. Brake failure), PSA evaluates the likelihood of undesired scenarios by assigning probabilities to the occurence of intermediate events (e.g. Detection System operational or not), including human actions. The probability of the outcome of human actions is evaluated in the same manner using an HRA Event Tree. In this example the probabilities of success and failure of human actions are supposed to be derived from the THERP database

outlined in this paper. In the next section Activity Theory is presented as such a candidate for the underlying theoretical framework.

3 Activity-Theoretic Framework

The proposed approach builds on the activity-theoretic approach to human behaviour. Activity Theory is rooted in the cultural-historical school of Soviet psychology and is commonly associated with the work of Vygotsky, Luria and Leontiev [ ], [ ]. Activity Theory has recently received a strong interest primarily in Europe (e.g. [ ], [ ]), but also in the US ([ ], [ ], [ ], Distributed Cognition approach [ ]).

3.1 Distribution of Knowledge

Humans are an essential and central part of any complex system, not just in operation, but also in maintenance and management, or earlier during design. In order to achieve the desired goals the humans are in constant interaction with each other and with the other existing resources of the system. According to the cultural-historical theory, human activity is mediated by artefacts. The term artefacts encompasses the general conception of tools as material objects, for example vehicles and instruments. However, it may be interpreted in more generality to include any representation used in the activity, whether internal or external to the subject. With the incorporation of artefacts into the activity, the human perceives the object not simply "as such", but rather within the possibilities and also the limitations set by the mediating artefact [ ]. According to Hutchins [ ], culture is an adaptive process that accumulates the partial solutions to frequently encountered problems. We may therefore view artefacts as the embodiment of these partial solutions, as the instantiation of historical knowledge of people who tried to solve similar problems before and shaped the artefact [1]. This historical knowledge is accumulated in the structural properties of an artefact (e.g. shape, size) as well as in the knowledge of how the artefact should be used [ ]. Artefact mediation represents a historical accumulation and transmission of social knowledge, which in turn implies that the knowledge required for achieving an objective is distributed over the human actor, the mediating artefacts, the rules which guide the use of the artefacts, as well as the environment within which they are used. The concept of artefact-mediated human activity has been portrayed traditionally as a triangle (see upper part of Fig. 2).

Humans are always part of varying communities, which themselves are part of a larger community or organisation. The relationship between an individual and the community is mediated by rules like norms, conventions, and social relations. Communities lead to a division of labour, which mediates the relationship between the community and the object. This involves for example the organisation of the community or the dynamic distribution of responsibilities. This systemic view on human activity was introduced by Engestrøm and is depicted in Fig. 2. It allows to understand the way knowledge is distributed and used in human activities.

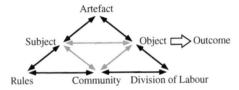

Fig. 2. The systemic view of human activity after Engestrøm. The basic mediation triangle shows the relationship between the subject, an object and the mediating auxilary means. The extended mediation triangle accounts for the fact that humans are always part of communities. Therefore the relationship between the subject and the community which is mediated by social rules is shown, as well as the relationship between the object and the community which is mediated by the division of labour.

3.2 SHEL-Model

In order to understand the interaction of the individual resources and the way in which knowledge is distributed throughout a complex system, it is important to

---

[1] Consider for example the Roman and the Arabian enumeration systems. Both are equally well suited for enumerating people, sheep, or whatever needs to be counted. However, into the Arabian system is incorporated the principle of iterative addition which reflects the need of people for an artefact supporting multiplication.

view the complex system in its entirety as a single unit of consideration. We can arrive at this holistic view on complex systems by extending the above principles to the system level as depicted in Fig. 3. For reasons of convenience we have used a graphical representation and the corresponding well-known denominator SHEL of the resource model introduced in [ ] and superimposed on it the findings about the distribution of knowledge discussed above.

In this extended or re-interpreted SHEL-model the resources over which knowledge in any complex system is distributed are grouped into three classes. The *H*ardware resource contains traditional hardware artefacts and tools, while the *S*oftware resource contains rules, procedures and work practices. The human resources in their relational and communicational aspects comprise the *L*iveware. The arrangement of different resources always operates in an *E*nvironment defined by political and social factors.

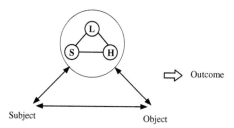

Fig. 3. Visualisation of a complex system according to the activity-theoretic conception. The liveware resource contains human aspects of the system, like the humans working in the system, the communities they belong to or the social rules that govern their interaction. In the hardware resource are grouped all artefacts like vehicles or signs. The software resource finally comprises all the procedures and rules that determine how the work is carried out. The knowledge is distributed over all the resources and their interaction takes place in an evironment. We refer to this model as the (extended) SHEL model. The original SHEL was first introduced by Edwards [ ]

Every process within a complex system is performed by a combination of hardware, software and liveware resources in the SHEL-space. This specific combination of resources and the knowledge the resources keep is not static, but changes over time as the process evolves. Considering the contribution of the resources over a given period of the life-cycle of a complex system, it is easy to observe that in general the knowledge associated with the hardware and software resources degrades over time, so that they need maintenance (in case of hardware) or have to be adapted (software) by humans. The same is only partially true for the human resources, who also have a great potential to increase their knowledge over time. Humans may need re-qualification or training to maintain their skills. More importantly, however, they can create new knowledge, which is needed to manage the evolving processes and which belongs only to the humans.

This knowledge is created in response to breakdowns in the existing knowledge distribution, and to meet the continuously evolving demands of other systems or changes in the environment. This new knowledge is embodied in the human practices and the interaction among people and the interaction with artefacts, and does not yet belong to the organisation.

3.3   Example

For illustration of the principle of differing resource combinations let us consider the following example which is taken from a case study with the Italian National Railways (FS). For a more detailed description of the case study see [ ]. The work analysed in the case study concerned the control and reactive management of the train movements within a certain control zone of the FS network (Tirrenica Sud). In general, the line supervisors are responsible for an efficient stock circulation. They observe the train movement, compute the deviation of the traffic situation from the theoretical schedule, and take actions such as the resolution of priority conflicts in order to avoid or minimise inconveniences. We were able to observe the same process (i.e. the real-time train scheduling) being performed by three different resource combinations. In the technologically least advanced work environment of Roma - Grosseto most of the knowledge required is kept by the humans. The responsible operators (Dirigente Centrale) acquire the information about the train movement via telephone communication. They record this information on a time/station matrix, i.e. a hardware artefact which will keep the knowledge in a physically durable way over time and contribute later in the problem solving process. In the more advanced environments of Roma - Formia and Roma - Chiusi this knowledge has been shifted to an automatic system which monitors and records the train movements. However, when problems with the automatic system are encountered, the process is performed by "falling back" to the configuration of the less advanced environment. For this reason the knowledge kept by the automatic system is replicated continuously and stored in a redundant way in a printed time/station matrix which the operators can use as the basis for their own recordings. Nothing is done (like training, etc.) to keep this knowledge alive in the operators, as it is thought that their long experience will do so by itself.

4   Formulation and Application of the Approach

In a project with the Italian National Railways (Ferrovie dello Stato FS) we aimed to identify and resolve problems in relation to human factors in the management and operation of the railways traffic. The multi-disciplinary approach we adopted was based mainly on the ideas presented in section 3. Thus, we were concerned with the distribution of knowledge among the different resources, like the humans in the system, hardware artefacts like vehicles, signs and instruments, and software artefacts like procedures, rules and practices.

The proposed approach to dependability evaluation we put forward in this paper is based on the same ideas, and should be an integral part of the overall design process. It consists of three main steps:

- Definition of the process (Model)
- Identification of critical issues (Method)
- Evaluation (Method)

Below each step will be described in more detail.

4.1 Definition of the Process

Abstract representations of work always leave a semantic gap to the actual working practices. Therefore, a thorough understanding of the actual human activites, and the way in which each resource contributes to performing the process is a prerequisite not just for dependability evaluation, but for the entire design process. In order to achieve this the involvement of the relevant stakeholders becomes a necessary and valuable tool. They can provide direct information about how the work is actually conducted. As was discussed, the humans are the only truly adaptive resource and the only resource capable of producing new knowledge. This knowledge needs to be documented and mapped to SHEL-models and will serve as the basis for the following design and evaluation. Techniques which may be useful for the analysis include ethnographic studies, video recordings, interviews, document analysis, etc.

SHEL-models in their basic form are descriptions of how the different resources contribute over time to the execution of the process. Any process description is always a way to segment a continuous flow of state transformations depending on one or more resources. A description of the three-dimensional SHEL-space would be needed to represent the modifications of all three resources. Since this proves to be hard to visualise and to be extremely time-consuming, it may be more reasonable to hook the process description to the modifications occurring in the human (liveware) resources. Every time a human engages in an activity or the actor changes a step in the process is defined. Human activity is always mediated by the hardware and software resources, and this contribution is documented in the model with descriptions, references, snapshots, location maps, etc. This first general model can then be further specified by descriptions of the interaction occuring within a specific activity.

The results of the analysis can be mapped to scenarios of different granularity according to the generic structure given in Tab. 1. Scenarios are verbal descriptions of the SHEL-models, and are an efficient means for communicating within a multi-disciplinary team, and especially with the stakeholders, each of which may in turn have a completely different background. In general, a collection of scenarios of varying complexity and detail, and with varying viewpoints is needed to describe one SHEL-model. The complete set of scenarios for a SHEL-model would be too lengthy to be included here. Note that in general, the set of scenarios includes for different viewpoints a general description of the specific activity, an explanation of the knowledge distribution, the functionality assigned to and performed by the individual resources, and an overview of the different roles involved.

Table 1. Template for scenarios describing a SHEL-model

General Description
Description of the process to be supported and the corresponding viewpoint.
Description of Specific Situation
Verbal description of the unfolding of the activity.
Description of Supporting Artefacts
Description of:
– knowledge contained in the artefacts and reference to other resources where the same knowledge (or parts thereof) is contained (e.g. graphical representation of station layout, parts of which may be memorised by the human)
– functionality explicitly assigned to the artefacts (e.g. point-to-point communication device)
– functionality actually supported by the artefacts (e.g. above device used during actual operation in a way mimicking a community-casting device)
Description of Knowledge Belonging to Humans, only
Description of knowledge which is contained in the humans, only (e.g. who is involved in a particular situation).
Description of Roles Involved
Description of the human stakeholders and their roles in performing the process.

The exemplar SHEL-model of the preparation process for a train for departure is shown in Fig. 4. Note that for a complete process representation both descriptive scenarios and the SHEL-model are needed.

The combination of SHEL-models and descriptive scenarios results in an augmented and improved process description, which can be used as the basis of both design and evaluation. By itself this first step is already valuable not only for qualitative but also for quantitative dependability assessment. Standard techniques like FTA or FMECA will benefit from such a representation, which describes the actual working practices in a more adequate way, and explains the dynamics of a complex system in a theoretically better grounded way than would be possible by employing exclusively abstract modelling techniques. The same applies to traditional HRA approaches which are provided more concrete information on which to base their human error probablility estimation.

4.2   Identification of Critial Issues

The next step attempts to identify "critical issues", i.e., facts or events which the humans working within the system experience as major criticalities, where they

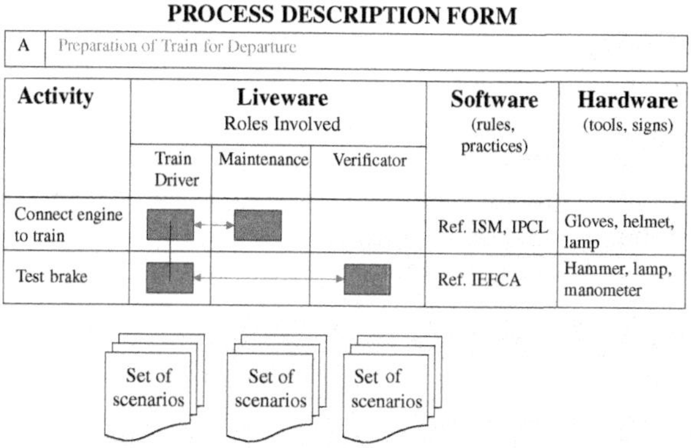

PROCESS DESCRIPTION FORM

A	Preparation of Train for Departure

Activity	Liveware Roles Involved			Software (rules, practices)	Hardware (tools, signs)
	Train Driver	Maintenance	Verificator		
Connect engine to train	■	→ ■		Ref. ISM, IPCL	Gloves, helmet, lamp
Test brake	■	◄───	──► ■	Ref. IEFCA	Hammer, lamp, manometer

Set of scenarios   Set of scenarios   Set of scenarios

Fig. 4. SHEL-model of the preparation process. The process description is hooked to the changes occuring in the human resources (liveware). In the columns Software and Hardware are shown the mediating artefacts supporting the activity. Descriptions of the activity in general, of the knowledge distribution, the functionality, and the different roles are included in the complementing scenarios

encounter problems and where they see the opportunity for improvement. These critical issues correspond to the concept of contradictions in Activity Theory. During the analysis we discovered not only various sources of breakdowns due to an insufficient or inadquate knowledge distribution, but also indications of affective problems. We have discussed in detail the issue of affective problems in system operation elsewhere [ ].

Identification of criticalities is done by interviewing stakeholders, and by accessing corresponding data bases of past incidents. The interviews are conducted openly, i.e., they provide the stakeholders with the opportunity to relate whatever they think relevant. The general structure of the interviews is derived from the SHEL-model. This implies that we are concerned with criticalities which the humans experience in the interaction with the hardware, the software and other humans (liveware). For each class is provided a set of very general questions (see Tab. 2), and each question is in turn refined to a set of more specific questions which the stakeholders can be asked. As was pointed out, these questions are used only as a general guideline. The stakeholders are free to mention anything that is important to them, and of course the interviewer is supposed to follow any interesting issue in sufficient detail.

Frequently reported as criticalities in the case study were missing, incomplete, contradictory, or out-of-date procedures to support the activity. Further major criticalites were in relation to communication among people, and the corresponding communication tools for collaboration like forms for maximum speed of a train under special circumstances (M40). This particular form was charac-

Table 2. Structure of a generic questionnaire derived from the SHEL-model

SOFTWARE
Rules, procedures, practices for performing the activities
S1 Is the knowledge required for performing the activity covered in sufficient and adequate detail by the available rules and procedures?
S2 Are the actual work practices consistent with those prescribed in the rules and procedures?
S3 Is the specific knowledge required for performing the activity sufficient and adequate?
HARDWARE
Machines, instruments, manuals, signals available for performing the activites
H1 Do the hardware artefacts perform the functions for which they were introduced reliably and efficiently?
H2 Do the hardware artefacts support the actual activity adequately?
H3 Does the physical environment (climate, spatial layout, etc.) permit a comfortable execution of the activity?
LIVEWARE
People, roles, and their relationship within the activities
L1 Is the communication flow adequate and efficient to support the activity?
L2 Is the distribution of the work between humans and the allocation to the single person instrumental in supporting the activity?

terised as "misleading and confusing" and "disturbing" by several train drivers, and was identified as one of the contributing factors in accidents.

By itself the identification of critical issues can contribute substantially to the success of standard evaluation techniques. Critical issues elicited in this way could, for example, serve as the starting points in an Event-Tree-Analysis (ETA). Likewise, they could serve to inform the application of Hazards and Operability Analysis (HAZOP). In our case, critical issues are the key points to be focused on during the following evaluation.

4.3 Evaluation

The evaluation is based on simulation and qualitative assessment. The simulation uses the scenarios, the critical issues identified and possible solutions proposed to enact the process performance with the relevant stakeholders. The scenarios are supposed to set the scene for the criticality of interest. The stakeholders can work with and evaluate mock-ups (e.g. paper-based mock-ups or more detailed prototypes) of proposed solutions in the setting of the criticality given in the scenarios. A simulation of this kind looks more like "role-playing" in the beginning and takes the form of detailed system simulation later on.

A major advantage of a simulative evaluation like this is that the dynamics of the interactions can be taken into account. It is by no means necessary to assume a static binary type of human behaviour. Rather, this approach allows to assess real human behaviour in the context of the realistic work setting. As a complex system is characterised by the interaction of its resources, the effects the changes in one resource induce in the other resources needs to be evaluated. Being based on a theory of evolutionary system change, also this is possible to some extent with the proposed method. For example, if a hardware artefact is changed, the human working with the artefact will experience the object of his or her intentionality in a different way as was discussed in section 3.1. This in turn may lead to changing practices, i.e. a modification of the software resource or also of the social interaction of the humans, which will introduce changes in the liveware resource. The stakeholders can provide feedback about the adequateness of a proposed solution to achieve the desired objective, they can point out criticalities, and they can anticipate and demonstrate the possible changes that are likely to occur.

Other factors which can be qualitatively assessed by this approach are, for example, the establishment of a safety-culture or affective influences. Usability studies are not sufficient to discover and point to contradictions within a complex system, such as a human's disappointment because he or she was not questioned adequately, or because a different type of support would have been prefered, or even due to fears that the new support system will act as a competitor or supervisor [ ].

Though the approach presented is of a qualitative nature, it is of course possible to integrate the findings into a PSA study, if so required, and thus arrive at a quantitative assessment. This will be discussed in the next section together with a brief summary.

5   Discussion

Complex systems, like the management of train traffic, which served as the case study in this paper, are highly dynamic entities, which have evolved over time and are undergoing a continuous adaptation process. The success of such systems is strongly dependent upon a smooth integration and effective co-operation of the available resources (the humans in the system, mediating artefacts, rules, procedures, etc.).

We have proposed a model and a method to dependability evaluation based on Activity Theory. The model is thus grounded in a sound psychological theory of human behaviour, and provides a framework within which many aspects, which have formerly been studied separately, can be united.

The method tries to identify criticalities in the system configuration, and allows to evaluate possible solutions. The evaluation is not just a static assessment of the system, but rather takes account of the evolutionary nature being an inherent characteristic of complex systems, and qualitatively assesses the intrinsic system capability to adapt to changes and novel situations.

Often a good qualitative assessment should be sufficient, since also probablilities need to be interpreted more in a qualitative way rather than as absolute values. Our approach is of a qualitative nature, this not withstanding we have outlined, however, how the approach can be integrated with traditional methods to yield a quantitative evaluation if so desired. The model will be beneficial to all methods, and the identification of critical issues can be combined with approaches like ETA or HAZOP.

The approach focuses on the overall system dependability centered around the concept of human actors. Therefore, it does not render studies of hardware and software (in the traditional sense) reliablity obsolete, but rather it is complemented by such techniques.

References

1. L. J. Bannon and S. Bødker. Beyond the Interface: Encountering Artefacts in Use. In J. Carroll, editor, *Designing Interaction*, chapter 12. Cambridge University Press, 1991. 409

2. C. Cacciabue. Human Reliability Assessment: Methods and Techniques. In F. Redmill and J. Rajan, editors, *Human Factors in Safety-Critial Systems*, chapter 3. Butterworth-Heinemann, 1997. 407

3. M. Cole. *Cultural Psychology*. Harvard University Press, 1996. 409

4. E. Edwards. Introductory Overview. In E. L. Wiener and D. C. Nagel, editors, *Human Factors in Aviation*. San Diego: Academic Press, 1988. 411

5. Y. Engeström. Learning by expanding: an activity-theoretical approach to developmental research. Helsinki: Orienta-Konsultit, 1987. 409

6. R. L. Helmreich. Managing human error in aviation. *Scientific American*, pages 40–45, May 1997. 407

7. E. Hollnagel. *Cognitive Reliability and Error Analysis Method*. Elsevier Science, 1998. 407

8. E. Hutchins. *Cognition in the Wild*. MIT Press, 1995. 409

9. An analysis of root cause failures in 1983 significant event reports. Atlanta, GA: Institute of Nuclear Power Operations, 1984. 407

10. V. Kaptelinin and B. Nardi. The activity checklist: A tool for representing the space of context. Technical report, Department of Informatics, Umea University, 1997. 409, 410

11. J. G. Kemeny. Report of the President's Commission Three Mile Island. US Government Accounting Office, Washington, D. C., 1979. 406

12. A. N. Leontev. *Activity, Consciousness, and Personality*. Prentice-Hall, Englewood Cliffs, NJ, 1978. 409

13. N. G. Leveson. *SAFEWARE: System Safety and Computers*. Addison Wesley, 1995. 407

14. N. G. Leveson and C. Turner. An investigation of the Therac-25 accidents. *IEEE Computer*, pages 18–43, 1993. 406

15. M. R. Lyu. *Handbook of Software Reliability Engineering*. McGraw-Hill, 1995. 407

16. B. Nardi. *Context and Consciousness*. MIT Press, Cambridge, MA, 1996. 409

17. USSR State Committee on the Utilisation of Atomic Energy. The accident at the Chernobyl nuclear power plant and its consequences. Report presented at AIEA Experts Metting, Vienna, August 1986. 406

18. J. T. Reason. *Human Error*. Cambridge University Press, Cambridge, UK, 1990. 407

19. M. A. Sujan, A. Pasquini, A. Rizzo, P. Scrivani, and M. Wimmer. Activity theory as a framework to consider human affect in the design. In *Proceedings of the IEEE Int. Conf. on Systems, Man and Cybernetics*, volume 1, pages 726–731, Tokyo, Japan, October 1999. IEEE Press. 415, 417

20. A. D. Swain and H. E. Guttman. Handbook of human reliability analysis with emphasis on nuclear power plant applications. NUREG CR-1278. SAND 80-0200 RX, AN. Final Report., 1984. 407, 408

21. L. S. Vygotsky. *Mind in Society*. Harward University Press, Cambridge, MA, 1978. 409

22. J. Wertsch. *The Social Formation of Mind*. Harvard University Press, Cambridge, MA, 1985. 409

23. M. Wimmer, A. Rizzo, and M. A. Sujan. A holistic design concept to improve safety related control systems. In *Proceedings of the Safecomp 99*, pages 297–309, Toulouse, France, September 1999. Springer-Verlag. 412

Forensic Software Engineering and the Need for New Approaches to Accident Investigation

Chris Johnson

Department of Computing Science, University of Glasgow
Glasgow, G12 8QQ, UK.
Tel: +44 (0141) 330 6053 Fax: +44 (0141) 330 4913
johnson@dcs.glasgow.ac.uk
http://www.dcs.gla.ac.uk/~johnson,

Abstract. Accident reports are intended to explain the causes of human error, system failure and managerial weakness. There is, however, a growing realization that existing investigation techniques fail to meet the challenges created by accidents that involve software failures. This paper argues that existing software development techniques cannot easily be used to provide retrospective information about the complex and systemic causes of major accidents. In consequence, we must develop specific techniques to support forensic software engineering.

1   Introduction

The Rand report into the "personnel and parties" in National Transportation Safety Board (NTSB) aviation accident investigations argues that existing techniques fail to meet the challenges created by modern systems:

> "As complexity grows, hidden design or equipment defects are problems of increasing concern. More and more, aircraft functions rely on software, and electronic systems are replacing many mechanical components. Accidents involving complex events multiply the number of potential failure scenarios and present investigators with new failure modes. The NTSB must be prepared to meet the challenges that the rapid growth in systems complexity poses by developing new investigative practices." [1]

The Rand report reveals how little we know about how to effectively investigate and report upon the growing catalogue of software induced failures. By software "induced" accidents we include incidents that stem from software that fails to perform an intended function.   We also include failures in which those intended functions were themselves incorrectly elicited and specified.   The following pages support this argument by evidence from accident investigations in several different safety-related industries [2].   These case studies have been chosen to illustrate failures at many different stages of the software development lifecycle.   As we shall see, the recent NTSB investigation into the Guam crash has identified a number of problems in

F. Koornneef and M. van der Meulen (Eds.): SAFECOMP 2000, LNCS 1943, pp. 420-429, 2000.
© Springer-Verlag Berlin Heidelberg 2000

requirements capture for Air Traffic Management systems [3]. Software implementation failures have been identified as one of the causal factors behind the well-publicised Therac-25 incidents [4]. The Lyons report found that testing failures were a primary cause of the Ariane-5 accident [5]. The South-West Thames Regional Health Authority identified software procurement problems as contributory factors in the failure of the London Ambulance Computer Aided Dispatch system [6].   A further motivation was that all of these incidents stem from more complex systemic failures that cross many different stages of the software lifecycle.

2   Problem of Supporting Systemic Approaches to Software Failure

It can be argued that there is no need to develop specific forensic techniques to represent and reason about software "induced" accidents. Many existing techniques, from formal methods through to UML, can be used to analyze the technical causes of software failure [7]. For instance, theorem proving can be used to establish that an accident can occur given a formal model of the software being examined and a set of pre-conditions/assumptions about the environment in which it will execute [8]. If an accident cannot be proven to have occurred using the formal model then either the specification is wrong or the environmental observations are incorrect or there are weaknesses in the theorem provide techniques that are being applied. Unfortunately, there are many special characteristics of accidents that prevent such techniques from being effective applied. For example, there are often several different ways in which software might have contributed to an accident.   Finding one failure path, using formal proof, symbolic execution or control flow analysis will not be sufficient to identify all possible causes of failure.   There are some well-known technical solutions to these problems. For instance, model checking can be used to increase an analyst's assurance that they have identified multiple routes to a hazardous state. These techniques have been applied to support the development of a number of complex software systems. However, they have not so far been used to support the analysis of complex, software-induced accidents [9].

There are a number of more theoretical problems that must be addressed before standard software engineering techniques can be applied to support accident investigation. Many development tools address the problems of software complexity by focussing on particular properties of sub-components.   As a result, they provide relatively little support for the analysis of what has been termed "systemic" failure [8]. The nature of such failures is illustrated by the NTSB's preliminary report into the Guam accident:

> "The National Transportation Safety Board determines that the probable cause of this accident was the captain's failure to adequately brief and execute the non-precision approach and the first officer's and flight engineer's failure to effectively monitor and cross-check the captain's execution of the approach. Contributing to these failures were the captain's fatigue and Korean Air's inadequate flight crew training.   Contributing to the accident was the Federal Aviation Administration's intentional inhibition

of the minimum safe altitude warning system and the agency's failure to adequately to manage the system." (Probable Causes, Page 3, [3]).

It is unclear how existing software engineering techniques might represent and reason about the Captain's fatigue and the inadequate briefings that left the crew vulnerable to the failure of air traffic control software. Such analyses depend upon the integration of software engineering techniques into other complementary forms of analysis that consider human factors as well as organizational and systems engineering issues. There are a number of requirements engineering techniques that come close to considering the impact that these diverse systemic factors have upon systems development. Finkelstein, Kramer and Nuseibeh's viewpoint-oriented approaches are a notable example [10]. However, existing requirement analysis techniques tend to focus on the generic impact of management and organizational structures on future software systems. They provide little or no support for situated analysis of the reasons why a specific piece of software failed on a particular day under specific operating conditions.

3   Problems of Framing any Analysis of Software Failure

The problems of identifying multiple systemic causes of failure are exacerbated by the lack of any clear "stopping rule" for accident investigations that involve software failures. This problem is particularly acute because many different causal factors contribute to software "induced" accidents. For example, at one level a failure can be caused because error-handling routines failed to deal with a particular condition. At another level, however, analysts might argue that the fault lay with the code that initially generated the exception. Both of these problems might, in turn, be associated with poor testing or flawed requirements capture. Questions can also be asked about the quality of training that programmers and designers receive. These different levels of causal analysis stretch back to operational management and to the contractors and sub-contractors who develop and maintain software systems. Beyond that investigators can focus on the advice that regulatory agencies provide for suitable development practices in safety related systems [2]. This multi-level analysis of the causes of software failure has a number of important consequences for accident analysis. The first is that existing software engineering techniques are heavily biased towards a small section of this spectrum. For example, Software Fault Trees provide good support for the analysis of coding failures [11]. Requirements analysis techniques can help trace software failures back to problems in the initial stages of development [10]. However, there has been little work into how different management practices contribute to, or compound, failures at more than one of these levels [12, 13].

The Therac-25 incidents provide one of the best-known examples of the problems that arise when attempting to frame any analysis of software failure. Leveson and Turner's [4] accounts provide detailed analyses of the technical reasons for the software bugs. They also emphasize the point that iterative bug fixes are unlikely to yield a reliable system because they address the symptoms rather than the causes of software failures. It is instructive, however, that many software engineers remember this incident purely for the initial scheduling problems rather than the subsequent inadequacies of the bug fixes:

> "in general, it is a mistake to patch just one causal factor (such as the software) and assume that future accidents will be eliminated. Accidents are unlikely to occur in exactly the same way again.   If we patch only the symptoms and ignore the deeper underlying cause of one accident, we are unlikely to have much effect on future accidents.   The series of accidents involving the Therac-25 is a good example of exactly this problem: Fixing each individual software flaw as it was found did not solve the safety problems of the device" (page 551, [4]).

A range of different approaches might, therefore, be recruited to identify the many different causal factors that contribute to major software failures.   Such an approach builds on the way in which standards, such as IEC61508 and DO-178B, advocate the use of different techniques to address different development issues.   There are, however, several objections to this ad hoc approach to the investigation of software induced accidents.   The most persuasive is Lekburg's analysis of the biases amongst incident investigators   [14]. Analysts select those tools with which they are most familiar.   They are also most likely to finding the causal factors that are best identified using those tools.   In the case of software engineering, this might result in analysts identifying those causal factors that are most easily identified using formal methods irrespective of whether or not those causal factors played a significant role in the course of the accident. A more cynical interpretation might observe that particular techniques might be selectively deployed to arrive at particular conclusions.   In either case, the lack of national and international guidance on the analysis of software failures creates the opportunity for individual and corporate bias to influence the investigation of major accidents.

4   Problems of Assessing Intention in Software Development

It is not enough for analysts simply to document the requirements failures or the erroneous instructions or the inadequate test procedures that contribute to software "induced" accidents.   They must also determine the reasons WHY software failed. Why was a necessary requirement omitted?   Why was an incorrect instruction introduced?   Why was testing inadequate? For instance, the Lyons report spends several pages considering the reasons why the inertial reference system (SRI) was not fully tested before Ariane flight 501:

> "When the project test philosophy was defined, the importance of having the SRI's in the loop was recognized and a decision was made (to incorporate them in the test).   At a later stage of the programme (in 1992), this decision was changed.   It was decided not to have the actual SRI's in the loop for the following reasons: the SRIs should be considered to be fully qualified at equipment level; the precision of the navigation software in the on-board computer depends critically on the precision of the SRI measurements.   In the Functional Simulation Facility (ISF), this precision could not be achieved

by electronics creating test signals; the simulation of failure modes is not possible with real equipment, but only with a model; the base period of the SRI is 1 millisecond whilst that of the simulation at the ISF is 6 milliseconds. This adds to the complexity of the interfacing electronics and may further reduce the precision of the simulation" (page 9, [5])."

Leveson's recent work on intent specifications provides significant support for these forensic investigations of software failure [15].   She argues that there will be significant long-term benefits for team-based development if specifications supported wider questions about the reasons why certain approaches were adopted.   For instance, programmers joining a team or maintaining software can not only see what was done, they can also see why it was done.   This approach is an extension of safety case techniques.   Rather than supporting external certification, intent specifications directly support software development within an organization. Accident investigators might also use these intent specifications to understand the reasons why software failures contribute to particular incidents.   Any forensic application of Leveson's ideas would depend upon companies adopting intent specifications throughout their software lifecycle.   For example, maintenance is often a contributory factor in software induced accidents.   Intent specifications would have to explain the reasons why any changes were made.   This would entail significant overheads in addition to the costs associated with maintaining safety cases for external certification [16]. However, it is equally important not to underestimate the benefits that might accrue from these activities.   Not only might they help accident investigators understand the justifications for particular development decisions, they can also help to establish a closer relationship between the implemented software and the documented design. The report into the failure of the London Ambulance Computer-Aided Dispatch System emphasizes the problems that can arise without these more formal documentation practices:

> "Strong project management might also have minimised another difficulty experienced by the development. SO, in their eagerness to please users, often put through software changes "on the fly" thus circumventing the official Project Issue Report (PIR) procedures whereby all such changes should be controlled. These "on the fly" changes also reduced the effectiveness of the testing procedures as previously tested software would be amended without the knowledge of the project group. Such changes could, and did, introduce further bugs." (paragraph 3082, [6]).

Many industries already have certification procedures for software maintenance. This helps to avoid the ad hoc procedures described in the previous quotation.   Safety cases go part of the way towards the intent specifications that are proposed by Leveson.   However, there is little room for complacency.   Kelly and McDermid argue that many companies experience great difficulties in maintaining their software safety cases in the face of new requirements or changing environmental circumstance [16]. As a result there is no documented justification for many of the decisions and actions that lead to software failure.   These have to be inferred by investigators in the aftermath of major accidents when a mass of ethical and legal factors make it particularly difficult to assess the motivations that lie behind key development decisions.

5   Problems of Assessing Human and Environmental Factors

Simulation is an important tool in many accident investigations.   For example, several hypotheses about the sinking of the MV Estonia were dismissed through testing models in a specially adapted tank.   Unfortunately, accident investigators must often account for software behaviors in circumstances that cannot easily be recreated. The same physical laws that convinced the sub-contractors not to test the Ariane 5's inertial reference systems in the Functional Simulation Facility also frustrate attempts to simulate the accident [5]. The difficulty of recreating the conditions that lead to software failures has important implications for the reporting of software induced accidents.   Readers must often rely upon the interpretation and analysis of domain experts.   Unfortunately, given the lack of agreed techniques in this area, there are few objective techniques that can be used to assess the work of these experts.   Given the complexity of the coding involved and the proprietary nature of many applications, accident reports often provide insufficient details about the technical causes of software failure.   As a result, readers must trust the interpretation of the board of inquiry.   This contrasts strongly with the technical documentation that often accompanies reports into other forms of engineering failure.   It also has important implications for teaching and training where students are expected to follow vague criticisms about the "dangers of re-use" rather than the more detail expositions that are provided for metallurgic failures and unanticipated chemical reactions.

The interactive nature of many safety-critical applications also complicates the simulation of software "induced" accidents.   It can be difficult to recreate the personal and group factors that lead individuals to act in particular ways. It can also be difficult to recreate the ways in which user interface problems exacerbate flaws in the underlying software engineering of safety-critical applications.   For example, the London Ambulance system required "almost perfect location information" [6].   As the demands on the system rose, the location information became increasingly out of date and a number of error messages were generated.   These error messages are termed "exceptions" in the following quotation.   The rising number of error messages increased the users' frustration with the software.   As a result, the operators became less and less inclined to update essential location and status information.   This, in turn, led to more error messages and a "vicious cycle" developed.   Accident analysts must, therefore, account both for the technical flaws in any software system but also for emergent properties that stem from the users' interaction with their system:

> "The situation was made worse as unrectified exception messages generated more exception messages. With the increasing number of "awaiting attention" and exception messages it became increasingly easy to fail to attend to messages that had scrolled off the top of the screen. Failing to attend to these messages arguably would have been less likely in a "paper-based" environment." (Paragraph 4023, [6])

It is not always so easy to understand the ways in which human behavior contributes to the failure of computer based systems. This is a complex topic in its own right. Behavioral observations of interaction provide relatively little information about WHY individuals use software in particular ways.   It is also notoriously difficult to apply existing human error modeling techniques to represent and reason about the mass of contextual factors that affect operator performance during a major accident [17]. The London Ambulance report provides a further illustration of these problems. There were persistent rumors and allegations about sabotage contributing to the failure of the software.   Accident investigators could never prove these allegations because it was difficult to distinguish instances of deliberate "neglect" from more general installation problems.

6   Problems of Making Adequate Recommendations

Previous paragraphs have argued that accident investigators must address the systemic factors that contribute to and combine with software failures during major failures.   They must also consider the scope of their analysis; software failures are often a symptom of poor training and management.   It can also be difficult to identify the motivations and intentions that lead to inadequate requirements, "erroneous" coding and poor testing.   Finally, we have argued that it can be difficult to determine the ways in which human factors and environmental influences compound the problems created by software failures in major accidents.   There are also a number of further problems.   In particular, it can be difficult for accident investigators to identify suitable recommendations for the design and operation of future software systems.   This is, in part, a natural consequence of an increasing emphasis being placed upon process improvement as a determinant of software quality.   Once an accident occurs, this throws doubt not only on the code that led to the failure but also on the entire development process that produced that code.   At best, the entire program may be untrustworthy.   At worst, all of the other code cut by that team or by any other teams practicing the same development techniques may be under suspicion. Readers can obtain a flavor of this in the closing pages of the Lyons' report into the Ariane 5 failure.   The development teams must:

> "Review all flight software (including embedded software), and in particular: Identify all implicit assumptions made by the code and its justification documents on the values of quantities provided by the equipment.   Check these assumptions against the restrictions on use of the equipment."
> (Paragraph R5, [16]).

This citation re-iterates the importance of justification and of intent, mentioned in previous paragraphs.   It also contains the recommendation that the must identify "all implicit assumptions made by their code".   Unfortunately, it does not suggest any tools or techniques that might be used to support this difficult task.   In preparing this paper, I have also been struck by comments that reveal how little many investigators appreciate about the problems involved in software development.   This is illustrated by a citation from the report into the London Ambulance Computer Aided Dispatch system.

> "A critical system such as this, as pointed out earlier, amongst other prerequisites must have totally reliable software.   This implies that quality assurance procedures must be formalised and extensive. Although Systems Options Ltd (SO) had a part-time QA resource it was clearly not fully effective and, more importantly, not

independent. QA in a project such as this must have considerable power including the ability to extend project time-scales if quality standards are not being met. This formalised QA did not exist at any time during the Computer Aided Despatch development. (Paragraph 3083, [13]).

It is impossible by any objective measures to achieve total software reliability, contrary to what is suggested in the previous paragraph. It may be politically expedient to propose this as a valid objective.   However, to suggest that this is a possible is to completely misrepresent the state of the art in safety-critical software engineering.

7   Conclusion and Further Work

A number of agencies have argued that existing techniques cannot easily be used to investigate accidents that involve the failure of software systems [1, 2].   This paper has, therefore, gone beyond the high level analysis presented in previous studies to focus on the challenges that must be addressed by forensic software engineering:

1.   There are no existing techniques that enable analysts to represent and reason about the systemic factors that stem from and lead to software failures.

2.   There are no agreed means of framing the scope of accident investigations that involve software.   This results in considerable differences in the quality of many reports.   Some focus on individual programmer error and even on differences in programming "style".   Others ignore these issues and focus on managerial and regulatory supervision.   Very few consider the interaction between these different contributory factors to software failure.

3.   The lack of guidance about appropriate analytical tools opens up the opportunity for subjective bias and major problems in recreating the analytical techniques that support particular conclusions.

4.   Software re-use creates particular problems in the aftermath of an accident because investigators may be forced to question all of the assumptions that were made about the safety of any modification to a new environment or platform.

5.   Accident investigators are concerned to understand not just how a program failed but also WHY that failure went undetected during subsequent stages of the software life cycle.   This makes it increasingly important that intentional techniques and safety cases are better integrated into all software development practices.

6.   It is impossible to run empirical tests or to simulate the operating conditions that lead to many software failures. This makes it imperative that analysts are explicit about the techniques that they use, and assumptions that they make, during the analysis of major software failures.   Other professionals must be able to assess the validity of their findings.

7.   The lack of integration between human factors and software engineering techniques makes it difficult to identify the ways in which "emergent behaviors" can lead to failure [17].   As a result, we have learnt remarkably

little about the nature of the human computer interaction during major accidents.

8. The lack of objective measures of software quality has led to a focus on development practices. As a result, the occurrence of even a single software failure can throw doubt upon an entire system. This makes it difficult for accident investigators to limit the potential scope of the recommendations in an accident report.

9. The greatest challenge for forensic software engineering is to educate other investigators, and ultimately the general public, about the nature of safety critical systems. Until this issue is addressed then we will continue to read accident reports that urge companies to develop "completely reliable software".

It should be stressed that this is a partial list. Additional factors complicate the analysis of software induced failures. It is also important to stress that this paper has not proposed any detailed solutions to the problems of assessing the role that software plays in major incidents and accidents. The lack of previous research in this area makes such proposals premature. However, it is possible to suggest directions for future research. For instance, many of the issues in the previous list are addressed by recent work on intentional forms of software engineering [4]. As mentioned, these not only specify what a system is intended to do but **why** that requirement is important. These approaches help investigators to distinguish between failures to achieve appropriate intentions, through poor coding, and the more fundamental problems that stem from inappropriate intentions. A second area for research focuses on the maintenance of safety cases and other design documents following software re-use [16]. Previous sections have argued that accident investigators must often piece together the reasons why software "failed" within new contexts of use, such as new hardware platforms or control environments. An analysis of software failures can provide insights about the threats that software re-use can create for existing safety-cases. Such an analysis might not only guide subsequent accident investigations but might also provide valuable guidelines for engineers and developers who want to re-use safety-critical software.

Jim Hall, the president of the US National Transportation Safety Board recently announced the foundation of an accident investigation academy. This is motivated by the criticisms of the Rand report that were cited at the start of this paper. The academy will train investigators to better assess the contribution that software failures make to major incidents. Perhaps the greatest indictment of our research is that we can offer relatively little practical advice about the curriculum that they should adopt. The thousands of papers that have been published on the constructive design of complex safety-critical software far outweigh the handful of papers that have been published on the analysis of software in major incidents and accidents.

References

[1]   C.C. Lebow, L.P. Sarsfield, W.L. Stanley, E. Ettedgui and G. Henning, *Safety in the Skies: Personnel and Parties in NTSB Accident Investigations.* Rand Institute, Santa Monica, USA, 1999.

[2]   US Department of Health and Human Services, Food and Drug Administration, Guidance for the Content of Premarket Submissions for Software Contained in Medical Devices. Report Number 337, May 1998.

[3]   National Transportation Safety Board, Controlled Flight Into Terrain Korean Air Flight 801 Boeing 747-300, HL7468 Nimitz Hill, Guam August 6, 1997. Aircraft Accident Report NTSB/AAR-99/02, 2000.

[4]   N.G. Leveson, Safeware: System Safety and Computers, Addison Wesley, Reading Mass. 1995.

[5]   J.L. Lyons, Report of the Inquiry Board into the Failure of Flight 501 of the Ariane 5 Rocket. European Space Agency Report, Paris, July 1996

[6]   South-West Thames Regional Health Authority. Report of the Inquiry Into The London Ambulance Service Computer-Assisted Despatch System (February 1993) Original ISBN No: 0 905133 70 6

[7]   C.W. Johnson, *A First Step Toward the Integration of Accident Reports and Constructive Design Documents.* In M. Felici, K. Kanoun and A. Pasquini (eds), Proc. of SAFECOMP'99, 286-296, Springer Verlag, 1999.

[8]   C.W. Johnson, *Proving Properties of Accidents*, Reliability Engineering and Systems Safety, (67)2:175-191, 2000.

[9]   J. Rushby, Using Model Checking to Help Discover Mode Confusions and Other Automation Surprises. In D. Javaux and V. de Keyser (eds.) Proc. of the 3rd Workshop on Human Error, Safety, and System Development, Liege, Belgium, 7--8 June 1999.

[10] A. Finkelstein, J. Kramer and B. Nuseibeh, Viewpoint Oriented Development: applications in composite systems.   In F. Redmill and T. Anderson (eds.) Safety Critical Systems: Current Issues, Techniques and Standards, Chapman & Hall, 1993, 90-101.

[11] N.G. Leveson, S.S. Cha and T.J. Shimeall, Safety Verification of Ada Programs using Software Fault Trees, IEEE Software, 8(7):48-59, July 1991.

[12] P. Benyon-Davies, Human Error and Information Systems Failure: the Case of the London Ambulance Service Computer-Aided Despatch System Project. Interacting with Computers, (11)6:699-720.

[13] J. Reason, Managing the Risks of Organizational Accidents, Ashgate, 1998.

[14] A. K. Lekburg, Different Approaches to Incident Investigation – How the Analyst Makes a Difference. In S. Smith and B. Lewis (eds), Proc. of the 15th International Systems Safety Conference, Washington DC, USA, August 1997.

[15] N.G. Leveson, Intent Specifications: An Approach to Building Human-Centered Specifications. Accepted for IEEE Trans. on Software Engineering (2000).

[16] T.P. Kelly and J.A. McDermid, *A Systematic Approach to Safety-Case Maintenance,* M. Felici, K. Kanoun and A. Pasquini (eds.) SAFECOMP'99, LNCS 1698, Springer Verlag, 1998.

[17] C.W. Johnson, Why Human Error Analysis Fails to Support Systems Development, Interacting with Computers, (11)5:517-524, 1999.

Author Index

Lecture Notes in Computer Science

For information about Vols. 1–1872
please contact your bookseller or Springer-Verlag